Histories
of Drug Trafficking
in Twentieth-Century
Mexico

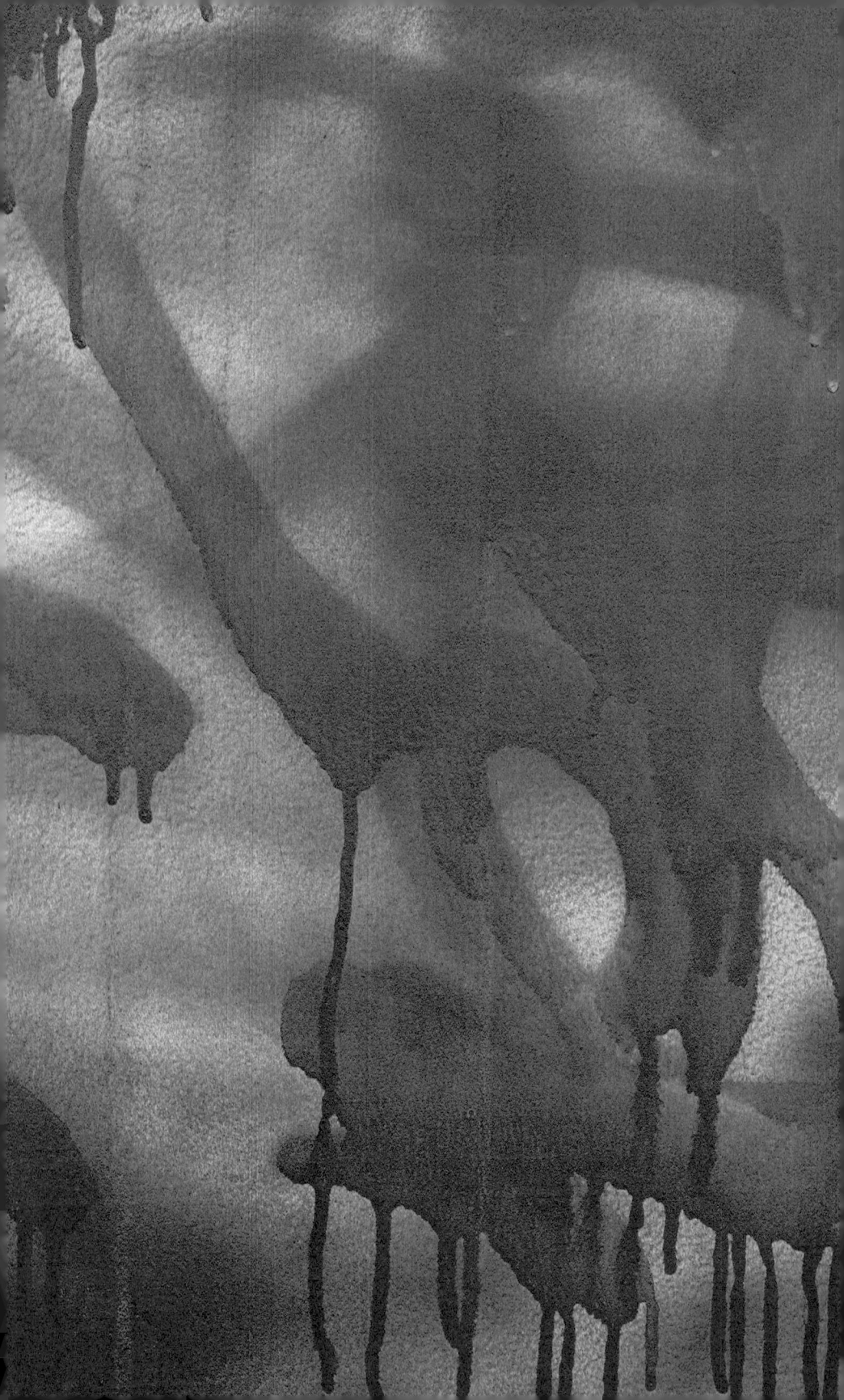

Edited by Wil G. Pansters and Benjamin T. Smith

HISTORIES OF DRUG TRAFFICKING IN TWENTIETH-CENTURY MEXICO

University of New Mexico Press / Albuquerque

© 2022 by the University of New Mexico Press
All rights reserved. Published 2022
Printed in the United States of America

First paperback printing 2024

ISBN 978-0-8263-6358-9 (cloth)
ISBN 978-0-8263-6736-5 (paper)
ISBN 978-0-8263-6737-2 (ePub)
ISBN 978-0-8263-6359-6 (PDF)

Library of Congress Control Number: 2022930087

Founded in 1889, the University of New Mexico sits on the traditional homelands of the Pueblo of Sandia. The original peoples of New Mexico—Pueblo, Navajo, and Apache—since time immemorial have deep connections to the land and have made significant contributions to the broader community statewide. We honor the land itself and those who remain stewards of this land throughout the generations and also acknowledge our committed relationship to Indigenous peoples. We gratefully recognize our history.

Cover illustration: Chicago, Illinois. USA, May 18, 1987 © 2019
     Mark Reinstein/Shutterstock.
Designed by Mindy Basinger Hill
Composed in 11/14 pt Garamond Premier Pro and Eurostile Regular

Contents

List of Illustrations / *ix*

1   Writing Twentieth-Century Mexico's Drug Histories / *1*
    WIL G. PANSTERS AND BENJAMIN T. SMITH

PART I *The Emerging Prohibition Regime /*
Policies, Policing, and Popular Vices

2   "Pressure-Response" and the Origins of Mexican Drug Prohibition,
    1912–1920 / A Reassessment / *43*
    ISAAC CAMPOS

3   Popular Vices and Revolutionary Restrictions / Drugs and Mexican
    Society, 1910–1920 / *67*
    RICARDO PÉREZ MONTFORT

4   Drugs, Control, and Corruption / The Antinarcotics Police
    in Mexico City, 1920–1947 / *88*
    NIDIA A. OLVERA HERNÁNDEZ

PART II *Drug Trafficking, Social Relations, Political Protection, and Law Enforcement during the Mexican Miracle*

5. **La Nacha, the Godmother of Border Trafficking** / Transnational Drugs and Gendered Power in Ciudad Juárez, 1920–1960 / *109*
ELAINE CAREY

6. **Highs and Lows** / Drug Trafficking in Baja California, 1930–1960 / *127*
BENJAMIN T. SMITH AND WIL G. PANSTERS

7. **Policing the Drug Trade** / U.S. Narcotic Agents in Mexico, 1936–1963 / *147*
CARLOS A. PÉREZ RICART

8. **"Rayando la Bola, Cortando la Rama"** / The Production of Opium and Marijuana in Sinaloa, 1940–ca. 1975 / *174*
JUAN ANTONIO FERNÁNDEZ VELÁZQUEZ

9. **With a Little Help from His Friends** / Juan N. Guerra, Smuggling, and Drug Trafficking in Tamaulipas and Nuevo León, 1940s–1960s / *193*
CARLOS ANTONIO FLORES PÉREZ

PART III *Drug Trafficking, the Drug War, the Dirty War, and the Unintended Consequences*

10. **Caciques, Traffickers, and Soldiers** / Drug Trafficking in the *Cardenista* Territory of Michoacán, 1960–1970 / *217*
SALVADOR MALDONADO ARANDA

11. **The War on Drugs, Counterinsurgency, and the State of Siege in the Golden Triangle, 1977–1982** / *240*
ADELA CEDILLO

12. **Grupo Sangre** / Drugs, Death Squads, and the Dirty War Origins of Mexico's Drug Wars / *263*
ALEXANDER AVIÑA

13. **Heroin, the Herreras, and the "Chicago Connection"** / The Drug Trade in Durango, 1950–1985 / *287*
NATHANIEL MORRIS

PART IV *Conclusions*

14   Drugs, Crime, and Violence in Modern Mexico / *317*
     ALAN KNIGHT

Contributors / *345*

Index / *349*

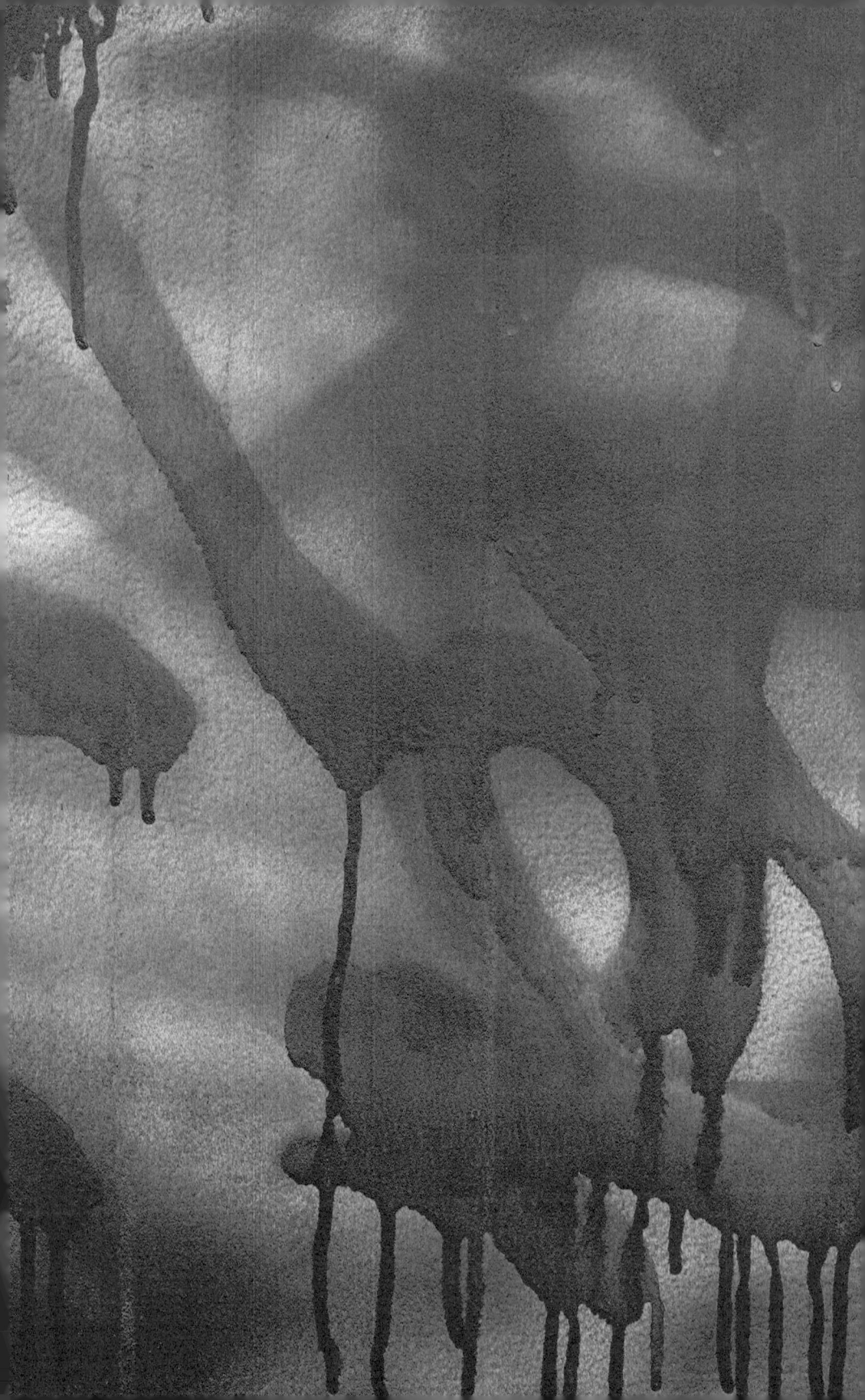

Illustrations

MAP 1 Map of Mexico / *4*

MAP 2 Map of Baja California / *130*

MAP 3 Map of Sinaloa / *178*

MAP 4 Map of Tamaulipas and Nuevo León / *197*

MAP 5 Map of Michoacán / *221*

MAP 6 Map of Guerrero / *266*

MAP 7 Map of Durango / *291*

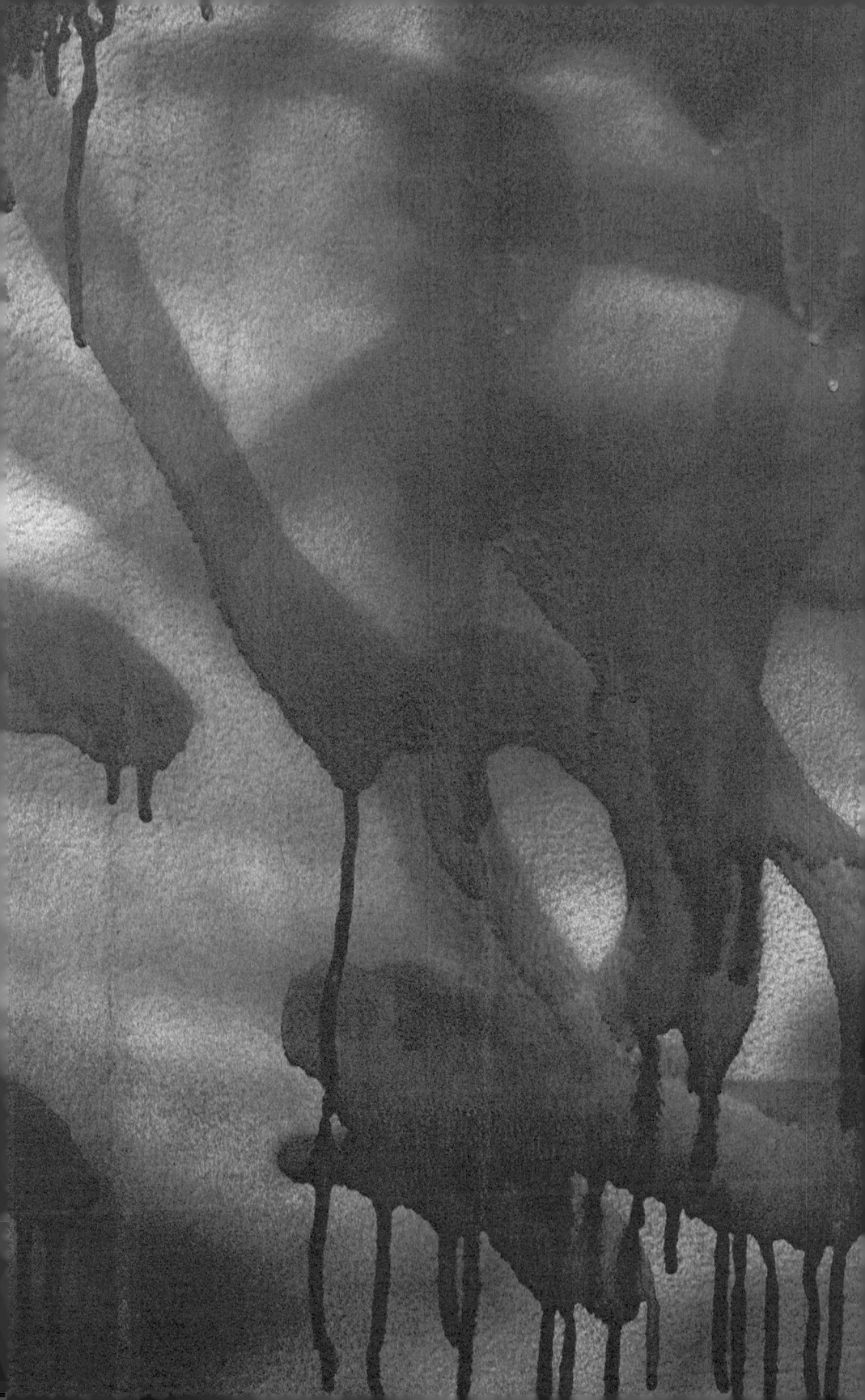

1

Writing Twentieth-Century Mexico's Drug Histories

WIL G. PANSTERS AND BENJAMIN T. SMITH

Over the past fifteen years, tales of drug trafficking and drug violence have dominated coverage of Mexico. Since President Felipe Calderón (2006–2012) declared war on the country's cartels, images of headless torsos, swinging corpses, and mass graves have dominated the front pages of national and international newspapers. Many onlookers now view the country and the continent at large through the warped prism of Netflix's fictionalized series *Narcos* or *El Chapo*, or its documentaries such as *Inside the Real Narcos*. In addition to mass media productions, many books have been published about Mexican drug trafficking and the fallout of the War on Drugs. Most accounts have concentrated on the confrontations between rival criminal organizations or between law enforcement agencies and organized crime groups. Particularly after 2006, journalists and commentators have published many books about particular criminal or drug trafficking organizations, the intrigues among *capos* and their extended families, or about the economics and politics of drug trafficking and violence in particular regions of the country.[1] Brimming with detailed information, these publications help contemporary readers to make sense of shifting alliances and conflicts within the world of drug crime, and of the unstable connections among organized crime, law enforcement, and politics. But overall, they tend to be more descriptive than analytical.[2]

No doubt some have moved away from the alleged certainties of true crime. They have started to document the tragic social consequences of violence endemic to Mexico's War on Drugs.[3] Reporting from the multiple epicenters of grief caused by *la guerra contra el narco*, they expose how "headline stories" of internecine criminal violence, feuds among ruthless cartel capos, and the supposed Manichean battles between state forces and organized crime mean havoc, destruction, and pain for countless individuals, families, and communities.[4] Unsurprisingly, and acknowledging notable exceptions, both types of publications don't really engage the political, social, or economic contexts of drug-related conflicts.[5] They are also not strong on historical contextualization. To a large extent, scholarly work from political science, criminology, and security studies has employed a similar perspective, mostly using secondary sources.[6] Most of this work also lacks critical socioeconomic, political, and, especially, historical contextualization.[7]

If this journalistic and scholarly work is helpful in coming to terms with the complex and fluctuating manifestations of drug trafficking, organized crime, violence, and insecurity in contemporary Mexico, it also reveals the essential empirical, methodological, and analytical challenges to doing such work. These challenges also apply to writing drug histories, perhaps even a fortiori. What can we know about the illicit world of drug trafficking and organized crime (who, what, where?) and their relations to assorted state actors and society at large (connections, coalitions, complicities)? How can we establish acceptable levels of certainty about what is occurring at present and, above all, what occurred in the past? Which sources are available? How is the world of drugs and crime related to broader social, economic, political, and cultural processes, and how have these relations transformed over time? Which analytical frameworks and scholarly debates should be brought to bear on them?

This chapter consists of two parts. The first part consists of two sections and addresses general theoretical and methodological issues concerning drugs research, and identifies ways forward. The first section discusses methodological problems intrinsic to drug research and critically reviews different branches of what we see as essentially constructivist approaches to drugs history. The second section builds on the accomplishments of different branches of constructivism and lays out ways forward by bringing together a new generation of historians and archival sources. We claim it is possible to write bottom-up (subnational) social, economic, and political histories of drug trafficking in twentieth-century Mexico. We also draw attention to the junctures linking the local, regional, national, and global realities and representations of drug trafficking.

The second part lays out the main historical trends and themes pertinent to the drug trade in Mexico and their connections to wider societal processes and scholarly debates. It is also divided in two. The first section examines the key actors and forces that shaped the organization and regulation of drug production, trafficking, and policies during twentieth-century Mexico and lays out a basic narrative. The second section discusses what the new drugs scholarship in general and this volume in particular contribute to broader thematic debates about twentieth-century Mexico. We focus on U.S.-Mexican relations, policing, state making, and regional developments and cultures. The historical, societal, and scholarly contextualization of the drug trade enables us to go beyond much of the existing work, increase our understanding of the phenomenon, and identify new avenues of research.

WRITING DRUG HISTORIES: CHALLENGES AND WAYS FORWARD

Constructivist Drugs Research: A Review

Piecing together even contemporary narratives of trafficking, violence, and insecurity is a tough job. Uncovering bribery, corruption, and state protection can even be fatal. Over the past two decades, state forces and cartel hit men have killed more than a hundred Mexican journalists just for trying.[8] This has led certain scholars to point at the intrinsic problems of such empirical endeavors. Luis Astorga, for example, has argued that "discovering the precise connections between the [traffickers] and the leaders in the fields of politics and economics" is a "sterile" and "fruitless" activity. Knowledge of such links can rarely be gleaned and is only "reserved for the initiated."[9]

The methodological problems Astorga highlights have generated a broad range of constructivist approaches to the drug business. Below we identify and briefly discuss three strands. More than focusing on the material and social organization of drug cultivation, trafficking, and use, constructivism privileges the study of historically shifting cultural understandings of drugs and how they guide medicinal, legal, and political approaches to the substances. The emphasis falls on the discourses, languages, and "readings" of the drug world. While we recognize the performative effects of representations and narratives, it is fair to say that in constructivist approaches the representations of the drug world take precedence over its social realities. All branches of constructivism combine the significance of how charged narratives and representations insert themselves in writing histories and anthropologies of drugs, with a cautiousness or even skepticism toward what really can be known about the economic and political realities of drug cultivation and trafficking.[10]

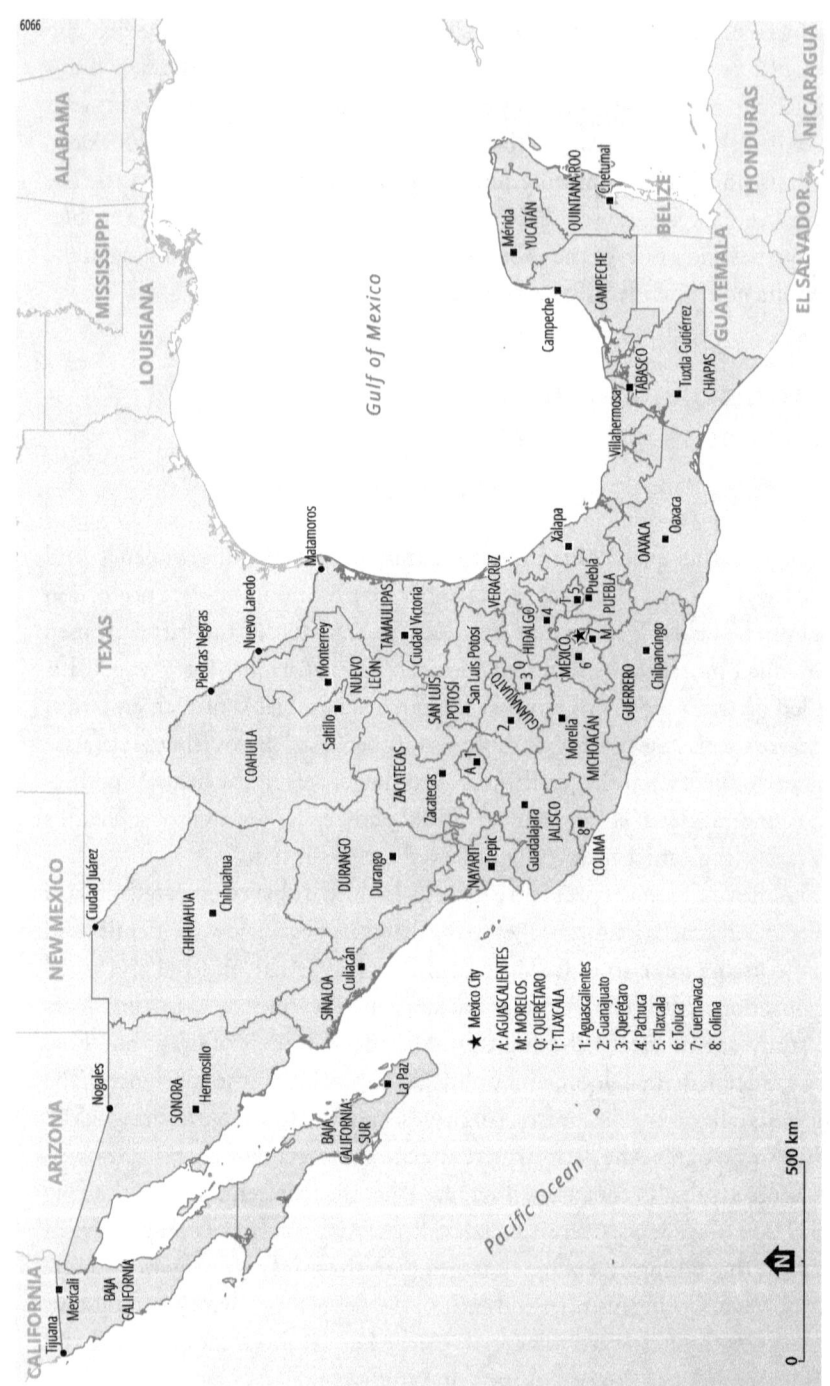

MAP 1 Map of Mexico (credits: UU-Geo-C&M–Carto).

In their timely special issue of the *Hispanic American Historical Review*, Gootenberg and Campos brought together essays that exemplify the cultural branch of constructivist drug history.[11] These examined the creation of a drug problem by legal and medical experts in Cold War Argentina, the nationalization of *vallenato* music in 1970s Colombia, and the cultural encounters around psychedelic drugs among indigenous shamanism, psychiatry, and pleasure-seeking hippies in 1960s Oaxaca. To these, one could add Dawson's fascinating study of how peyote was symbolically constructed as a boundary between indigenous and non-indigenous subjects and policed by ecclesiastical, legal, and scientific authorities.[12]

The second branch of the constructivist approach does not focus so much on how changing moral, legal, and medicinal repertoires frame particular drugs, or on how the drug world shapes certain cultural products. Instead it dissects the standard accounts of contemporary drug trafficking, organized crime, and violence produced by global policy makers, national politicians, security experts, and journalists. Some years ago Mexican sociologist Fernando Escalante published a powerful book that argued that government documents, reports, news bulletins, and press declarations constructed a "new language or narrative," which claimed to explain the recent history and features of the Mexican world of drug trafficking and the threats it posed to Mexico and the United States. This narrative—in effect—legitimized the punitive and militarized "War on Drugs." During the Calderón presidency, this new way of speaking about drug trafficking and organized crime "was naturalized, and impose[d] itself with the weight of the obvious."[13] It became part of a commonsense framework reiterated by the mass media. And it operated as a filter that gave meaning to daily events in the War on Drugs.

This filter had four key features: it assumed the existence of recognizable and separate social groups exclusively and professionally dedicated to crime and integrated in large stable and hierarchically structured organizations called cartels; it emphasized the entrepreneurial features of these organizations, their multinational scope, and business rationality (costs, markets, competition, profit margins, etc.); it stressed their use of violence to regulate an increasingly diversified criminal portfolio (now also including human trafficking, extortion, kidnapping); finally, it supposed that criminal enterprises controlled territories. Such control entailed not only the production, trafficking, and domestic sale of drugs, but also the regulation of informal markets, the extortion of licit businesses, and the sale of protection. The idea of territorial control—in particular—constituted the cornerstone of the government narrative of the war against organized crime. Cartels were invading armies; they could only be confronted by militarization. This—in turn—caused increasing violence.[14] The imaginary construction of organized crime and drug trafficking contains "exaggerations, distortions, inconsistencies, and unfounded and doubtful claims."[15] The entrenchment of this narrative came with militarization and a catastrophic increase of violence.[16] The problem of Mexico's security crisis was in large part one of the language used to describe it.[17]

Escalante's constructivist critique compels us to examine and historicize the languages of the state, the private security industry, and drug war agencies. Furthermore, there is a strong moral component to this: the incorporation of daily stories and images of violent executions, massacres, and mass graves in the standard narrative of state-cartel or intercartel confrontations not only normalizes violence but also suggests the guilt of the deceased. Just as journalists reporting from Mexico's most violent areas have noted, a handful of political scientists have observed that this framing of the War on Drugs pushes many to excuse deaths and disappearances with the comforting story that the victims were in some way *metidos* [involved] in the trade.[18]

In addition to the cultural and narrative strands of constructivist approaches, Escalante's work also raises some epistemological questions. Numbers float around about the value of international drugs markets, the profit margins of criminal organizations, the amount of drug money laundered through the financial system, and even the net worth of concrete individuals (see Chapo Guzmán's 701 spot on the 2009 Forbes list with his alleged fortune of $1 billion!). These numbers are reported on and quoted, but they often appear to be based more on what policy makers want them to be than on verifiable empirical and statistical data, or even logical extrapolations.[19] Similar to Astorga's concerns about the empirical verification of corruption networks, these epistemological concerns urge researchers to remain critical of numerical claims regarding illegal economies. The temptation of interested parties and agencies to inflate numbers that convey risks or threats to society and the state is simply too big. The archives of the Federal Bureau of Narcotics, for example, abound with references to "major" and "important" drug traffickers or rings, even if suspects are arrested with minor quantities of narcotics. It raises legitimate questions about the limits of what researchers can know.

Such skepticism also holds also true for concepts. Terms like "sicario," "cartel," and "plaza" (or "rings" and "syndicates" during the 1940s and 1950s) are routinely trotted out to explain confrontations and murders without proper attention to what they actually mean. Was the Guadalajara "Cartel" really a monolithic, hierarchical organization directed by a trio of Sinaloa exiles? Did the Zetas Cartel effectively control the "plaza" of Monterrey, a large industrial city of over a million people? What is a plaza exactly, and where does it begin and end? All these terms carry with them the leading assumptions of the standard "War on Drugs" language. Some authors have no doubt about the intent of all this mystification. Drug war language is just a symbolic device that functions to conceal the real networks of (state) power that control drug trafficking and enhance the interests of extractive industries. After all, why else would the state embark on halting a nonexistent war among cartels that don't exist either?[20]

Lessons Learned, Ways Forward

To what extent has the constructivist emphasis on the cultural and imaginary representations of drug trafficking prevented scholars from posing hard questions about the realities of the trade? Does it explain why, despite the contemporary fascination with Mexican narcotics, we still know little about the history of the trade or its regulation? Acknowledging the insights from cultural constructivist approaches to drug history, and the critical lessons about the contemporary history and sociology of the drug trade in particular, we believe that the answers to both questions are affirmative. But we also believe it is possible and essential to move this debate forward. To do so, this volume proceeds from the following considerations.

First, it acknowledges the concerns articulated by these constructivist approaches and builds on their insights. It is impossible to write histories of drug trafficking without incorporating the shifting cultural, political, and moral representations of drugs and giving them the analytical weight they deserve, as they shape human behavior and choices. It is, however, equally important to ask specific questions about the mechanics of the drugs industry: the what, who, when, where, and how. In fact, as this volume makes abundantly clear, it is both feasible and productive to integrate constructivist and empirically grounded histories and anthropologies of drug trafficking. Morris's chapter about the Herrera heroin drug ring in Durango, for example, not only historically reconstructs the socioeconomic organization of the ring, but also pays attention to how U.S. intelligence agencies created narratives about the Herrera clan as an international narco-empire or "cartel" that processed huge—in fact vastly inflated—amounts of heroin and money, controlled entire regions, and employed a massive army of farm laborers. The leaking of such exaggerations to the media served to boost the nascent DEA's own profile and budget and to embarrass the Mexican government.

Second, this volume pushes beyond the confines of such constructivism by focusing for the first time on a plethora of new historical sources. Such emphasis allows the authors to go beyond the standard top-down narratives that are encased in official documents and national newspapers. On the one hand, they have started to study the bottom-up perspectives of small-time smugglers, farmers, and regional wholesalers that can be retrieved from regional papers, interviews, and Mexico's state, local, and judicial archives. On the other hand, they have also begun to investigate declassified documents slowly released by both U.S. and Mexican institutions, including the Bureau of Narcotics (popularly known as the FBN), the DEA, the Dirección Federal de Seguridad (DFS), and the CIA. Together these new sources allow the contributing scholars to see beyond the common tales of cops and criminals and assemble more cogent, multivalent histories of the drug trade, the War on Drugs, and their broader political and socioeconomic ramifications.

One variant of these histories employs a political-economic approach, which prioritizes examining the drug trade above all as an economic process that involves supply and demand, pricing and profits, and networks of economic actors from peasant producers to intermediaries to wholesalers, financiers, and lawyers. This approach also looks at how local illicit economies relate to the structural features of socioeconomic systems in general. In this respect Morris, Fernández Velázquez, and Smith and Pansters argue that early drug economies did not emerge from the milieu of organized crime properly speaking but from more recognizable worlds of highland rancher clans, ambitious merchants, and border town grifters. In recent years, an influential political economic approach has grown out of the concept of global commodity chains. These were first employed to trace the economic and spatial pathways of export goods—such as silver, coffee, and rubber—across the globe and thereby "interlocking processes of production, transport, commercialization, and consumption."[21] Paul Gootenberg has employed them to pick apart the exogenous and endogenous forces that shaped the shifting commercial networks of Peruvian cocaine.[22] Similarly, a recent study places the 1970s marijuana boom in northeastern Colombia in a long regional history of agrarian export commodities (banana, cotton) and modernization, integration with U.S. markets, nation-state formation, and cultural identification.[23]

Another variant of drug histories privileges a political-institutional approach. This focuses on the relations between criminal organizations and formal institutions like federal and local authorities, the police, the armed forces, and political parties, as well as informal institutions like caciques and business networks. Flores Pérez, Morris, Aviña, and Cedillo, in particular, examine the complex and shifting relations between criminal organizations, political elites at different administrative levels, and law enforcement agencies. Alternatively, Olvera Hernández, Pérez Ricart, and Maldonado Aranda examine the ideological, organizational, and operational aspects of different law enforcement agencies involved in combatting drug trafficking: the Mexico City Narcotics Police in the 1920s, the FBN during the second third of the century, and the Mexican army during the 1960s.

Third, this volume elaborates the methodological contours of the "new drug history of Latin America," which emphasize the connections between "different levels and geographies of power."[24] Drugs are commodities that obtain most of their value by virtue of their movement across spatial, legal, and political borders. After all, the bulk of drugs cultivated and produced in particular areas is consumed elsewhere, most often in distant places. Opium, heroin, marijuana, cocaine, and, more recently, fentanyl have been truly global commodities.[25] The life histories and trajectories of these drugs are embedded in networks of local, national, and global actors and fashioned by layers of political forces and cultural imaginations. While writing drug histories should be attentive to the interconnections between local, regional, national, and global realities, integrating these scales constitutes a methodological challenge.

Most of the drug histories of twentieth-century Mexico brought together in this volume can easily speak to the principles of global ethnography—in many ways akin to fine-grained historiography—that aims to "strategically locate itself at critical points of intersection of scales and units of analysis and [...] examine the negotiation of interconnected social actors across multiple scales."[26] More specifically, this volume studies how social actors and places are caught up in global forces beyond their influence, which are mediated by particular actors (e.g., smugglers) who construct strategies of adaptation, avoidance, or contestation. It also examines how social actors may seize opportunities and expand their geographic and political boundaries by building translocal and global connections. The entrepreneurial spirit of Sinaloa rancheros who stepped up opium production during the 1940s or of the pioneers of the marijuana trade in the Colombian Guajira peninsula during the 1970s spring to mind. Finally, it studies how differentially situated social actors produce, negotiate, and contest the imaginations of these forces, processes, and connections, drawing upon distinctive and often conflictive political and legal resources.[27]

While anthropologists may use multisited ethnographic fieldwork, historians can consult and combine sources ranging from international diplomatic records, through national archives, to regional judicial collections and to local newspapers and interviews. Looking at the histories of drugs through the lens of the (global) forces, connections, and imaginations is particularly rewarding if we realize that these manifest themselves in political-economic, political-institutional, and cultural domains, and in their complex linkages. Examining drugs from a global commodity chain perspective creates insights into the extensive spatial pathways that link drug cultivation, production, transportation, and distribution and into the connections between the latter and migration networks. Heroin production by the Herrera clan during the 1960s and 1970s in the Santiago Papasquiaro region in western Durango developed in conjunction with migration networks that connected Durango through Ciudad Juárez to Southside Chicago, where various cells of the extended Herrera family organized wholesale distribution.[28] More recently, cheap black tar heroin from Xalisco, Nayarit, was distributed through sophisticated marketing and retail delivery systems run by young members of extensive family-based migrant networks linking the small town in western Mexico to cells across the United States.[29] Transnational migration flows and closely knit connections among Chinese migrant communities were instrumental in the origins of the heroin trade between northwestern Mexico and the United States in terms of production, markets, and knowledge transfer. Border peddler Mike Barragán was originally from Michoacán. First, he migrated to California. Then he returned and used his cross-border contacts to become a prominent marijuana and heroin dealer in Tijuana during the 1950s and 1960s.[30] Drug history is part of this social history of mobility.

Meanings, discourses, and ideas about drugs equally travel and form interconnected layers of production, negotiation, and contestation at different scales. It is not always easy to distinguish in which direction meanings and discourses move and shape behavioral outcomes or policy choices. Contrary to the widely held belief that prohibitionist discourses and regulations were forced upon Mexico by a U.S.-led global campaign, Campos argues that at the time of the first-generation war on drugs during the 1910s, Mexico had autonomously developed a widely accepted moral code concerning the use of certain intoxicants. With respect to marijuana, negative Mexican stereotypes in fact traveled north, while a "narcophobic discourse" centered on Chinese opium use journeyed across the globe.[31] While Pérez Montfort points at persistent U.S. pressures on the Mexican government during the 1910s and early 1920s to enact antidrug measures—which appears to dispute Campos's claim—he also notes that by 1920 the effective enforcement of a prohibitionist regime had failed. At the time, Mexican health officials themselves expressed their concerns about drug use, and soon an invigorated U.S. prohibitionist campaign resonated with Mexico's postrevolutionary governments. The combination of U.S. pressures and Mexico's homegrown concerns and political interests leave little room for linear causality.

As the prohibitionist regime consolidated during the 1930s and 1940s, specialized agencies were founded that exchanged information, set up mostly informal mechanisms of bureaucratic cooperation, and carried out joint undercover antinarcotics operations. Information exchanges about international criminal networks, discussions about policies and operations, training programs, and informal agreements between U.S. and Mexican law enforcement agencies and specific agents were at least partially guided by the views of U.S. drug agencies about Mexico. These views "were oversimplified and full of stereotypes" and were molded, it seems, above all after New York–based Italian crime syndicates.[32] At the same time, the moral values and ideological positions that underpinned prohibitionist discourses and translated into massive intervention campaigns in drug-producing areas also collided with regionally based moral economies of peasant and ranchero communities. Fernández Velázquez, in particular, demonstrates how drugs cultivation and trafficking in the Sinaloa highlands was above all a product of community-based solidarity and reciprocity and the outcome of rational livelihood strategies. When Mexican and U.S. law enforcement agencies descended on these highlands to eradicate poppy and marijuana fields and clashed with local communities, it was not only a matter of material interests, but also one of moral repertoires and localized meanings of (il)licit behavior. Stopping growing opium might have been obeying the law, but it was also letting down your compadre.

The collision of meanings and morals is by no means specific to Mexico. In Colombia the marijuana trade and the commodity itself were considered "legitimate, albeit illegal." Once repressive policies intensified at the end of the 1970s, just as they did in northwestern Mexico, they also "materialized as a discursive battle to define the divide between what was legal and what was legitimate."³³ In Afghanistan, the adoption of stringent antinarcotics policies in the late 1950s went against "local norms of opium production, use, and trade; in this way the drug ban reinforced the profound disconnect" between local communities and the state. The elimination of a "culturally accepted and economically vital commodity" antagonized local communities, alienated them from the global antinarcotics discourse, delegitimized the national state, and ultimately stimulated the expansion of drugs production in subsequent years.³⁴ As Cedillo and Aviña show in this volume, punitive antinarcotics interventions in producing areas became even more ideologically charged and antagonistic to the material and moral economies of local communities when the former connected to global Cold War counterinsurgency ideologies.

In sum, this volume builds on the accomplishments of cultural and discursive constructivism and acknowledges the epistemological concerns. It brings together a new generation of historians and works with numerous archival sources, which are instrumental in writing Mexico's bottom-up subnational histories of drug trafficking, either privileging political-economic or political-institutional perspectives. In doing so, it strongly claims that it is possible to write social, economic, and political histories of drug trafficking in twentieth-century Mexico. Finally, the chapters in this volume pay attention to the connections and junctures between the local, regional, national, and global realities and representations of drug trafficking.

HISTORICAL TRENDS, THEMATIC DEBATES

The Organization and Regulation of the Mexican Drug Trade (1910–1985)

The integration of international, national, and local perspectives and the attendant blending of three levels of sources offer both a clearer narrative of the drug trade and a more nuanced picture of the war against it. No doubt, changing U.S. appetites have provided the principal impetus for the Mexican narcotics industry. For example, from around the early 1960s onwards cannabis production spread throughout the western slopes of the Sierra Madre in lockstep with the development of the U.S. counterculture.³⁵ U.S. pop culture marked its growth. In 1967 Rainy Daze celebrated the power of "Acapulco

Gold." Three years later Jefferson Airplane lamented that a "small-headed man" called "Richard [Nixon]" now had Mexico "under his thumb" and had ended the "tons of gold and green, comin' up here from Mexico: 'A donde esta la planta, mi amigo, del sol?'"[36] But other forces also shaped Mexican production. They included homegrown Mexican appetites. These were much more limited than U.S. demands and in general less concerned with hard drugs. But they existed. They also included changes in global narcotic production. Just like any other domestic good, Mexican drugs were buffeted by the ups and downs of the world market and the shifting policies of the big international players. From 1976 onwards Mexican marijuana production fell partly due to Operation Condor and partly to the U.S. scare over paraquat poisoning.[37] But most importantly, it was victim to the competition from better quality weed being produced in Colombia, Thailand, and Jamaica.[38] Mexican heroin production witnessed a similar dip in 1948 and again in 1978. Underprocessed "Mexican brown" could neither match the purity nor the price of rival products from Europe and Southeast Asia.[39]

As U.S. markets, global supply, and domestic demand have molded the Mexican drug trade, each of the three major narcotics (marijuana, opiates, and cocaine) has its own unique rhythm of production. During the late nineteenth century, marijuana production was limited, used to feed a market of soldiers and prisoners with limited access to alcohol.[40] Though this is difficult to track, it seems that production increased during the Revolution as Mexicans were dragooned into the army and faced with a limited supply of standard pain relief drugs.[41] From the 1940s through the 1960s marijuana production dropped. As early as 1940, the army reported very few cases of marijuana "intoxication." Regiments that did report some were—interestingly—based in places like Atlixco, Puebla, and Ameca, Jalisco, where marijuana had a history of production.[42] Media reports of marijuana use also slid. The *Siglo de Torreón* went from around a mention a week during the early 1930s to barely one every two months from 1956 to 1965.[43] In the subsequent decade, production grew again, this time exponentially. Busts went from a few dozen kilos to few dozen tons, and by the mid-1970s the DEA estimated that Mexico was producing up to six thousand tons a year.[44] For many villages it became the sole retail crop. In San Juan, Sinaloa, peasants competed to see who could grow the tallest plants.[45] Yet it was a boom, not a sustained industry. By 1982, Mexican youths sniffed paint thinner rather than smoked weed and Mexico produced 6 percent of U.S. supply.[46]

The Mexican opiate trade has been similarly up and down. During the 1910s Mexico served as a transition point for large quantities of imported raw and smoking opium.[47] Baja California governor Esteban Cantú famously taxed the product and used the money to build roads and schools.[48] Yet the declining use of smoking opium and the reopening of European sources of processed narcotics like morphine and heroin ate into the trade.[49] By the mid-1930s, the opiate trade was reduced to a handful of European entrepreneurs, a few surviving Chinese businessmen, and some farmers in Sonora's El Altar valley.[50] World War II resuscitated the trade. European and Asian sources of narcotics stopped, and by 1943, the U.S. Customs Office reported that Mexico was now "the principal source of supply of prepared opium to the illicit traffic in the United States."[51] Furthermore, Mexico had started to produce its own. The following year U.S. Customs officials reported that they were also seizing both morphine and heroin on the Mexican border. The drugs were "definitely of Mexican origin."[52]

As Pérez Ricart argues, the U.S. and Mexican authorities congratulated themselves that it was hard-nosed antinarcotics tactics that ended the boom in heroin "hecho en México."[53] In reality it was international competition from new European sources of heroin (particularly Italy and France).[54] Yet the boom left a legacy, a heavy concentration of growers, processors, and traffickers in the so-called "Golden Triangle," the mountains connecting the states of Sinaloa, Chihuahua, and Durango. During the 1950s and 1960s, these small-scale heroin dealers—captured for posterity in the first work of narcolit *Diario de un narcotraficante*—fed Mike Barragán's Tijuana dealers and La Nacha's Ciudad Juárez shooting galleries.[55] What is less known is that they increasingly teamed up with international French Connection dealers to ferry through larger quantities of European heroin.[56]

The counterculture persuaded some of these traffickers to experiment with other narcotics, including marijuana and, by the late 1960s, cocaine. Yet others stuck firmly to what they knew. And from 1973 onwards U.S. addicts reacquainted themselves with underprocessed "Mexican mud." In 1972, 80 percent of U.S. heroin came from France; within four years most came from Mexico. Yet again, like the 1940s, the boom was short-lived. By the beginning of the 1980s, Mexico had returned to producing just over 30 percent of America's heroin.[57]

For decades U.S. drug authorities speculated that Mexican traffickers sought to grow coca plants, particularly in the isolated mountains of Chiapas.[58] But evidence of cocaine "hecho en México" is sparse; any attempts there ended in failure. Processing coca paste into cocaine was done. And from the 1970s onwards police busted small-scale cocaine laboratories throughout Mexico.[59] But in general cocaine was always imported; Mexico was a region that cocaine was trafficked across and to a much lesser extent snorted in. There was a small market for cocaine in bohemian circles in 1920s Mexico City, where one flapper compared her use of the drug to her love of classical music: "When I am very bored, very bored, so bored that neither Grieg nor Chopin nor Beethoven nor Debussy will suffice, I take ether or coc[aine]."[60] And there was a small market among border thrill seekers. Just less than 10 percent of drug arrests in Mexicali and Tijuana from 1922 to 1923 were for cocaine.[61] In both cases the product came from European pharmaceutical companies and was imported by European smugglers.[62]

Again the counterculture changed things. Traffickers increasingly used Mexican smuggling routes to get their product across to the United States. (It might have been marijuana that Billy and Wyatt were smoking in *Easy Rider*, but it was cocaine they were smuggling out of Mexico at the beginning of the film.) Cedillo cites the DEA estimate that by 1977 30 percent of Peruvian cocaine came through Mexico. Some was brought by freelance Americans who were previously involved in the weed business,[63] and some was brought in by the Golden Triangle's former heroin traffickers.[64] But much of it appears to have passed through official channels. In 1976, a Miami grand jury indicted the federal judicial police commander, Arturo "el Negro" Durazo Moreno, on five counts of orchestrating the smuggling of cocaine from Colombia, through the Mexico City airport, to the United States. As elections were approaching and Durazo was the PRI presidential candidate's campaign security chief, the accusations were quietly dropped.[65]

Taking this three-tier approach not only allows us to map out the contours of the trade, it also helps us understand the chronology, the intensity, and the focus of counternarcotics policies. Most social scientists are still wedded to a dynamic of drug prohibition that views Mexican efforts as a direct U.S. imposition. It is commonly referred to as the "pressure-response" model. Certain set pieces back this up. In 1940, U.S. threats to withhold pain-relief opiates ended Mexico's experiment with a state-run maintenance program for addicts. And in 1969, President Nixon's exhaustive border check—Operation Intercept—forced Mexico into adopting a more aggressive stance as well as more prohibitive laws on drug prohibition.[66]

Yet such an approach tells only part of the story. Mexican antidrug policies were not simply foreign imports. They—like the drugs—were also "hecho en México." The cultural prejudices that framed and fed decades of counternarcotics policies were often national in scope. Sometimes they were fit for export like the homegrown biases over marijuana smoking, which Anslinger happily adopted for his own anticannabis campaign.[67] Sometimes they were national prejudices shared by a broad swath of modernizing nations, like the Sinophobic bigotry that nourished the antiopium campaigns of the 1920s and 1930s.[68] Sometimes they were distinctly regional preconceptions of class and race, like those wheeled out by the political elites of Guerrero, Sinaloa, and Chihuahua during the 1970s to excuse the imprisonment, torture, forced displacement, and murder of hundreds, maybe even thousands.[69]

The political motives for drug policies were also distinctly homegrown. They often shaped the timing, the focus, and the manner of antidrugs policies. Venustiano Carranza's efforts to control opium imports obeyed U.S. diktats and rested on a Mexican version of degeneration theory. But they also undercut the funding and the credibility of the autonomous Baja California governor, Esteban Cantú.[70] By the 1960s, as Maldonado shows, similar concerns over the political independence of the Tierra Caliente (and its links to the influential former president Lázaro Cárdenas) precipitated a military campaign against local marijuana and opium growers.[71] And fifteen years later anxieties over regional autonomy, peasant activism, and guerrilla insurgency finally pushed the federal government into supporting the mix of military intervention, crop spraying, and police crackdown that the United States had been encouraging for more than six years.[72]

Furthermore, not all of these initiatives came from the top down. Though it is rarely acknowledged—and subsequently often regretted—the political impetus for antidrugs policies also came from regional representatives of civil society on both sides of the border. Moral panics in California and Texas pushed the crackdown on Mexican border drug sales during the late 1950s. But America's wordy moralizers were not alone. As Cedillo points out, it was the Sinaloa elites that eventually called on the Mexican army to occupy Culiacán at the end of 1976. In the 1950s and again in the 1980s, PAN politicians, especially in the north, used accusations of collusion between local politicians and traffickers to undergird social movements and push PRI representatives from power.[73] In fact, it could be argued that Felipe Calderón's post-2006 campaign had its roots as much in these pious anticorruption efforts as contemporary issues of realpolitik.

The integration of these three levels of analysis also offers a much more accurate picture of the links between drug traffickers and the different layers of the state. Again a narrative emerges. From the 1910s to the 1930s certain border governors, including Esteban Cantú but also Abelardo Rodríguez (Baja California) and Rodrigo Quevedo (Chihuahua) extorted drug sellers and drug traffickers.[74] At times, the money went into public coffers.[75] But a lot went into their private bank accounts. In Mexico City during the 1920s, the head of the capital's police protected dealers in return for cash. By the following decade, as Olvera shows, this role had fallen to the Health Department's narcotics police.[76]

The 1940s boom and the extension of opium cultivation to the Sierra Madre shifted state-trafficker relations. These changes were often accompanied by violence. At first, municipal policemen in league with local military regiments protected and extorted the growers. But by the early 1940s, the state authorities attempted to take control using the state judicial police. In Sinaloa, the attempted takeover led to the high-profile murder of the head of the state police, Alfonso Leyzaola Salazar, by Badiraguato traffickers in 1941.[77] It also probably precipitated the assassination of the governor of Sinaloa at the Mazatlán carnival three years later.[78] Yet by the mid-1940s, at least in the northwestern states, an arrangement was reached. State governors would protect the trade using the state judicial police in return for a cut of the profits.[79] Growers and traffickers would keep a low profile and avoid bloody squabbles. If they failed to do this, protection ended. This arrangement would last for at least three decades and reached its apogee under the governor of Sinaloa, Leopoldo Sánchez Celis, who appointed some of Mexico's most feared *pistoleros* to protect the trade.[80]

In the northeast, as Flores Pérez observes, a slightly different arrangement emerged. In Tamaulipas and Coahuila, drugs were not grown, but transported. Former alcohol smugglers and *fayuqueros*, like Juan N. Guerra, dominated the trade. To work, they needed protection of the border checkpoints and the states' major federal roads. Broader territorial control was unnecessary. At first, as in the northwest, state governors took an interest. Hugo Pedro González protected the Nuevo Laredo trafficker, Alfonso Treviño, and even ordered the local authorities to let him out of jail in the evenings to visit the local cabarets (he used the prison, one paper claimed, as a "dormitory"). But in 1947, things changed. Governor González was sacked and the old *camarilla* surrounding former president Emilio Portes Gil was unceremoniously dumped from power. From the late 1940s, an alliance of local military commanders (like Tiburcio Garza Zamora and Bonifacio Salinas Leal) and federally appointed customs officials controlled the checkpoints and the roads and as a result protected both the drug trade and the smuggling of duty-free contraband.[81] Again, it was an arrangement that lasted until the 1970s.[82]

It should be noted that what happened in Tamaulipas may have been part of a broader attempt by Mexico's federal authorities to take control of the burgeoning trade. There is ample evidence that in 1947 the newly created Dirección Federal de Seguridad (DFS) tried to muscle in on the narcotics business. Some more conspiratorially minded writers have drawn the conclusion that the DFS protected the trade from the Alemán presidency until the institution's implication in the Camarena murder nearly forty years later.[83] But there is no evidence of this. If there was an attempt, it failed. After 1948, U.S. accusations of DFS complicity disappear completely. Furthermore, for at least the next thirty years the organization was so underpowered, it seems extremely unlikely it had the time, the manpower, or the powers of coercion to corral and extort Mexico's drug dealers.[84]

No doubt, during the 1970s something changed. Profits from the trade grew exponentially. The protection rackets run by the state governments boomed. Yet this upset relations with Mexico's federal powers. On the one hand, the trade was too big to ignore, and the United States started to take an increasingly aggressive role on drug prohibition. On the other hand, and perhaps just as worryingly, certain state governments were starting to become increasingly autonomous. The drug trade was effectively decentralizing the Mexican state. In the early 1970s, for example, Sinaloa had a state judicial police force with perhaps as many as five thousand badge-carrying members.[85] In comparison the federal judicial police [Policia Judicial Federal or PJF]—Mexico's official counternarcotics force—numbered less than three hundred and could only enter the region with state government permission. "We got a clear message from the [PJF] that we needed to leave as soon as possible," one former DEA agent complained.[86]

The antidrug campaigns of the 1970s were designed to counteract this increasing regional autonomy. An expanded, armed, and well-funded PJF supported by the army went in, arrested traffickers, harried, tortured, and murdered growers and dismantled the state government protection rackets. It is tempting to question the Mexican government's statistics on fields sprayed and crops destroyed. But by 1978 the marijuana and heroin industries were in free fall, albeit as much for reasons of global competition as counternarcotics efforts.

The question of what came next remains open to debate. We know that by 1985, the DFS provided protection for the cocaine trafficking and marijuana production of the so-called Guadalajara Cartel.[87] Yet such an arrangement did not emerge overnight. From the end of the 1970s onwards, different federal institutions, including the army, the DFS, and the Attorney General's Office and their police force, the PJF, jockeyed for control of a radically diminished and hence less visible trade.[88] The initial winners seem to have been the Attorney General's Office under former Chihuahua governor Oscar Flores Sánchez. He was backed up by the head of the PJF (and former Ciudad Juárez hit man) Raúl Mendiolea Cerecero, the Mexican police chief Arturo "El Negro" Durazo and his right-hand man, Francisco Sahagún Baca. Together they started to control the smuggling of cocaine through Mexico City and up to the United States.[89] Only with the 1982 election of Miguel de la Madrid, the public fall of Durazo, and a fair amount of interagency violence did control of the trade swing into the hands of the DFS.[90]

Drugs, U.S.-Mexican Relations, Policing, and State Making: Thematic Reflections

The new drugs scholarship tells us a lot about the historical dynamics of the organization and regulation of the trade and its subnational variations. It also speaks to several broader scholarly debates concerning Mexico. The latter is based on a simple but critical idea, itself borne out by recent scholarship: the drug trade is deeply rooted in and entangled with other major societal domains, and as a result it shapes and is shaped by the processes taking place in these domains. In contrast to approaches that view the drug trade as a phenomenon in itself, enclosed in its own illicit world, a quintessential *Fremdkörper* to "normal" social relations, we understand histories of drug trafficking as part and parcel of wider histories. Focusing on narcotics can be useful for understanding processes and relations beyond the "underworld," not least because much of it occurs in the "upper" world. So, unsurprisingly, its study will produce insights relevant for our understanding of economic development, politics and state making, cultural production, social hierarchies, and international relations in twentieth-century Mexico.

In the most basic terms, this book attempts to shift the focus of drug studies from the confines of the state of Sinaloa. For nearly three decades, discussion of the relationship between the state's rancher class and its peasant opium growers has dominated the scholarship.[91] There is good reason for this. As Fernández Velázquez demonstrates, clans of Sinaloa opium wholesalers and chemists dominated the opium trade during the 1940s and 1950s.[92] They developed their own distinct *narcocultura* replete with songs, dress code, and a narco-saint[93]; during the 1970s they were the focus of Operation Condor's most brutal repression[94]; and during the next decade they linked up with state security forces to form what became known as the Guadalajara Cartel.[95] Yet Mexican drug culture has always been more than a silk shirt, a Stetson, and a Jesús Malverde medallion. As Pérez Montfort demonstrates, there were various distinct cultures of drug users in postrevolutionary Mexico.[96] These ranged from down-at-heel weed smokers to Chinese immigrant opium smokers to upper-class cocaine users. There were also regional variations in drug smuggling networks. Some—like the Sinaloans—seemed to have been based on a combination of rural links and chemical know-how. Others, like Durango's Herrera family or the Mexican American traffickers of the 1970s, relied much more strongly on connections to sales points in the United States.[97] There are also distinct regional cultures of border drug peddlers. Up until the 1970s, in Baja California and Chihuahua, narcotics dealers focused on selling small quantities of narcotics to a market of predominantly U.S. border addicts in the vice zones of Tijuana, Mexicali, or Ciudad Juárez.[98] In Ciudad Juárez, Ignacia "La Nacha" Jasso made sure that many of these were women.[99] In contrast, drug dealers in the northeast concentrated on smuggling heroin and marijuana through unguarded desert towns and into the markets of Texas and the East Coast.[100] These differences, in turn, shaped distinct regional protection rackets. In Sinaloa, they were dominated by the state governments, which had a degree of influence both in the sierra and the urban laboratories of Culiacán. In the border towns of Tijuana and Ciudad Juárez, state governments and the municipal authorities shared in the profits from the vice industry. In Tamaulipas and Coahuila, however, it was the customs agents and military detachments that controlled the major highways and that dominated payoffs from the drug business.[101]

The new drug scholarship also adds to our understanding of U.S.-Mexican relations. Previously, diplomatic historians and international relations specialists either left counternarcotics policy to one side or dealt with it as a separate set of negotiations.[102] They also tended to concentrate on policies, treaties, summits, bilateral agreements (an impressive forty-seven of which were signed between the late 1930s and mid-1980s!).[103] While important for understanding Mexico's place in bilateral, hemispheric, and global regulatory frameworks, they also limit analysis. As Pérez Ricart demonstrates, the scope and extent of the U.S. policing presence in Mexico was a highly controversial issue. Tacit federal permission often bumped up against the authority of local governments, as well as public outrage, on both sides of the border. It was a rolling problem. New protocols were constantly being discussed at national and state levels. At the same time, both the U.S. and the Mexican governments clearly used counternarcotics policies as pawns in bigger games of bilateral chess. Anslinger's overt bullying of Mexico at the 1947 UN's Commission on Narcotic Drugs meeting was designed to push the new government toward harsher drug laws, toward more wide-ranging counternarcotics campaigns, and toward taking drug policing out of the hands of the health authorities. In the short term it worked.[104] Yet it probably only did so because President Miguel Alemán needed U.S. support for an ailing economy and an increasingly defiant union movement.[105] It ushered in a period between the late 1940s and the early 1960s seen by some as "the golden epoch" of bilateral cooperation between the United States and Mexico in combating drug trafficking.[106] Since most of these years featured, as we observed before, a significant decrease in Mexico's production and export of marijuana and heroin, this is perhaps not that surprising. Almost half a century later, the huge economic interests involved in the negotiations and implementation of NAFTA (and the 1995 peso crisis) led to far-reaching cooperation in matters of drug trafficking at the end of the century.

Furthermore, other chess games are still to be understood. How did Operation Condor and the militarization of counternarcotics efforts link into other contemporary foreign policy debates over the economy, the oil boom, and migrants?[107] How did Mexico's brief flirtation with morphine dispensaries in 1940 fit into bigger narratives of bilateral relations? Was it just an example of Anslinger's intransigence over drug laws?[108] Was it, as Campos argues, an instance of poor Mexican institutional coordination?[109] Or was it one of *cardenista* Mexico's diplomatic weapons of the weak?[110] Did the Mexican authorities push it and then rapidly back down from it in order to persuade the United States to make more important concessions over—say—repayment for oil expropriation? Was it simply a coincidence that the U.S. decision to enter into arbitration with Mexico over expropriation occurred in the same month as Mexico's climb down from the morphine dispensaries?[111]

A particularly interesting contribution of recent drugs scholarship is going beyond formal (diplomatic) relations and policies. The Mexican drug trade has also shaped and been shaped by other, popular appreciations of the neighboring country. During the 1950s, Californian middle-class concern about Mexican American drug peddlers preying on white, suburban girls kick-started a moral panic over borderlands narcotics trafficking.[112] This, in turn, led to mass arrests and public drug burnings in Mexicali and Tijuana.[113] In contrast, at least some of drug trafficking's appeal in Mexico has come from the fact that the narcotics have tended (until recently) to be sold up north rather than to domestic addicts. It is the subaltern counterpunch, the second half of the twentieth century's version of peasant nationalism. It is expressed in narcocorridos.[114] And it is occasionally reflected in the offhand comments of cornered traffickers. During the Michoacán antinarcotics operations of the late early 1960s one local poppy planter rebuked the soldiers: "Tell me another way to take revenge for what happened in 1947 [the year the United States led a controversial nationwide livestock cull to wipe out foot-and-mouth disease] if it isn't poisoning the gringos. . . . Instead of putting me in jail, you should act like a good Mexican and give me better seeds."[115] In times of NAFTA, as Knight observed ironically, successful drug traffickers may represent "a more genuinely nationalist national bourgeoisie than many in modern neoliberal Mexico who might claim that title."[116]

Studying drugs also allows us to reconfigure how we understand state-society relations. For decades, U.S. historians—in particular—have viewed much of the interaction as occurring in the arena of culture. Discussions happened in schools, secular ceremonies, and municipal meetings. They were conducted by teachers, anthropologists, and the participants of cultural missions.[117] Yet for most of the twentieth century, Mexicans interacted most frequently with another, rather less friendly, state emissary: the cop. The prominent roles that the police play in these new drug histories contrast with the scant works on the history of this Mexican institution.[118] In fact, among the coercive state institutions, we may know more about the army and the intelligence services than about the police.[119] In such a vacuum the new drug scholarship proves a major advance. It suggests the essential paradox at the heart of Mexican policing. Cops were meant to keep order and enforce the law but they were also meant to do so without incurring significant costs and with at least a degree of social approval.[120] Usually this was resolved through some sort of controlled corruption. Olvera demonstrates how the postrevolutionary sanitary police mixed employing drug laws to clean the streets of vagrants with the increasingly well-remunerated protection of certain favored peddlers. There were similar policies in 1920s Baja California, where the local government shielded certain traffickers but arrested others, collecting an impressive 26,000 pesos in fines in just eighteen months.[121] Or in San Luis Potosí, where Gonzalo Santos tried to win back the favor of the Potosino elites by corralling all the street *marihuanos* into the local jail.[122]

Such roles often led many police officials to go full time into the trade. The career move from cop to capo was frequent. At the end of the 1920s, the chief of police in Ciudad Juárez, Jesus Soza, and Edmundo Herrera of the state judicial police were actively involved in the drugs and prostitution business, enjoying the protection of the municipal president and military zone commander.[123] Since the mid-1960s, Jaime Herrera Nevárez worked as an officer of the State Judicial Police in Durango. As Morris shows, his rise as a major heroin trafficker ran parallel to his rise through the ranks of the police.[124] In the 1970s, Mexico City police chief and childhood friend of the president, Arturo "el Negro" Durazo, was a "known narcotics trafficker."[125]

In more general terms, analyzing the police, in turn, speaks to broader discussions about the historiography of twentieth-century state making, in which the framework that privileges hegemonic rule and cultural negotiations is effectively challenged by one that underscores the role of coercion, violence, repression, and (organized) crime in state making. The latter argues that the decrease in violence at the national level and the consolidation of institutional mechanisms of social and political control was, at least in part, conditioned by the displacement of violence and coercion to provincial towns and villages. In fact, grassroots violence and repression facilitated "the more ostensibly peaceful conduct of national politics."[126]

It is also possible to bring together these views on diplomacy and on the police in illuminating new ways. In particular, the combination of U.S. diplomatic pressure and U.S. policing methods upset delicate—some may argue unsustainable—balances. Pérez Ricart shows how FBN buy-and-busts might have caught border peddlers but also incited considerable public outrage and the eventual legal clampdown on such maneuvers. In this volume, Aviña, Cedillo, and Morris all suggest that U.S. antidrug pressure not only forced the military into an increased policing role but also rolled out federal police forces throughout the Mexican provinces. Such pressure transformed the local equilibriums forever. The federal judicial police and the DFS now competed with the state and municipal cops for the income from the drug trade. In view of the absence of accessible national police archives, archival sources concerning the drug trade provide valuable insights into the features and functioning of police forces at different administrative levels, into their complex and often contradictory relations, and into their significance for state making at local, regional, and national levels.

Looking at drug trafficking also offers insights into the evolution and changing features of Mexico's political system. In particular, the shifting balance between political centralization and regional power has been the subject of considerable debate. An influential theory has been that the consolidation of one-party rule and its corporatist structures was key for federal power holders to subdue powerful regional political and military interests that had emerged from the armed phase of the Revolution. Centrally run economic and fiscal policies strengthened this trend. Although this historical trend was never linear across the national territory nor irreversible (think of the formal politics of decentralization and the de facto re-emergence of powerful regional elites in the face of weakened federal institutions since the 1980s), the overall argument still seems valid.

Yet new drugs scholarship impinges on this debate in at least two ways: What role have resources from the drug business played in shaping the balance of power between local/regional and federal interests during particular conjunctures? Governors or local strongmen with pockets filled with drug money are less likely to bow to directives or incentives from higher political or state echelons. We can think of examples running from Esteban Cantú Jiménez, governor of Baja California during the 1910s, through Leopoldo Sánchez Celis, governor of Sinaloa in the 1960s, to Tomás Yárrington Ruvalcaba, governor of Tamaulipas at the start of the twenty-first century. All confronted the federal authorities and managed—at least temporarily—to gain a degree of state autonomy.

The other way to approach this theme is to investigate the dynamics of local/regional and centralized control of the illicit drug business itself. Which political or law enforcement agencies were associated with drug traffickers, and how did those coalitions shift through time? It has sometimes been suggested—parallel to the general argument concerning political centralization—that Mexico's drug business was since the late 1940s controlled by the national intelligence agency and by national political elites, until the grip of the latter on the political system weakened. There is, however, evidence that if such a more or less centrally controlled system of trafficking and state protection ever existed it was not until the late 1970s, and only for a brief period. The historical evidence instead shows that during a large part of the twentieth century the drug trade system was relatively small-scale, integrated into regional socioeconomic hierarchies, and regulated by municipal or state police forces. By the mid-1970s, increased competition among drug growers and traffickers, spurred by the new scale of the trade from the 1960s onwards, in combination with the heavy-handed intromission of federal law enforcement agencies into the regions, lead to fierce competition about who would control markets and state-sponsored protection rackets (local, state, and federal agencies), a pluralization of armed actors and a dominance of federal law enforcement agencies (the army, federal police, and DFS).

Caciquismo has long played a critical role in constructing informal political and social relations between different levels of government and the state. While its phenomenology changed through time, as caciques gradually became more absorbed into the new institutional environment, while maintaining their informal power, their essential role as mediators remained crucial for postrevolutionary state making. How to approach the relations between caciquismo and the worlds of drug trafficking and organized crime? It is possible to think about the development of these connections along two routes: established cacique power structures articulate with illicit (drug) economies; the other route works in reverse when drugs-based "primitive accumulation" and power, coercive muscle, and territorial control morph into broader cacicazgos. Both scenarios may lead to what we could call "narco-caciquismo," a modality of local authority and mechanisms of intermediation, built at least partially on the revenues of drug trafficking, generally set in regional societies in which drug trafficking or organized crime are socially and economically significant.

Although there are many studies about local and regional cacicazgos in postrevolutionary Mexico, hardly any touch upon the role of drug trafficking. Local illicit drug economies were rarely factored into the original research questions.[127] It is likely also related to the availability of relevant archival sources. We nevertheless expect that future bottom-up histories of drug trafficking will encounter the figure of the "narco-cacique." In fact, recent scholarship has started to investigate the relationship between the formation of cacicazgos and the world of drugs. Fernández Velázquez has shown that during the 1940s through 1960s peasants in highland Sinaloa combined the cultivation of marijuana and poppies with subsistence crops and cooperated in family- and place-based networks, which later developed into the clans that ran drugs cultivation in the highlands and trafficking routes in the lowlands and beyond.[128] Informal networks were crucial for protection. Melesio Cuén Cásarez had been municipal president of Badiraguato, Sinaloa, on several occasions during the 1930s and early 1950s. His political influence included the appointment of judges, police officers, and civil servants: "tuvo el mando en el puño y todo lo que ahí pasaba tenía que ver con él" [he held power in his hands and everything that happened there had to do with him].[129] His cacicazgo originated in substantial economic influence. Cuén had business interests in commerce, mining, real estate, tortilla factories, a pharmacy, and a funeral home. As a prominent merchant, he became the best-informed and best-connected man in town, who arranged marriages, resolved quarrels, and advised people in all matters.[130] For one local author he was the "cacique deseado" of the town.[131] Federal law enforcement agents probably disagreed when they reported Cuén's involvement in poppy cultivation in 1938.[132] He sold protection to local producers. By the 1930s, Cuén had become a kind of narco-cacique, whose local authority was based on a mixture of licit and illicit businesses, formal political authority, informal networks, and social capital.

Others were classic revolutionary caciques, who harnessed their military record, their control of armed men, and their contacts with urban politicians to carve out areas of local influence. By the 1940s, with the money to buy up opium and the political power to escape prosecution, they were able to become caciques-turned-opium wholesalers.[133] There are no reasons to think that similar cacicazgos would not have formed in the Chihuahuan sierras or in the southern states of Jalisco, Nayarit, Michoacán, or perhaps, above all, in Guerrero and Oaxaca. What can we learn if we look through the lens of caciquismo at the Herrera clan in Santiago Papasquiaro, Durango, in many ways a "traditional" local ranchero leader, but with access to a "modern" migrant network in Chicago?

Several contributions to this volume make clear that the drug trade shaped political processes and state making during particular conjunctures. For example, during the mid-1940s, and most importantly from the 1970s onwards, the increasing competition among traffickers and the repressive interventions by different law enforcements agencies caused waves of conflict and violence. The latter added another source of conflict, contestation, and instability, mostly overlooked so far, to an already complicated landscape of social conflicts and radicalization. In the rural Mexico of the 1970s, sources of discontent and conflict multiplied as the state abandoned the countryside, leaving it in the hands of caciques, corrupt government officials, and agrarian capital. Meanwhile, electoral channels clogged and had almost unvarying outcomes: "victories for the PRI and ... the requisite supermajorities, rooted in formal and informal electoral manipulation, to block all but glacially incremental institutional change."[134] As social tensions and contradictions mounted, the Cold War, especially the Cuban Revolution, provided a language of polarization and radicalization to discontented opposition groups and entrenched state and party elites alike.[135] Armed conflicts and guerrilla movements emerged, and the Mexican state unleashed a dirty war. Regions with major forms of social, often radical, activism often overlapped with drug cultivation hotspots. For many peasants, marijuana or poppy cultivation provided a livelihood option amidst overwhelmingly depressive economic opportunity structures. It provided cash to escape rural poverty and the associated racial and social hierarchies.[136] But drug trafficking also overlapped with local mestizo elites, such as in Guerrero, where the trade funded armed state-affiliated paramilitaries like the Grupo Sangre. What had started as the "*gran campaña*" against drug cultivation and trafficking in 1948 became a major source of violence in the second half of the 1970s, mainly in the form of Operation Condor.[137] In Sinaloa, Chihuahua, Michoacán, and Guerrero counternarcotics operations became entangled with counterinsurgency: distinguishing between combating guerrillas, social activism, and drug trafficking became impossible, especially from the perspective of local communities. In sum, during the 1960s and 1970s, the Mexican political system was overwhelmed by the accumulation and mutual reinforcement of several large (national) social conflicts and myriad sources of contestation and resistance, including those resulting from the progressively violent world of drugs.

Violence and Mexico's Singularity: Some Final Reflections

No doubt, readers will ask what our historical case studies can tell us about Mexico's contemporary drug-related violence? Well, in some ways, not very much. This volume suggests that until the 1970s crackdown, the Mexican drug trade was relatively pacific. It was not simply a matter of "state control" as many political scientists assert, nor, one should add, of the breakdown of (central) state control in subsequent decades as the "prize of democratization" and political pluralization.[138] The trade was often based on a more deep-seated blend of cooperation, family ties, community alliances, and, when needed, due deference. Competition was rare, drug-related murders rarer, and when they did occur, they were often caused by outsiders (like the American mafiosi who washed up in wartime Tijuana). In the 1970s, the violence associated with the drug trade did increase, as did the volumes and resources involved in the trade. Though we have no systematic criminal violence data set for that period, the qualitative evidence we do have goes some way to corroborating contemporary examinations of drug violence.[139] Yet, as Aviña and Cedillo argue, aggressive, unforgiving policing has always been ineffective and counterproductive. Military involvement has been even more destructive. In this sense, this volume's historical studies corroborate the main conclusions of political scientists and other scholars about more recent developments. One anthropologist found that in the early 2000s concerted law enforcement interventions triggered a cycle of lethal violence and disorder in eastern Peru.[140] In Mexico, after 2006, all-out militarization and law enforcement tactics such as the kingpin strategy combined to create criminal fragmentation and a vortex of violence.[141] Harsh policing and militarization not only produced violent responses and divisions among trafficking organizations, it also encouraged corruption among federal institutions. This in turn resulted in competition between different layers of the state over the control of a more and more valuable trade. And this caused more violence. Conjunctures of intrastate rivalries and spikes in violence, such as those during late 1940s Tamaulipas (Flores Pérez) and 1970s Sinaloa (Cedillo), provide historical evidence for Durán-Martínez's political economy approach to drug violence in post-1980 Colombia and Mexico, which argues that the diminishing cohesion of state security apparatuses instigates the escalation and visibility of violence.[142]

Readers may also wonder about Mexico's singularity (or not). While we strongly believe in the value of fine-grained and in-depth studies of subnational histories of drug trafficking, we also see great scholarly merit in examining parallels with the history of Mexico's drug trade. No doubt, such parallels abound. In particular, recent works argue that drug production emerged in regions of failed midcentury state development projects. In South American countries, including Bolivia, Peru, and Colombia, these projects were Cold War attempts to stave off land reform by colonizing regions of the Amazon. In Afghanistan it was the vast Helmand Valley Development Project.[143] As

Maldonado argues, similar processes of initial state-backed growth followed by declining state support and depressed agricultural prices pushed many Tierra Caliente peasants to start growing marijuana and opium. Decades before, the decline of the Sinaloan mining industry and the grinding poverty of the state's sierras propelled many highland peasants toward drugs cultivation. The growth of border vice zones—like Tijuana and Ciudad Juárez—with their own semiautonomous drug markets parallel the establishment of similar spaces first in the African American areas of U.S. cities and then by the 1950s overseas in places like Havana. The logic—of fulfilling American desires while minimizing the visible damage to white America's morality—was the same.[144]

Mexican drug traffickers also built networks on existing smuggling connections both in the wake of Prohibition and again following the 1960s fayuquero boom in moving untaxed commercial goods.[145] Similar, relatively simple job swaps undergirded the expansion of drug trafficking in Colombia from the Caribbean coast of Colombia through highland Medellín to the jungle of Caquetá, where former goods smugglers pioneered the narcotics trade.[146] In addition, Mexico's northern desert-like border region shares certain features with the tropical "narco-frontiers" of Colombia's northern coast, Peru's Upper Huallaga valleys, and Bolivia's Chapare "borderlands."[147] Finally, stories of the Mexican government allowing counterinsurgency specialists to build up the state security apparatus and their own private bank accounts with the proceeds from drug trafficking chime with similar Cold War practices pioneered in Southeast Asia (by the French SDECE and the CIA) and then carried on in Guatemala, Brazil, Bolivia, Chile, and Colombia.[148]

Yet despite these parallels, Mexico also stands alone. We briefly highlight three features. First, the evolution of drug trafficking and its broader political and social ramifications and articulations are mediated by particular historical trajectories of power configurations, regime types, and institutional arrangements. Although not the centralized Leviathan outlined by a previous generation of scholarship, Mexico's peculiar dominant party regime provided the state with a comparatively stronger cohesion and coercive capacity than, say, the Colombian state that faced prolonged armed conflict in substantial parts of the national territory.[149] Second, most nations only play one role in the drug trade. They are predominantly producers (like Peru), or chemists (like 1960s France) or traffickers (like 1950s Canada or 1980s Colombia), or zones of drug consumption (like 1950s Havana or 1970s Amsterdam). From the 1920s onwards, Mexico has always played all four. Mexicans have grown the raw materials, made them into marketable narcotics, and then either taken them up north or provided spaces for consumers to take them in Mexico. Finally, such multitasking is—of course—the result of sitting on the frontier with the United States. So far from God, so close to a country which consumes 70 percent of the world's cocaine. It has given the Mexican drug trade a history, culture, and a durability that most countries lack. But it is also a multitasking that has combined at different times in multiple ways to throw up diverse, regional drug trafficking cultures.

NOTES

1. Malcolm Beith, *The Last Narco. Inside the Hunt for El Chapo, the World's Most Wanted Drug Lord* (New York: Grove Press, 2010); José Blancornelas, *El Cártel. Los Arrellano Félix: La mafia más ponderosas en la historia de América Latina* (Mexico City: Delbolsillo, 2002); Francisco Cruz, *El Cártel de Juárez* (Mexico City: Planeta, 2008), *Tierra narca* (Mexico City: Temas'dehoy, 2010); Al Cimino, *Drug Wars: The Bloody Reign of the Mexican Cartels* (Heatherton, Victoria: Hinkler, 2014); Michael Deibert, *In the Shadow of Saint Death. The Gulf Cartel and the Price of America's Drug War in Mexico* (Guildford: Lyons Press, 2014); Jorge Fernández Menéndez, *El otro poder: las redes del narcotráfico, la política y la violencia en México* (Mexico City: Suma de Letras, 2004); Jorge Fernández Menéndez, *De los maras a los Zetas: los secretos del narcotráfico, de Colombia a Chicago* (Mexico City: Random House, 2006); Alejandro Gutiérrez, *Narcotráfico. El gran desafío de Calderón* (Mexico City: Temas'dehoy, 2007); Jerry Langton, *Gangland: The Rise of the Mexican Drug Cartels from El Paso to Vancouver* (Ontario: Harper Collins, 2013); Omar Millán, *Viajes al este de la ciudad: una crónica de la guerra contra el narco en Tijuana* (Mexico City: Trilce, 2015); Humberto Padgett, *Guerrero. Los hombres de verde y la dama de rojo. Crónica de la Nación Gomera* (Barcelona: Ediciones Urano, 2015); Humberto Padgett, *Tamaulipas. La casta de los narcogobernadores: Un eastern mexicano* (Barcelona: Ediciones Urano, 2016); Ricardo Ravelo, *Los capos: las narco-rutas de México* (Mexico City: Debolsillo, 2006); Ricardo Ravelo, *Narcomex: historia e historias de una guerra* (Mexico City: Grijalbo, 2013); Ricardo Ravelo, *Osiel: vida y tragedia de un capo* (Mexico City: Debolsillo, 2013); José Reveles, *El cartel incómodo. El fin de los Beltrán Leyva y la hegemonía del Chapo Guzmán* (Mexico City: Grijalbo, 2010); Rafael Rodríguez Castañeda, ed., *El México Narco* (Mexico City: Temas'dehoy, 2009).

2. Publications by specialists from think tanks, government agencies, and security consultancy firms also tend to focus on the interactions of drug trafficking organizations and state agencies. These institutions include STRATFOR, the Center for Strategic & International Studies, the Congressional Research Center, and the Woodrow Wilson

Center Mexico Institute in the United States, and the Instituto para la Seguridad y la Democracia (Insyde), the Consejo Ciudadano para la Seguridad y la Justicia Penal, and the Instituto para la Acción Ciudadana in Mexico.

3. Judith Torrea, *Juárez en la sombra. Crónicas de una ciudad que se resiste a morir* (Mexico City: Aguilar, 2010); Sandra Rodríguez Nieto, *Fábrica del crimen* (Mexico City: Temas'dehoy, 2012); Marcela Turati, *Fuego cruzado: las víctimas atrapadas en la guerra del narco* (Mexico City: Random House, 2011); Javier Valdez Cárdenas, *Los morros del narco: Historias reales de niños y jóvenes en el narcotráfico mexicano* (Mexico City: Aguilar, 2011).

4. In 2011, the poet and activist Javier Sicilia called Ciudad Juárez the "epicenter of pain" and ominously predicted that the whole of Mexico would become like Juárez if the situation of violence were not addressed. See *Excélsior*, June 10, 2011.

5. Ioan Grillo, *El Narco: Inside Mexico's Criminal Insurgency* (New York: Bloomsbury, 2012); Diego Osorno, *La guerra de los Zetas: viaje por la frontera de la necropolítica* (Mexico City: Grijalbo, 2012); J. Jesús Esquivel, *La CIA, Camarena y Caro Quintero: la historia secreta* (Mexico City: Grijalbo, 2014); Terence Poppa, *Drug Lord: The Life & Death of a Mexican Kingpin. A True Story* (Seattle: Demand Publications, 1998 [1990]); Charles Bowden, *Down by the River: Drugs, Money, Murder, and Family* (New York: Simon & Schuster, 2004), *Murder City: Ciudad Juárez and the Global Economy's New Killing Fields* (New York: Nation Books, 2011).

6. George W. Grayson, *Mexico: Narco-Violence and a Failed State?* (New Brunswick, NJ: Transaction Publishers, 2009); George W. Grayson, *La Familia Drug Cartel: Implications for U.S.-Mexican Security* (Carlisle, PA: U.S. Army War College Press, 2010); George W. Grayson and Samuel Logan, *The Executioner's Men: Los Zetas, Rogue Soldiers, Criminal Entrepreneurs, and the Shadow State They Created* (New Brunswick, NJ: Transaction Publishers, 2015); Robert J. Bunker, ed., *Narcos over the Border: Gangs, Cartels and Mercenaries* (New York: Routledge, 2011); Paul Rexton Kan, *Cartels at War: Mexico's Drug-Fueled Violence and the Threat to U.S. National Security* (Washington, DC: Potomac, 2012).

7. We acknowledge the existence of methodologically and conceptually more sophisticated research such as that of Nathan P. Jones, *Mexico's Illicit Drug Networks and the State Reaction* (Washington: Georgetown University Press, 2016); Paul Kenny and Mónica Serrano, with Arturo Sotomayor, eds., *Mexico's Security Failure: Collapse into Criminal Violence* (London: Routledge, 2011).

8. Vidriana Rios, "Quién mata a los periodistas?" *Nexos*, August 1, 2013.

9. Luis Astorga, *Mitología del "narcotraficante" en México* (Mexico City: UNAM/Plaza y Valdés, 1995), 89.

10. Paul Gootenberg and Isaac Campos, "Towards a New Drug History of Latin America: A Research Frontier at the Center of Debates," *Hispanic American Historical Review*, 95, no. 1 (2015): 22.

11. See the Special Issue of *Hispanic American Historical Review* 95, no. 1 (2015).

12. Alexander S. Dawson, *The Peyote Effect. From the Inquisition to the War on Drugs* (Oakland: University of California Press, 2018). This type of cultural history easily bleeds into the scholarly work produced by cultural studies about the representation of drug trafficking and violence in literature, cinema, and other forms of artistic mediation. See e.g. Shaylih Muehlmann, *When I Wear My Alligator Boots. Narco-culture in the U.S.-Mexico Borderlands* (Oakland: University of California Press, 2014).

13. Fernando Escalante Gonzalbo, *El crimen como realidad y representación* (Mexico City: El Colegio de México, 2012), 104.

14. Oswaldo Zavala, *Los cárteles no existen. Narcotráfico y cultura en México* (Barcelona: Malpaso, 2018), 20.

15. Escalante Gonzalbo, *El crimen*, 107.

16. Zavala, *Los cárteles no existen*, 20.

17. Escalante Gonzalbo, *El crimen*, 238.

18. Torrea, *Juárez en la sombra*; Andreas Schedler, *En la niebla de la guerra. Los ciudadanos ante la violencia criminal organizada* (Mexico City: CIDE, 2015).

19. See also Peter Andreas and Kelly M. Greenhill, *Sex, Drugs, and Body Counts: The Politics of Numbers in Global Crime and Conflict* (Ithaca, NY: Cornell University Press, 2008).

20. Zavala, *Los cárteles no existen*, 14, 21, 23. The controversial and empirically weak argument of the War on Drugs as an instrument to depopulate areas in favor of extractive industries can also be found in Guadalupe Correa-Correa, *Los Zetas Inc. Criminal Corporations, Energy, and Civil War in Mexico* (Austin: University of Texas Press, 2017); Federico Mastrogiovanni, *Ni vivos, ni muertos. La desaparición forzada en México como estrategia de terror* (Mexico City: Grijalbo/Proceso, 2014), 35–44; Dawn Paley, *Drug War Capitalism* (Oakland: AK Press, 2014).

21. Gootenberg and Campos, "Towards a New Drug History," 20; the quotation is from Steven Topic, Carlos Marichal, and Zephyr Frank, "Commodity Chains in Theory and in Latin American History," in *From Silver to Cocaine. Latin American Commodity Chains and the Building of the World Economy, 1500–2000*, ed. Steven Topik, Carlos Marichal, and Zephyr Frank (Durham, NC: Duke University Press, 2006), 8.

22. Paul Gootenberg, "Cocaine in Chains: The Rise and Demise of a Global Commodity, 1860–1950," in *From Silver to Cocaine. Latin American Commodity Chains and the Building of the World Economy, 1500–2000*, ed. Steven Topik, Carlos Marichal, and Zephyr Frank (Durham, NC: Duke University Press, 2006), 321.

23. Lina Britto, *Marijuana Boom. The Rise and Fall of Colombia's First Drug Paradise* (Oakland: University of California Press, 2020).

24. Gootenberg and Campos, "Towards a New Drug History," 19.

25. Frank Dikötter, Lars Laaman, Zhou Xun, *Narcotic Culture. A History of Drugs in China* (London: C. Hurst & Co., 2016 [2004]); Paul Gootenberg, *Andean Co-*

caine. *The Making of a Global Drug* (Durham, NC: Duke University Press, 2008); Ben Westhoff, *Fentanyl, Inc. How Rogue Chemists Are Creating the Deadliest Wave of the Opioid Epidemic* (London: Scribe, 2019).

26. Zsusa Gille and Seán Ó Riain, "Global Ethnography," *Annual Review of Sociology* 28 (2002): 279.

27. Gille and Ó Riain, "Global Ethnography," 279, and Michael Burawoy, "Introduction. Reaching for the Global," in *Global Ethnography. Forces, Connections and Imaginations in a Postmodern World*, ed. Michael Burawoy et al. (Berkeley: University of California Press, 2000), 28–32.

28. See Morris, chapter 13 in this volume.

29. Sam Quiñones, *Dreamland. The True Tale of America's Opiate Epidemic* (New York: Bloomsbury Press, 2015).

30. Smith and Pansters, chapter 6 in this volume.

31. Campos, chapter 2 in this volume; Dikötter, Laaman, and Xun, *Narcotic Culture*, 2.

32. Pérez Ricart, chapter 7 in this volume.

33. Britto, *Marijuana Boom*, 209, 217.

34. James Tharin Bradford, *Poppies, Politics, and Power. Afghanistan and the Global History of Drugs and Diplomacy* (Ithaca, NY: Cornell University Press, 2019), 109, 112.

35. For Sinaloa, see Juan Antonio Fernández Velázquez, "El Narcotráfico en los Altos de Sinaloa" (PhD thesis, Universidad Veraruzana, 2016). For Michoacán and Guerrero, see Maldonado and Aviña, chapters 10 and 12 in this volume.

36. From the record "Mexico," released 1970, RCA Victor. Translation: "Where, my friend, is the plant of the sun?"

37. Cedillo, chapter 11 in this volume. Britto shows that decreasing marijuana production in the early 1970s in Mexico and increasing U.S. demand prompted the marijuana boom in northeastern Colombia. *Marijuana Boom*, 77.

38. Peter Maguire, *Thai Stick: Surfers, Scammers and the Untold Story of the Marijuana Trade* (New York: University of Columbia Press, 2013); *High Times*, August 7, 1978.

39. Alfred W. McCoy, *The Politics of Heroin: CIA Complicity in the Global Drug Trade, Afghanistan, Southeast Asia, Central America, Colombia* (New York: Lawrence Hill Books, 2003), 44–45.

40. Isaac Campos, *Home Grown: Marijuana and the Origins of Mexico's War on Drugs* (Chapel Hill: University of North Carolina Press, 2012).

41. For examples, Casa de la Cultura Júridica de Tijuana, caja 1, exp. 13, Mauro López Mendez, 1946, and caja 4, exp. 96, Enrique Durán Granados, 1943.

42. Jorge Segura Millan, *Marihuana* (Mexico City: Costa-Amic, 1971), 250–66.

43. *Siglo de Torreón*, online database.

44. *Washington Post*, January 29, 1975.

45. Fernández Velázquez, "El Narcotráfico," 130.

46. National Narcotics Intelligence Consumers Committee (NNICC), *Narcotics Intelligence Estimate* (Washington, DC, 1984).

47. Campos, chapter 2 in this volume.

48. James A. Sandos, "Northern Separatism during the Mexican Revolution: An Inquiry into the Role of Drug Trafficking, 1910–1920," *The Americas*, 41, no. 2 (1984): 191–214; James A. Sandos, "Prostitution and Drugs: The United States Army on the Mexican-American Border, 1916–1917," *Pacific Historical Review* 49 (1980): 621–45; Antonio Ponce Aguilar, *El Coronel Esteban Cantú en el Distrito Norte de Baja California, 1911–1920* (Mexico City: n.d.), 69–82; Joseph Richard Werne, "Esteban Cantú y la Soberanía Mexicana en Baja California," *Historia Mexicana* (July–September 1980): 1–32.

49. David T. Courtwright, *Dark Paradise, A History of Opiate Addiction in America* (Cambridge, MA: Harvard University Press, 2001).

50. Archivo Histórico del Departamento del Distrito Federal, Sección Jefatura de Policía, serie Investigación y Seguridad, Servicio Secreto, caja 2, exp. 11, 20 Apr. 1932–20 Feb. 1937; NARA, RG59, Report re. Poppy Growing around Altar, 18 Apr. 1936.

51. NARA, RG170, box 23, Collected FBN Reports on Mexico, 1940–1947.

52. NARA, RG170, box 23, Collected FBN Reports on Mexico, 1940–1947.

53. Carlos Pérez Ricart, chapter 7 in this volume.

54. For the upsurge in European heroin, see McCoy, *Politics*, 44–67.

55. A. Nacaveva, *Diario de un narcotraficante* (Mexico City: Costa-Amic, 1994 ed.)

56. Tribunal Superior de Justicia, Amparos, 2967, 1967, Arturo Izquierdo Ebrard.

57. National Narcotics Intelligence Consumers Committee (NNICC), *Narcotics Intelligence Estimate* (Washington, DC, 1984).

58. Wikileaks, COCA CULTIVATION IN MEXICO. GFTA-75–8056, 2/24/1978 [Consulted February 25, 2021].

59. NARA, RG59, Secretary of State Telegrams, 24 Feb. 1978; *Alarma*, May 15, 1984.

60. Ricardo Pérez Montfort, ed., *Hábitos, normas y escándalo. Prensa, criminalidad y drogas durante el porfiriato tardío* (Mexico City: Fondo de Cultura Económica, 1997), 173.

61. NARA, RG59, 1910–1929, Mexicali Consul to Secretary of State, July 5, 1923.

62. NARA, RG59, 1930–34, R. Walton Moore to JD, August 8, 1934.

63. Cedillo, chapter 11 in this volume.

64. In 1980, Jaime Buelna confessed that he had been buying kilos of the stuff from heroin trafficker Jorge Favela as early as 1972. See Tribunal Superior de Justicia, Amparos, 1242, 1980, Jaime Buelna Aviles.

65. *Proceso*, July 14, 1984.

66. Campos, chapter 2 in this volume.

67. Campos, *Home Grown*, 19.

68. Pérez Montfort, chapter 3 in this volume; Elaine Carey, *Women Drug Traffick-*

ers: Mules, Bosses, and Organized Crime (Albuquerque: University of New Mexico Press, 2014), 38–45.

69. According to the Culiacán mayor, the traffickers had "come down from the sierra," were "particularly ignorant and spendthrift," and were "easily recognizable by their peculiar form of clothes and walk." *El Noroeste*, April 30, 1977.

70. Campos, chapter 2 in this volume.

71. Maldonado, chapter 10 in this volume.

72. Aviña and Cedillo, chapters 12 and 11 in this volume.

73. Wil G. Pansters and Benjamin T. Smith, "U.S. Moral Panics, Mexican Politics, and the Borderlands Origins of the War on Drugs, 1950–62," *Journal of Contemporary History* 55, no. 2 (2018): 364–87.

74. José Alfredo Gómez Estrada, *Gobierno y casinos: El origen de la riqueza de Abelardo L. Rodríguez* (Mexico City: Instituto Mora, 2002), 101–45; Nicole Mottier, "Drug Gangs and Politics in Ciudad Juárez: 1928–1936," *Mexican Studies/Estudios Mexicanos*, 25, no. 1 (Winter 2009): 19–46.

75. Enrique Fernández, the Ciudad Juárez dealer, funded multiple schools in the Juárez Valley. *La Prensa* (San Antonio), July 5, 1931, March 5, 1932.

76. Olvera, chapter 4 in this volume; AGN, DGIPS, 46/5, Reports of Agent 1a, August–December, 1924.

77. Fernández Velázquez, "El Narcotráfico."

78. NARA, RG84, Mazatlán, Consul to Secretary of State, January 23, 1945.

79. For the best evidence of this see the story of journalist Danton de los Rios negotiating with the governor's secretary for 50 kg of opium in 1947. NARA, RG170, Delagrave to Commissioner of Customs, August 20, 1947.

80. AGN, DFS, Versión Pública, Leopoldo Sánchez Celis; Nicolas Vidales Soto, *El Hombre del Paliacate* (Mexico City: SEP, 2006), 154.

81. Flores Pérez, chapter 9 in this volume.

82. AGN, DFS, Informe "El tráfico de armas, drogas etc," July 2, 1974.

83. Peter Dale Scott, *American War Machine: Deep Politics, the CIA Global Drug Connection, and the Road to Afghanistan* (Lanham, MD: Rowman & Littlefield, 2010), 49.

84. Sergio Aguayo Quezada, *La Charola: Una historia de los servicios de inteligencia en México* (Mexico City: Sextil, 2014).

85. *Últimas Noticias*, February 20, 1978.

86. Anonymous DEA agent, interview, September 2018.

87. Elaine Shannon, *Desperados: Latin Drug Lords, U.S. Lawmen, and the War America Can't Win* (New York: Viking, 1988).

88. Cedillo, chapter 11 in this volume.

89. AGN, DFS, Versión Pública, Raúl Mendiolea, Informe sobre Oscar Flores Sánchez, n.d.; NARA, RG59, 1930–1934, Anon to Josephus Daniels, March 5, 1934;

Wikileaks Telegram, August 26, 1976, https://wikileaks.org/plusd/cables/1976MEXICO10988_b.html; Wikileaks, Telegram, December 8, 1976, https://wikileaks.org/plusd/cables/1976MEXICO15494_b.html; José González G., *Lo Negro del Negro Durazo* (London: Editorial Posada, 1983).

90. *Proceso*, July 14, 1984.

91. Luis Astorga Almanza, *El Siglo de las Drogas* (Mexico City: Espasa Calpe, 1996); Astorga, *Mitología*.

92. Fernández Velázquez, chapter 8 in this volume.

93. Jorge Alan Sánchez Godoy, "Procesos de institucionalización de la narcocultura en Sinaloa," *Frontera Norte* 21, no. 41 (2009): 77–103.

94. Francisco Ortiz Pinchetti, Miguel Cabildo, Federico Campbell, and Ignacio Rodríguez, *La Operación Condor* (Mexico City: Proceso, 1991).

95. José Alfredo Andrade Bojorges, *La Historia Secreta del Narco: Desde Navolato Vengo* (Mexico City: Grijalbo, 1999).

96. Pérez Montfort, chapter 3 in this volume.

97. Morris, chapter 13 in this volume; René Cárdenas Barrios, *Narcotráfico, S. A.* (Mexico City: Diana, 1977).

98. Smith and Pansters, chapter 6 in this volume; Carey, chapter 5 in this volume.

99. Analysis of drug crimes from 1930 to 1950 listed in the Casas de la Cultura Júridica in Tijuana, Mazatlán, and Ciudad Juárez backs this up. In Ciudad Juárez 15 percent of drug offenders were women. In Tijuana it was less than 4 percent. In Mazatlán it was 2 percent.

100. Flores Pérez, chapter 9 in this volume.

101. Flores Pérez, chapter 9 in this volume; Smith and Pansters, chapter 6 in this volume.

102. Lorenzo Meyer and Josefina Zoraida Vazquez, *The United States and Mexico* (Chicago: Chicago University Press, 1995 edition), contains one sole reference to narcotics. For stand-alone treatments see Maria Celia Toro, *Mexico's "War" on Drugs, Causes and Consequences* (London: Lynne Reiner, 1995); Guadalupe González and Marta Tienda, eds., *The Drug Connection in U.S.-Mexican Relations* (San Diego: Center for U.S.-Mexican Studies, 1989); William O. Walker, *Drug Control in the Americas* (Albuquerque: University of New Mexico Press, 1989).

103. Octavio Herrera and Arturo Santa Cruz, *Historia de las relaciones internacionales de México, 1821–2010. América del Norte* (Mexico City: Secretaría de Relaciones Exteriores, 2011), 388.

104. See Pérez Ricart, chapter 7 in this volume.

105. Benjamin T. Smith, *The Mexican Press and Civil Society, 1940–1976: Stories from the Newsroom, Stories from the Street* (Chapel Hill: University of North Carolina Press, 2018), 81–114.

106. Herrera and Santa Cruz, *Historia*, 391.

107. Carlos Rico, *México y el mundo. Historia de sus relaciones exteriores: Vol. 8,*

Hacía la globalización (Mexico City: El Colegio de México, 2010), 67–114. This is an excellent introduction to José López Portillo's foreign policy. There is, however, one sole mention of drugs and no mention at all of Operation Condor.

108. Walker, *Drug Control*, 122.

109. Isaac Campos, "A Diplomatic Failure: The Mexican Role in the Demise of the 1940 Reglamento Federal de Toxicomanías," *Third World Quarterly* 39, no. 2 (2018): 232–47.

110. John J. Dwyer, *The Agrarian Dispute: The Expropriation of American-Owned Rural Land in Postrevolutionary Mexico* (Durham, NC: Duke University Press, 2008), 194–231. Again, drugs are mentioned once and in passing.

111. *La Prensa*, April 10, 1940.

112. Matthew D. Lassiter, "Pushers, Victims and the Lost Innocence of White Suburbia: California's War on Narcotics during the 1950s," *Journal of Urban History* 41, no. 5 (2015): 787–807.

113. Pansters and Smith, "U.S. Panics, Mexican Politics."

114. Muehlmann, *When I Wear My Alligator Boots*, 74–76.

115. Salvador Maldonado, *Los Márgenes del Estado Mexicano: Territorios ilegales, desarrollo y violencia en Michoacán* (Mexico City: Colegio de Michoacán, 2010), 351.

116. Alan Knight, "Narco-Violence and the State in Modern Mexico," in *Violence, Coercion, and State-Making in Twentieth-Century Mexico. The Other Half of the Centaur*, ed. Wil G. Pansters (Stanford, CA: Stanford University Press, 2012), 133.

117. E.g., Gilbert Joseph and Daniel Nugent, eds., *Everyday Forms of State Formation: Revolution and the Negotiation of Rule in Modern Mexico* (Durham, NC: Duke University Press, 1994); Mary Kay Vaughan, *Cultural Politics in Revolution: Teachers, Peasants, and Schools in Mexico, 1930–1940* (Tucson: University of Arizona Press, 1997).

118. Diane Davis, "Policing and Mexican Regime Change: From Post-Authoritarianism to Populism to Neo-Liberalism," in *Violence, Coercion, and State-Making in Twentieth-Century Mexico. The Other Half of the Centaur*, ed. Wil G. Pansters (Stanford, CA: Stanford University Press, 2012), 68–90; Diane Davis, "Policing and Populism in the Cárdenas and Echeverría Administrations," in *Populism in Twentieth Century Mexico: The Presidencies of Lázaro Cárdenas and Luis Echeverría in Mexico*, ed. Amelia M. Kiddle and María L. O. Muñoz (Tucson: University of Arizona Press, 2010), 135–58. Studies about current Mexican policing include María Eugenia Suárez de Garay, *Policías: una averiguación antropológica* (Guadalajara: ITESO/UDG, 2006); Daniel M. Sabet, *Police Reform in Mexico. Informal Politics and the Challenge of Institutional Change* (Stanford, CA: Stanford University Press, 2012); Niels Uildriks (with the collaboration of Nelia Tello Peón), *Mexico's Unrule of Law. Implementing Human Rights in Police and Judicial Reform under Democratization* (Lanham, MD: Lexington Books, 2010).

119. About the army see, e.g., the recent studies by Thomas Rath, *Myths of Demili-*

tarization in Postrevolutionary Mexico, 1920–1960 (Chapel Hill: University of North Carolina Press, 2013), and Ben Fallaw and Terry Rugeley, eds., *Forced Marches. Soldiers and Military Caciques in Modern Mexico* (Tucson: University of Arizona Press, 2012); about the intelligence services see Aaron Navarro, *Political Intelligence and the Creation of Modern Mexico, 1938–1952* (University Park: Penn State University Press, 2010), and Sergio Aguayo Quezada, *La charola. Una historia de los servicios de inteligencia en México* (Mexico City: Grijalbo, 2001).

120. As Pablo Piccato has demonstrated, the crime pages of the tabloid press were influential sites for demonstrating public displeasure. See *A History of Infamy: Crime, Truth, and Justice in Mexico* (Oakland: University of California Press, 2017), 63–103.

121. Gómez Estrada, *Gobierno y casinos*, 55–56.

122. Casa de la Cultura Júridica, San Luis Potosí, Delitos contra la salud, 1943–1944.

123. Report of agent nr. 10, May 25, 1928, AGN, DGIPS, 1928, file 19.

124. Chapter 13 in this volume.

125. The López Portillo Cabinet: A Political Assessment, December 8, 1976, see https://wikileaks.org/plusd/cables/1976MEXICO15494_b.html.

126. Alan Knight, "Habitus and Homicide. Political Culture in Revolutionary Mexico," in *Citizens of the Pyramide. Essays on Mexican Political Culture*, ed. Wil G. Pansters (Amsterdam: Thela Publishers, 1997), 123.

127. They sometimes were. See the following two extraordinary works, which all feature narco-caciques. George Arthur Genz, "Entrepreneurship and Caciquismo: A Study of Community Power in a Mexican Gulf Coast Village" (PhD diss., Michigan State University 1975); Patricia Arias Lucia Bazan, *Demandas y Conflicto: El Poder Político en un pueblo de Morelos* (Mexico City: CIS-INAH, 1979).

128. Chapter 8 in this volume.

129. Modesto Aguilar Alvarado and Wilfrido Ibarra Escobar, *Desarrollo empresarial y liderazgo político. Melesio Cuén Cázares: empresario y líder de Badiraguato* (Culiacán: Universidad Autónoma de Sinaloa, 2013), 53.

130. Alvarado and Escobar, *Desarrollo empresarial*, 55, 37.

131. Translation: "the preferred cacique." Enrique Ruiz Alba, "Don Melesio Cuén o el cacique deseado," in *18 Encuentros con la historia: Badiraguato*, part 1, ed. José Ma. Figueroa and Gilberto López Alanís (Culiacán: Gobierno del Estado, 2002), 69–70; see also Aguilar and Escobar, *Desarrollo empresarial*, 28.

132. AGN, DGIPS, box 128, exp. 17, Atwood to Jefe del Depto. de Salubridad, November 25, 1938.

133. An interesting example is that of the revolutionary Carabineros of Santiago, Sinaloa. See AGN, DGIPS, box 128, file 17, Atwood to Jefe del Departamento de Salubridad, November 25, 1938. Carlos Manuel Aguirre, *Los Carabineros de Santiago* (Culiacán: n.p., 1992).

134. Paul Gillingham, "'We don't have arms, but we do have balls.' Fraud, Violence, and Popular Agency in Elections," in *Dictablanda. Politics, Work, and Culture in*

Mexico, 1938–1968, ed. Paul Gillingham and Benjamín T. Smith (Durham, NC: Duke University Press, 2014), 166.

135. Renata Keller, *Mexico's Cold War. Cuba, the United States, and the Legacy of the Mexican Revolution* (Cambridge: Cambridge University Press, 2015).

136. On his wanderings through rural Mexico during the 1960s, Jerry Kamstra found firsthand evidence of "rational economic" peasant behavior when switching to drugs cultivation; see *Weed. Adventures of a Dope Smuggler* (Santa Barbara, CA: Ross-Erikson Publishers, 1984 [1973]).

137. For an early informative article see Richard B. Craig, "La Campaña Permanente: Mexico's Antidrug Campaign," *Journal of Interamerican Studies and World Affairs* 20, no. 2 (1978): 107–31.

138. Gustavo Duncan's political analysis of drug trafficking in Colombia and Mexico understands the latter's war on drugs as an "unintended consequence of the process of democratization." See his *Más que plata o plomo. El poder político del narcotráfico en Colombia y México* (Mexico City: Debate, 2014), 144. Although the plain "democratization argument" has many followers, we sympathize with the more cautious position adopted by Angélica Durán-Martínez ("democratization... may potentially—though not inevitably—increase criminal violence"). After all, would the vastly increased volume of drug trafficking since the late 1970s not have unsettled a nondemocratic PRI regime as well? See Durán-Martínez, *The Politics of Drug Violence. Criminals, Cops, and Politicians in Colombia and Mexico* (New York: Oxford University Press, 2018), 65.

139. One suspects that the hiding of bodies in combination with the throttling of the press would make an attempt at such a data set redundant. For recent decades, Guillermo Trejo and Sandra Ley use data from Mexican newspapers to assess levels of drug-related violence from 1997 onwards. See their *Votes, Drugs and Violence, The Political Logic of Criminal Wars in Mexico* (Cambridge: Cambridge University Press, 2020).

140. Mirella van Dun, "Exploring Narco-Sovereignty/Violence: Analyzing Illegal Networks, Crime, Violence and Legitimation in a Peruvian Cocaine Enclave (2003–2007)," *Journal of Contemporary Ethnography* 43, no. 4 (2014): 395–418.

141. See Mónica Serrano, "Mexico. A Humanitarian Crisis in the Making," and Laura Carlsen, "Effects of Militarization in the Name of Counter-Narcotics Efforts and Consequences for Human Rights in Mexico," both in *Beyond the Drug War in Mexico. Human Rights, the Public Sphere and Justice*, ed. Wil G. Pansters, Benjamin T. Smith, and Peter Watt (London: Routledge, 2018), 53–75, 76–94. For a comparative analysis, see Benjamin Lessing, *Making Peace in Drug Wars: Crackdowns and Cartels in Latin America* (Cambridge: Cambridge University Press, 2018). See also Javier Osorio, "The Contagion of Drug Violence: Spatiotemporal Dynamics of the War on Drugs," *Journal of Conflict Resolution*, 59, no. 8 (2015): 1403–32.

142. Durán-Martínez, *The Politics of Drug Violence*.

143. Paul Gootenberg and Liliana M. Dávalos, eds., *The Origins of Cocaine: Colo-*

nization and Failed Development in the Amazon Andes (London: Routledge, 2019); Bradford, *Poppies, Politics*, 180–213.

144. Joseph Spillane, "The Making of an Underground Market: Drug Selling in Chicago, 1900–1940," *Journal of Social History* 32, no. 1 (Autumn 1998): 27–47; Eduardo Sáenz Rovner, *The Cuban Connection: Drug Trafficking, Smuggling and Gambling in Cuba from the 1920s to the Revolution*, trans. Russ Davidson (Chapel Hill: University of North Carolina Press, 2008).

145. As well as the articles in this volume the point is made in George T. Díaz, *Border Contraband: A History of Smuggling across the Rio Grande* (Austin: University of Texas Press, 2015). For *fayuqueros* see Efrén Sandoval, "Economía de la fayuca y del narcotráfico en el noreste de México. Extorsiones, contubernios y solidaridades en las economías transfronterizas," *Desacatos*, no. 38 (2012). Also Flores Pérez, chapter 9 in this volume.

146. Francisco Thoumi, "Why the Illegal Psychoactive Drugs Industry Grew in Colombia," *Journal of Interamerican Studies and World Affairs* 34, no. 3 (1992): 37–63; Britto, *Marijuana Boom*, 57–67.

147. Teo Ballvé, "Narco-Frontiers: A Spatial Framework for Drug-Fuelled Accumulation," *Journal of Agrarian Change* 19, no. 2: 211–24; Britto, *Marijuana Boom*; Mirella van Dun, "Narco-Territoriality and Shadow Powers in a Peruvian Cocaine Frontier," *Terrorism and Political Violence* 31, no. 5: 1026–48. Andrew C. Millington, "Creating Coca Frontiers and Cocaleros in Chapare. Bolivia, 1940 to 1990," in *The Origins of Cocaine: Colonization and Failed Development in the Amazon Andes*, ed. Paul Gootenberg and Liliana M. Dávalos (London: Routledge, 2019), 84–113, speaks of Chapare as the "borderland" between highland and lowland people and economies.

148. McCoy, *The Politics of Heroin*; Teresa Caldeira and James Holston, "Democracy and Violence in Brazil," *Comparative Studies in Society and History* 41, no. 4 (1999): 691–729; Allan Gillies, "Theorising State–Narco Relations in Bolivia's Nascent Democracy (1982–1993): Governance, Order and Political Transition," *Third World Quarterly* 39, no. 4 (2018): 727–46; Trejo and Ley, *Votes, Drugs and Violence*, 42–45.

149. Paul Gillingham and Benjamin T. Smith, eds., *Dictablanda. Politics, Work, and Culture in Mexico, 1938–1968* (Durham, NC: Duke University Press, 2014), esp. 1–43. For comparative studies about drug trafficking in Mexico and Colombia, see Durán Martínez, *The Politics of Drug Violence*, and Duncan, *Más que plata o plomo*, 143–247.

PART I

The Emerging Prohibition Regime
Policies, Policing, and Popular Vices

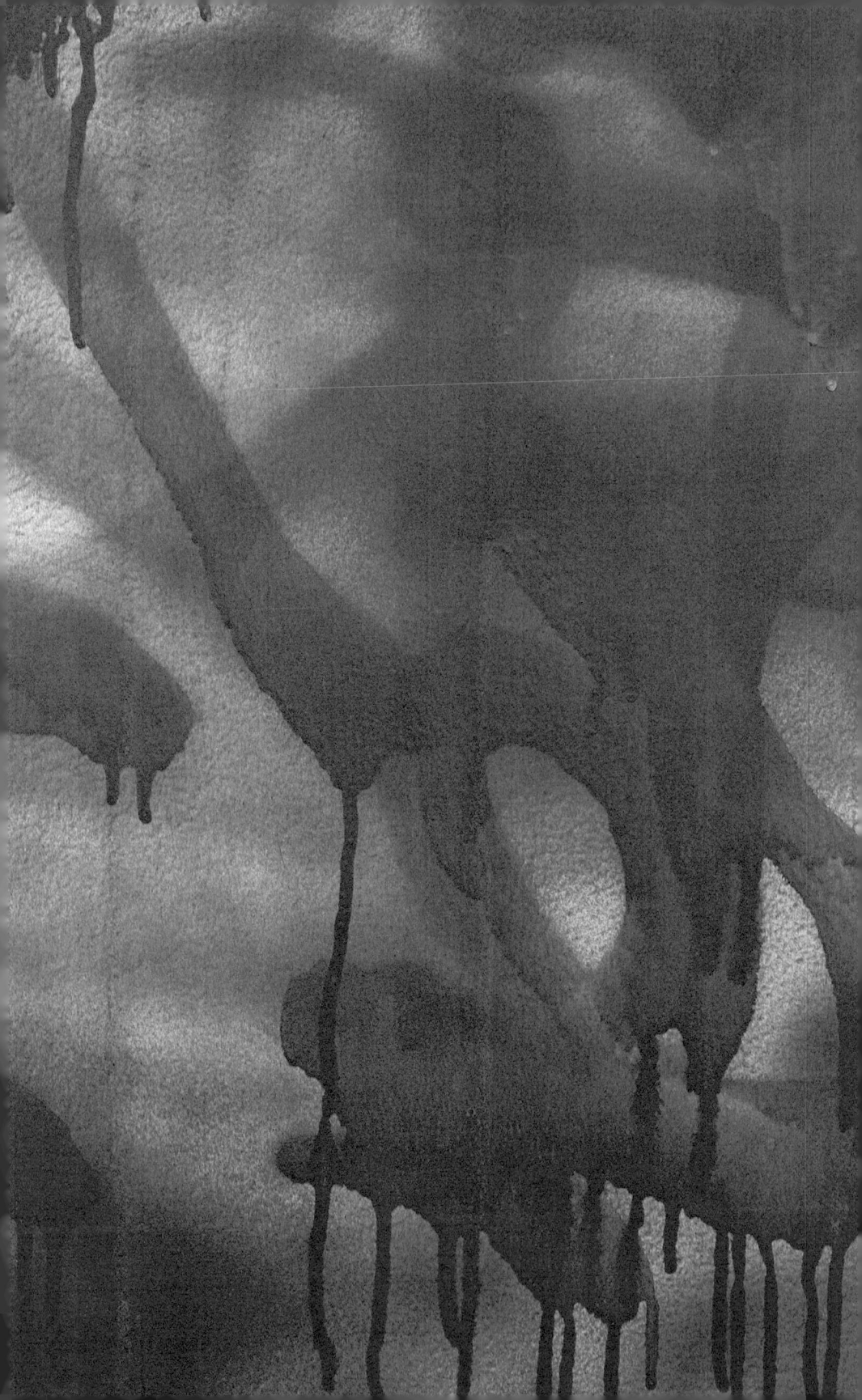

2

"Pressure-Response" and the Origins of Mexican Drug Prohibition, 1912–1920
A Reassessment

ISAAC CAMPOS

INTRODUCTION

Over the past fifteen years, upwards of 200,000 Mexicans have died as a result of their government's commitment to drug prohibition.¹ While the body count is horrific, it is only one part of a larger tableau of harms, from corruption and damaged institutions, to the long-term psychological scars left on countless orphans and other survivors.² Drug prohibition, in short, has been a disaster for Mexico. So who is to blame?

Here I examine the very beginnings of Mexico's prohibitionist policy during a decade—the 1910s—that is far more famous for another historic convulsion of violence in that country. Despite an ongoing Revolution, that decade saw numerous prohibitionist watersheds, from Mexico's adherence to the 1912 Hague International Opium Convention, to the insertion of drug-fighting provisions into the Constitution of 1917, a decision that was itself sandwiched between a 1916 opium restriction and a 1920 law that established Mexico's peacetime prohibitionist policy. Along with all this, there were additional policy directives in the fall of 1912 and summer of 1914.

Why then did Mexico go down this road at that time, in the midst of so much else that was happening? And who is to blame for Mexico's initial steps down the prohibitionist path?

Scholars have largely attributed the erection of this prohibitionist system to outside pressures. Forty years ago, pioneering drug historian William Walker suggested that this period saw a radical shift in antidrug attitudes in Mexico. At the turn of the century, he argued, Mexicans, in contrast to their neighbors to the north, had a relatively tolerant attitude toward intoxicants, one that "led to few demands for legal restriction." Yet he also noted that by the 1920s, "upper echelon leaders in Mexico seemingly possessed antidrug sentiments similar to those held in the United States," while, among the nations of the Western Hemisphere, Mexico's drug-control system ranked second only to that of the United States in terms of its severity.[3] Scholars have since explained this shift as the result of so-called "pressure-response," with the United States and Britain applying diplomatic pressure and Mexico responding with new drug laws.[4]

Elsewhere I have challenged Walker's foundational premise by demonstrating that antidrug attitudes, along with regulations controlling domestic drug distribution, were already well-developed by the turn of the twentieth century in Mexico.[5] Here, drawing on evidence mined in British, Mexican, and U.S. archives, I expand my challenge to the "pressure-response" thesis by arguing that Mexico was from the beginning an enthusiastic participant in international drug control. Indeed, there was little reason for any other orientation to the problem. The ideology of Mexico's leadership at the time was in harmony with that of antidrug, progressive reformers in the United States, and Mexico, in contrast to say Peru or Bolivia, had no financial interest in the opiates or cocaine, the substances targeted by the period's emerging international drug-control regimes.[6] I also demonstrate, however, that Mexican officials were caught off guard by global market shifts that suddenly turned Mexico into an international drug-smuggling hub. This, along with the inefficiencies that surely resulted from the country's ongoing civil war, was sometimes misinterpreted by foreign diplomats as intransigence, and those views have been echoed by later scholars. But the Mexican records demonstrate that, in truth, Mexico was a willing drug-fighting partner from the very beginning.

MEXICO'S NEW TRAFFICKING ROLE AND THE HAGUE CONVENTION (1909-1912)

Mexican drug policy only became of interest to foreign powers after 1909. Prior to that year, Mexico had played no role in the illicit international market for opium or any other drug.[7] But the situation changed suddenly and radically as global opium markets entered a period of great volatility. At the center of all of this were China, Great Britain, and the United States. China was of course the world's greatest consumer of "prepared" opium, that is, opium manufactured for smoking purposes, and Great Britain was the world's most notorious supplier of that drug. In both countries there were highly energized movements to wipe out the opium trade altogether.[8] Meanwhile the United States, driven in part by the controversy over opium in China and Britain's role in purveying it, was busy spearheading a new global crusade aimed at stamping out "the opium evil throughout the world," as Teddy Roosevelt put it.[9] In 1907, Britain pledged to reduce exports of Indian opium to China by 10 percent per year over the next decade. In exchange, China vowed to gradually stamp out its own production of the drug.[10] Two years later, the U.S. Congress passed the Opium Exclusion Act, which made it illegal to import prepared opium into the United States. Similar prohibitions were also initiated in Canada and Australia.[11]

These forces combined to put enormous pressure on opium's traditional trade circuits and sent shock waves through the economies of various opium suppliers. Half of government revenue in Hong Kong, for example, was derived from opium sales.[12] The Portuguese colony of Macao also felt the economic strain. Prior to the U.S. import ban of 1909, 70 percent of Macanese opium exports went to San Francisco. The Opium Exclusion Act, along with the growing restrictions on the Chinese market, brought Macao's opium "farming" system—whereby a particular syndicate purchased monopoly distribution rights from the Macanese government—into crisis.[13] Within a month of the ban, Macao's "opium farmer" was forced to close shop, obliging the government to take over the opium trade directly.[14] This intense pressure on both opium consumers and suppliers inspired a wave of new smuggling, and, as a result, Mexico became a major player in global illicit drug markets for the first time.

Suspiciously, as these new market restrictions went into effect, Mexico's opium imports spiked from just under 5,000 kg to more than 9,000 kg. In 1910 the number rose again to nearly 13,000 kg. This despite official Mexican assurances that the country's annual legitimate opium requirements were about half that. It seemed that much of this surplus was destined to be smuggled into the United States.[15] Meanwhile, Macanese export figures suggested even greater exports to "Mexico," though British officials suspected that the numbers reflected phantom shipments that were in fact routed to China. As the director general of the Portuguese Colonial Office admitted, "the Macao Government had no proof that opium, presumed to be exported to Mexico, actually reached that country."[16] Some of it clearly didn't. In 1916, for example, a ship carrying 132 chests of "opium" destined for Mexico turned out instead to have 132 chests of molasses packed in old opium tins, the actual opium surely having been smuggled into China.[17] Thus the unsettled conditions in revolutionary Mexico, and resulting inefficiencies, seem to have made it not only an ideal staging area for actual trafficking into the United States, but as a straw destination for opium that was really destined for China.

As Mexico's new role came to the attention of the world's first drug warriors, outside observers and diplomats often presumed, for whatever reason, that Mexicans had permissive attitudes toward drug smuggling and might be resistant to cooperation with emerging international drug-control regimes. But they also presumed that, once pressured, Mexico and other Latin American countries would quickly fall into line with U.S. objectives. In short, Mexico was seen as both potentially recalcitrant and utterly pliable. This is perhaps best illustrated by the events surrounding Mexico's decision to sign the 1912 Hague International Opium Convention. In the run-up to the 1911–12 Hague conference, Henry Finger, a Hague delegate for the United States as well as a California state drug regulator, argued that Mexico should be invited to participate in the conference because its attitude toward smuggling was "deplorable."[18] That perception seems to have been derived mostly from prejudice (not unusual for Finger), though as we will see, such misreading of Mexican drug attitudes would become increasingly common.[19] Nonetheless, pioneering drug warrior Hamilton Wright's response to Finger's suggestion is telling: "I at one time . . . did suggest to [Secretary of State] Knox that Mexico be invited to the Conference but on second thoughts we decided not to do so, for the reason that should we invite Mexico there would be a danger of all the other Latin American countries applying for admission to the Conference. That would never do as it would appear to the European powers that we were trying to stack the Conference."[20] In other words, the rest of the world would assume that the Latin American nations felt obliged to vote with the United States. It seems that presumptions about "pressure-response" have a very long history.[21]

Though Mexico would not participate in the initial conference, it was soon invited, along with the several dozen other nations who had not attended, to sign the convention. As agreed in the treaty, this process was carried out by the Dutch, who, on March 6, 1912, invited Mexico to send a delegate to The Hague to sign the new accord. Based on nothing more than a general description of the purpose of the convention and the need for all powers to sign the treaty to make it effective, on March 26 President Francisco Madero designated Federico Gamboa, minister plenipotentiary to Belgium and the Low Countries, as Mexican representative. His orders were simple: sign the agreement.[22] Six weeks later, on May 6, U.S. ambassador Henry Lane Wilson also asked Mexico to designate a delegate to The Hague to sign the accord. Mexico had of course already done so and it informed the United States of this on the 15th. The next day, at 3 p.m., Gamboa signed the convention, making Mexico the second Latin American nation to do so.[23]

Almost six months later, on November 3, 1912, Huntington Wilson, acting secretary of state in Washington, received the news that Mexico had signed. He then instructed the U.S. chargé d'affaires, Montgomery Schuyler Jr., to offer a thank you on behalf of the President of the United States, while thanking the embassy for its work on the problem. "The Department desires to express its appreciation of the Embassy's action on its instruction of April 15, last, which resulted in the prompt adherence of Mexico to the International Opium Convention."[24] Presumably this was the instruction given to Henry Lane Wilson that led him, on May 6, to ask Mexico to send a delegate to sign the document. But, as we've seen, Madero had made the decision to sign six weeks earlier. U.S. officials simply presumed it had been their efforts that had inspired Mexico's adherence. This episode again hints at just how commonsensical the idea of pressure-response has been since the beginning with respect to drugs in the bilateral relationship, though clearly it did not play a role here.

Why then did Mexico sign the convention? While the basic vision of the treaty and most of its specific provisions were in perfect harmony with Mexican drug policy down to this point, Madero's decision does not seem to have been based on the content of the convention itself, which, it appears, he was not yet privy to when he ordered Gamboa to sign it.[25] This might suggest that appearances on the international stage were the real motivation. Though if international appearances were the key, why then did Madero fail to even mention Mexico's signing of it in his State of the Union address in September? This was a tedious speech that British diplomats described as being of "inordinate length, owing to the incorporation of reports from the seven Ministries of State, with a multiplicity of detail which, in former years was not considered necessary." Indeed, Madero, in this speech that is always watched closely by foreign diplomats, mentioned seemingly every diplomatic initiative of the previous year except its signing of the Hague Convention, from Mexico's role at the International Conference of Jurisconsults in Rio, to the Hague conference on the unification of the Law of Exchange, and the upcoming Conference on International Maritime Law.[26] Thus the more simple explanation—that Madero believed in the cause, and perhaps international cooperation more generally—appears more plausible. Beginning in the fall of 1912, however, the story would become increasingly complex, as domestic motivations for policy innovations sprang up almost simultaneously with British and U.S. inquiries about Mexican drug control.

DOMESTIC MOTIVATIONS VS. INTERNATIONAL PRESSURES (1912–1920)

The events in question began on October 13, 1912, when three Chinese residents of Mexico City penned a letter of complaint to the city governor. Their countrymen, they insisted, were being cheated. The Chinese in Mexico regularly imported prepared opium, a practice that was perfectly legal, as indicated by the 3.20 peso import duty they paid per kilogram. Yet they were routinely arrested for distributing it to their countrymen for whom the stuff, they insisted, was merely medicine. The Chinese began smoking it at a tender age, they argued; later they simply needed to continue using for their own health: "it is a medicine for them, just as it is a medicine for many other ailments that occupy medical science."[27]

The request provides some insight into the discourse and the related moral geography surrounding drugs in Mexico at the time, for these men clearly presumed that Mexican authorities would look askance at the request unless it included some key restrictions: First, that these sales would be for *medicinal* rather than recreational use, the latter clearly presumed already by this time to be a nonstarter, and, second, that this commerce would be directed at Chinese rather than native-born Mexicans. They also sought to appeal to both Mexico's financial interest and the typical Europhilia of that era's Mexican elite, emphasizing not only that opium imports were lucrative, but that they came from "England and various European nations."[28]

It was a savvy argument but nonetheless doomed to failure. Since the colonial era, Mexican law had distinguished between dangerous and other drugs, the sale of the former being limited to trained and licensed physicians or pharmacists. Opium had long been categorized as "dangerous," and Mexico's sanitary code and related pharmacy regulations were quite specific on this point.[29] The Chinese did raise the distinction between "prepared" and raw opium, a difference that had never before come to the attention of Mexico's sanitary authorities, though neither would this help their cause. As I illustrate in more detail below, by this time in the West, prepared or "smoking opium" was widely recognized as the world's dangerous drug par excellence.

Indeed, Mexican sanitary authorities alluded to that global reputation in a relatively rapid response to the Chinese petition. On October 18, the city government forwarded it to the city's Consejo Superior de Salubridad (Superior Sanitary Council)—which I will refer to hereafter simply as Salubridad—the public health agency in charge of such matters, and from there it was handed over to the council's Apothecary Commission. On November 15 that body delivered a ruling. Though opium distribution was already restricted, the commission emphasized that opium prepared for smoking was a distinct substance from the medicinal variety. The opium referred to by the petitioners was used exclusively for smoking, and since "its use in this way is universally recognized as having noxious results," it should be included under Article 230 of the Sanitary Code, which gave Salubridad the right to ban harmful "medications or cosmetics." Therefore the requested license for its sale must of course be rejected, and locations where it was used (i.e., "opium dens") should be suppressed. The commission also recommended that Article 50 of the Sanitary Code, which allowed Salubridad to ban the import of noxious substances, should be invoked in order to prohibit its importation. Both proposals were quickly approved and forwarded to the Ministries of the Interior (Gobernación) and of Revenue (Hacienda).[30]

Here a contingent and local event triggered a quick and decisive prohibitionist response from Mexican sanitary authorities, one that reflected decades of precedent and what was by then a relatively clear and widely accepted moral code regarding intoxicant use. Given that prepared opium was "universally recognized to have noxious results," it should clearly be banned. This statement also demonstrates the informal influence of broader global discourses on drugs, particularly the story of China's famous prostration before the British as a result of the opium trade. As the story went, the British had forced the drug on the Chinese in two "Opium Wars," and the subsequent spread of addiction had gradually eroded that great civilization. Though scholars now challenge the simplicity of this original narrative, it was nonetheless extraordinarily influential at the time. As Frank Dikötter, Lars Laamann, and Zhou Zun have put it in their revisionist history of opium in China: "During the first decades of the twentieth century . . . the image of China as opium slave became the *locus classicus* of the modern drug debate, the cornerstone of the antiopium movement."[31]

That broader discourse, which flourished in both Mexico and the United States, was one part of the shared ideology that was so crucial to this story. In both countries, controversy regarding the Chinese and opium dated to at least the 1860s, as advocates of Chinese immigration (as a source of cheap labor) were met with rebuttals that rarely failed to emphasize the Chinese link to vice, including opium smoking. These debates touched a number of sensitive nerves in Mexican intellectual life in part due to the growing dominance of degeneration theory as a framework for understanding social problems. The Chinese were viewed, like Mexico's Indians, as a textbook example of degeneration in action. Indeed, the two discourses were closely related. Each saw a once great race supposedly degenerated by imperial intervention and vice. In Mexico the bogeyman vice was overwhelmingly alcohol, but the basic narrative was roughly the same. And while both discourses provoked a certain amount of sympathy for the plight of these degenerated peoples, in the main the stories inspired calls for aggressive governmental intervention to treat the social cancer.[32]

Thus in both Mexico and the United States, the Chinese were the archetypal cautionary tale about drugs, though to be sure other factors fueled antidrug sentiment on both sides of the Rio Grande. While in Mexico degeneration theory played an enormous role, in the United States concerns about false advertising and the unseemly practices of patent medicine manufacturers gave the American antidrug discourse a decidedly progressive-era hue.[33] Race and class were also key factors on both sides of the border, though they played out in different ways, with Mexican newspapers hyping concerns about Indian atavisms and mestizo violence, while in the United States it was often foreigners, including Mexicans, who were the objects of concern.[34] But in the end the result was the same: a general transnational moral code on drugs that made recreational use largely unacceptable. Alcohol of course was the exception for many Mexicans and Americans, though the most radical tended to see alcohol in the same light as these other drugs. Hence the eventual prohibition of alcohol in the United States and the various state-level prohibitions by Carrancista "proconsuls" during the Revolution in Mexico.[35]

But despite Mexican officials' relatively clear-cut response to the Chinese request of October 1912, the story quickly becomes much more complicated, for in a case of truly extraordinary timing, it was that very month that the British, in their efforts to discover where all of that excess Macanese opium was actually going, decided that inquiries should be made to Mexico regarding its opium import policy and its annual opium requirements. On October 3, Francis Henry May, governor of Hong Kong, informed Francis Stronge, minister plenipotentiary in Mexico, that for the year ending June 30, 1912, Macanese statistics showed that 340 chests (roughly 12,500 kg) of prepared opium had been exported to Mexico. For comparison's sake, Hong Kong, with a Chinese population of 450,000, required about 500 chests of opium per year for local consumption.[36] Mexico's Chinese population, which we might assume (as British officials routinely did) used the majority of the prepared opium smoked in Mexico, numbered about 13,000 at that time.[37] In other words, the numbers suggested that Mexico was importing 68 percent as much opium as was used in Hong Kong for a Chinese population that was 3 percent as large. "It would be interesting to know," concluded May, "whether this amount was actually imported into Mexico during that period."[38] Stronge followed up again in early November: "It [would] certainly help us to know what Mexico considers her legitimate requirements [and] incidentally if we were to ask this question of the Mexican government they might exchange some info as to whether they contemplated taking any steps in the near future in compliance with art. 7 of the 1912 opium Convention to which they acceded last May."[39] Art. 7 obliged signatories to "prohibit the import and export of prepared opium."[40]

On November 6, just three weeks after the Chinese request to Mexican authorities, Stronge began following through on these orders. In two separate communications to Pedro Lascurain, Mexico's secretary of foreign relations, Stronge asked how much opium Mexico annually imported, how much it legitimately needed, and whether Mexico was "prepared to take steps to prevent its importation in accordance with the convention of 1912." Concretely he suggested that perhaps Mexico might develop a system wherein those who wanted to import prepared opium would need to acquire, on each occasion, permission from the Mexican government.[41]

Of course at that very moment Salubridad was considering the Chinese request from October and arriving at the decision that imports of prepared opium should be totally banned. The evidence suggests, however, that British inquiries had no impact on that decision. In fact, given the delays in communication that were standard during these years (see the various examples below), it's unlikely that officials at Salubridad were even aware of the British inquiry before their decision on November 15. And more directly to the point, the meeting minutes from November also completely fail to mention it. Furthermore, while by mid-December Salubridad had passed its ruling along to Gobernación, which then passed it on to Hacienda for implementation, the British would not be informed of any of this until mid-January.[42] On January 9, Stronge complained that he had "repeatedly brought the matter to the attention of the Mexican Government, but have only succeeded, at last, in eliciting from them the figures for the import of opium for the last five years."[43] Five days later Stronge responded to another inquiry from London, noting, "I have never ceased to press the Mexican Govt. both verbally and in writing for reply but so far without success."[44] In sum, the evidence hardly suggests that Mexico was trying to appease the British with this new legislation.

Meanwhile, on January 15, Hacienda had written Salubridad to inform it of its desire to implement the new import restrictions, but wondered how customs agents were supposed to distinguish at points of entry between prepared opium, which was banned, and the medicinal opium that could still be legally imported. Implementation would thus be delayed until Salubridad could provide an answer.[45] It was only on January 22 that Mexican officials informed the British of what was going on, noting both the November decision to ban the import of prepared opium and Hacienda's estimate that Mexico's legitimate opium requirements were about 6,000 kg a year.[46]

The various figures sent by Mexico confirmed what the British had been suspecting, for the Macanese and Mexican numbers did not match. According to Macao, it had exported the majority of its opium, 416 of 740 total chests, to Mexico. But Mexican figures indicated that opium imports from all sources combined during the same period equaled only 363 chests, or about 2,000 kg less than the Macanese claims. Still, the Mexican records showed that it was annually importing about twice the opium it needed for legitimate purposes.[47] In short, Mexico appeared to be playing a key role in illicit markets eight thousand miles apart: as a site for actual opium imports that were then smuggled into the United States; as a straw buyer for opium that was actually destined for China's newly restricted market; and, of course, as a country with its own small internal prepared-opium market.

Meanwhile, despite Hacienda having put the November decision on hold, the ruling went partially into effect. Apparently unaware of Hacienda's misgivings, on June 2, 1913, Gobernación informed the Postal Service (Correos) of Salubridad's November ruling. That was enough for Correos to conclude that it was now illegal to ship opium through the mail, given that "according to Mexico's postal legislation, it is prohibited to send poisons by mail, a prohibition that extends to opium since it is [now] included in that classification."[48] Correos thus went ahead with the ban. Through this process, it soon discovered the problems that Hacienda had anticipated months before. As shipments of opium continued to arrive in the mail marked simply as "drugs," postal authorities began to detain them, leading to complaints from shippers that the opium was medicinal and should be allowed to reach its destination. Correos thus asked Salubridad to clarify, "with the most detail possible" and "as fast as possible," how postal officials were supposed to distinguish between prepared and medicinal opium in the mail.[49]

As Correos waited for a response, the British continued to press Mexico for firmer answers on the two questions it had already answered back in January, namely, if Mexico would consider a system whereby prepared opium dealers would have to gain the government's permission on each occasion that they sought to import the drug, and what Mexico's legitimate opium needs were. It's not clear if they were dissatisfied with the 6,000 kg estimate that had been offered in the winter, or if they'd simply lost track. At this point it seems there was plenty of confusion on all sides. With respect to the proposed system of imports, the communication acknowledged Salubridad's November ruling on the subject, but it wanted to know if Mexico would be fully adopting these or other restrictions.[50] In September Mexico responded, relaying the problems Hacienda had identified and noting that because of this it had been forced to delay implementation until Salubridad could provide some means of distinguishing between prepared and medicinal opium at the border. Beyond this, the Mexican response was vague: "With respect to the arrangement proposed as desirable by His Britannic majesty's Minister in his above mentioned Note . . . this Ministry considers that these are matters for regulation which the Government must, in due course, determine upon in such manner as they consider that the nature of the case demands." British frustration mounted. "The note," one official briefly summarized, "contains no information whatsoever."[51]

In November, Correos, waiting since mid-August for its answer, informed Salubridad that various packages of opium had long been in its custody and that, by law, they would soon have to be returned to sender.[52] Further demonstrating that long delays in response were not reserved for foreign powers, Salubridad took another month to respond, noting that the study underway had not yet been completed and that the packages should therefore be turned over to their destination "as long as the recipients prove they are drug merchants and they bear witness that the packages in question are of medicinal opium."[53]

In other words, despite the problems, the ban on smoking opium had become the de facto law with respect to the drug's shipment through the mail.

Then, in late January 1914 the commission that had been assigned to resolve this matter concluded that it could not proceed until it was given a copy of the Hague Convention, for while it was aware that Mexico had signed the document, it did not yet know what it mandated. The commission then penned a resolution asking the leadership of Salubridad to request from the foreign secretariat, via Gobernación, an exact copy of the convention, though it's not clear if this request was carried out.[54] Interestingly, the original draft of the resolution emphasized, incorrectly, that the convention had been accepted by all the nations of the world and suggested that Mexico should perhaps subordinate all of its pertinent laws, even its Regulation for the Sale of Medicinal Substances, to it. The final, edited version struck this section and replaced "all of the nations" with the "principal nations," and then noted that Mexico's laws should conform to the convention as long as the latter didn't clash with Mexico's existing legislation.[55] Here we see that though Mexico was clearly a willing and even enthusiastic participant in the international drug control movement, within the bureaucracy there were voices that remained vigilant about balancing those commitments with Mexican sovereignty.

This would prove to be a tricky balance, for the Hague Convention itself gave more commercially powerful nations a tool by which they might leverage their dominance of the international pharmaceutical market to demand adherence to the convention's various requirements. That tool was found in Article 13, which mandated that convention signatories only allow the export of opiates and cocaine to other convention signatories if the latter had laws on the subject of the kind mandated by that accord (i.e., requiring special permits for the import of these drugs).[56]

Thus, in order to comply with this article, on January 17, 1914, the U.S. Congress passed an amendment to the 1909 Opium Exclusion Act that prohibited the export of opium and cocaine to countries that did not have laws regulating their import, while completely banning exports of prepared opium.[57] The law also required the secretary of state to "request all foreign Governments to communicate through the diplomatic channels copies of laws and regulations promulgated in their respective countries which prohibit or regulate the importation of the aforesaid drugs." On March 11, 1914, U.S. diplomatic officers were directed to inquire as to the laws in effect regulating the import of these products throughout the Americas, and on April 1, that request was made to

Mexico.⁵⁸ On May 7, the request was passed along to Salubridad, which then dealt with the question another month later, at its June 10 meeting.⁵⁹

There the Apothecary Commission presented its proposed response to the U.S. request, noting that it was prepared to send copies of Mexico's Sanitary Code and Regulation for the Distribution of Medicines, emphasizing that in addition to the requirements that opiates and cocaine could only be distributed by prescription, opium dens had long been persecuted in Mexico as "immoral establishments." Furthermore, the response emphasized that in November 1912 the council had moved to ban the introduction of prepared opium altogether, but the measure had been held up by problems distinguishing between prepared and medicinal opium at ports of entry. Finally, Mexico currently had under study further restrictions due to the growth in use within the Chinese colony and the "exaggerated customs" of certain sectors of society, especially prostitutes, who were given to snorting cocaine, but that this was all pending in expectation of receiving the complete Hague Opium Convention for reference. The president of the council, Ramón Macías, then added a clarification: "that if the Council had not previously moved to specifically limit the import of opium to Mexico, it was because until recently the drug was only used [in Mexico] for medicinal purposes."⁶⁰

Meanwhile the British had continued to ask about Mexico's opium import restrictions, with their most recent inquiry coming on March 30 and then passed on to Salubridad on June 11, the day after the response to the United States had been agreed upon. On June 13, the Apothecary Commission responded that it had reached a conclusion that, if approved, would provide the result sought by the British.⁶¹

On June 17, the commission finally presented its formal proposal in two articles. Article 1 completely banned the import of prepared opium under Article 50 of the Sanitary Code, just as it had attempted to do in November 1912. Article 2 allowed the import of all other opium and cocaine products by authorized establishments for medicinal use with advanced permission on each separate import occasion from Hacienda. This clearly fit with the guidelines of the Hague Convention and thus with the related British proposal of 1912 as well. This was to apply to both official customs entry points and the customs sections of the postal service. In its explanation, the commission recounted how it had sought to make a similar ban almost two years earlier but that Hacienda "gave an interpretation that was contrary to the desire [*ánimo*] of the council."

In any case, the commission explained that its long delay in acting after Hacienda's ruling was due both to being away from the capital and because it was waiting on a copy of the Hague Convention, eventually having been shown it by the American chargé d'affaires. It also noted that the British had made several inquiries on this and thus recommended that action be taken so that it would not appear that Mexico had made no decision on this matter, and because convention signatories were not to ship opium to countries that did not have regulations controlling commerce in the drug. Hacienda's lawyer agreed with the urgency of the matter given that Mexico had signed the convention, and emphasized that the measure should be forwarded as quickly as possible to Gobernación so that it could pass through all the necessary legal hoops.[62] Notes were then sent to the British government, Correos, and Hacienda explaining the new regulation, though nothing would be sent to the United States, which would continue until 1919 to list Mexico among the countries whose opium laws were "unknown."[63]

The commission also finally responded to Hacienda's concerns, which had been raised originally in January 1913, insisting that these were now essentially moot. Given that the new ruling mandated that opiates could only be imported by authorized dealers, and those dealers would know that these substances could only be distributed for medicinal purposes, and that, furthermore, prepared opium imports were banned, there would be no attempts to import prepared opium to Mexico.[64] Once again, however, these recommendations were stillborn as President Huerta was overthrown and the country descended deeper into civil war.

Then, eighteen months later, on January 11, 1916, E. A. González, Mexican consul in San Diego, informed U.S. officials that "the importation of opium into Mexico has been prohibited."[65] As a result, U.S. officials began holding up all opium shipments from crossing the border.[66] This created considerable controversy among legitimate medicinal opium dealers who were, quite predictably, confused by a ruling banning all opiates (rather than simply prepared opium). For months the United States sought a straight answer from Mexican officials to confirm the opium ban, receiving mixed messages along the way and no definitive answer, though one Mexican official explained that a circular telegram had been sent out by the Mexican government on December 20, 1915, banning "opium imports" effective January 1.[67]

Though this information was never shared with U.S. officials, the "ban" stated the following:

> Given the immoderate importations of opium that are presently occurring with the end of employing it, most of the time, for non-medicinal purposes, which seriously damages society, the Ministry of Revenue (Hacienda), with the goal of preventing this, has provided by decree of the Citizen First Chief of the Constitutionalist Army, who is in command of the Nation's Executive Power, that Customs authorities be told that beginning on the first day of January, and until subsequent orders, the importation of opium in all of its kinds and extracts is prohibited ... with the knowledge that only with special authorization of the same, Ministry of Revenue, will the import of that product be allowed, permission for which interested parties will in each case request from that same Secretariat.[68]

This law is often cited as Mexico's first national prohibition,[69] but, as we've seen, Mexico had prohibited prepared opium imports on two previous occasions. This measure, by contrast, did not distinguish between prepared and medicinal opium, while leaving Hacienda in charge of decisions to approve or reject any import requests. Subsequent regulations (see below) did insist that the drug only be imported by licensed pharmacists and physicians, which suggests that it may have been presumed that only "medicinal" opium imports would be authorized by Hacienda. But that point is not explicit in the order. The law's origins also remain obscure. Ricardo Pérez Montfort has recently argued that the law was an "authoritarian reaction" to developing international prohibitions and an effort to send a moralizing message to Mexican society.[70] Though we don't have any direct evidence on this point, the latter is certainly plausible, as it fit with other directives taken by Carranza, including his banning of opium smoking as governor of Coahuila in 1911.[71] Froylán Enciso has similarly speculated that Carranza "took the decision due to the fear of losing control of the border and as a message to these local authorities. His order was ignored by some like Esteban Cantú, at the time the governor of Baja California."[72] There may also be something to this latter theory, for Cantú was profiting from the manufacture of opium products there and the Carranza government was plotting his overthrow.[73] It could also be simply that Carranza was finally carrying out part of the Salubridad recommendation of June 1914, or some combination of all of these motivations.

Whatever the case, medicinal opium could still be legally imported as long as permission had been granted by Hacienda. Indeed on July 31, 1916, Carranza declared a new tariff on the import of opium that would go into effect on

November 1 of the same year, limiting imports to five kilograms, and additionally requiring the permission of Salubridad, which would only extend such authorization to licensed physicians and pharmacists.[74] In the fall, Salubridad began receiving, and approving, requests from pharmacists to import opiates.[75] Even before that tariff was announced, Salubridad had received a request from a certain Luis Chopson to manufacture opium products and alkaloids. The request was approved with the stipulations that the factory be under the direction of a licensed pharmacist, that the product of the work adhered to the guidelines of Mexico's Pharmacopeia, and that the opiates be sold exclusively to licensed pharmacies and drugstores.[76] Yet in November 1916, due to the failure of Mexican officials to explain the new restrictions, the United States was still holding tens of thousands of dollars of raw opium destined for Mexico.[77] If Mexico had crafted this legislation to demonstrate its willing bilateral cooperation, it was certainly doing a poor job of advertising it.[78]

In January 1917, José María Rodríguez, president of Salubridad and also Carranza's personal physician, would successfully argue that the new Mexican Constitution should include authorization for a nationwide "sanitary dictatorship," a case he made largely with reference to the problems of alcoholism and the use of other habit-forming drugs. In 1920, Mexico passed new legislation that formally prohibited marijuana—a drug that was not yet on the international control agenda—banned the cultivation of opium, and only allowed the import of the opiates and cocaine by specially authorized dealers who in turn were only permitted to sell the drug to licensed and authorized medical distributors. The law, which addressed both domestic concerns and Mexico's international commitments, was the first major drug legislation passed under the Constitution of 1917. It was also developed and promulgated with no direct foreign interference whatsoever.[79]

CONCLUSION

Pressure implies coercion. Pressure also cannot develop without resistance. Mexico was not pressured into the content of its foundational drug policy during these years because there was nothing in the emerging international control regimes that violated the reigning ideology on drugs in Mexico. Tellingly, while Mexico would not ratify the Hague Convention until 1927, it immediately looked to craft its laws in accordance with that treaty's provisions, though it had no obligation to do so.[80] A specific law on cocaine imports, for example, would probably not have been proposed in 1914 had it not been for the requirements of the Hague Convention, but not because of any Mexican resistance to such a measure, but merely because problematic cocaine imports had never come to the attention of Mexico's sanitary authorities before then.

The notion that Mexico needed to be pressured, and that it would eventually go along with whatever the United States demanded of it, nonetheless has deep roots. U.S. officials themselves incorrectly took credit for Mexico's decision to sign the Hague Convention. As illicit drug traffic suddenly sprang up along the border after 1909, Henry Finger of California's Pharmacy Board assumed Mexican attitudes on these matters to be "deplorable," though this traffic was a new development that had sprung from recent U.S. prohibitions. The tendency of Mexican officials to take months to respond to correspondence surely reinforced these preconceptions. It must be emphasized, though, that such delays do not appear to have been orchestrated as passive resistance to outside pressure, for they clearly existed between Mexican departments as well. There was, after all, a civil war going on.[81]

What is clear is that the sudden changes to global drug markets during these years combined with Mexico's geographic position and ongoing civil war to make it an ideal location for illicit drug activity. Since then we've seen that even with the return of peacetime order, the length of the border and the profits to be gained from the illicit supply of drugs to the huge U.S. market have made efforts to halt the traffic quixotic at best, even when billions of dollars in manpower and technology are dedicated to the cause. That fact, along with some high-profile instances of U.S. drug-war imperialism in 1940 and 1969,[82] has made it easy for observers to presume that Mexico has resisted efforts to control drugs and thus has been coerced by the United States on these matters from the beginning. But this was clearly not the case. At this foundational moment of the War on Drugs, Mexican and U.S. officials largely saw these substances through a similar lens that ultimately generated highly compatible policy approaches.

NOTES

1. Estimates of course vary. In 2016 the death toll was reported to be 170,000. In 2018 some claim it as high as 250,000. See Human Rights Watch, "Mexico: Events of 2016," https://www.hrw.org/world-report/2017/country-chapters/mexico; Brianna Lee and Danielle Renwick, "Mexico's Drug War," https://www.cfr.org/backgrounder

/mexicos-drug-war; Estrategia fallida: 250.000 asesinatos en México desde el inicio de la "guerra contra el narco," https://actualidad.rt.com/actualidad/272788-mexico-llega-250000-asesinatos-inicio-guerra-narcotraficoReferences; "In Mexico, Not Dead. Not Alive. Just Gone," https://www.nytimes.com/2017/11/20/world/americas/mexico-drug-war-dead.html.

2. See, for example, "Ten Years of Militarised Drug Policies in Mexico: More Violence and Human Rights Violations," https://www.opendemocracy.net/en/ten-years-of-militarised-drug-policies-in-mexico-more-violence-and-human-rights-violati/.

3. William Walker, *Drug Control in the Americas* (Albuquerque: University of New Mexico Press, 1981), 1–2, 48–49, 59.

4. On "pressure-response," see Daniel Weimer, *Seeing Drugs. Modernization, Counterinsurgency and U.S. Narcotics Control in the Third World, 1969–1976* (Kent, OH: Kent State University Press, 2013), 177–78. In part this view reflects a general sense that the War on Drugs has been a U.S. export to the rest of the world. See Jurg Gerber and Eric L. Jensen, "The Internationalization of U.S. Policy on Illicit Drug Control," in *Drug War American Style: The Internationalization of Failed Policy and Its Alternatives*, ed. Jurg Gerber and Eric L. Jensen (New York: Garland Publishing, 2001), 1–2; H. Richard Friman, *Narcodiplomacy: Exporting the U.S. War on Drugs* (Ithaca, NY: Cornell University Press, 1996), 4. For Britain as another source of pressure, see William B. McAllister, *Drug Diplomacy in the Twentieth Century* (London: Routledge, 2000); Arnold H. Taylor, *American Diplomacy and the Narcotics Traffic, 1900–1939: A Study in International Humanitarian Reform* (Durham, NC: Duke University Press, 1969); Peter D. Lowes, *The Genesis of International Narcotics Control* (Geneva: Librairie Droz, 1966). On Mexico specifically, see William Walker III, *Drug Control in the Americas* (Albuquerque: University of New Mexico Press: 1981), 1–2, 48–49, 59; Maria Celia Toro, *Mexico's "War" on Drugs: Causes and Consequences*, vol. 3 of *Studies on the Impact of the Illegal Drug Trade* (Boulder, CO: Lynne Rienner Publishers, 1995), 6–7; Luis Astorga, *Drogas sin fronteras* (Mexico City: Grijalbo, 2003), 353; Ricardo Pérez Montfort, *Tolerancia y prohibición: Aproximaciones a la historia social y cultural de las drogas en México, 1840–1940* (Mexico City: Penguin Random House, 2016), 120, and chapter 3 in this volume; Froylán Enciso, "Los fracasos del chantaje: Régimen de prohibición de drogas y narcotráfico," in *Seguridad nacional y seguridad interior*, ed. Arturo Alvarado and Mónica Serrano (Mexico City: El Colegio de México, 2010), 67–68; Guadalupe González, "The Drug Connection in U.S.-Mexican Relations: Introduction," in *The Drug Connection in U.S. Mexican Relations*, ed. Guadalupe Gonzalez and Marta Tienda (San Diego: Center for U.S.-Mexican Studies, 1989), 2. For the view that, along with U.S. pressure, increasing drug abuse inspired prohibition in Mexico, see Fernando Martínez Cortés and Xóchitl Martínez Barbosa, *Del Consejo Superior de Salubridad al Consejo de Salubridad General*. Vol. 3 of *Historia del Consejo de Salubridad General* (Mexico City: SmithKline Beecham, 2000), 231–32. See also José de Jesús Emmanel Valero Palacios, "Formación de una región productora de

enervantes" (BA thesis, Escuela Nacional de Antropología e Historia, 2001), 24, and Axayácatl Gutiérrez Ramos, "La prohibición de las drogas en México: La construcción del discurso jurídico, 1917–1931" (MA thesis, Instituto de Investigaciones, 1996), 38. Elsewhere, Ricardo Pérez Montfort has argued that "international pressures and tendencies" and the self-interest of Mexican politicians (i.e., the desire to profit from the illicit trade) combined to produce drug prohibition there. See his "Fragmentos de historia de las 'drogas' en México 1870–1920," in *Hábitos, normas y escándalo: Prensa, criminalidad y drogas durante el porfiriato tardío*, ed. Ricardo Pérez Montfort (Mexico City: Plaza y Valdés, 19997), 163. A slight exception to the rule is Richard Craig, who argues that U.S. pressure was "belated" since "unofficial Mexican efforts against illicit opium cultivation began early in [the twentieth century]." See his "U.S. Narcotics Policy toward Mexico: Consequences for the Bilateral Relationship," in *The Drug Connection in U.S. Mexican Relations*, ed. Guadalupe Gonzalez and Marta Tienda (San Diego: Center for U.S.-Mexican Studies, 1989), 72. Similarly, see Olga Cárdenas de Ojeda, *Toxicomanía y narcotráfico: Aspectos legales* (Mexico City: Fondo de Cultura Económica, 1976).

5. Isaac Campos, *Home Grown: Marijuana and the Origins of Mexico's War on Drugs* (Chapel Hill: University of North Carolina Press, 2012).

6. On the general ideological harmony between U.S. and Mexican policy makers, see Alan Knight, *U.S.-Mexican Relations, 1910–1940: An Interpretation* (San Diego, CA: Center for U.S.-Mexican Studies, 1987), 4–9, 19, 111–13. On the interests of Peru and Bolivia in coca and cocaine, and their resulting resistance to international control regimes, see Paul Gootenberg, *Andean Cocaine: The Making of a Global Drug* (Chapel Hill, NC: University of North Carolina Press, 2008), 211–17.

7. Consider, for example, Mexico's total absence in the 1909 *Report of the International Opium Commission*.

8. Lowes, *The Genesis*, 74–75; Gregory Blue, "Opium for China: The British Connection," in *Opium Regimes: China, Britain, and Japan, 1839–1952*, ed. Timothy Brook and Bob Tadashi Wakabayashi (Berkeley: University of California Press, 2000), 40.

9. Lowes, *The Genesis*, 117.

10. Blue, "Opium for China," 41.

11. Lowes, *The Genesis*, 100–101. Various correspondence, Foreign Office (FO) 371/1925, paper #17949, National Archives of the UK, London, England (hereafter cited as TNA).

12. Blue, "Opium for China," 43.

13. On the tradition of opium and other commodity "farms" in colonial Asia, see Carl A. Trocki, "Opium and the Beginnings of Chinese Capitalism in Southeast Asia," *Journal of Southeast Asian Studies* 33, no. 2 (2002): 297.

14. Campbell to the Inspector-General, 7/18/1912 (this was Enclosure #2 in Jordan to Grey, 9/14/1912), FO, 371/1333, paper #41323, TNA; May to Harcourt, 10/151912, FO, 371/1333, paper #49724, TNA.

15. Stronge to Grey (Received 2/6/1913), 1/22/1913, FO, 371/1596, paper #5655, TNA. See also, Department of State, *Papers Relating to the Foreign Relations of the United States with the Annual Message of the President Transmitted to Congress December 3, 1912* (Washington, DC: Government Printing Office, 1919), 214.

16. "Minutes of the Third Meeting," 2/12/1913, FO, 371/1596, paper #7800, TNA; Campbell to the Inspector-General, 7/18/1912 (this was Enclosure #2 in Jordan to Grey, 9/14/1912), FO, 371/1333, paper #41323, TNA; "Minutes of a Meeting to discuss the Opium Traffic at Macao," 1/13/1913, FO, 371/1596, paper #2200, TNA.

17. Colonial Secretary, Hong Kong, to Finance Department, Govt. of India, 9/22/1916, FO, 371/2650, paper #228474, TNA.

18. Ibid., 172.

19. For more on Finger, see Dale Gieringer, "The Forgotten Origins of Cannabis Prohibition in California," *Contemporary Drug Problems*, 26, no. 2 (1999): 250–52.

20. As quoted in Lowes, *The Genesis*, 172.

21. For a more famous version of this presumption, see Thomas J. Fleming, *The Illusion of Victory: America in World War I* (New York: Basic Books, 2003), 463. This of course mirrors the way some historians have characterized U.S.-Mexican relations during these years, particularly with respect to drug policy. Knight also notes a remarkable similarity between presumptions about U.S.-Mexican relations during the Revolution and those that appear later in the historiography. See his *U.S.-Mexican Relations*, 112.

22. Foreign Minister of the Netherlands to the Secretaría de Relaciones Exteriores (SRE), 3/6/1912, contained within letter from SRE to Gamboa, 4/15/1912, III-502-5(I), SRE. From Madero, 3/26/1912, III-502-5(I), SRE.

23. Lascuráin to Wilson, Ambassador, 5/15/1912, and Gamboa to Lascuráin, 5/17/1912, III-502-5(I), SRE. The SRE later would say this occurred on May 15. See "Convención Internacional del Opio," III-502–5(I), SRE. Costa Rica was first to sign. List of signatories to the Hague Convention, 7/18/1912, III-502-5(I), SRE.

24. Huntington Wilson, Acting Secretary of State, to Montgomery Schuyler Jr., American Chargé d'Affaires, Mexico City, 11/8/1912; 811.4; Vol. 0454, Correspondence File for Mexico City; Records of Foreign Service Posts, RG 84; National Archives II, College Park, MD (hereafter cited as NARA).

25. On the compatibility of Mexican drug law with the Hague Convention, see Campos, *Home Grown*, 181–93.

26. Stronge to Grey, 9/21/1912, FO 371/1398, Paper # 41886, TNA.

27. Shin, Chío and Twong to the Government of the D.F., 10/13/1912, Salubridad Pública (hereafter cited as SP)/Congresos y Convenciones (hereafter cited as CyC), c. 11, exp. 12, Archivo Histórico de la Secretaría de Salubridad y Asistencia, Mexico City (hereafter cited as AHSSA).

28. Ibid., 164.

29. Campos, *Home Grown*, 184–93.

30. Acta de la sesión, 16 Nov. 1912, SP/Presidencia (hereafter cited as P)/Actas de Sesión (hereafter cited as AS), c. 16, exp. 2, AHSSA. Continuation of Chinese request, 15 Nov. 1912, SP/CyC, c. 11, exp. 12, AHSSA.

31. Frank Dikötter, Lars Laamann, and Zhou Zun, *Narcotic Culture: A History of Drugs in China* (Chicago: University of Chicago Press, 2004), 1–2. For another revisionist account, see R. K. Newman, "Opium Smoking in Late Imperial China: A Reconsideration," *Modern Asian Studies* 29, no. 4 (1995): 765–94.

32. Axayácatl Gutiérrez Ramos, "Consumo y tráfico de opio en México, 1920–1949" (BA thesis, UNAM), 108. José Jorge Gómez Izquierdo, *El movimiento antichino en México (1871–1934): Problemas del racismo y del nacionalismo durante la revolución mexicana* (Mexico City: Instituto Nacional de Antropología e Historia, 1991), 46, 95; Grace Peña Delgado, *Making the Chinese Mexican: Global Migration, Localism, and Exclusion in the U.S.-Mexico Borderlands* (Stanford, CA: Stanford University Press, 2012), 30–31, chap. 4. Robert Chao Romero discusses these issues at length but with more emphasis on the 1920s and 1930s. See his *The Chinese in Mexico, 1882–1940* (Tucson: University of Arizona Press, 2010), especially chap. 4. Similarly, see Schiavone Camacho, *Chinese Mexicans: Transpacific Migration and the Search for a Homeland, 1910–1960* (Chapel Hill: University of North Carolina Press, 2012), chap. 2.

33. Joseph F. Spillane, "The Road to the Harrison Narcotics Act: Drugs and Their Control, 1875–1918," in *Federal Drug Control: The Evolution of Policy and Practice*, ed. Jonathon Erlen and Joseph F. Spillane (Binghamton, NY: Pharmaceutical Products Press, 2004), 1–24.

34. Campos, *Home Grown*, especially chap. 6; David F. Musto, *The American Disease: Origins of Narcotic Control* (New York: Oxford University Press, 1999), 294–95.

35. Alan Knight, *The Mexican Revolution: Counter Revolution and Reconstruction*, vol. 2, (Cambridge: Cambridge University Press, 1986), 501–3. Mexico did not prohibit alcohol nationally because Carranza insisted that the federal treasury was too dependent on alcohol revenue. See Campos, *Home Grown*, 105, 197–201.

36. Minutes of a Meeting to discuss the Opium Traffic at Macao, 1/13/1913, FO 371/1596, paper #2200, TNA.

37. Gómez Izquierdo, *El movimiento antichino*, 75.

38. May to Stronge, 10/3/1912, FO 371/1333, paper #49724, TNA. Macanese internal consumption numbers also seemed quite out of proportion to the population of Chinese there. See the note From May (Hong Kong) to (the Foreign Office?), included in correspondence received 10/26/1912, FO 371/1333, paper #45560, TNA.

39. Cover Sheet, "Opium Traffic at Macao," 10/26/1912, FO 371/1333, paper #45560, TNA.

40. "International Opium Convention," in the *American Journal of International Law* 6, no. 3 (1912) 177–92.

41. The details of these inquiries (the second on November 9) are scattered through various documents. See Gobernación to Salubridad, 6/11/1914, SP/CyC, c. 11, exp.

12, AHSSA. See also, Stronge to Grey, 1/9/1913, FO, 371/1596, paper #3982, TNA; Hacienda to SRE, FO, 371/1596, paper #5655, TNA; Gobernación to Salubridad, 8/28/1913, SP/CyC, c. 11, exp. 12, AHSSA. On November 9, Sir Edward Grey himself had cabled Stronge and reiterated May's request: Grey to Stronge, 11/9/1912, FO, 371/1333, paper #45560, TNA.

42. FO, 371/1334, paper #53957, TNA.
43. Stronge to Grey, 1/9/1913, FO, 371/1596, paper #3982, TNA.
44. Cover sheet, 1/15/1913, FO, 371/1596, paper #2103, TNA.
45. Gobernación to Salubridad, 1/15/1913, SP/CyC, c. 11, exp. 12, AHSSA.
46. Stronge to Grey (Received February 6), 1/22/1913, FO, 371/1596, paper #5655, TNA.
47. "Minutes of the Third Meeting, held at the Foreign Office on 12 Feb. 1913, to discuss the Opium Traffic at Macao," FO 371/1596, paper #7800, TNA. Cover sheet, FO, 371/1596, paper #3982, TNA.
48. Comunicaciones to SRE, 6/14/1913, III-502-5(I), SRE.
49. Correos to Salubridad, 8/11/1913, and related correspondence, SP/CyC, c.11, exp. 12, AHSSA.
50. Gobernación to Salubridad, 8/28/1913, SP/CyC, c.11, exp.12, AHSSA.
51. 9/9/1913, FO, 371/1601, paper #44800, TNA.
52. 11/21/1913, SP/CyC, c.11, exp.12, AHSSA.
53. Salubridad to Correos, 12/19/1913, SP/CyC, c.11, exp. 12, AHSSA. Before receiving this response, Correos followed up again on December 20, emphasizing the urgency of the matter. Correos to Salubridad, SP/CyC, c.11, exp.12, AHSSA. On December 31, Correos thanked Salubridad for its response: Correos to Salubridad, SP/CyC, c.11, exp. 12, AHSSA.
54. Acta de la sesión, 1/24/1914, SP/P/AS, c. 17, exp. 2, AHSSA. This presumably was the Apothecary Committee, though the documents are not explicit on this point.
55. Draft of Committee request, 1/24/1914, SP/CyC, c.11, exp. 12, AHSSA.
56. "International Opium Convention."
57. The U.S. law was actually more inclusive than the original Hague provision, the latter having only required such restrictions with respect to convention signatories.
58. Circular Telegram, Osborne for the Sec. of State, 3/11/1914, 811.4, vol. 0612, Correspondence File for Mexico City; Records of Foreign Service Posts, RG 84, NARA.
59. Gobernación to Salubridad, 5/7/1914, SP/CyC, c.11, exp. 12, AHSSA.
60. Acta de la sesión, 6/10/1914, SP/P/AS, c.17, exp. 2, AHSSA. The original report by the Apothecary Commission claimed with respect to the November 1912 rulings on prepared opium imports that "indeed they have been carried out." See the ruling 6/10/1914, SP/CyC, c.11, exp.12, AHSSA. This contradicts earlier documents. As noted above, the minutes also suggest that this was on hold as the commission awaited the text of the Hague Convention, though it does not explicitly say that the order was not carried out. Correspondence on the Macao side, however, confirms that

there were no restrictions beyond a $3.00/kilo duty for opium imports. 4/17/1914, FO, 371/1927, paper #34757, TNA.

61. 6/12/1914, SP/CyC, c.11, exp. 12, AHSSA.

62. Acta de la sesión, 6/17/1914, SP/P/AS, c. 17, exp. 2, AHSSA.

63. Ibid. Division of Far Eastern Affairs, "Memorandum on Control of Importation and Exportation of Narcotic Drugs," 11/7/1919; 800.114/149, box 7173; Department of State, Central Decimal File, 1910–29, RG 59, NARA.

64. Proposal, 6/22/1914, SP/CyC, c.11, exp.12, AHSSA.

65. Gonzales to the U.S. Customs Collector, 1/11/1916, r.135, 812.114/Narcotics/9, Records of the Department of State Relating to Internal Affairs of Mexico, 1910–29 (hereafter cited as RDSMEX).

66. Polk to McAdoo, 4/7/1916, r.135, 812.114/Narcotics/7, RDSMEX.

67. Aguilar to Arredondo, 6/2/1916, III-502–5(I), SRE; Aguilar to the British Chargé d' Affaires, 5/19/1916, III-502–5(I), SRE; Mexican Govt. Representative to Lansing, 13 May 1916, r. 135, 812.114/Narcotics/10, RDSMEX.

68. Secretaría de Hacienda y Crédito Público.

69. See, for example, Walker, *Drug Control*, 22; Toro, *Mexico's "War" on Drugs*, 7; Pérez Montfort cites the first part of the order, but leaves out the final section indicating that permission can be granted by Hacienda, *Tolerancia y prohibición*, 119–20.

70. Pérez Montfort, *Tolerancia y prohibición*, 120.

71. Douglas W. Richmond, *Venustiano Carranza's Nationalist Struggle, 1893–1920* (Lincoln: University of Nebraska Press, 1983), 33.

72. Enciso, 'Los fracasos,' 68.

73. XI/481.5/15, Archivo de Cancelados, Dirección General de Archivo e Historia, Secretaría de la Defensa Nacional, Mexico City.

74. Cabrera to Sumerlin, U.S. Chargé d'Affaires, 10/20/1919, 811.4, vol. 0612, Correspondence File for Mexico City; Records of Foreign Service Posts, RG 84, NARA.

75. Actas de la sesión, December 2, 13, and 16, 1916, SP/P/AS, c.18, exp. 3, AHSSA.

76. Acta de la sesión, 7/5//1916, SP/P/AS, c. 18, exp. 3, AHSSA.

77. *San Diego Union*, 11/16/1916, r. 135, 812.114/Narcotics/15, RDSMEX.

78. Just after Carranza's December 20 decree, Mexican postal officials came to an agreement with their U.S. counterparts to not ship opium through the mail either to or via the United States. Peters to the Secretary of State, 12/31/1915, 811.4, vol. 51, Correspondence File for Guadalajara, Consular Posts, Records of Foreign Service Posts, RG 84, NARA. The Hague Convention called for the Universal Postal Union to establish such regulations. "International Opium Convention," 191. Though, as we've seen, Correos, back in the summer of 1913, was the first department to implement the November 1912 opium restrictions.

79. Campos, *Home Grown*, 197–201.

80. Cárdenas de Ojeda notes that it was typical of Mexico during the twentieth century to begin adhering to such treaties before ratifying them, while also enacting

laws that were more severe than what was required by the agreements. *Toxicomanía y narcotráfico*, 35–36, 48–49.

81. We might also note that Gobernación would take six months to supply Salubridad with a copy of the Hague Convention. Gobernación to Salubridad, 7/7/1914, SP/CyC, c.11, exp.12, AHSSA.

82. Kate Doyle, "Operation Intercept: The Perils of Unilateralism," http://nsarchive.gwu.edu/NSAEBB/NSAEBB86/, accessed December 4, 2015; Walker, *Drug Control*, 122–33.

3

Popular Vices and Revolutionary Restrictions
Drugs and Mexican Society, 1910–1920

RICARDO PÉREZ MONTFORT

THE BEGINNINGS OF PROHIBITION IN MEXICO

One of the first restrictive government rulings on the use of drugs in Mexico in the twentieth century was decreed during the early days of the Mexican Revolution in the state of Coahuila, whose governor, Venustiano Carranza, would become a convinced promoter of the "campaign against vice." During the first decades of the twentieth century, the commercial and pharmaceutical companies of Torreón, along with the Banco Americano, freely imported opium and its derivatives, distributing them primarily through Chinese street vendors. In October 1911, shortly after Carranza became governor, the importation and trade of opium for smoking was outlawed while gambling was also prohibited, for fear that these vices would "contaminate" the rest of the population.[1] A special awareness of the international news then published about drugs—mainly opium consumption and its consequences—had been growing since the late nineteenth century, although without much concern on the part of Mexican authorities. The fashionable consumption in affluent sectors did not pose any problem. It was a habit that even seemed linked to the social prestige of the *dolce far niente* of the high bourgeoisie. But it was the impact that opium consumption had on the working classes—especially those linked with Chinese migrants in railroad construction and extensive agriculture—that generated the first wake-up call in government circles.

The ban on opium importation nationwide was decreed at the end of 1912, shortly prior to the bloody events of the Ten Tragic Days, which prevented the provision from being fully implemented. For example, even in August 1913, the Post Office General reported that they were frequently receiving in their offices "postal parcels from abroad containing opium, with statements on the packages with the word 'Drugs' ... for which reason they were not delivered ... but recipients claim that the imported opium is for medicinal purposes."[2] The Board of Health insisted on the prohibition and supposedly only allowed the importation of medicinal opium by drug and pharmaceutical companies.

Most of the opiates and other drugs, such as cocaine and heroin, entered Mexico by way of English and German ships. That is why during 1913 and 1914, there was an intense diplomatic exchange among the United Kingdom, the German Empire, and the government of General Victoriano Huerta, which focused on the interests that were affected by the prohibition of the entry of these substances into Mexico. The Commission of Drugstores, which part of the controversy referred to, suggested the issuing of "a law that restricts the importation of opium and its derivatives made from the alkaloids of that drug, cocaine and salts of those alkaloids, to the exclusive medicinal use of these drugs."[3] The representative of the United Kingdom, like the German envoy, were relatively satisfied when they were informed that the intentions of the Mexican prohibition were not entirely restrictive. It was only a reorientation of the market. And it would actually strengthen their commercial monopolies over chemical products, which now could only be distributed for medical and hospital purposes.

Although during those years the international drug and narcotics trade still were not severely restricted, U.S. pressures already were beginning to align some sectors of the Mexican government in favor of the International Opium Convention that had been adopted at The Hague in 1912. This convention was the continuation of a previous one held in Shanghai in 1909. There, the U.S. representative, Rev. Charles Henry Brent, who had been the bishop of Manila and governor of the Philippines, marked the beginning of his international crusade against drugs. The U.S. government tried to impose worldwide restrictions and prohibitions that had been established in its territory a few years before. In their desire to criminalize opium and other drugs widely used for extra-medicinal and recreational purposes, they used the pretext of wanting to support China in eradicating consumption in that country. And it was the same Reverend Brent who promoted these international debates between 1909 and 1912 with the support of the governments of Theodore Roosevelt and William Howard Taft. The second debate was held in The Hague, where twelve nations tried to reach an agreement that sought "the gradual eradication of the abuse of opium, morphine and cocaine."

Both Serbia and Turkey, as producers and distributors of these substances, refused to sign such an agreement. So did the German Empire and the United Kingdom, both of whom put conditions on their obligation. Germany refused to submit to the convention, as it did not want to harm the interests of its pharmaceutical companies. The United Kingdom made its signature conditional on the German government's doing the same. Furthermore, it was established that the agreements would enter into force as soon as thirty-five nations supported the prohibition. That was not achieved until several years later.[4]

By that time the Mexican regime of Victoriano Huerta received multiple interventionist pressures from the United States, including one that insisted that opium traffic from Mexico into the United Sates be limited to several border cities.[5] The promise to enact an antidrug law responded to U.S. pressure and was soon supported by Germany and the United Kingdom, which realized the possibility of a substantial price increase on their pharmaceuticals if the prohibition was carried out. But after the increase in tensions in Mexico-U.S. relations, and after the occupation of the Port of Veracruz by U.S. Marines in April 1914, the government of Victoriano Huerta was overthrown before the restrictive law was expedited, so the issue of control and drug prohibition was also not resolved in Mexico during those years.

By then, the tradition of smoking opium in the Chinese communities was seen as an intolerable "vice" and on various occasions aroused the intransigent mood of some authorities in certain sectors in Mexico. The anti-Chinese xenophobia that peaked during the late Porfiriato and throughout the Revolution shaped the social rejection of the open consumption of opium.[6]

In some regions of the country, however, particularly along the northern border and in the cities of Tijuana and Mexicali, opium dens did not seem to have any restrictions. The governor of Baja California, Esteban Cantú, who had been a supporter of Huerta in 1913 and joined the constitutionalists when the latter's government fell, maintained a situation of relative peace in the region. His power was based on his alliance with the California-Mexico Land and Cattle Company and on his own ability to do business with, and have partners in, several businesses dedicated to recreational habits.[7]

By mid-1914, Tijuana and Mexicali had definitely become a "land of fun and entertainment" for North Americans, Europeans, Mexicans, and Chinese. The

400,000 hectares that the California-Mexico Land and Cattle Company had around Mexicali were worked mainly by Chinese migrants who had brought the consumption of opium with them. In Mexicali's downtown alone, during 1914, forty sites for fun and pleasure were registered, including numerous smoking dens or "recreational rooms."[8] And a year later, Cantú legalized the processing and marketing of opium in the region, claiming he lacked the funds and police forces to exercise real control. It was decided to collect taxes from the importers and manufacturers, thus establishing a lucrative business for the local government. The concessions paid monthly quotas from 250 pesos to 1,000 pesos in gold to the government of the districts of Mexicali, Tijuana, and Ensenada. In Mexicali, it was even said that there was an opium den on every block. One of the most important ones belonged to Chan Fu, who also had his own laboratory that processed the raw material. Ten percent of the profits of Chan Fu's business went directly into the pockets of Cantú.[9]

It seems that the same authorities lacked a strategy to deal with the issue of consumption and manufacture of opium, until in 1914 the Department of Health definitively decided to try and forbid its import.[10] The matter was driven by an anti-Chinese xenophobia that was strongly perceived, although it clearly revealed the lack of a precise position in relation to the production, distribution, and consumption of most of the drugs.

Between 1910 and 1915, regulations and controls on the domestic markets, both of pharmaceutical substances and products as well as plants and herbs, started to unravel. Due to the Revolution, the gradual deterioration of the institutions responsible for the local and national restrictions as well as those on foreign trade made it possible to reactivate the production and circulation of these substances. These institutions were barely moving closer to the codes of prohibition that were being sought internationally, and the limitation and restriction of its production, circulation, and consumption were therefore nearly impossible to enforce. In addition, the war and militarization itself broadened the socialization processes of the use and abuse of drugs, and their application became more and more common among physicians and pharmacists.

POPULAR CONSUMPTION OF DRUGS

The indulgence in military and civilian environments—as well as the easing of restrictions and state constraints, coupled with a loss of both bourgeois and Christian ethical and moral values—led to an increase in the consumption of narcotics and even the rise of a liberal attitude toward them. For example, in September 1912 the newspaper *El Mundo Ilustrado* of Mexico City openly published the emergence and unrestricted sale of a few "cannabis sativa cigarettes" called "Cuentos Nacionales" (National Stories), produced by one Ignacio Alcocer in the Saltillo Prison.[11] While it is true that there are no reliable statistics or hard data in this regard, the increase in the open use, and without major restrictions, of drugs and narcotics could be proven by the significant increase in references to it appearing in newspapers and magazines, in the popular theaters, and literature of the time.

The circulation of drugs—at least of the inevitable cannabis and Asian "chandoo"—was manifested in the news stories announcing the discovery of marijuana shipments going to prisons and the army.[12] It was also visible in direct allusions to the marijuana habit of dictator Victoriano Huerta and his collaborators; the recurrent appearances of weed in the work of Federico Gamboa, like *La Llaga*, published in 1912; the narratives of the playwright Marcelino Dávalos, the classic Mariano Azuela novel *Los de abajo*, first published in 1915; and the cases about opium smuggling followed by the reporters of *Excélsior* during 1918 and 1919.

Since the early years of the Revolution many newspaper notes and news releases dealt with an almost unrestricted circulation of "pharmacy" drugs, like morphine, heroine, and cocaine in various Mexican cities. And there was also a sort of omnipresence of marijuana smoking in military headquarters, jails, and popular circles. The gutter press constantly indicated that almost every misdemeanor or crime that was committed had "surely something to do with opium or marijuana."[13] Shortly after 1911 the large amount of newspaper clippings and documents prove that there was a practically uncontrolled consumption of marijuana inside the military and civil jails. And the same impression could be obtained by reading the reports of the different popular armies. Campfire corridos contained the following verses:

> One fresh morning
> coming in from the orchard
> one can hear the notes of the bugle call
> played in the barracks,
> to the Juan [the soldier]
> they taste like honey,
> the same as marijuana.[14]

It was hardly a secret that Gen. Victoriano Huerta, a respected military authority during the late Porfiriato and the early revolutionary period, had a special fondness for Hennessy cognac and marijuana. After the coup of February 1913 against president Madero, popular corridos would mention Huerta with verses like these:

> Here comes the chant of the louse
> of the famous Mexican
> it is a modern corrido
> entitled "El Mariguano" (Pothead)

> The stoner, sirs
> will tell a certain thing
> it is none other than a bad Mexican:
> Victoriano Huerta

> The stoner, the stoner,
> that's the name of this little song
> that tells the verses
> the things of this little soldier.[15]

Some tragic moments in city life that were provoked by the collapse of urban order and the corruption of the authorities during the worst years of the Revolution were also related to marijuana and other drugs. For example, the famed armed robbers of the Banda del Automóvil Gris, which preyed on the capital's wealthy sectors, were soon linked with the consumption of "Doña Juanita." One of its leaders, Francisco Oviedo, was a known abuser of marijuana, a habit that made one of the news reporters write that people who smoke that weed "behaved sometimes like fierce lions and some other times like peaceful lambs."[16]

Some of the best chronicles of the everyday consumption of marijuana and other drugs in military environments and jails are found in the literary testimonies of those revolutionary years. Authors like Marcelino Dávalos and Ramón Puente wrote about the habit of marijuana smoking in the federal army. In his book ¡*Carne de Cañon!* (Cannon fodder), published in 1915, Dávalos writes the story of four soldiers that end up in a terrible fight because one of them confuses malaria with being stoned. In the story, titled "Marijuano," Samuel, the soldier with malaria, is killed by Natividad, who is addicted to marijuana and loses his temper easily when provoked.[17]

Also trying to question the ethical weakness of the federal army, Ramón Puente wrote the novel *Juan Rivera*, in which he described the military atmosphere among the former Porfirian troops during the first stages of the Revolution. Those troops were forced to support Madero's regime and finally turned against him when Victoriano Huerta led his coup d'etat in 1913. In this novel, a student, Juan, joins the army and gradually falls into hopelessness, which he relieves by smoking marijuana and drinking alcohol. During a trip to Quintana Roo, Puente describes how:

> Juan had a new taste for marihuana. The veteran with the big scars in his face had introduced him to this vice of the military quarters. Many of the officers and even the commander were addicts. Some of them used pot to ease their pains, others had perverse tendencies, others were curious, but it degenerated all of them.
>
> Learn to drag your namesake—the rude veteran told him once, fixing a cigarette and drawing it to his lips to show him how he could smoke it in a soldier's style.
>
> La Juanita (the weed) is a good friend; if you learn to deal with her, she will make you sleep and have beautiful visions.[18]

But not everything was violence or despair when drugs showed up in those military environments. Other authors refer to marijuana in a more playful and festive way. During the Revolution it was maybe the pen of Francisco L. Urquizo that revealed with most eloquence the smell of "toasted tortilla" among the army troops. He called his novel *La Tropa Vieja* and wrote the story of young Espiridión Sifuentes, who was first recruited in Nuevo León and spent most of the Revolution in the federal army. Thanks to his journalist friend Otamendi, Sifuentes gets to know the effects of smoking marijuana:

> Little liberating weed! Consolation of the overwhelmed, the sad one and the afflicted one. You must be a relative of death, since you have the power to make people forget the miseries of life, the tyranny of the body and the discomfort of the soul.... You get rid of the heavy feeling of time; you make people fly and dream about what the Supreme Being could be. You are the comfort of the unhappy prisoner, balm of the heart and the ideas. White smoke that rises like an illusion, music of a song that sings about a man that enjoys a vast freedom. Holy weed, God's creature that grows in the field to feed the souls and make them rise up to Him!

Urquizo described some of the hallucinations that Sifuentes presumably experienced:

> First, I felt a sort of astonishment, afterward I went blind; a very strong buzz in my head, and afterward I experienced something like a rare but very beautiful awakening, I had no body and felt no urge at all, as if I had everything I wanted. I was walking in the air without making a noise: I flew over the barracks, the towns, across the walls. And a sun. What a sun! A sun shining with all the colors: blue, green, yellow, red, crimson. Little singing birds, music in everything, happy sounds, songs. Such may be the Glory, very soft: with all the colors and all the sounds. If somebody shot me now, if they killed me, I wouldn't mind: I would keep flying, hearing and watching. What could be better?[19]

Unlike Ramón Puente or Marcelino Dávalos, Urquizo depicted the evasion from violent reality produced by marijuana smoking more as a ritual and mystic experience than as an intoxication. He recognized that getting high was not approved of by the army authorities, but Urquizo does not condemn the habit and views it essentially as a way to forget about everyday dangers. As a military novelist he noted that even little children held in arms by the *soldaderas* took part in providing the weed to the troops to facilitate a popular way to escape from war's horrible reality.

Another long account of the use of marijuana in prison and military circles can be found in Federico Gamboa's novel *La llaga*, published first in 1910 and then again in 1912. The leading character, Gregorio, is sent to San Juan de Ulua's prison. One of his companions, Eulalio, promises Gregorio that he will experience a surprising performance "unique and impressive" as soon as the evil weed "la mota" arrives. Gamboa describes a "satanic session" with abundant marijuana smoking infested with barbaric violence that serves as a good example of the recurrent prejudices and stereotypes the Porfirian aristocracy turned to when they stuck their nose in the world of the poor and the marginalized. The author shows some knowledge of orientalism by comparing the "grifa" used in the Mexican jailhouses with other substances that produced altered consciences: "It was marijuana: the cursed weed known to the Egyptians and Marco-Polo; the 'pot' or Indian hemp, that naturalists classify the same as hashish, the substance that drives you crazy. It stands in contrast with opium that makes you sleep, or alcohol that momentarily excites and then induces depression and astonishment."

After describing a "whirlpool of bloodthirsty bodies" that attacked each other with roaring laughter and curses, Gamboa quoted the lines of a song that was popular in the late nineteenth century and belonged to the marijuanero repertoire:

> When I'm stoned
> I'm not able to lift my head
> I have very red-colored eyes
>
> The oldest Devil, with his twenty-five brothers
> are going to take away the fleet of potheads . . .
>
> Here went passing
> the little weed that gave me consolation.[20]

This terrible scene ends when the guards violently burst in and the authorities confiscate the weed, trying to find out who bootlegged it into the prison and how. The major then discovers that the package of marijuana cigarettes had a label that identified the product as manufactured by a common and legal tobacco factory. He read: "Fábrica del Mosquetero—*Cannabis Indica*—Cigarros medicinales contra el asma, la tos y la ronquera—La Regeneración, de Pachuca, E. de H."[21] (Mosquetero's Factory—*Cannabis Indica*—Medicinal cigarettes to prevent asthma, cough, and sore throat). This seems to confirm that during the late Porfiriato and the early Revolution, it was easy to obtain marijuana cigarettes that could have therapeutic purposes but could also be used recreationally.

But some of the most eloquent testimonies of popular marijuana use during the Revolution can be found in two classic references of Mexican literature. One is Mariano Azuela's *Los de abajo*, which was published in 1915, and the other is Francisco Castillo Nájera's long "corrido" titled *El Gavilán* (The hawk), which was written during the revolutionary years but not published until 1939. While Azuela's novel describes the popular background of the revolutionary army led by Demetrio Macías, Castillo Nájera's poem tries to recover, with a popular language, the experience of a young man from Durango, Jesús Cienfuegos, who is carried away by the social commotion of the Revolution. In *Los de abajo* being a "marijuano" or "grifo" is almost an affirmative quality of a popular member of the revolutionary troops. For example, a humble Zapatista commander, Antonio Barona, was known as "El Grifo" and was renowned as one of the fiercest enemies of Victoriano Huerta's federal army.[22]

On the other hand, Castillo Nájera's *El Gavilan* wasn't as obliging toward marijuana smokers. He used his long poem to describe his own experience as a military doctor during the Revolution and found that many "marijuanos" had to lead a terrible life with their habit. In the chapter called "Marijuana," he wrote the following verses, which ended by stating that the herb was the devil's weed:

Very sad, because he was discharged from the army,
Jesús, again a peasant
started to gamble
and became a pothead

He smokes frequently
Juanita (the weed) is his ball, he likes her, it's his party,
he fools around with the weed

In circles, with gangs
the gatherings end badly
and the most beautiful parties end up as nightmares

If you don't know how to sweeten your pot
and then taste your blow
it is very difficult to appreciate the delight
of your puff

You have burns in your eyes
your mouth is dry,
but how many misfortunes
are driven away by this common weed

The pot is a poison
More dangerous than wine
A good man is transformed by it
into a murderer

You see ferocious monsters
that is better not to remember
you hear thunder and voices
and the pothead starts to tremble

> He feels cramps, he becomes delirious, he gets crazy and afraid
> he burns, he feels cold
> he soaks in sweats
>
> If a dude gets high
> It passes on to the others
> and the bewitched weed
> is the devil's weed.[23]

Other mentions of marijuana occur in the folk songs the soldiers sang during that violent period. Folklorist Vicente T. Mendoza classified those songs as "soldier folklore," and one of the most popular quatrains belonged to the well-known "jarabito": "La Cucaracha":

> The cockroach, the cockroach
> can't walk any further
> because it lacks
> the blow of marijuana . . .

MEXICO AND THE UNITED STATES: UNEASY RESTRICTIONS

In military hospitals and improvised sanatoriums, there was an indiscriminate use of opiates, particularly morphine, and on occasions heroin, which was recorded in the U.S. punitive persecution campaigns in the north of the country during 1916 and 1917. Among the troops under the command of Gen. John J. P. Pershing, organized against the forces of Pancho Villa after the attack on Columbus, it was reported that hundreds of soldiers used drugs with relative frequency.[24]

In the United States by 1916 not all legal restrictions on drugs had been fully implemented, although attempts at regulation had already begun. Trains that supplied the punitive expedition passed through El Paso, Texas, and Columbus itself, and among them several Chinese and Mexican traders offered the troops all kinds of alcohol and drugs.[25] The same lack of control also meant that access to these substances by occasional or habitual consumers was made relatively easy, both in pharmacies and in illegal trade. According to one estimate, of the 10,000 men who made up the punitive expedition, about 2 percent were habitual drug users, and of the 106,000 U.S. soldiers guarding the border, probably about 12,000 consumed other narcotics in addition to alcohol.[26] And there was a strong suspicion that all these substances came from Mexico. A news story that appeared in *El Demócrata* in July 1916, for example, claimed that "lately there have been large quantities of smoking opium in transit to the United States. The drug has been received in packages deposited in Mexican post offices." For this reason and in response to U.S. pressure, the Post Office issued instructions to establish greater vigilance "in order to prevent the shipment of the product of reference."[27]

Perhaps as a radical reaction to the inability of the Mexican governments to enforce the restriction on drugs pushed by the U.S. government—which lasted at least from 1911 to mid-1916—the provisional government of Venustiano Carranza decreed the prohibition of the import of "opium of all kinds and its extracts" throughout Mexico in December 1915.[28]

The decree said that the Ministry of Finance alone was authorized to permit such importation, and in the event of the discovery of fraud or smuggling, this should be referred to the Customs Office. The newspaper *El Constitucionalista* published the provision on January 7, 1916. And by the middle of that year, the prohibition against other drugs, like cocaine and marijuana, was also included.

Carranza launched this decree not only as an authoritarian reaction to the course prohibition was taking at the international level, but also as an act that had a clear moralistic message directed at the armed forces and Mexican society in general.[29] Carranza's ideology contained the fundamental premise that social reforms could only be imposed by combating vice. In their political, economic, and military actions, the Carrancistas sought to eliminate these anomalies and attacked basic pleasures. Pablo González prohibited dancing, music, and alcohol on his way through Matamoros in early 1916.[30] In Sinaloa and Chihuahua, the death penalty was decreed for anyone selling alcoholic beverages during the years 1916 and 1917. It was thus not surprising that Venustiano Carranza would undertake a crusade against drugs, banning first the import and exportation of opium, and then the production, distribution, and consumption of other narcotic substances.[31] In Baja California, however, although the restriction and outlawing of the trade and consumption of opium was accepted, its distribution was not outlawed, and until the end of 1919 opium could still be openly obtained and consumed on every block in Mexicali.[32]

The argument in favor of these restrictive provisions was that they were a way to prevent the "degeneration of the race." It was also argued that they would prevent the Mexican people from falling into the hands of those who "poisoned society." This was argued with much greater precision in the debates of the Constituent Congress held in late 1916 and early 1917 in Querétaro. The criterion for imposing a "social cleansing"—without the vices or poisons that affect the "race"—would have an enormous weight on any drug provision from then on.[33]

We must not forget that since the nineteenth century ideas about human races had spread globally. Taking classifications in mineralogy and biology as models, the identification of human groups "whose members possessed in full the typical or peculiar features of the same, which are transmitted from generation to generation" seemed plausible. This certainly generated countless polemics about racial superiority and justifications for actions rife with racism, which increased during the first thirty years of the twentieth century.[34]

The decree issued by Venustiano Carranza was far from being enforced in reality, in part because of the generally unstable situation in the country and in part because producers and importers, particularly pharmacists and merchants themselves, invariably found ways to negotiate with authorities and evade the restrictions. Imports of German, French, and English chemicals were rarely seized. And stories of drug taking abounded. For example, in March 1917, the newspaper *El Universal* reported that in Guadalajara, nine individuals in an opium den on Leandro Valle street were taken by surprise, and in November of the same year another article claimed that in the city of Oaxaca "the immoral habit of snorting heavy doses of cocaine has spread among middle class youth and many in the upper classes with fatal consequences."[35]

With regard to marijuana in Mexico City, it was reported in August of that same year (1917) that the weed "arrived in large quantities to the prisons, for a short time now," and authorities were asked to intervene in the matter.[36] Between May and December of the following year, the general police inspector of the Federal District arrested forty-eight individuals who were trying to smuggle marijuana into the Lecumberri prison.[37] By the end of the next year, however, *El Universal* once again published an article reporting that the police had discovered "500 sacks of the weed that were stored in a house in the Colonia Hidalgo."[38] Also during 1919, at least twenty-five drug-related cases were reported in the major newspapers of the capital.[39]

In addition to a scandalous case of the smuggling of several tons of opium that involved the Board of Health itself and a German merchant called Walter Hermann, the increase in drug consumption toward the end of the government of Venustiano Carranza led to the launching of a campaign against "intoxication by injections." By the end of World War I, once again U.S. prohibitionist pressures started their influence on the Mexican government. In July 1919, the Health Department launched a propaganda operation against "the more or less artistic, more or less vulgar intoxication that is reaching a huge increase among us, especially middle-class youth." The campaign was directed at pharmacies and drugstores in order to limit "the sale of all these substances that are used to get high (*enervarse*)" and had become a "true national calamity."[40] Even though this campaign seemed exaggerated, it is clear that by the end of the second decade of the twentieth century, the existence of opium dens in several cities across the country, the almost unrestricted circulation of "pharmaceutical" drugs like morphine, heroin, and cocaine, and almost certainly the pervasive presence of marijuana in barracks, prisons, and working-class neighborhoods, went far beyond the intentions of state control. Attempts to promote and enforce restrictive and punitive measures during the revolutionary decade had failed dramatically, as they have done until today with local and global initiatives and circumstances.

During the debates of the Constituent Congress held in Querétaro at the end of 1916 and early 1917, Coahuila deputy Dr. José María Rodríguez suggested that following the guidelines inspired by the U.S. provisions outlined in the the Hague Convention, a single body—the General Health Council—should be responsible for the regulation of drugs throughout the country. The premise that drugs "degenerate the race" had already been discussed since the first prohibition under the Carranza government and seemed to influence the additions to Article 73 of the Constitution.

Once Carranza was declared constitutional president, Dr. Rodríguez became the head of the Health Council, the institution that would dictate health policies at the federal level. Between 1917 and 1920, two epidemics—typhoid and Spanish influenza—ravaged the country, which is why the issue of drugs became less important to those responsible for Mexican public health.[41]

But on March 2, 1920, while the Carranza government was losing support, Edmundo G. Aragón, general secretary of the Department of Public Health, established a series of limitations "on the trade of products that can be used to encourage the vices that degenerate the race and on the cultivation of plants that can be used for the same purpose." These provisions were published in the *Diario Oficial* on March 15, 1920, and established that anyone who wanted to import opium, morphine, heroin, or cocaine needed special permission from the Department of Health. The marketing of these products could only take place in medical dispensaries, which were also required to keep careful records of their movements. The strict prohibition of the cultivation and trade of marijuana and opium poppy was also included in these provisions. Violations of these mandates were punishable with fines of up to five thousand pesos.[42]

Even though the attempt at state control of these substances was established when the Carranza regime was facing great uncertainty, the authorities that came to power after his fall decided to adopt the same measures and expand them with other elements taken from previous projects. In late 1920, it was established that as of the first of January 1921, no pharmacy could continue dispatching if it did not have a qualified pharmacist.[43]

The United States exercised pressure through diplomatic channels to promote the prohibition of alcohol and drugs. Therefore, it would not have been strange for members of the Mexican Health Council to follow this same trend, as many viewed the U.S. crusade against vice with particular sympathy.[44] But, unlike what happened in the United States, the Mexican government never prohibited the manufacture or sale of alcohol during those years.

From the early 1920s, the international crusade against "hallucinatory and recreational drugs" intensified, and the Mexican government formed part of a multinational alliance intolerant of the free movement of these drugs. In 1919, the Volstead Act, or Prohibition Act, was launched in the United States as part of a prohibitionist barrage by antialcohol groups, led by the Anti-Saloon League, whose commander was Senator Wayne Wheeler. U.S. pressure to continue a similar course in Mexico was felt immediately, to the extent that the reports by Ernest H. Cherrington, secretary general of the World League Against Alcoholism, hinted at the possibility that the Mexican government would end the cultivation of the maguey, used to make pulque and mezcal.[45] Needless to say, Cherrington's expectations were never fulfilled and instead a lucrative business at various points of the Mexican-U.S. border appeared: the smuggling of alcohol.

Clashes between Mexican smugglers and U.S. agents on the border soon became daily news. In Ciudad Juárez, Chihuahua, in March 1921, for example, a well-known case involving the smuggling of opium, tequila, and other liquors kept both the local population and newspaper readers busy. The battle between smugglers and U.S. troops received a lot of international attention, since, according to the news published in Mexico, New York, Arizona, and Texas, between twenty-five and forty Mexican traffickers "kept fending off their enemies... until they finally withdrew taking all their cargo with them."[46]

According to a Mexican newspaper, such clashes were becoming common since "large shipments of tequila and opium" often crossed the border to be sold as "articles that have a huge demand in the southern part of the United States and, therefore, they are sold at very elevated prices."[47]

And of course, it did not take long before corridos about the so-called "bootleggers" appeared as well as local legends about cross-border heroes. Some mentioned the tension between Mexican smugglers and illegal U.S. traders, while at the same time recommending certain discretion in order to do good business:

> Since prohibition
> Took away our spirits
> The old resellers
> Sell it with more cynicism.
>
> They are called bootleggers
> Gentlemen, very persecuted
> By the cops and women
> Who always end up bitten...
>
> What a business, what a business
> It is to make a good drink,
> You don't need a partner
> Simply sell it quietly.[48]

Small-time smuggling was perhaps most widely practiced by those who saw a way to benefit from prohibition. The traders of Mexican alcohol, identified as *tequileros*, were also the subjects of corridos and regional mythologies. Their battles against the rangers, or *rinches*, appeared as the central themes of those early adventures of cross-border traffic. Smuggling was conducted in many ways, but apparently the most common was organizing small groups that crossed international borders with casks of wood, metal, or leather filled with tequila or *aguardiente*. Of course, there were also those who crossed the border with sacks of marijuana or cans of opium.

With the prohibitionist laws, U.S. authorities fanned the flames of a transnational and intercultural conflict. A hot dispute in those regions put the border patrol on alert. U.S. troops and patrols often ambushed Mexican smugglers in the classic style of the gunmen of the Old West.[49] Their myths and legends became globally known.

But the restrictions on the production, sale, and consumption of alcohol, which had serious consequences in U.S. society in the 1920s, was preceded by the initiatives of religious groups, mostly Protestants, that saw drunkenness as a sin and bars as centers of moral and political corruption. Drug use was also a target of Methodist and Lutheran intolerance. The aforementioned Rev. Charles Henry Brent, along with Hamilton Wright and Francis Burton Harrison, were the main promoters of the U.S. prohibitionist principles that stated emphatically that "any non-medical use of drugs was immoral." This principle—along with a clear racist identification of drug users and their activities—determined the beginning of the U.S. campaign against drugs from the early years of the 1920s. Brent, Wright, and Harrison associated drug use with the alleged inferiority of some "minorities" who were gradually occupying positions of greater economic importance in U.S. society. In this way, they said that opium converted Asians into men unfit for work, marijuana made Latinos crazy, and cocaine transformed African Americans into criminals. Therefore, prohibition was directed mainly at these minorities, as a racist policy that had to be gradually installed throughout the entire world.[50]

In 1918, the prohibitionist campaign regained strength when the U.S. Treasury Department appointed a special committee in charge of the fight against drugs.[51] In 1919, at the end of World War I, Article 295 of the Treaty of Versailles required signatory nations to strictly follow the agreements of the 1912 Hague Convention and promote the laws necessary to control drugs in their respective countries.[52]

The prohibitionist spirit of Brent and his followers found an echo among Mexican revolutionary and postrevolutionary governments that gradually was formalized in decrees and policies, as demonstrated by government regulations in the early and mid-1920s. In the beginning, this eagerness justified the need for a state control of drugs, which also responded to the attempts to reorder the basic structures of postrevolutionary Mexico and the reorientation of existing cultural patterns. With these measures, the revolutionary governments also sought to end the "decadence" of those who were responsible for the social injustices and the "enlightened despotism" of the Porfiriato.

But it is fair to say that postrevolutionary Mexican "antinarcotic" provisions were often linked to the U.S. ones in their racist dimension. In this sense, it is impossible to deny that state restrictions imposed on the use of opium were tied to the anti-Chinese policies of the time that affected both Mexicans and North Americans.[53] But more than concern over the harm that opium could cause to an addict's health, the reason for making this substance illegal was because it was the habit of an ethnic and racial group considered inferior and undesirable. During the postrevolutionary years, there were frequent allusions to the Chinese as "vicious people who corrupted our traditions" or as "a people who have become degenerate as a result of the delusionary effects produced by opium."[54]

Nevertheless, in social circles with a more cosmopolitan influence, drug consumption had more ambiguous connotations. And in some places there was admiration, curiosity, and a morbid fascination over narcotics, despite their social stigma. But they also provoked commiseration and indulgence. In 1920, for example, in a feature written by the famous actress Mimí Derba titled "El Fifí," an addict was judged as a "social outcast . . . even though they mostly belong to good families." The account followed an individual one night to a well-known coffee shop called "El Globo" on Avenida Madero. There the actress and a friend witnessed the following ritual:

> From one of the pockets of his waistcoat he takes out a little round box, opens it, and with his clumsy fingers of an old man he takes out a small dose of a white and shiny powder, brings it to his nose and absorbs it with delight. What are you taking?—my friend asks me with her eyes wide open. Cocaine—I quietly respond.[55]

The author then described the way cocaine enhanced everday experiences. In a moment of candor she confessed she too was human and that maybe one day a habit or vice such as the one they had just observed "would be able to destroy her in its claws."[56]

This short story talked about the cocaine habit with great spontaneity, as if the person she had described was one of the many urban characters one could find in the enormous social mosaic that was Mexico City by the time the Revolution was almost over. The "Fifí" was an aristocrat, part of the old world of the dictatorship that was on the way out and was giving way to a new model of a country that would restore hope for the people. In the end, many continuities remained and the new man that was supposed to appear after the Revolution wasn't that different after all. Restrictions on drugs stayed in place and the tensions between individual freedom and the responsibilities of the revolutionary state remained an important issue.

NOTES

1. Douglas W. Richmond, *La lucha nacionalista de Venustiano Carranza 1893–1920* (Mexico City: Fondo de Cultura Económica, Mexico, 1986), 57.
2. Richmond, *La lucha*, 57.
3. Richmond, *La lucha*, 57.
4. Richard Davenport-Hines, *La búsqueda del olvido. Historia global de las drogas 1500–2000* (Mexico City: Turner-Fondo de Cultura Económica, 2003), 196–97; Antonio Escohotado, *Majestades, crímenes y víctimas* (Barcelona: Editorial Anagrama, 1987), 117–28.
5. Berta Ulloa, *La Revolución intervenida* (Mexico City: El Colegio de México, 1971), 205–42.
6. Juan Puig, *Entre el río Perla y el Nazas: la China decimonónica y sus braceros emigrantes, la colonia china de Torreón y la matanza de 1911* (Mexico City: CONACULTA, 1993).
7. Linda B. Hall, "El liderazgo en la frontera: Los casos de Sonora y Baja California," *Boletín Fideicomiso Archivos Plutarco Elías Calles and Fernando Torreblanca* 21 (1996): 10–12.
8. José Alfredo Gómez Estrada, *Gobierno y casinos. El origen de la riqueza de Abelardo L. Rodríguez* (Mexicali: UABC, 2002), 43.
9. Gómez Estrada, *Gobierno*, 43.
10. Archivo Histórico de la Secretaría de Salud (AHSS), Fondo Salubridad Pública, Sección Congresos y Convenciones, leg. 11 exp. 12.
11. *El Mundo Ilustrado*, September 29, 1912.
12. *El Universal*, November 9, 1918; *Excélsior*, March 10, 1919.
13. *El Universal*, February 6, 1920.
14. Armando de María y Campos, *La Revolución Mexicana a través de los corridos populares* (Mexico City: INEHRM, 1962), 1:407. All the translations are by the author.
15. De María y Campos, *La Revolución Mexicana*, 1:294–95.
16. *El Universal*, December 21, l915.
17. Marcelino Dávalos, *¡Carne de cañón! (Cuentos)* (Mexico City: n.p., 1915).
18. Ramón Puente, *Juan Rivera, Novela del pensamiento revolucionario* (Mexico City: Editorial Botas, 1936), 115–17.
19. Antonio Castro Leal, *Novela de la Revolución Mexicana* (Mexico City: Editorial Aguilar, 1960), 2:402–3.
20. Federico Gamboa, *La llaga* (Mexico City: Eusebio Gómez de la Puente, 1910), 38, 206, 208, 209.
21. Gamboa, *La llaga*, 211.
22. Arturo Langle, *Vocabulario, apodos, seudónimos, sobrenombres y hemerografía de la Revolución Mexicana* (Mexico City: UNAM, 1966), 100.

23. Francisco Castillo Nájera, *El Gavilán (Corrido grande)* (Mexico City: Editorial Mexico Nuevo, 1939), 33–36.

24. James Sandos, "Prostitution and Drugs. The United States Army on the Mexican-American Border, 1916–1917," *Pacific Historical Review* 49, no. 4 (1980): 621–45.

25. Sandos, "Prostitution," 639–41.

26. Sandos, "Prostitution," 642–43.

27. *El Demócrata*, July 9, 1916.

28. The decree was signed in December 1915 but implemented the following year. Venustiano Carranza, *Codificación de los decretos del C. Venustiano Carranza*, (Mexico City: Imprenta de la Secretaría de Gobernación, 1915), 423–24; Richmond, *La lucha*, 231.

29. Olga Cárdenas de Ojeda, *Toxicomanía y narcotráfico* (Mexico City: Fondo de Cultura Económica, 1976), 35–36; AHSS, Fondo Salubridad Pública, Sección Servicio Júridico, caja 2, exp. 3.

30. Richmond, *La lucha*, 230.

31. Richmond, *La lucha*, 231–32.

32. Pedro Castro, *Adolfo de la Huerta. La integridad como arma de la Revolución* (Mexico City: Siglo XXI, 1998), 101.

33. Isaac Campos Costero has noted with particular clarity the importance of this argument. See Isaac Campos Costero, "Marijuana, Madness, and Modernity in Global Mexico, 1545–1920" (PhD diss., Harvard University, 2006), 222–35. Also see Beatriz Urías Horcasitas, "Fisiología y moral en los estudios sobre las razas mexicanas: continuidades y rupturas (siglos XIX y XX)" *Revista de Indias* 65, no. 234 (2005): 355–74.

34. Juan Comas, *Razas y racismo* (Mexico City: SEP-Setentas, 1972), 14.

35. *El Universal*, March 12, 1917; *El Universal*, November 14, 1917.

36. *El Universal*, August 17, 1917.

37. Archivo Histórico de la Ciudad de México, Policia, Penitenciaría, Presos, no. 3664 and 4158.

38. *El Universal*, September 11, 1918.

39. *El Universal*, January 3, 1919; *Excélsior*, April 11, 1919, July 6, 1919, July 20, 1919; *El Universal*, June 12, 1919, *Excélsior*, June 9, 1919, June 7, 1919.

40. *Excélsior*, July 8, 1919.

41. Mario Ramírez Rancaño, "La epidemia de influenza española en México: 1918," *Revista 20/10* 4 (2009): 69–92.

42. AHSS, Fondo Salubridad Pública, Sección Servicio Júridico, caja 2, exp. 3.

43. AHSS, Fondo Salubridad Pública, Sección Servicio Júridico, caja 2, exp. 4.

44. Dr. Gabriel Malda, who took over the Health Department in 1920, showed a particular admiration for the advances in the control of epidemics in the United States. Ann Emanuelle Birn, *Marriage of Convenience. Rockefeller International Health and Revolutionary Mexico* (New York: University of Rochester Press, 2006).

45. Ernest H. Cherrington, "Worldwide Progress Toward Prohibition Legislation in 1923," *The Annals, Academy of Political and Social Science* CIX (1929): 211.
46. *Excélsior*, March 19 and 20, 1921.
47. *Excélsior*, March 20, 1921.
48. Guillermo Hernández, ed., "The Chicano Experience," in *Una historia de la música de la frontera. Texas-Mexican Border Music*, vol. 14, Folcloryc Records, 9021, n.d.
49. Américo Paredes, *A Texas-Mexican Cancionero* (Urbana: University of Illinois Press, 1976), 42–44.
50. Escohotado, *Majestades*, 198, 114.
51. David F. Musto, *The American Disease. Origins of Narcotic Control* (New Haven, CT: Yale University Press, l973), 134–36.
52. Davenport-Hines, *La búsqueda del olvido*, 213–14.
53. Moisés González Navarro, *Población y sociedad en México* (Mexico City: UNAM, 1974), 57–77.
54. José Jorge Gómez Izquierdo, *El movimiento anti-chino en México (l871–1934). Problemas de racismo y nacionalismo durante la Revolución Mexicana* (Mexico City: INAH, 1992), 103–8; Axayácatl Gutiérrez, "Trafico y consumo de opio en México 1920-1940," (BA thesis, UNAM, 1996), 23; Macrina Rabadán Figueroa, "Chinos: entre la historia ancestral y la imagen desfavorable," in *La ciudad cosmopolita de los inmigrantes*, ed. Carlos Martínez Assad (Mexico City: Gobierno del DF, 2009), 1:263–81.
55. Mimí Derba, *Realidades* (Mexico City: Tipografía F. E. Graue, 1921), 77–79.
56. Derba, *Realidades*, 77–79.

4

Drugs, Control, and Corruption
The Antinarcotics Police in Mexico City, 1920–1947

NIDIA A. OLVERA HERNÁNDEZ

On April 12, 1938, Luis Huesca de la Fuente, the chief of the Narcotics Police of the Department of Public Health (DSP), was put in Lecumberri jail. He was charged with abuse of authority, false declarations, and narcotics offenses. Less than a week earlier, two narcotics officers had detained a girl in the Merced market with ninety-eight wraps of what appeared to be heroin and took her to the station. Two women eventually arrived to take the girl back home. They too were detained. At this point, Luis Huesca intervened. He phoned the station and ordered the three detainees and the narcotics to be taken to his home.[1]

Here, in the house of the chief of the Narcotics Police, the two agents handed over the prisoners and the drugs. Huesca seemed annoyed and said that the detention of the girl had put at risk a much larger operation. This one was a "question of kilos" and involved a big target—the Mexico City dealer Dolores Estévez Zulueta, aka Lola la Chata.[2] He ordered the women to stay in his house, told the agents to take the young girl away, and claimed that the drugs actually belonged to an addict called Esperanza López. The agents, however, refused and instead told the man in charge of the Campaign against Alcoholism and Drug Addiction, Leopoldo Salazar Viniegra.[3] The story soon hit the press: "Chief of Narcotic Police in prison." "He substituted abundant cocaine. This was collected from one woman, and he changed it for bicarbonate."[4] "Captain Huesca is in prison."[5] At the same time, they published Huesca's own declarations in which he claimed the accusations were "slander and intrigue" and actually the result of his own discovery that his agents were "taking bribes" as well as a personal conflict with Salazar Viniegra.[6]

Leónides Almázan, the head of the DSP, denied that he had authorized Huesca to release the two women. In fact, he had ordered exactly the opposite. Huesca was to proceed with "all energy possible to exterminate the social plague of drug trafficking."[7] For his part, Salazar Viniegra declared that he didn't approve of the way the Narcotics Police had acted and that the institution itself had too much autonomy and wasn't working according to an established plan.[8]

The scandal surrounding Huesca brought into focus a police agency that for more than twenty years had been in charge of controlling illicit drugs in Mexico. The agency stood at the threshold between an approach to drugs that focused on health care and safety and a prohibitionist approach, which stressed policing and punishment. But as the Huesca case outlined, corruption ran through the institution. He was not the first narcotics policeman to be accused of it and he would not be the last.

In this chapter, I offer an introduction to the history of what was first called the Sanitary and then renamed the Narcotics Police. I will examine its principal functions, its organization, and its action in eradicating the "pernicious trafficking and consumption of drugs." I will also look at the discretionary way it executed new laws on narcotics, often indulging in corrupt and illegal practices.[9]

Informed by work on state formation and its links to both violence and coercion, I examine both the formal practices of policing and the informal practices or the "dark side" of policing.[10] In Mexico in particular the role drug trafficking has played in the formation of the state has always been characterized by violence and the "incestuous relationship" between crime and the state apparatus.[11] At the same time, here I also look at how the trade in illicit substances, as well as the legal regimes of control, acquired transnational dimensions.[12] This can help us understand the growing global policies of prohibition and their links to state formation in the local context of Mexico City.

ORIGIN AND ORGANIZATION OF THE ANTINARCOTICS POLICE IN MEXICO

The origins of the Sanitary Police can be found in the notion of medical police.[13] These were created for the administration of public health and included the supervision of hygiene, the control of food and drink, and in general the improvement of sanitary conditions in the cities. In general, these efforts were also connected to the extension of state power.[14] In Mexico, since the nineteenth century, the authorities claimed the need for a Sanitary Police as part of "the administration's obligations towards the people."[15] This organization was under the supervision of medical science professionals.[16]

Medical ideas at the time were heavily influenced by hygenicist thought and the notion of "degeneration." This helped justify state control of narcotics.[17] The same doctors that had first defended the therapeutic use of drugs soon started to attribute to them negative properties and started to create the "symptoms of a new disease."[18] They began to flag the risks of consuming certain substances and to catalogue their uses and abuses as manias. And in the last years of the nineteenth century they conducted various investigations into the pernicious effects of opium, heroin, and morphine.[19] They also started to investigate the relationship between "marihuanismo" and violent crime, concluding that the plant produced a "true mania."[20]

The doctors proposed measures to prevent the consumption of drugs and avoid the supposed degeneration of the population. The strategies that were employed to try to avoid the problem of "toxicomanías" were of two types. First there were the treatments for those that had acquired the vice. Second there were the prophylactic measures. The former included the detoxification of patients,[21] or the prescription of pharmaceutical medicines designed to reduce the symptoms of drug withdrawal.[22] They also included imprisonment in psychiatric institutions or other medical establishments or even prisons. Due to the difficulties with such therapeutic treatments, the doctors also considered prevention to be the best strategy to avoid an increase in addicts. And included among the prophylactic measures were educational campaigns to show the population the risks of drug consumption, mechanisms to impede access to the substances such as restrictive legislation, and the execution of these laws by the police.

During the postrevolutionary period, the government created a formal Sanitary Police specializing in narcotics. Among the first regulations of the new body were the "Dispositions about products that degenerate the race," published in 1920. This established restrictions on the cultivation of poppies, the introduction and sale of opium, morphine, heroin, and cocaine, and the commerce in and sale of marijuana.[23] These regulations as well as those published afterwards responded to the need of the postrevolutionary regime to impose social control. From now on the authorities would be in charge of supervising the production, sale, and consumption of products they designated as narcotics.[24]

In 1925 the authorities established the Department of Public Health (Departamento de Salubridad Pública, or DSP), which was in charge of making sure that sanitary laws were followed. The department was also in charge of "running campaigns against alcoholism and the direct sale of substances that poisoned the individual and degenerated the race." The regulations also stated that each one of the sanitary services would have at its disposal a group of agents and inspectors.[25] The Sanitary Police was officially set up in the same year as the department; soon after, the first inspector general was appointed. It was subdivided into different branches, each with its own specialized agents. There were branches in health, food and drink, milk, markets and plazas, and veterinary hygiene, and there were agents who specialized in the control of drugs, the Narcotics Police.[26]

Soon afterwards the Narcotics Police established an office and purchased a car so they could expand their sphere of action within Mexico City. The agents received credentials and the "implements of the Service so that they came across no obstacle . . . to pursue with determination traffickers and addicts."[27] This included a badge, a pistol, and an electric lamp. These credentials were particularly useful and allowed agents to "penetrate commercial establishments, factories and industrial sites as well as houses."[28]

In 1928 the DSP published internal regulations for the Sanitary Police in which it was demanded that the members would be "models of orderliness and decency." They were to refrain from "establishing differences between the persons with which they deal, being equally respectful and active both with the humble and the powerful." In general they were obliged to "show in their person and their habits that they are worthy of the confidence that the Nation has deposited in them." They were also prohibited from using violence, from consuming alcohol both on and off the job, from getting involved in political and religious matters during their hours of work, and from "accepting payoffs." If they did the latter, they would be immediately sacked.[29] The authorities also thought the agents needed an education, so they provided the police with their own library and obliged the agents to attend the DSP school.[30] In 1929 the school offered courses on reading maps of Mexico City, on street names, on sanitary legislation, alcoholism, tobacco use, and diverse drug addictions.[31]

In 1930 the Sanitary Police was composed of a chief of police, nine deputy chiefs, and 220 agents. Only 12 belonged to the narcotics branch. The chief of police suggested that the latter be extended to 24 agents due to the "great quantity of addicts and traffickers" that existed in the capital. The personnel of this service were charged with visiting houses where they knew people traded in drugs, arresting traffickers and decommissioning narcotics, surveilling addicts and traffickers to find the places where they met to inject, and visiting drugstores and pharmacies.[32] There was, it seems, an ambiguity in their role. They were meant to supervise the world of official medicine but also the everyday world of street addicts and peddlers.

From its earliest days there were accusations of corruption and irregularities in the Sanitary Police. In the first reports of the DSP, it was admitted that certain men had infiltrated the corporation who "although they apparently lend their magnificent help, in the end what interests them is their individual interest."[33] In 1925 there was the case of doctors Gabriel Malda and Alfonso Pruneda, who were the chief and the secretary general of the DSP respectively. They were both investigated by the Ministry of the Interior's Confidential Department due to a letter that had accused them of committing "immoralities" and getting involved in the trafficking of heroin.[34] The investigation discovered that Pruneda was "an upstanding family man on which no suspicion should fall." Malda, however, was of "doubtful morality" and had "tried to commit indecorous acts with señoras and señoritas who attended his sanatorium." He was also a notorious drinker who often hung out with the military commander Norberto Olvera and committed "true orgies." The investigation did not find any explicit evidence of trafficking but it did mention that the DSP's controls were so weak that it was certainly possible.[35]

These accusations against the DSP were relatively constant. And many focused on the Sanitary Police in particular. Between 1925 and 1929, 40 percent were accused of some sort of irregularity.[36] Certain deputy chiefs were charged with trafficking in narcotics and covering up for traffickers.

In 1929, for example, Jesús Merza Terán, the chief of the DSP's internal affairs, wrote a report on investigations into the Narcotics Police. In it he claimed that he knew of at least eight cases where agents had arrested traffickers and then released them. In their stead they arrested a group of addicts. In return they paid Raúl Camargo, the chief of the Narcotics Police, a quota in order to continue trafficking. Meza Terán asserted he had copious proof that Camargo had "become the protector of drug sellers, through funds which he received." He had even received gifts from traffickers "with no scruples and in the presence of all of his agents."[37] In response to the report, Rául Camargo was sacked from his post.

CONTROL AND REPRESSION OF DRUG ADDICTS IN MEXICO CITY

New laws increasingly defined the Sanitary Police's role in attempting to clamp down on the drug business. First with the penal codes of 1929 and 1931 the authorities advanced the national criminalization of narcotics and established sanctions against the acquisition, selling, or trafficking of narcotic plants. In 1931 they also published the Federal Regulation against Drug Addicts, which defined an addict as "any individual that without therapeutic end habitually uses any drug."[38] At the same time it showed the need to establish hospitals for treating addicts. Later in 1931 they also published the Regulations of the Sanitary Police. This established the organization, faculties, and tasks of the police agents, which involved the "investigation and vigilance over the complying with the Sanitary Code, its regulations and other dispositions about health." At the same time, it determined that the agents should have a certificate from the school of the DSP, sit for an exam, and comply with their jobs "with honor and good conduct."[39]

Although there is evidence of people being arrested for crimes related to marijuana and opium since the first decade of the twentieth century,[40] a careful revision of documentary sources indicates that it was in the 1930s that the arrests for crimes connected to narcotics really increased.[41] They indicate that at least 1,117 persons were in Lecumberri on drugs charges in the 1930s and 1,625 persons in the following decade.[42]

It is important to point out that during the period it was not simply the agents of the Narcotics Police that collaborated in tracking down drug criminals. Other local authorities also got involved. They included the Judicial Police linked to the attorney general, members of the Secret Service of the Federal District, members of the Dirección General de Investigaciones Políticas y Sociales, and from 1947 onwards even members of the Dirección Federal de Seguridad.[43]

Although the agents of the Sanitary Police had federal badges and were allowed to police other parts of the country, for the most part they stayed in Mexico City. They were occasionally sent to the border or to port cities when they had direct information on drug rings. But this was rare. Within Mexico City, they concentrated their work in the poorer neighborhoods, where they apprehended both consumers and peddlers. According to the press, this resulted in a "big blow in all the *barrios bajos* against addicts and traffickers."[44] Among the barrios that were most targeted were La Merced, Tepito, Candelaria de los Patos, and other marginal areas in the center of the city. Other areas that were frequently raided included the fields around the Colegio Militar, which were famed for marijuana selling, and the fields around Tlalpan and Xochimilco, where some farmers grew both poppies and marijuana.

Although the addicts were legally mandated to receive medical attention before they were put before the judicial authorities, this didn't exclude them from the attention of the Sanitary Police. Rather the targets were arrested, brought to the offices of the Sanitary Police, and forced to undergo a medical checkup to determine whether they were addicts or not. From there the Legal Department of the DSP had to make the decision whether to release the suspects, subject them to detoxification, or prosecute them for narcotics crime. The chief of the Legal Department, Manuel Rueda Magro, explained the method used:

> The Sanitary Police of the country . . . exercises a constant and strict vigilance over the known addicts with the end of surprising their suppliers. After arresting an addict or a trafficker, he is consigned first to the Sanitary Authority, which proceeds to decommission the drugs found in their power, doing an analysis of these. Then we will put out a report in which we list the circumstances of the detention and the declarations obtained from the detained person and the others involved. Then the Sanitary Authority . . . proceeds to send the detainee to the Federal Attorney General, sending all the drugs found, and also does an analysis, with the aim of doing a full investigation and sending the suspect to a judge, who is able through the Penal Code to impose up to seven years prison and 5,000 pesos in fines.
>
> The addicts are generally sent to the Hospital de Toxicómanos where they are subject to treatment with the aim of weaning them off the drugs and once done they are set free and are not prosecuted but kept under strict vigilance. Those addicts and traffickers found guilty are imprisoned, tried, and sent to prison.[45]

To reach their objectives, the agents of the Sanitary Police raided the houses of "known traffickers" or the places where they "knew that drugs were sold." For example, on March 1, 1930, José Pedroza and José Monroy kept a watch on Magdalena Mixhuca and followed her to the house of her dealer, Herlinda Sánchez. They staked out her house, and when Herlinda noticed they were watching she threw two papers on the floor, which had 3.30 grams of heroin.

The woman was sent to the Sanitary Police station and was processed. She confessed that she did sell narcotics as she needed the money to maintain her children. She received a sentence of one year and a fine.[46]

As well as staking out houses, the police were accustomed to doing thorough house and body searches to look for drugs. This was the case with Agustín Campos González, a forty-three-year-old shoemaker who had just had a stint in prison on drugs charges. In October 1932 three agents were patrolling the barrio of La Merced when they saw "a well-known trafficker of marijuana." This was Agustín. They started by doing a series of searches of the suspect. "The first were superficial and the last the most thorough. In the part of the left leg at the height of the knee and inside the underpants, which had a drawstring, they found a packet secured by a lace which contained 7 cigarettes of marijuana."[47] And although the suspect denied they were his, he was sentenced to a year in prison and fined fifty pesos.

Another strategy that was commonly practiced among the agents was the so-called "hook [*gancho*] method." This consisted of using an addict as an informant and telling the addict where to find the main local peddlers. This was what Luis Huesca was supposed to be doing. He wanted to use the child and the two women to try to get closer to the main trafficker of Mexico City, Lola "la Chata," or at least so he claimed. At the same time in 1937, an agent named Luis Polina Limón detained an addict called Pedro Elizalde, who was in turn used to capture the trafficker Conrado Lugo with thirty papers of drugs. But Elizalde, in fear of being taken to the Hospital de Toxicómanos and "making the most of the liberty that 'hooks/ganchos' were allowed," decided to flee.[48] Many of these ganchos, however, did not flee. And they were paid for their service. In the same year, Rafael Ham was paid fifty pesos for his help in decommissioning two thousand pesos worth of opium.[49]

The detentions related to the smuggling of illicit substances became increasingly complicated. The police were using more and more force against suspects, and at the same time traffickers were fighting back. Peddlers and traffickers increasingly carried arms.[50] For example, in 1935 three agents approached the house of Hilario Desseusa and his wife Virginia Coronado. They suspected that Hilario was selling narcotics from his property. When they entered the house, they found Virginia Coronado "busy dividing up the drugs," but this woman, on seeing the police, threw thirty papers of heroin over the floor and attacked one of the agents, beating him and biting him on the arm. Then when Hilario arrived he also tried to beat the police.[51]

At the end of the 1930s, during the government of Lázaro Cárdenas (1934–1940), the authorities also put into practice the so-called National Campaign against Alcoholism and Other Addictions, under the direction of Dr. Salazar Viniegra. Although this campaign was in the hands of the DSP, they sought help from the Ministry of the Interior, the attorney general's office, and even the army.[52] Also inside the DSP there were discussions on the need to restructure the corporation and iron out irregularities in the Sanitary Police. In particular they wanted to get rid of the frequent practice of taking bribes.[53]

In 1938 Luis Huesca de la Fonte took charge of the Narcotics Police and announced that he was going to take it in a new direction. He was now going to go after the "big traffickers."[54] At the same time within a week of taking charge he claimed that he had sent forty peddlers to prison and three hundred addicts to the Hospital de Toxicómanos.[55] Within three months, however, he was arrested for the scandal involving the young girl and sent to Lecumberri jail.[56]

Though Huesca was sacked, he only spent a few days in jail. The judge decided that he was able to get bail for the crimes of abuse of authority. And there was not enough evidence to prosecute him for the narcotics offenses. What is more, the drugs discovered were not even really drugs. Instead they contained a form of antiseptic.[57]

THE END OF THE NARCOTICS POLICE

In the following years the discussion of the drug problem only intensified. The antinarcotics agents continued to apprehend traffickers and addicts. At the same time Leopoldo Salazar Viniegra started to push for the treatment of addicts as sick people rather than as criminals.[58] In 1940 the authorities even passed a new law, the Federal Regulations of Drug Addicts, which attempted to establish state-run morphine clinics for addicts.[59] But the new regulation didn't prosper and eventually collapsed due to Mexican disorganization and U.S. pressure.[60] After a few months, the entire project was suspended.[61]

Although there had always been U.S. pressure on Mexican drug policy, after the Second World War this increased. Harry Anslinger, the head of the FBN, pushed for countries to enact harsher drug laws.[62] In Mexico he was extremely successful. The focus on policing and punishment consolidated while health care approaches to the drug problem were shelved.[63] The Mexican government agreed to cooperate with the United States and operate eradication campaigns and greater prosecution of suspects.[64] As intolerance toward drugs deepened, so did the official antidrug rhetoric, and violence and corruption also escalated.[65]

A few days after Manuel Avila Camacho became president, the DSP presented a plan to restructure the Sanitary Police. In this it pushed the need to "combat endemic diseases and epidemics, and also the trafficking of narcotics and toxic substances which degenerate and annihilate the human race."[66] The document was approved and published at the end of 1940.[67]

In 1945 it was agreed that the campaigns against drugs would be implemented by the attorney general's office, the Ministry of National Defense and the Health Ministry (the new version of the DSP).[68] In the campaigns of the following years, an agent of the U.S. Treasury Department, Salvador Peña, was also involved. Peña also joined a 1946 aerial survey of drug growing regions, accompanied by a member of the Narcotics Police, military officials, politicians, a cameraman, and a mechanic.[69] That same year the Federal Judicial Police (PJF) created a group of twenty agents dedicated exclusively to the investigation and prosecution of "crimes against health." They were now also sent north to arrest suspected traffickers on the border.[70]

Although drug eradication concentrated in the northwest of the country, it also came to the fields south of Mexico City. In February 1946 agents arrived at the barrio of San Cristobal, Xochimilco, and destroyed poppy plantations in the area. The peasants sent a letter to Avila Camacho in which they complained about suffering large losses. They said that the blooms were not for the production of opium but rather to sell as decorative flowers. They were just traditional adornments for April festivities.[71] In response the sanitary authorities designated a pair of inspectors to investigate the poppy plantations of Xochimilco and whether they were being used to extract opium. The agents returned and said that the plants were grown in plain sight and there was no evidence that they were being harvested for their narcotic qualities.[72] But despite this the authorities went ahead with banning cultivation of these plants.

During the government of Miguel Alemán (1946–1952) there were substantial changes to the mechanisms of drug control. In 1947 the authorities changed the penalties for drug offenses. They reformed articles 193, 194, and 197 of the Penal Code and incorporated the crime of proselytism (encouraging the consumption of drugs) among the legal definitions of drug crimes.[73] These modifications were put in place during a new National Campaign against Enervantes. The National Army and the Air Force, local and state police forces, the PJF, and the Narcotics Police of the Health Department participated in the campaign, and the number of people arrested for drug offenses increased dramatically.[74] These were all dependent on the attorney general's office.[75] The Alemán government also created a new state security force, the Dirección Federal de Seguridad. At first this agency was also allowed to intervene in matters of narcotics,[76] but this was soon dropped when the United States suspected that they were also involved in shaking down traffickers.[77]

In the barrios of Mexico City, the members of the judicial police and the local police increased investigations of drug crimes. And for several more years agents of what would be called the Federal Narcotics Police continued to ply their work. Those they arrested, due to the new regulations, could expect longer jail time and bigger fines. For example, María Luisa Moreno got four years and a five-hundred-peso fine at the end of 1947. After agents raided her house they found thirty-two marijuana cigarettes hidden in a bag of *ixtle* and some loose weed, all of which amounted to a kilo of drugs. This was her second drug offense and so the judge decided on such a high penalty. Two years later she was moved to the Islas Marías with others the authorities deemed hardened offenders.[78]

The acts of corruption also continued. A former head of the Narcotics Police, Gastón Vaca Corella, made the most of his experience to get into the trade himself. He started to help produce "black heroin" in Mexico, which he sought to export to the United States. He was eventually caught and consigned to prison in late 1947.[79]

Vaca was apprehended when José García Cantín, a Spanish chemist, claimed it was Vaca who provided him with the raw opium necessary to make morphine and heroin in his Guadalajara lab. The other persons Cantín named as distributors were María Rubio Tamayo and a "person from Sinaloa, whose name he refused to give as he estimated that his life would be under threat."[80] The press referred to the former head of the Narcotics Police as the "maximum chief of the bands of cultivators of poppies and of the traffickers of opium" and "a millionaire." They called him the "most dangerous among the capitalists involved in this business."[81]

In his declarations Vaca claimed that when he was chief of the Narcotics Police during Avila Camacho's presidency (1940–1946) he had made various trips to Sinaloa as part of the eradication campaigns. There he had realized the fabulous wealth that could be generated by the drugs business and decided to go into it himself. He employed a chemist, Cantín, who knew how to extract the opium from the plant. Despite the confession, Vaca clearly still had connections. After only six months in prison he received an *amparo* and was released. Cantín had less influence and was kept in jail for five years.[82]

The antinarcotics operations were now in the hands of the attorney general's office. Their acts were characterized by an increased use of force and the inevitable increase in violence. The press started to announce that even the growers were being handed guns to defend their crops,[83] and they started to use them on some of the police. In early 1948 the newspapers reported that a PJF agent called Reinaldo Beltrán was "vilely assassinated" by a band of traffickers near Tehuixtitlán, in the State of Mexico, after the young police officer had managed to seize fifty kilos of marijuana.[84]

This happened just two hours from Mexico City in a rural zone where marijuana grew in great amounts. It was described as "a native vernacular herb, whose shrubbery covers the foothills of the Popocatépetl and Iztaccíhuatl [volcanoes] like long hair" According to the press, a mafia had already come to power and "control[led] the cultivation and sale" of the plant.[85] Reinaldo Beltrán had tried to acquire the drugs before arresting the traffickers through a *gancho* and two friends who would act as buyers of the weed. After this had been arranged two cars and a truck left the attorney general's office carrying eight agents. However, Beltrán went ahead of the rest to track down the offenders. Once he had found the place where they were storing the marijuana he opened fire. The traffickers returned fire and he was shot.[86] For the PGR "the sacrifice of agent Beltrán" would mark a step up in their efforts to stop drug crime. The deputy attorney general gave a speech at his funeral, in which he claimed that Beltrán "constituted an example and a painful stimulus."[87]

The official reports show that during the 1950s the Narcotics Police continued to participate in the campaign against drugs. For example between September 1951 and August 1952 the corporation sent eighty-seven men and twenty-eight women to jail for trafficking.[88] Still in 1958 it was reported that this police force had "intensified vigilance of the trade in narcotic products from their entrance into the country in primary form or as manufactured product, up to its prescription and employment to the sick."[89] At that point, however, the functions of the institution had moved under the control of the PGR.[90]

FINAL COMMENTS

After decades of prosecutions, arrests, seizures, and other means of control, the Narcotics Service of the Sanitary Police disappeared. The prohibition of drugs, however, persisted and other police bodies and the military got involved in the campaigns against drugs. The same strategies of keeping a watch on traffickers, raiding houses, doing searches, and using ganchos were kept up.

The study of the Narcotics Police demonstrates the attempts of the post-revolutionary state to regulate and control certain activities of the population. In these early years, while Mexican institutions were still being built and the global prohibition regime was only starting to consolidate, this led to the partial, irregular, and arbitrary policing of the narcotics business. Informal practices, including the abuse of authority and corruption, were frequent.

The cases examined here have demonstrated that from the early years Sanitary Police officers and other authorities involved in drug control were engaged in illegal and murky arrangements. These ranged from demanding and accepting bribes, through protecting traffickers, and even to being directly involved in the production and commercialization of drugs. Although many of these policemen were sacked, the majority managed to avoid formal justice. None of the officers mentioned here were found guilty and in the worst cases only spent a few months in prison, which stands in stark contrast to the plight of ordinary citizens prosecuted and sentenced for "crimes against health."

At least three thousand persons were detained for drug crimes in Mexico City between 1920 and 1947. These had to pay fines, and they often got sentences of years in prison. These punishments—along with the antinarcotics propaganda of the press—probably dissuaded many from getting involved in drug consumption and trade. As Salazar Viniegra mentioned, however, prohibition could result in "an incentive, especially in the case of drugs like opium, which has been surrounded, from time immemorial, by an aura of mystery."[91] At the same time, the premonitions of Salazar Viniegra were made reality: the addicts were left without an alternative and had to rely on illicit commerce, which created "a situation of advantage and privilege for the trafficker."[92]

NOTES

1. Archivo Histórico de la Ciudad de México (AHCDMX), Penitenciaría, Cárceles, caja 402, exp. 1304, "Luis Huesca"; Luis Astorga, *Drogas sin fronteras* (Mexico City: Penguin Random House, 2015), 230; Ricardo Pérez Montfort, *Tolerancia y prohibición: aproximaciones a la historia social y cultural de las drogas en México, 1840–1940* (Mexico City: Penguin Random House, 2016), 284.

2. Elaine Carey, *Women Drug Traffickers. Mules, Bosses and Organized Crime* (Albuquerque: University of New Mexico Press, 2014), 91–125.
3. AHCDMX, Penitenciaría, Cárceles, caja 402, exp. 1304, "Luis Huesca."
4. *El Universal*, April 10, 1938.
5. *El Universal*, April 12, 1938.
6. *Excélsior*, April 14, 1938.
7. *El Nacional*, April 14, 1938.
8. AHCDMX, Penitenciaría, Cárceles, caja 402, exp. 1304, "Luis Huesca."
9. Guillermina Seri, "Discrecionalidad policial y ley no escrita: gobernando en el estado de excepción," in *Mirada (de) uniforme. Historia y crítica de la razón policial*, ed. Diego Galeano and Gregorio Kaminsky (Buenos Aires: Editorial Teseo, 2011), 356; Stephen D. Morris and Charles H. Blake, *Corruption and Politics in Latin America: National and Regional Dynamics* (Boulder, CO: Lynne Rienner Publishers, 2010), 3–4.
10. Wil G. Pansters, "Zones of State-Making. Violence, Coerción and Hegemony in Twentieth-Century Mexico," in *Violence, Coercion and State-Making in Twentieth-Century Mexico. The Other Half of the Centaur*, ed. Wil G. Pansters (Stanford, CA: Stanford University Press, 2012), 8; Diane Davis, "Policing and Regime Transition. From Postauthoritharianism to Populism to Neoliberalism," in *Violence, Coercion and State-Making in Twentieth-Century Mexico. The Other Half of the Centaur*, ed. Wil G. Pansters (Stanford, CA: Stanford University Press, 2012), 69.
11. Alan Knight, "Narco-violence and the State in Modern Mexico," in *Violence, Coercion and State-Making in Twentieth-Century Mexico. The Other Half of the Centaur*, ed. Wil G. Pansters (Stanford, CA: Stanford University Press, 2012), 115–34.
12. Isaac Campos and Paul Gootenberg, "Introduction: Toward a New Drug History of Latin America. A Research Frontier at the Center of Debates," *Hispanic American Historical Review* 95, no. 1 (2015): 18–19.
13. George Rosen, *De la policía médica a la medicina social* (Mexico City: Siglo XXI, 2005), 150–64.
14. Rosen, *De la policía médica*, 180.
15. José María Castillo, *Ensayo sobre el derecho administrativo mexicano, 1874* (Mexico City: Instituto de Investigaciones Jurídicas, UNAM, 1994), 216.
16. Nicolás Mendiola, "Consideraciones sobre la actual organización de las secciones médicas de las inspecciones de policía" (Thesis, Facultad de Medicina de México, 1885).
17. Isaac Campos, "Degenerations and the Origins of Mexico's War on Drugs," *Mexican Studies/Estudios Mexicanos* 26, no. 2 (2010): 379–408.
18. Fernando Tenorio Tagle, *El control social de las drogas. Una aproximación social a las imágenes que han proyectado sus discursos* (Mexico City: Instituto Nacional de Ciencias Penales, 1991), 156.
19. Francisco Sánchez, "Apuntes sobre la morfinomanía" (Thesis, Facultad de Medicina de México, 1883); José Olvera, "¿Los morfinomaniáticos son aptos para ciertas acciones civiles? ¿Son responsables de sus actos?" *Gaceta Médica de México* XXI (1886):

205–10; Antenor Lescano, "Contribución al estudio de la morfinomanía" (Thesis, Escuela Nacional de Medicina, 1898).

20. Genaro Pérez, "La marihuana. Breve estudio sobre esta planta" (Thesis, Facultad de Medicina de México, 1886), 53–59.

21. Albrecht Erlenmeyer, *On the Treatment of the Morphine Habit* (Detroit: George S. Davis, 1898); "Tratamiento de las narcomanías: reseña," *Boletín de la Oficina Sanitaria Panamericana* (1933): 1206.

22. "Tratamiento de las narcomanías," 1206–14.

23. *Diario Oficial de la Federación*, March 15, 1920.

24. *Diario Oficial de la Federación*, June 26, 1923; *Diario Oficial de la Federación*, July 28, 1923. Domingo Schievenini, "La criminalización del consumo de marihuana en México (1917–1961)" (PhD thesis, UNAM, 2017), 252.

25. *Diario Oficial de la Federación*, January 2, 1925.

26. Policía de Salubridad, *Memoria de los trabajos realizados por el Departamento de Salubridad Pública, 1925–1928* (Mexico City: Ediciones del DSP, 1928), 447–49.

27. Narcóticos, *Memoria de los trabajos realizados por el Departamento de Salubridad Pública 1925–1928*, tomo II (Mexico City, Ediciones del DSP, 1928), 449–50.

28. Archivo Histórico de la Secretaría de Salubridad y Asistencia (AHSSA), Fondo Salubridad Pública, Sección Expedientes Personales, caja 8, exp. 2.

29. *Reglamento para la Inspección de la Policía de Salubridad,* 16/05/1928, AHSSA, Fondo Salubridad Pública, Sección Servicio Jurídico, caja 15, exp. 1.

30. María Gudiño-Cejudo et al., "La Escuela de Salud Pública de México: su fundación y primera época 1922–1945," *Salud Pública de México* 55 (2013).

31. AHSSA, Fondo Salubridad Pública, Sección Presidencia, caja 11, exp. 28, "Informe anual reglamentario de las labores de la Escuela de Salubridad durante 1928," DSP, México, 1929.

32. AHSSA, Fondo Salubridad Pública, Sección Servicio Jurídico, caja 26, exp. 01, "Informe de las labores que desarrolla el personal de la Policía Sanitaria," February 13, 1930.

33. Policía Sanitaria, *Memoria de los trabajos realizados por el Departamento de Salubridad Pública, 1925–1928*, tomo II (México: Editorial Cultura, DSP, 1928) 452.

34. AHSSA, Salubridad Pública, Expedientes Personales, caja 45, exp. 25.

35. Archivo General de la Nación (AGN), Direccion General de Investigaciones Políticas y Sociales (DGIPS), caja 50, exp. 7.

36. Pérez Montfort, *Tolerancia y prohibición*, 185.

37. AHSSA, Salubridad Pública, Servicio Jurídico, caja 17, exp. 14.

38. DSP, *Reglamento Federal de Toxicomanías, Diario Oficial de la Federación*, October 27, 1931.

39. DSP, *Reglamento de Policía Sanitaria, Diario Oficial de la Federación*, October 7, 1932.

40. AGN, Tribunal Superior Juridca del Distrito Federal, (TSJDF), caja 0484, folio 085477; AHCDMX, Cárceles, Cárcel de Belem, libro 16.

41. AHSSA, Fondo Salubridad Pública, Sección Servicio Jurídico; AGN, TSJDF; AGN DGIPS; AHCDMX, DDF, Jefatura de Policía; AHCDMX, Cárceles, Cárcel de Belem; AHCDMX, Cárceles Lecumberri.

42. AHCDMX, Cárceles, Lecumberri.

43. AHSSA, Fondo Salubridad Pública, Sección Servicio Jurídico, 5/10/1935, caja 43, exp. 4, "Dictamen en relación a la policía especializada en la lucha contra el tráfico de drogas nocivas."

44. *El Universal*, August 1, 1937.

45. AHSSA, Fondo Salubridad Pública, Sección Servicio Jurídico, 10/05/1935, caja 43, exp. 4, "Dictamen en relación a la policía especializada en la lucha contra el tráfico de drogas nocivas."

46. AGN, TSJDF, caja 2332, folio 430103, Herlinda Hernández, delitos contra la salud, 1930.

47. AGN, Dirección General del Gobierno, vol. 83, exp. 1.322.1(29)597, Agustín Campos González, delito contra la salud, 1932.

48. AHSSA, Fondo Salubridad Pública, Sección Servicio Jurídico, caja 49, exp. 4, Carta al Jefe de la Campaña contra las Toxicomanías, 8/3/1937.

49. AGN, Secretaría de Salubridad y Asistencia (SSA), caja 931, exp. 2, Memorándum de acuerdo de gratificación a Rafael Ham.

50. Pérez Montfort, *Tolerancia y prohibición*, 251.

51. AGN, DGG, vol. 87, exp. 1.322.1(29) 1188/1192, Hilario Desseusa y Virginia Coronado, delito contra la salud y ultrajes, 1935.

52. *El Nacional*, February 23, 1937.

53. AHSSA, Fondo Salubridad Pública, Sección Servicio Jurídico, caja 51, exp. 18, "Estudio relativo a la Policía Sanitaria," 9/28/1938.

54. *El Nacional*, February 1, 1938.

55. *El Gráfico*, February 5, 1938; *La Prensa*, February 7, 1938.

56. *El Universal*, April 10, 1938; *Excélsior*, April 14, 1938.

57. AHCDMX, Penitenciaría, Cárceles, caja 402, exp. 1304, "Luis Huesca."

58. Magali Ocaña Salazar y Nidia Olvera Hernández, "El psiquiatra que luchó contra los cuerdos para despenalizar las drogas," May 24, 2018, available at https://chacruna-la.org/el-psiquiatra-que-lucho-contra-los-cuerdos-para-despenalizar-las-drogas/.

59. DSP, *Reglamento Federal de Toxicómanos, Diario Oficial de la Federación*, February 17, 1940; Mariana Flores, "La alternativa mexicana al marco internacional de prohibición durante el Cardenismo" (BA thesis, El Colegio de México, 2013); Pérez Montfort, *Tolerancia y prohibición*, 265–308, Isaac Campos, "A Diplomatic Failure: The Mexican Role in the Demise of the 1940 Reglamento Federal de Toxicomanías," *Third World Quarterly* 39, no. 2 (2018): 232–47.

60. Campos, "A Diplomatic Failure."

61. DSP, *Decreto que suspende la vigencia del Reglamento Federal de Toxicomanías, Diario Oficial de la Federación*, July 3, 1940.

62. Paul Gootenberg, *Andean Cocaine. The Making of a Global Drug* (Chapel Hill: University of North Carolina Press: 2008), 22; William Walker III, *Drug Control in the Americas* (Albuquerque: University of New Mexico Press, 1981); Ethan Nadelmann, *Cops across Borders. The Internationalization of U.S. Criminal Law Enforcement* (University Park: Pennsylvania State University Press, 1993); María Celia Toro, *Mexico's "War" on Drugs: Causes and Consequences* (Boulder, CO: Lynne Rienner Publishers, 1995); Carlos Pérez Ricart, "Las agencias antinarcóticos de los Estados Unidos y la construcción transnacional de la guerra contra las drogas en México (1938–1978)" (Doctoral thesis, Freie Universität Berlin, 2016).

63. Froylán Enciso, "Los fracasos del chantaje. Régimen de prohibición de drogas y narcotráfico," in *Seguridad nacional seguridad interior. Los grandes problemas de México*, ed. Mónica Serrano and Arturo Alvarado (Mexico City: El Colegio de México, 2010), 74–79.

64. Benjamin T. Smith, "Public Drug Policy and Grey Zone Pacts," in *Drug Policies and the Politics of Drugs in the Americas*, ed. Bia Labate et al. (E-book: Springer, 2016), 43.

65. Pérez Montfort, *Tolerancia y prohibición*, 344.

66. AGN, SSA, Subsecretaría, caja 36, exp. 14, "Proyecto de reestructuración de la Policía Federal Sanitaria."

67. DSP, "Acuerdo que autoriza la formación de un Cuerpo de Policía Sanitaria Federal," *Diario Oficial de la Federación*, December 31, 1940.

68. *Excélsior*, January 5, 1945; SEGOB, "Decreto que crea la Secretaría de Salubridad y Asistencia," *Diario Oficial de la Federación*, October 18, 1943.

69. AHSSA, SSA, Subsecretaría, caja 08, exp. 16, Oficio del doctor Demetrio Mayoral de la Dirección General de Higiene de la Alimentación y Control de Medicamentos al Subsecretario de SSA, 3/18/1946.

70. PGR, *Memoria de la Procuraduría General de la República*, 161.

71. AGN, Presidentes, Manuel Ávila Camacho, caja 0933, exp. 564.3/12, Pobladores de Xochimilco to President, 2/27/1946.

72. AHSSA, SSA, Subsecretaría, caja 08, exp. 16, El Jefe del Departamento de Inspección al Subsecretario de SSA, 4/3/1946.

73. "Decreto que reforma y adiciona los artículos 193, 194 y 197 del Código Penal para el Distrito y Territorios Federales y en materia del fuero común y para toda la República en materia del fuero federal," 11/14/1947, *Diario Oficial de la Federación*, 2–3.

74. SEGOB, 'Decreto que crea la Secretaría de Salubridad y Asistencia,' *Diario Oficial de la Federación*, October 18, 1943.

75. *Memoria de la PGR 1947–1948* (Mexico City: PGR, 1948), 17–21.

76. Sergio Aguayo, *La Charola: Una historia de los servicios de inteligencia en México* (Mexico City: Grijalbo, 2001), 62.

77. Smith, "Public Drug Policy," 42; Stephen Niblo, *Mexico in the 1940s: Modernity, Politics, and Corruption* (Lanham, MD: Rowman & Littlefield, 1999), 259–60.

78. AHCDMX, Cárceles, Penitenciaría, caja 1069, exp. 9765, "María Luisa Moreno Soto, contra la salud," 1947.

79. AHCDMX, Cárceles, Penitenciaría, caja 402, exp. 1304, "Gastón Vaca Corella, contra la salud," 1947.

80. AHCDMX, Cárceles, Penitenciaría, caja 1090, exp. 1304, "José García Cantín, contra la salud," 1947.

81. *La Prensa*, April 1, 1947; *La Prensa*, January 27, 1948; *Magazine de policía*, March 1, 1948.

82. AHCDMX, Cárceles, Penitenciaría, caja 1090, exp. 1304, "José García Cantín, contra la salud," 1947.

83. *El Universal*, November 16, 1947.

84. *Memoria de la PGR* (Mexico City: PGR, 1948), 27.

85. *Suplemento de policía*, January 29, 1948.

86. *Memoria de la PGR* (Mexico City: PGR, 1948), 27.

87. *Memoria de la PGR* (México City: PGR, 1948), 27.

88. AHSSA, SSA, Subsecretaría, caja 36, exp. 14, "Informe de labores de la Oficina de Consignaciones 1951–1952."

89. AGN, SSA, Subsecretaría, caja 41, exp. 1, "Memoria del ejercicio de la Dirección de Control de Medicamentos," 9/3/1958.

90. AGN, SSA, Secretaría Particular, caja 918, "Proyecto de reestructuración de la Policía Federal Sanitaria," 1963.

91. *El Nacional*, October 13, 1938.

92. *El Nacional*, June 4, 1938.

PART II

Drug Trafficking, Social Relations, Political Protection, and Law Enforcement during the Mexican Miracle

5

La Nacha, the Godmother of Border Trafficking
Transnational Drugs and Gendered Power
in Ciudad Juárez, 1920–1960

ELAINE CAREY

In 1942, narcotics trafficker Ignacia Jasso la viuda de González, also known as Emma and La Nacha, made a critical error by stepping into a planned snare set by U.S. narcotics officers in El Paso, Texas. That move touched off a four-year firestorm between the United States and Mexico over drug trafficking. Harry J. Anslinger, the director of the U.S. Federal Bureau of Narcotics (FBN), demanded her extradition to stand trial in the United States for violation of the 1914 Harrison Narcotics Act.[1] The incident not only serves as a means for understanding U.S.-Mexican relations over the knotty issue of drug trafficking, but it also highlights La Nacha (and her family's) sophisticated understanding of politics and illicit narcotics markets in both countries. This understanding allowed her to adeptly manipulate the press, the people, and government officials. As a leader of a transnational organized crime syndicate on the U.S.-Mexico border, however, she ensured that she remained a major concern of both governments, who cast her as an enemy of both nations.

Jasso remains a pivotal figure in U.S.-Mexican narcotics relations because of her re-emergence in contemporary drug literature and the centrality of the border region in the War on Drugs.[2] Some scholars and journalists have stated that she built the first Mexican cartel. A product of a city known for its zone of tolerance, she operated out of Ciudad Juárez, supplying opium, morphine, and marijuana first to American soldiers and border residents and later to major U.S. cities. Her reach, so the papers claimed, extended as far north as

Seattle, Detroit, and New York City.[3] Until her death in the 1980s, La Nacha peddled and trafficked heroin, marijuana, and morphine. She lasted in the trade for over fifty years, surpassing many of her male peers in her longevity.

THE EXTRADITION OF LA NACHA

In 1942 two events triggered the arrest of Jasso. In the summer, police in El Paso detained two of her agents, Teodoro García and Guadalupe Gúzman, crossing the Santa Fe Bridge from Ciudad Juárez with nineteen cans of opium. In interrogations, the couple admitted that the cans belonged to Jasso. The previous April, La Nacha had appeared on the U.S. radar. The U.S. Federal Bureau of Narcotics, the Bureau of Customs, and the Mexican authorities had formulated a sting operation to arrest La Nacha. Two U.S. narcotics agents—H. B. Westover and W. H. Crook—approached La Nacha and claimed to be traffickers who sold opium and morphine to Oklahoman Indians. She demanded that they purchase 450 cans of smoking opium and a kilo of gummed opium.[4] Like any good dealer, Westover asked to sample her product. Her assistant Guadalupe Guzmán brought him a fruit jar full of smoking opium as well as a can of opium. La Nacha told Westover and Crook that she had a chemist who could extract morphine, but he was a five-hour drive from them. Westover told La Nacha that he wanted to think it over but that he would contact her soon.

A couple of weeks later, Westover and Crook returned to Ciudad Juárez to visit Jasso. She described a group of smugglers that trafficked her opium into the United States, and she argued that she had customers in places as far away in New York and San Francisco.[5] The assertion may have been more than an idle boast. With World War II, Mexico traffickers moved into the large-scale growing and also manufacturing of illicit drugs. Five years later, the United Nations Commission on Narcotic Drugs reported that a U.S. aerial survey had found at least 4,500 opium fields in the country. Most of the harvested gum ended up in the United States or Canada either as smoking opium, morphine, or increasingly "brown" heroin.[6] To prove her efficiency in transporting, she agreed to sell Westover a can so that he could gauge how fast her organization could deliver it to El Paso. There, he planned to have it tested by his own chemist on the U.S. side of the border.[7] Crook went back to El Paso to await delivery and to ensure that Jasso could indeed deliver on the U.S. side and to allegedly test the opium in El Paso.[8]

Once the opium was tested, the agents told her they could only obtain a small amount of morphine from the opium, but that they maintained their interests in doing business with her. Over time, they gained La Nacha's trust, and she escorted them to her poppy fields in the state of Jalisco and one of her morphine labs in Guadalajara, where the agents observed chemists working with crude opium weighing ten pounds. There they met two of her lieutenants, "The Chemist" Luis Manuel Vázquez and "The Lawyer" Alberto Torres Ibarra, who made an unwise offer to cut out La Nacha and sell directly to the agents.[9]

Seeing an opportunity, Westover and Crook made a deal with Vázquez and Torres. Ultimately, Vázquez and Torres traveled to San Antonio with fifty-five ounces of morphine hidden in a secret compartment in the gas tank of their car; they were arrested. They pleaded guilty in court and received sentences of five years in prison. In response to this case, in a speech before the United States Congress, Rep. John J. Cochran declared that Mexican poppy and opiates were the source of that distributed by the "Dutch" Schultz and Lucky Luciano gangs.[10] Whether the "remnants" of Schultz and Luciano dealt in Mexican opiates from Jasso remains opaque; U.S. and Canadian organized crime did distribute and sell opiates of Mexican origin.

Vázquez and Torres's betrayal meant La Nacha remained free, but she grew deeply suspicious of any attempted cross-border transactions. Pressure increased in her home city of Ciudad Juárez, where the police detained many of her runners and captured 125 ounces of smoking opium and 78 ounces of morphine.[11] These events culminated in a search of her café on the morning of November 4, 1942 where she was found with two addicts, Mariano Morales, "El Chamaco," and Regina Guzmán, "La Picuchi," both of whom she had allegedly injected. A toxicology report documented that indeed Morales and Guzmán were addicted to morphine and heroin, but Jasso's report showed no opiates in her blood. The ten-month attempt to arrest her finally ended with Jasso in the custody of the Ciudad Juárez police.[12] Recognizing that she had been the subject of a transnational sting, she told the chief of police, "I have been in tighter spots before, why shouldn't I be able to get out of this one?"[13] This one turned more complicated because the United States demanded her extradition.

Jasso's arrest made national news on both sides of the border. Two days later *El Continental Span* reported that the United States wanted Jasso de González to be extradited.[14] In Juárez and El Paso, rumors persisted that U.S. Narcotics and Customs agents had orchestrated the raid of her house and her subsequent arrest. Due to these rumors, the municipal president Antonio J. Bermúdez issued a public statement in the newspaper *El Mexicano* repudiating these claims and arguing that La Nacha was arrested by the chief of police Teodoro Pérez Rivas because her activities violated Mexican laws, not those of the United States. He further argued that extradition was not a matter of the municipal government but of the federal authorities.[15] Despite his claims, the United States State Department requested her extradition on November 9, 1942.[16]

Bermúdez's statements to the press may not have been completely transparent. On September 2, 1942, Ben Foster, United States attorney for the Western District of El Paso, had formally requested Jasso's extradition. On October 22, the United States embassy sent a formal request to the minister of foreign affairs, Ezequiel Padilla, to detain Jasso in preparation for extradition proceedings.[17] In the documents, La Nacha was described as forty-eight years old, standing 5-foot-5, weighing 170 pounds, and dressing poorly "when around home." Her arrest came two weeks later.

The argument for the extradition of Jasso touched off a crisis in Mexico and contributed to heated exchanges between officials on both sides of the border. On January 19, 1943, Anslinger wrote to Bermúdez following a meeting about La Nacha:

> We believe that the extradition of Ignacia Jasso González is of utmost importance in suppressing the illicit traffic in narcotics between Mexico and the United States. Mexico has now become the principal source of supply of opium and its derivatives throughout the United States. We find narcotic drugs of Mexican origin in New York, Washington, Chicago, and Detroit and in fact every large center of population. Those narcotics drugs are being distributed by organized gangs, which we are sending to prison, but as long as Mexico remains the source of supply and the traffic is not suppressed there, the traffic will increase. Before the war, Japan was the source of these drugs and this traffic was part of the Imperial policy of Japan to poison and weaken our people for conquest. The people of Mexico were also being poisoned by these drugs. We presented sufficient evidence to substantiate our charges before the Opium Advisory Committee of the League of Nations. It is unfortunate that we must now place before the world public the fact that Mexico has now become the source of smuggled narcotics.[18]

To encourage Mexican officials to avoid becoming a site that promotes "human slavery" and force them to extradite Jasso González, Anslinger threatened that the United States would publicize Mexico as a chief source of supply. This caused concern within the Mexican government because of their close economic ties and the strain on their relations that policies of land reform and oil nationalization had recently caused.[19] By February, the case of La Nacha came before the House of Representatives. On February 10, 1943, John J. Cochran, representative from Missouri, recognized the work of Anslinger and his men. In doing so, he insisted that Anslinger deserved "a medal of honor" for his work in attempting to rid the United States of drugs. In arguing this point, he read a statement about the case against La Nacha calling her the largest distributor of illicit drugs on the "Mexican frontier."[20]

In October of 1942, Anslinger made similar comments to George S. Messersmith, the U.S. ambassador to Mexico. Anslinger wrote in regards to Jasso: "This case is of unusual importance at this time because narcotic smuggling from Europe, the Near East, and the Far East has just ceased, and the traffic is switching to Mexico. We feel that potentially large traffic has been destroyed by the apprehension of this ring."[21] Anslinger's letter implied that Mexico had evolved into a key site not only of transshipment but also of production. According to Anslinger, Jasso had played an important role in that evolution.

In Mexico, Bermúdez immediately forwarded Anslinger's translated letter to President Ávila Camacho. He asked what they should do in the case of Jasso since her case could have negative ramifications on Mexico's global standing in light of their stained relations.[22] Mexican officials also began to investigate how to proceed with the extradition request.

Documents obtained from the Federal Bureau of Investigation (FBI) reveal that the pressure that Anslinger placed on Mexico initially appeared to work in the FBN's favor.[23] The U.S. Embassy in Mexico City reported that Padilla cooperated with Ambassador Messersmith. Messersmith adopted Anslinger's language and argued that Jasso's arrest would destroy a significant narcotic smuggling ring that not only endangered the United States but also Mexico. Moreover, the United States had offered to extradite Americans charged for crimes in Mexico, specifically the passing of bad checks.

Despite the support that Padilla and his legal advisors initially offered, U.S. officials were dubious. Internal exchanges claimed that corruption was rife among the Mexican police forces on the border. An FBI agent wrote:

> The officials of the Health Department of the Mexican government
> have been co-operating with the officials of the United States Treasury
> Department in Mexico City . . . in an effort to stamp out the international

dope traffic. However, one obstacle to this program is the fact that local officials in the border states and even the municipal police sometime "have a hand" in the growing of poppies. It has been rumored in several distinct pieces of correspondence that it might be difficult to keep Ignacia Jasso Gonzalez in jail because of the influence of local politicians, and even that the adverse decision of the trial judge in the initial extradition proceedings were strongly influenced by this factor.[24]

Furthermore, the United States had to contend with a growing Mexican campaign to prevent La Nacha's extradition. That campaign drew on long-standing criticisms of the U.S. government's meddling in domestic affairs, and it questioned the integrity and nationalism of Mexican politicians.

A letter from the farmers of Ciudad Juárez asked the president to cancel the pending extradition order. They admitted that Jasso's dead husband, the former police officer Pablo "El Pablote" González, had sold and trafficked drugs. Since his death, however, Jasso had lived an "absolutely moral" life supporting her children by growing cotton and selling clothes. They argued that the charges were just invented by her enemies in Ciudad Juárez and El Paso.[25]

Despite the claims, it is clear that La Nacha had continued her husband's business after his death. As husband and wife they had come to prominence in the local narcotics scene during the 1920s.[26] Urban myths circulated that they had secured their position by ordering the executions of eleven prominent Chinese distributors and traffickers.[27] Whether these myths were true or not, it is clear that the duo took advantage of anti-Chinese sentiment of the era.[28]

The husband-and-wife partnership is a common theme running through the history of narcotics. La Nacha and Pablote were perfect examples.[29] No doubt, Pablote's contacts in the drug world helped La Nacha's rise. While Pablote has been described as loud, boisterous, alcoholic, and spendthrift, La Nacha maintained a more discreet and respectable lifestyle.[30] The proponents of Jasso argued that Pablote forced his wife into the trade, but evidence suggests that even prior to his death, she controlled the finances of their emerging enterprise. Her home, surroundings, and life reflected a modest businessperson and farmer rather than a transnational trafficker. La Nacha probably saw drug smuggling as one of many strategies to keep her family financially afloat after her husband's death.

After Pablote's death, La Nacha consolidated and ran the criminal enterprise until the 1970s. In 1933, Daniel Minjares Perea and Daniel Rodríguez, leaders of the Confederation of Parents and Teachers in Ciudad Juárez, complained about La Nacha to state governor Rodrigo Quevedo. They wrote, "The sale of narcotics is being done shamelessly and with impunity in the house of a woman dubbed the Nacha with the knowledge of the Police chief, a man called Moriel, and the protection of the Municipal President who has exploited this business, not only in that (La Nacha's) house, but in several places where armed men who flaunt their impunity engage in the sale, who are nonetheless employees of the current administration."[31]

The confederation outlined a host of threats to the health of the nation: the showing of banned films, illegal licensing, prostitution, extortion from tourists, and government corruption. But La Nacha was presented as the main threat. By 1933 she seemed to have the protection of the local authorities. She was even reputed to use municipal employees as dealers. Such a franchise model noticeably ties in with more contemporary studies of the trade.[32]

Despite her reputation, there were men who attempted to displace Jasso, particularly when her children were younger. In 1939, American vice consul T. L. Lilliestrom wrote to the secretary of state and pointed out that La Nacha had long been the head of a prominent narcotics ring that operated in the El Paso–Ciudad Juárez area. In October of 1939, she fled Ciudad Juárez due to an impending arrest. In Torreón, Coahuila, two plain-clothes police officers beat her and told her she must pay twenty thousand pesos or General Alatorre, the commander of the garrison at Ciudad Juárez, would use the evidence he had against her to send her to the prison colony of Islas Marías. A relative of La Nacha approached Alatorre. Lilliestrom wrote, "The General made it clear to this individual that he had no part in the matter, but that to the contrary he deplored the underhanded treatment she had received. He further stated that the only action he could condone would be legal punishment, which might be meted out to her as a result of regular judicial procedure."[33]

Lilliestrom went on to explain that Alatorre deplored the behavior of his men, but he also recognized that La Nacha had a protector who was the sub-chief of police. As demonstrated in the other chapters, this communication further indicates that the police had a dual relationship with traffickers and peddlers. La Nacha went to jail in 1939 again. By 1940, however, Terry Talent, a Customs agent, informed Anslinger that La Nacha lived close to Ciudad Juárez and operated as "the source of supply for small peddlers."[34] In Talent's report, she was the only confirmed female drug dealer in Ciudad Juárez, but was joined by five other women who were under suspicion.

Jasso's 1942 arrest brought the possibility of seclusion in the island prison of Islas Marías or, worse, extradition to the United States. La Nacha remained in prison for more than three years, but never far from the public eye. In 1944, the *El Paso Herald Post* reported that with the psychological pressure over her possible extradition to the United States or a sentence to Islas Marías, she had become a born again Christian following the evangelical minister Pablo I. Delgado and his twelve-year-old son, Beto, a reported Bible prodigy.[35] Again, letters from followers of Delgado, Jasso's family, and her husband's mother and brother pleaded for her to be able to attend his revivals. Despite allowing her to attend family events such as funerals, prison authorities ultimately denied her request to attend the religious services. Instead, she called upon her fellow prisoners to listen to the sermons of Delgado and his son in the prison yard. She stated, "I accepted Christ after I heard the Bible messages. I have also found, through reading the Scripture, a consolation and peace of mind hard to describe." The newspaper published a photo of Jasso peering into the camera holding a Bible.

On April 27, 1945, Mexican president Manuel Ávila Camacho issued a presidential decree that waived constitutional guarantees in the cases of narcotics trafficking and permitted the immediate detention of peddlers and smugglers to federal penitentiary on the Islas Marías without first being tried in the Mexican courts.[36] The decree meant that Jasso—along with another famous female trafficker Lola la Chata—were to be sent to Islas Marías without due process.[37] Immediately upon notice, Jasso petitioned for an amparo to be released or permitted to remain in Ciudad Juárez. It is unclear if Jasso completely succeeded in her pleas. In an interview, an attorney for her family vehemently declared that she had never been sent to Islas Marías.[38] Evidence supports that she had been moved to Chihuahua City and later returned to the penitentiary in Ciudad Juárez without ever being sent to the island prison. In Chihuahua City and Ciudad Juárez, La Nacha received prominent visitors who were never checked prior to entering or leaving the jail, and she continued to sell marijuana and opiates in and outside the prison.[39] Newspapers reported that she went to Islas Marías in July 1945 and gained her release in 1946 or 1947, but the family, the evidence, and she herself argued that she never went.[40] The amparo had seemed to work.

Ultimately, Ávila Camacho and officials in Ciudad Juárez did not extradite her to the United States. The Mexican government denied the extradition request in 1943, but Anslinger's effort remained in the U.S. courts for three more years. In 1946, federal judge Boynton dismissed the case on the recommendation of Holvey Williams, assistant U.S. district attorney, due to the Mexican government's refusal to grant extradition of Jasso on the grounds that insufficient evidence existed. She had never been arrested in the United States nor had she committed a crime in the United States. The Americans were furious. "We convicted two of La Nacha's confederates on the evidence the Mexican Government says is insufficient," Mr. Williams explained. "However, extradition has been refused."[41]

Once released from prison, La Nacha continued to sell and distribute heroin, morphine, and marijuana, though some U.S. journalists reported that she returned to selling tortillas from a stall in Guadalajara.[42] That assertion reflected more wishful thinking than reality. American journalists embraced the state's punitive rhetoric on drug crime. In 1950, officials of the FBN documented Jasso as the potential source of a prominent California trafficker and dealer, an ex-prostitute from Ciudad Juárez that operated in the Los Angeles area.[43] In 1951, the mayor of Ciudad Juárez, Pedro García, told P. A. Williams, an FBI agent, that La Nacha lived permanently in Guadalajara. When she visited her sons in Ciudad Juárez, however, she always carried an "amparo," which the FBI agent described as a legal document prohibiting her arrest. Her children, Natividad, Manuel, Pabla, and Ignacia, continued to live and operate out of Ciudad Juárez. They ensured that her business interests and access to the international port of entry continued in Ciudad Juárez, whether she was physically present or not. Thus, prison or "exile" did not undermine her smuggling since her social networks ensured her economic survival. By the early 1950s, she could very well have been the supplier to her own children, who then supplied dealers in El Paso and beyond.

BORDER MENACE

In the mid-1950s, La Nacha and her children re-emerged in the United States as one of the primary sources of opiates in the Southwest. During what has come to be known as the Price Daniels hearings in Texas in October of 1955, the celebrated Chicano journalist Ruben Salazar gave testimony about La Nacha, reintroducing her to the United States Congress thirteen years after the attempt at her extradition.[44] From Salazar's testimony and coverage, he painted the history of a prominent woman in the trade, but his work also provided insight into other women operating on or close to the United States–Mexico border in the 1950s.

The hearings took place in New York, Pennsylvania, Texas, and California. Although the hearings began a year after the official end of McCarthyism, the Red Scare still loomed over the the hearings, since the House Un-American Activities Committee still existed despite the censure of Joseph McCarthy. Drug addiction, peddling, and trafficking had become associated with communism and behavior deemed un-American or a threat to American values. The hearings sought to link drug use and drug smuggling with a covert plot by "Red China" to poison Americans. The hearings also reflected clashes between the medical community and policing agencies on what to do about drug addiction. The New York hearings served as a platform to discuss efforts in the struggle against drug addiction; those held outside of Washington DC and New York featured more of regional focuses on the growing problems of the flow of drugs into major cities in the United States. Thus, in Chicago and Detroit, the hearings showed connections to Canada and the role of organized crime families.

During the Texas and Southern California hearings, Mexico was again portrayed as a dangerous site of drugs and drug trafficking. For the hearings, the Mexican government sent representatives to the hearings in California. In Texas, Senator Price Daniels of Texas sent an invitation to top diplomat Oscar Rabasa and attorney general Carlos Franco.[45] Both declined but outlined their ongoing commitment to the battle against drug trafficking. In part, Rabasa and Franco's reason for not attending the hearings came from the U.S. State Department. Because of the collaboration that had developed between Mexico and the United States regarding drugs, the State Department expressed concern then and again in hearings in Los Angeles in 1959 that Rabasa might be used as a political scapegoat. Lower-level Mexican officials attended the hearings in Southern California in 1955, and in 1959 they offered to meet in another state.[46]

A close reading of the testimony in front of the Daniels Commission of 1955 on Illicit Narcotics Traffic challenges much of the contemporary drug literature published from the 1970s to 1980s that continued to situate Mexico as a minor player in the international heroin trade. Through the numerous interviews and hearings, Mexico emerged as a major player in heroin and morphine trade in the 1950s, accounting for the majority of drugs used in the Southwest. The hearings went beyond the traditional focus on the East Coast, where much of the trafficking was controlled by Italian organized crime. Instead, the Texas and California hearings positioned Mexico not as an upstart in the heroin trade but rather a historical site of marijuana and heroin supply for years.

Jasso lurked in many of the hearings and interviews prior to Salazar's testimony. In the days prior to his appearance, people spoke about the La Noche Queen (The Night Queen) of Ciudad Juárez and suggested her reach into Texas and the Southwest. The moral panic that emerged in the hearings focused on ties between Ciudad Juárez's drug trade and Fort Bliss. Daniels and the other members of the committee heard about soldiers going to Juárez shooting galleries (*picaderos*) or those in El Paso supplied by Jasso and her sons. The Red Scare loomed large, and thus drug use became a threat to the integrity of the army and its ability to fight communists, whether in Korea, China, or Eastern Europe.

The most famous case of drug use among soldiers took place in El Paso, when the body of twenty-two-year-old paratrooper Daniel Barrera was found in a ditch. His death, apparently from a heroin overdose, served to heighten the moral panic associated with addiction among members of the armed forces. On the evening of August 23, Barrera had gone to the home of Antonio Tavárez Rodríguez, where he purchased and injected heroin. In an interview, Tavárez claimed that Barrera was already drunk before he injected himself. He immediately became ill and passed out, and Tavárez and Barrera's two female companions assumed he was asleep. When they failed to wake him the next morning, Tavárez hired a cab to take Barrera to the ditch, where he cut his throat and arms to hide the track marks.[47] The Juárez police arrested five people: Tavárez, two women, and the two drivers who disposed of the body.[48]

The issue of soldiers using narcotics had long been a concern of the Federal Bureau of Narcotics and other U.S. agencies since the Mexican Revolution, when soldiers sought companionship, alcohol, and drugs in the border cities. The argument that La Nacha had to be imprisoned during World War II to ensure that soldiers remained in fighting shape further added to her danger. Despite the focus on Mexico during World War II, with the end of the war and the low levels of addiction of returning veterans, Anslinger's attention turned to organized crime and drugs as a communist plot. The attention garnered to Mexico during the war diminished in the post–World War II era only to resurface again in the mid-1950s.

Salazar's testimony to the committee served as a lesson on the border. He highlighted the distance between the border and the Beltway. Despite being a veteran himself, Salazar had to establish his and Barrera's citizenship. While working with the *El Paso Herald Post*, Salazar covered El Paso and Ciudad Juárez as a local.[49] Born in Ciudad Juárez and naturalized as an American citizen who attended University of Texas-El Paso on the GI bill, Salazar knew both sides of the border. His own work as a journalist and his observations of addiction in El Paso and Ciudad Juárez led him to testify at the hearings. He also announced that he had told the mayor of Ciudad Juárez that he was scheduled to appear before the commission. Senator Daniels asked how he came to know La Nacha, and Salazar said that many people knew her in the border region. He stated that she had been trafficking for at least twenty-three years, a fact that shocked Daniels, who immediately inquired about her operations.[50]

Salazar's articles on Jasso also drew the attention of Senator Daniels. Salazar provided a number of 8 x 10 photos of places where drugs were sold in El Paso and Ciudad Juárez.[51] In turn, Salazar testified about Jasso during the commission hearings on drugs, and so did fifty-six other people, including male and female addicts, small-time traffickers and peddlers, narcotics agents, customs agents, and children of addicts.[52] Salazar established La Nacha's presence on the border. He wrote, "La Nacha is the dope queen of the border. She's big stuff. But she will sell you one *papel* (paper) of heroin for five dollars just like any other pusher on a street corner."[53] With a junkie named Hypo, he paid a visit to Jasso.[54] He described her as "fat, dark, cynical, and around 60." Salazar noted that her life in Ciudad Juárez was modest for a drug trafficker even in the 1950s. La Nacha lived in a barrio with unpaved roads, "a good house in a bad neighborhood." Salazar observed that her house had all the modern conveniences despite its location on an unpaved street.[55] She lived quite differently than her client, the heroin addict Hypo, who had sold all his furniture to pay for his ten-dollar-a-day addiction to heroin; he shared a filthy mattress on the floor with his wife and children.

In his articles, Salazar noted some commonalities of women involved in illicit trade. Jasso's daughters and sons worked with her. Her sons, Manuel and Natividad, owned bathhouses but also controlled shooting galleries on both sides of the border. Her daughters Ignacia and Pabla helped her in the trade. What is distinct about Jasso was despite her success and extensive control, she sold *papelitos* (little packs of heroin) from her home like any other pusher. She worked as a supplier and a distributor, but also as a peddler. Perhaps her protection in Ciudad Juárez gave her a sense of comfort that she did not feel the need to create such extensive distance from herself and the sale of the product, as was and is common among other traffickers. Instead, she earned a steady cash flow by selling directly from her house in the Bellavista barrio on

Violetas Mercurio. Salazar pointed out that her front door was in front of the truck in the foreground of the photo he submitted for evidence.

Jasso's life and her career became a component of the Daniels Committee in Texas since she not only peddled but also supplied key dealers throughout the state. Salazar verified that La Nacha had long been active and that the United States had previously attempted to control her drug dealing. He described how he heard about her: "I got to know some heroin addicts... who talked about La Nacha to me. I had heard La Nacha was not selling any more because during World War II, the Mexican government sent her to a penal colony because the United States pressured them to take her out of the border because we feared she would sell narcotics to our soldiers."[56]

Salazar described how he purchased heroin from Jasso and how she enjoyed some sort of legal protection, undoubtedly referring to the amparos she obtained on several occasions. The exchange between Salazar and Daniels demonstrates the committee's surprise and shock that she enjoyed legal protections:

> *Mr. Salazar*: I understand she had gotten an embargo, which is an injunction. This I cannot prove but I understand at one time she could buy protection from federal judges.
> *Senator Daniels*: Now, you mean by injunction that she has had injunctions issued restraining officers from arresting her?
> *Mr. Salazar*: That is right.
> *Senator Daniels*: Is it common knowledge around there in Juarez that has been the situation in the past?
> *Mr. Salazar*: Yes it is.
> *Senator Daniels*: She has had court orders enjoining officers from arresting her?
> *Mr. Salazar*: That is what I understand. I have never seen them, sir. It is common knowledge.
> *Senator Daniels*: Have you talked to the district attorney across the border of Juarez?
> *Mr. Salazar*: Right, sir. He says he has been district attorney a year and a half. She has not had an embargo during that time.[57]

After this exchange, Salazar informed the commission that Humberto Poncinon Solaranzo, the district attorney, told Salazar to tell the commission that President Adolfo Ruíz Cortines had established his own commission to investigate the drug trade in Ciudad Juárez. Agents from Mexico City went to Ciudad Juárez to assist the local authorities. Daniels expressed his pleasure that the Mexican federal government planned to investigate the narcotic problem. He noted, however, that the hearings were causing problems with the Mexican government because some officials denied that La Nacha sold drugs, while the Mexican federal government planned to investigate the border region. This drew considerable attention from diverse sectors in the United States and fueled the perception that Mexico was too lax on drug peddlers and traffickers, a theme that had echoed since the early 1900s and continues to the present.[58] Lastly, Salazar used a map along with photos to show the number of shooting galleries and dope pads in Ciudad Juárez and El Paso, and he provided names of other know sellers in the region.

Despite Salazar's testimony, Jasso remained stubbornly in place. Her ability to navigate and persevere in the drug economy for more than fifty years represents a profound example of the difficulty of policing, proving, and prosecuting such cases. Along the border, that space of contact led to constant renegotiations of power, law, and culture. Jasso truly represents the culture of *el ambiente fronterizo* of the twentieth century. With her husband, she recognized the potential of their proximity to the enormous drug market in the United States. After his death, she sought the potential markets beyond the immediate border region. World War II severed the transnational flows from Asia and Europe, giving her an economic advantage like never before. She had her own supply, labs, and distribution networks. Demand in the North remained high while supply had declined. Jasso represents the woman who continually seeks economic survival in a harsh environment.

La Nacha, like many other borderlanders, took advantage of the economic inequalities and other forms of marginality created by borders by spinning those boundaries and marginal spaces into sites for transnational entrepreneurial activities. In turn, Anslinger, Messersmith, Padilla, Bermúdez, and others demanded that she, like the border, be restrained, controlled, and enclosed. In the United States, she became a figure, like the border, to construct arguments to reinforce the "need" for strengthening policies and laws. These arguments echo today with similar demands for border fences, customs workers, policing agencies, and laws that reinforce such disparities across the region.[59]

La Nacha and other women of the border remained a focus of the Federal Bureau of Narcotics, the Bureau of Narcotics and Dangerous Drugs (BNDD), and politicians. More recently, they are drawing further analysis and scrutiny by border scholars and experts.[60] La Nacha's career established the importance of family in building an empire, but her location on the border made her all the more perilous for the United States and for Mexico and its relations with its northern neighbor. The constant shifts and reinterpretations of the border and its centrality in the wars on drugs may be read through Jasso's life. Despite her longevity, the multigeneration dynasty, and her physical location, she has rarely been mentioned by name in the historiography on drug trafficking until recently, even though the FBN, the FBI, the local police, journalists, the governors of Chihuahua, mayors of Ciudad Juárez, and the U.S. Congress saw her as a central threat beginning in the 1930s. Over the past couple of years, scholars have rediscovered her, and her dynasty has been reconceptualized as an important nexus between old forms of drug trafficking and the new forms that have triggered such violence in recent years.[61] Her ability to build a transnational organized crime family challenges many of the readings and analysis of such entities as exclusively masculine in nature. La Nacha, like countless other borderlanders involved in illicit trade, operated someplace between the United States and Mexico, legal and illegal, masculine and feminine, and real and imagined.

NOTES

1. Much of this article is drawn from my *Women Drug Traffickers: Mules, Bosses, and Organized Crime* (Albuquerque: University of New Mexico Press, 2014). I would like the thank the following people for their feedback and comments: Howard Abadinsky, Robert Chessey, Sterling Evans, José Carlos Cisneros Guzmán, Froylán Enciso, Paul Gootenberg, Andrae Marak, Tony Payán, and Larry Sullivan. Much of this research was completed under the Lloyd Sealy Research Fellowship at John Jay College of Criminal Justice and a Fulbright García-Robles.

For more on Anslinger and his interest in Mexico, see María Celia Toro, "The Internationalization of Police: The DEA in Mexico," *Journal of American History* 86, no. 2 (1999); Ethan Nadelmann, *Cops across Borders: The Internationalization of U.S. Criminal Law Enforcement* (University Park: Pennsylvania State University Press, 1993); William Walker, *Drug Control of the Americas* (Albuquerque: University of New Mexico Press, 1983).

2. *Dallas Morning News*, July 12, 2008; *Newspaper Tree*, March 6, 2006; Howard Campbell, "Female Drug Smugglers on the U.S.-Mexican Border: Gender, Crime, and Empowerment," *Anthropological Quarterly* 81, no. 1 (Winter 2008): 233–67.

3. *El Paso Herald*, April 23, 1943.

4. National Archives II–College Park (hereafter NACP), Record Group (RG)

59, Central Decimal Files, 1940–1944, 212.11, box 105, "Affidavit of H. B. Westover," 9/16/1942.

5. NACP, RG59, Central Decimal Files, 1940–1944, 212.11, box 105, "Affidavit of H. B. Westover," 9/16/1942. In 1944, a young woman named Hortensia Díaz was arrested crossing the bridge from El Paso to Ciudad Juárez carrying $24,000 dollars hidden in her brassiere. Díaz transported the money from New York in payment for opium. *Washington Post*, May 1, 1944.

6. United Nations, "Report to the Economic and Social Council on the First Session of the Commission on Narcotics Drugs Held at Lake Success, New York 24 July to 8 August 1947," 7.

7. NACP, RG59, Central Decimal Files, 1940–1944, 212.11, box 105, "Affidavit of H. B. Westover," 9/16/1942.

8. Ibid.

9. Ibid.

10. Penn State University, Special Collections, Harry J. Anslinger Archive, box 2, folder 20, Extension of Remarks of John J. Cochran, Congressional Record, Proceedings and Debate of the 78th Congress, First Session, vol. 89, no. 23, 2/10/1943.

11. NACP, RG59, Central Decimal Files, 1940–1944, 212.11, box 105, "Affidavit of H. B. Westover," 9/16/1942.

12. *Excélsior*, November 5, 1942.

13. *Diario de la Mañana*, November 15, 1942.

14. *El Continental Span*, November 6, 1942.

15. *El Mexicano*, November 11, 1942.

16. NACP, box 9656, Treaties and Other International Act Series, Extradition: Treaty Between the United States and Mexico, signed at Mexico City, 5/4/1978.

17. Department of Justice (DoJ), Federal Bureau of Investigation (FBI), "Ignacia Jasso Gonzalez W/As La Nacha," 3/25/1943, 64-22536-1, 5. Obtained under the Freedom of Information Act, July 16, 2009.

18. Archivo General de la Nación (AGN), Presidentes Manuel Ávila Camacho (MAC), 422/4, Anslinger to Bermúdez, 1/19/1943.

19. In 1938, Mexican president Lázaro Cárdenas nationalized Mexico's oil, triggering a fierce battle between oil companies and the executive branch. Linda B. Hall, *Oil, Banks, and Politics: The United States and Postrevolutionary Mexico, 1917–1924* (Austin: University of Texas Press, 1995).

20. Extension of Remarks of John J. Cochran, Congressional Record, Proceedings and Debate of the 78th Congress, First Session, vol. 89, no. 23, 2/10/1943.

21. DoJ, FBI, "Ignacia Jasso Gonzalez W/As La Nacha," 3/25/1943, 64-22536-1, 5.

22. AGN, MAC, 422/4, Anslinger to Bermúdez, 1/19/1943.

23. DoJ, FBI, "Ignacia Jasso Gonzalez W/As La Nacha," 3/25/1943, 64-22536-1, 5.

24. DoJ, FBI, "Ignacia Jasso Gonzalez W/As La Nacha," 3/25/1943, 64-22536-1, 3.

25. AGN, MAC, 422/2/, Higinio M. Reyes, et al. to Ávila Camacho, 1/1/1943.

26. NACP, RG84, Ciudad Juárez, John Dye, "Smuggling on the border between the United States and Ciudad Juarez consular district in Mexico," 4/25/1925.

27. Despite the lack of evidence to support the actual account, this myth continues to circulate in the press. It demonstrates a recognition of female power within the early drug market. See Howard Campbell, *Drug War Zone: Frontline Dispatches from the Streets of El Paso and Ciudad Juárez* (Austin: University of Texas Press, 2009). For the repeating of the myth, see *El Paso Times*, March 9, 2010.

28. Robert Chao Romero, *The Chinese in Mexico, 1882–1940* (Tucson: University of Arizona Press, 2010).

29. Tammy L. Anderson, "Dimensions of Women's Power in the Illicit Drug Economy," *Theoretical Criminology* 9, no. 4 (November 2005): 371–400; Alan Block, "Aw, Your Mother's in the Mafia: Women Criminals in Progressive New York," *Contemporary Crises* 1 (1977): 5–22; Campbell, "Female Drug Smugglers"; Eloise Dunlap and Bruce D. Johnson, "Family and Human Resources in the Development of a Female Crack Seller: Case Study of a Hidden Population," *Journal of Drug Issues* 26, no. 1 (1996): 175–98; Barbara Denton, *Dealing: Women in the Drug Economy* (Sydney: University of New South Wales, 2001); L. Maher and Ric Curtis, "Women on the Edge of Crime: Crack Cocaine and Changing Context of Street Level Sex Work in New York City," *Crime, Law, and Social Change* 18, no. 3 (1992): 221–58.

30. AGN, MAC, 422/2, Higinio M. Reyes, et al. to Manuel Ávila Camacho, 1/1/1943.

31. AGN, MAC, 525.3/189, Daniel Minjares Parea, Daniel Rodríguez, et al. to Governor of Chihuahua, 3/2/1943.

32. For a contemporary analysis see Anderson, "Dimensions."

33. NACP, RG170, box 23, T. L. Lilliestrom, Vice Consul, Ciudad Juárez to Secretary of State.

34. NACP, RG170, box 23, Terry A. Talent to H. J. Anslinger, 12/1/1947.

35. *El Paso Herald Post*, March 14, 1944.

36. NACO RG170, box 23, S. C. Peña, Special Employee, to Commissioner of Customs, 5/7/1945.

37. Elaine Carey, *Women Drug Traffickers: Mules, Bosses, and Organized Crime* (Albuquerque: University of New Mexico Press, 2014), 91–125.

38. Bob Chessey, interview with Joe Rey, El Paso, Texas, October 1, 2007.

39. NACP, RG170, box 23, American Consulate at Ciudad Juárez, 1/24/1945.

40. *American Weekly Magazine*, January 4, 1948.

41. *El Paso Herald*, February 21, 1946.

42. *American Weekly Magazine*, January 4, 1948.

43. NACP, RG170, box 29, Memorandum Report Bureau of Narcotics, El Paso, TX, 3/15/1950.

44. On Ruben Salazar, see Mario T. García, "Introduction," in Mario T. García and Ruben Salazar, *Border Correspondent: Selected Writings, 1955–1970* (Los Angeles: University of California Press, 2018), 1–31.

45. Price Daniels to Oscar Rabasa and Carlos Franco Sodi, October 1, 1955 reprinted in *Hearing Before the Subcommittee on Improvements in the Federal Code of the Committee on the Judiciary, United States Senate, 84th Congress. Illicit Narcotics Traffic Austin, Dallas, Forth Worth, Houston, and San Antonio Texas* (Washington, DC: Government Printing Office, 1956).

46. NACP, RG 170, box 28, Telegram from Consulate Mexico City to Department of State, 12/4/1959.

47. *El Paso Herald Post*, September 1, 1955.

48. *El Paso Herald Post*, October 2, 1955.

49. Mario T. García and Ruben Salazar, *Border Correspondent: Selected Writings, 1955–1970* (Los Angeles: University of California Press, 2018), 39–49.

50. *Hearing Before the Subcommittee on Improvements*, 3304–3324.

51. Some of these were published in the report, others were not. NACP, RG170, box 9, Price Daniels Committee—San Antonio Hearings, 12/14/1955.

52. NACP, RG170, box 9, Price Daniels Committee—San Antonio Hearings, 12/14/1955.

53. *El Paso Herald Post*, August 17, 1955.

54. *El Paso Herald Post*, August 17, 1955.

55. *El Paso Herald Post*, August 17, 1955.

56. *Hearing Before the Subcommittee on Improvements*, 3306.

57. *Hearing Before the Subcommittee on Improvements*, 3317.

58. Appendix 1, Second International Opium Conference, Senate doc. 733, 62nd Congress, 2nd session; AGN, Presidentes Obregón-Calles, "La resolución tomada por el Consejo S. de Salubridad relativa a la ratificación de la Convención Internacional sobre el Opio celebrada en la Haya el año de 1912."

59. Josiah Heyman, "U.S. Ports of Entry on the Mexican Border," *Journal of the Southwest* 43, no. 4 (2001): 681–700. Peter Andreas notes the symbiotic relationship between smugglers and states, arguing that it is the perception that smuggling (of goods or people) is a "growing threat that is most critical for sustaining and expanding law enforcement." See Peter Andreas, "Smuggling Wars: Law Enforcement and Law Evasion in a Changing World," in *Transnational Crime in the Americas: An Inter-American Dialogue Book*, ed. T. Farer (New York: Routledge, 1999). Moisés Naim similarly argues that the focus on sending countries is "politically profitable" and tools such as "helicopters, gunboats, heavily armed agents, judges, and generals" are more "telegenic" than focusing on demand. See Moisés Naim, *Illicit: How Smugglers, Traffickers, and Copycats are Hijacking the Global Economy* (New York: Bantam, 2005).

60. Campbell, "Female Drug Smuggler."

61. Campbell, *Drug War Zone*, 30–52.

6

Highs and Lows
Drug Trafficking in Baja California, 1930–1960

BENJAMIN T. SMITH AND WIL G. PANSTERS

For more than a century U.S. observers have portrayed the frontier between California and Baja California as the principal hub of the American drug trade. It has been described as a region where both the incessant movement of transborder trade has disguised the subterranean flow of narcotics and where U.S thrill seekers have gone to get high.[1] During the 1950s, concern among civil society organizations and politicians increased. A moral panic emerged as crusading journalists returned from Tijuana and Mexicali with alarmist tales of Southern Californian youths crossing the border to smoke and smuggle "secas" (weed), purchase some "H" (heroin) and have it injected at sleazy shooting galleries, or chomp a cornucopia of exotically named uppers like Green Dragons, Yellow Jackets, and Red Devils, sold openly in pop-up pharmacies.[2] Condemnation reached a peak with Ovid Demaris's *Poso del Mundo*, a racist diatribe against the mass murderers, "fat Indians," and "sadistic homosexuals" that flogged and smuggled the drugs that were poisoning America's hippies and hypes (heroin addicts).[3]

Despite the furor, we actually know very little about the mechanics of the drug trade in the border area before the arrival of the Arrellano Félix cartel during the 1990s.[4] We have the foundation stories of Baja California governor Esteban Cantú Jiménez (1915–1920), who funded roads, irrigation works, and schools by taxing the import, sale, and production of smoking opium first legally and then, when President Venustiano Carranza banned the practice, illegally.[5] We have the tales of his successor, Abelardo Rodríguez (1923–1930), who, less selflessly, funded his own fabulous wealth through protection of the trade.⁶ And we have a handful of more grassroots studies of U.S. drug smugglers and Chinese opium dealers, who not only established a network of dank opium dens underneath Mexicali's Chinatown during the first decades of the twentieth century but also used the trade to fund an array of licit commercial businesses.⁷

Yet if we understand little about the roots of the border's narcotics industry, we know much less about how it transformed and grew (even if never to the levels asserted by U.S. moralizers) in the subsequent decades. What were the drugs that flowed through the bodies and the border of Baja California? Where did they come from and how did they get there? Who took them? Who sold them? And who tried to take them over the border? Until recently, we had little opportunity and instead had to rely on either noisy, hysterical news pieces or the sketchy impressions of U.S. consuls, who would occasionally discover their inner Philip Marlowe, prowl the dingy basements of Mexicali's *la chinesca*, and send back horrified accounts of what they saw.⁸ The opening of new archives, however, has enabled historians to start to peer beneath these sporadic and often alarmist reports. In particular, the Casa de la Cultura Júridica in Tijuana not only contains hundreds of cases against both small-time users and dealers but also major judicial wranglings with some of the border's most powerful drug wholesalers and traffickers. Such findings—combined with U.S. Customs reports, Federal Bureau of Narcotics testimony, and careful reading of both U.S. and Mexican newspapers—offer a more nuanced, detailed, and accurate picture of how the drug trade actually worked and evolved in this quintessential corridor in the Mexican-U.S. drug trade.

Shifts in types of narcotics, their provenance, shipment routes, smuggling techniques, and the people involved in the trade now become apparent. During the 1930s, drugs were a small-scale, international, and maritime trade. Opium, morphine, heroin, and to a lesser extent cocaine arrived at the Pacific port of Ensenada before being transported to Tijuana or, more commonly, Mexicali. Here they were either taken or shipped northwards. Most of the opium and smoking opium came from Asia and most of the processed narcotics from factories in Europe. Those involved in the trade reflected the drugs' origins. European and U.S. pharmacists, dentists, doctors, and merchants dominated the wholesale purchase and transporting of the more processed narcotics; Chinese merchants specialized in smoking opium for use in Mexicali or U.S. dens. In the 1940s, things changed. World War II cut off traditional international flows; Mexico—particularly the region of the Sierra Madre covering the four states of Sonora, Sinaloa, Durango, and Chihuahua—provided most of the raw opium and by the mid-1940s also processed derivatives such as morphine and heroin. With the opening of the Sonora–Baja California railway, train, not boat, became the principal means of transport. And Mexicans rather than foreigners started to dominate the trade. Initially these joined with organized crime figures from the United States to smuggle the goods over the border, which caused a brief outbreak of violence as different gangs sought to form exclusive links with the U.S. criminals. But this was short-lived. The end of the war, the reopening of former narcotics routes, and to a lesser extent a joint U.S.-Mexican crackdown, saw Baja California decrease in importance. Ironically, during the 1950s, just as U.S. moralizers were whipping up a storm over Mexican drug smugglers, the regional trade had started to wind down. A handful of wholesalers still bought opium and heroin from inland. But they often supplemented this with more highly prized European heroin. Furthermore, violence decreased and cooperation rather than conflict became the defining characteristic of the trade.

THE 1930S: A LOCAL INDUSTRY

During the 1930s, the Baja California border was on the decline. The U.S. depression cut into the thousands of California high rollers that had crossed into Tijuana during the previous decade to bet on the horses, dodge Prohibition at one of the strip's seventy-five different bars, or gawk at Margarita Cansino (aka Rita Hayworth) as she danced flamenco beneath the garish architectural mishmash of the Agua Caliente Hotel and Casino.[9] It also completely suffocated the market in Imperial Valley agricultural workers who used to carouse, booze, and whore around the state capital of Mexicali every weekend.[10] In addition, the regional economy absorbed large numbers of Mexican workers deported from the United States. The cessation of the U.S. alcohol ban in 1933 made matters worse. And three years later, Mexican president Lázaro Cárdenas knocked the final nails into the border's festive reputation by banning gambling altogether.[11] While the party was now officially over, the federal government had difficulty responding to the "economic collapse" of the region and in establishing stable political control over the peninsula, which it only managed when Rodolfo Sánchez Taboada became governor in 1937.[12] A key objective of the Cárdenas administration was to "nationalize and mexicanize" the district of Baja California by incorporating it more closely

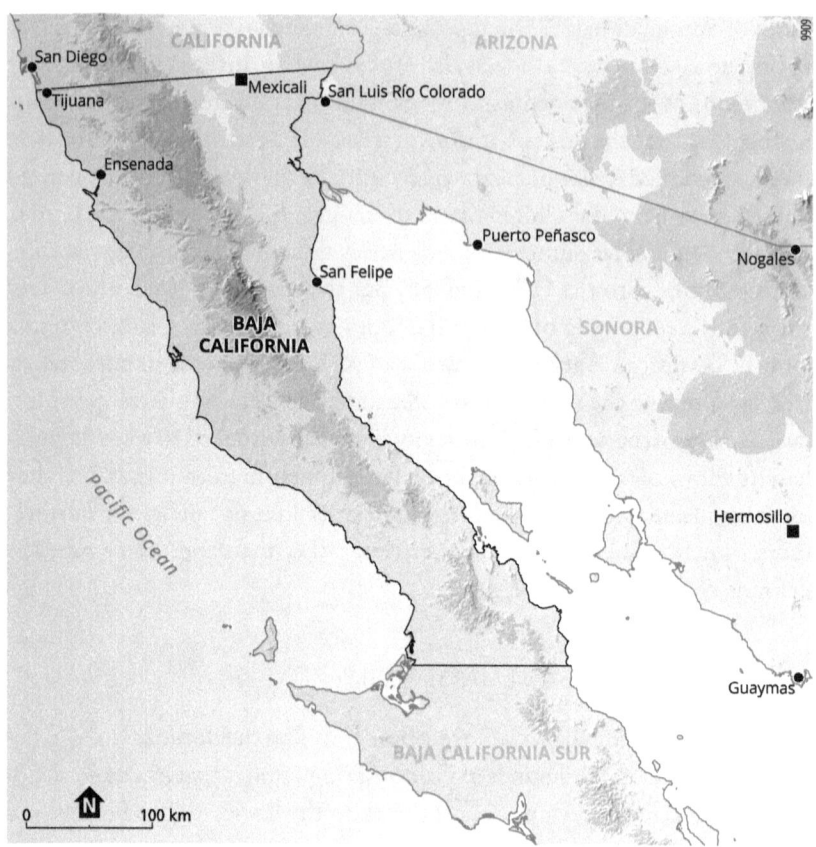

MAP 2 Map of Baja California (credits: UU-Geo-C&M–Carto).

in the national economy and polity.[13] The completion of the railway in 1938 that connected the peninsula to the national network through Sonora was crucial in this respect. It would affect the near future of the region's economy and society, including drug trafficking.

Such changes also changed the narcotics trade. The depression caused the local market in snorting, injecting, and toking weekend tourists to drop off. Perhaps more importantly, as organized criminals, mostly from New York, turned to importing opiates into the ports of the eastern seaboard, Mexico was marginalized.[14] Yet the trade staggered on, catering to a diminishing group of local addicts. At the head of this spluttering industry was a diverse group of Americans and Europeans, who used their links either to the pharmaceutical business or to the shipping trade to keep bringing drugs onto the Pacific coast. In Ensenada, the Latvian merchant Manuel Ezeroi went from humble shopkeeper to affluent merchant in a couple of years by importing and wholesaling opium.[15] Similarly, a U.S. dentist, J. W. Denny, was also involved in bringing in opium and selling it on to poor foreigners or what the United States described as "aliens and the Chinese within Mexico" or what the Mexican authorities dismissed as a "class of persons . . . who were of little or no interest to the government."[16]

But perhaps the family that best demonstrated how non-Mexicans used kin networks on both sides of the border to dominate the drug trade were the notorious Hussong brothers. The Hussongs were imposing characters, giant, heavy-set men of German extraction with wavy hair and thin waxed mustaches. Their father, Percy Hussong, had arrived in Ensenada in the late nineteenth century and made his money first as a gun for hire and then a cantina owner and merchant.[17] His intrepidness (and his disregard for the law) was clearly passed on. Two of his sons—Walter and Richard—stayed in Ensenada and ran the Hussong bar, a small fleet of fishing boats, a service station, and a bank of holiday bungalows. The ships—including one rather cheekily named *Black Gold* (slang for opium)—brought the drugs into Ensenada or down the coast in San Pedro. The opium was then moved by land or sea to San Diego, where another brother ran a shoe shop, or to Tucson, where another ran a nightclub called The Last Round Up.[18]

If the major importers of narcotics were Europeans, the drug peddlers, especially of opium and its derivatives, remained predominantly Chinese. Though Baja California witnessed substantial Sinophobia during the late 1920s and early 1930s, unlike in Sonora or Sinaloa the government did not engineer the wholesale expulsion of the Chinese population.[19] As a result, some remained in the game. Yon Kee, an Ensenada shopkeeper, was involved in small-scale drug trafficking for years, but appeared to limit his operations to move small quantities of opium bought from the Europeans to his countrymen in the border cities. On the border a Chinese man nicknamed "El Cucho" was rumored to be the main source for Mexicali's la chinesca's subterranean dens.[20] Though some of the judicial cases against Chinese dealers were clearly setups motivated by racist policing (on April 25, 1938, for example, five Chinese were arrested and prosecuted for effectively living in a house where police found a grand total of 0.5 milligrams of opium extract), he was probably not alone.[21]

More than a quarter of those picked up with opiates in Baja California between 1930 and 1939 were born in China.[22] But the problem with the Chinese side of the trade was not only persecution but also quality. The opium imported into Ensenada was just not up to the standards expected by Chinese communities on the West Coast of the United States; it only really had a local market.[23] In 1936, one U.S. Customs officer concluded that the Mexicali trade, at least, consisted of little more than "petty peddlers selling to a few addicts on the Mexican side, with little, if any on the American side."[24]

No doubt, high politicians got involved in the trade. Drugs were still a money earner, albeit a less lucrative one than during the 1910s and 1920s. In 1935 the U.S. consul claimed that the governor of the district, Gen. Agustín Olachea, had dismissed his police chief for mistakenly interfering in the regular shuttling of opium from one of the foreign Ensenada importers to his own ranch outside Tijuana.[25] (It was a business Olachea would continue when he moved to run the southern district of Baja California in the mid-1940s).[26] But long-term monopoly control, like that exercised by Cantú or Rodriguez, was tough. Governors in 1930s Baja California didn't last long; between 1930 and 1937, there were eight, including Olachea, who ruled the district twice. Instead, protection was small-scale and at the local level. U.S. authorities—admittedly always keen to point the finger—claimed in 1931 that the Ensenada mayor's secretary was involved in the trade, in 1933 that the mayor and the postmaster of Tijuana were also involved, and in 1936 that the assistant chief of the Mexican Immigration Service was actively engaged in narcotics smuggling to Los Angeles and San Diego.[27]

The most convincing exposé and the one that best demonstrated the localized and competitive free-for-all that characterized the 1930s trade concerned a federal health official, Bernardo Bátiz. Bátiz was charged with both regulating the food, pharmaceutical, and prostitution industries and prosecuting the illegal narcotics trade. Known as a "cruel and vicious racketeer," Bátiz especially extorted prostitutes and shook down saloons and grocery stores. Women were expected to pay him seven pesos per week; foreign workers five to six pesos, and grocers, shopkeepers, and dealers an unspecified cut of their profits. Those that wanted to avoid Bátiz's racket had two options: pay protection to the local military commander or the city's chief of police. But they also faced the threat of Bátiz arresting them.[28]

THE 1940S: BOOM TIMES AND BLOODSHED

World War II proved a boom time for the Baja California drugs trade, one that was not surpassed until possibly the hippie heyday of the early 1970s, and more probably the cocaine bonanza of the 1990s. Hostilities in both Europe and Asia cut off traditional sources of opiates to the United States. At first the trickle was slow. In 1941 a lot of U.S. opiates were still arriving in East Coast ports. But by 1943, the U.S. Customs Office reported that Mexico was now "the principal source of supply of prepared opium to the illicit traffic in the United States."[29] By the middle of the decade, Mexican-run laboratories produced morphine and even heroin for the U.S. market. In the states of Sinaloa, Sonora, Durango, and Chihuahua, the shift encouraged poppy growing, opium harvesting, and eventually narcotics production on a scale never seen before.[30] But on the border, especially in Baja California, the changes were just as dramatic. Mexicans, often from these producing states, displaced Europeans and the Chinese as wholesalers, smugglers, and dealers. They now fed a growing market not only over the border but also in Tijuana, where U.S. sailors from the San Diego Naval Base migrated south at every opportunity. Such profits looked attractive, and soon figures from U.S. organized crime entered the industry and sought to cement links with certain smuggling networks. This caused both intergang violence and, starting in 1944, a series of U.S. and Mexican crackdowns.

During the first few years of the 1940s, the judicial cases demonstrate a clear decline in the number of Europeans and Chinese busted for drug-related crimes. In contrast, the number of Mexicans arrested, for opiates especially, rose dramatically. The increasing influence and participation of Mexican traffickers is not only visible in arrests, the quantities confiscated also show a marked upward trend. In 1942, three women from Sinaloa were arrested after they each brought three kilos of opium from Culiacán. In 1944, two women were arrested with approximately ten kilos of opium in cans hidden on their bodies.[31] And in 1945, Francisco Suárez Buelna was ordered to take nine kilos of opium to Mexicali by one Leoncio López, a shop owner from the Sinaloan town of Surutato, north of Badiraguato in the sierra. He would receive a commission of around fifty-five pesos per kilo for the job. Another man in the party, Venancio López, was arrested with a load of opium he brought from Mocorito on the western slopes of the Sierra Madre in Sinaloa.[32] The largest seizure occurred in 1943. It involved the arrest of Justo Arias, originally from La Piedad, Michoacán, and Juan Acuña Carmona, from Sinaloa, after they landed in an aircraft in Mexicali coming from Hermosillo. They carried 4 kilos of opium on their bodies, but hid another 10.7 kilos in their luggage.[33]

A general analysis of the Casa de la Cultura Jurídica files in Tijuana underscores the shift. Whereas during the decade of the 1930s there was one large bust involving five kilos of raw opium and many more busts with small quantities, during the 1940s, the police seized almost sixty-three kilos of opium. Of the thirteen people caught with more than one kilo in their possession, eight were from Sinaloa and one each from Michoacán, Jalisco, Durango, China, and the United States.[34] Production and trafficking was not only large-scale, it was now almost wholly homegrown. The latter was the outcome of a cautious trend initiated during the 1930s that changed the source of opium distributed in and through Baja California. Whereas at the time the majority of (crude) opium still came from overseas, hence the importance of the port city of Ensenada, U.S. reports from the 1930s contained concerns about poppy production in the peninsula, which proved incorrect, and in the mainland highlands of Sonora and Sinaloa, which was true. Large poppy fields were found around Cajeme in central Sonora, and from there crude opium was shipped through the port of Guaymas to San Felipe on Baja California's eastern seaboard and from there to Mexicali. Guaymas also functioned as the exit point for opium grown in Sinaloa.[35] By 1938, local peasants cultivated poppies farther south near coastal Huatabampo, Sonora. By the 1940s, this development had shifted the trade routes from the Pacific coast, centered above all on Ensenada, toward the southeastern states of Sonora, Sinaloa, and Durango. There is little doubt that the peninsula's integration into Mexico's national railroad system facilitated the shift.

Though this chapter concentrates on opiates, there was a similar upscaling in the trafficking of marijuana. It was closely connected to the resurgence of Tijuana as a vice center for U.S. sailors on shore leave. Almost nineteen kilos were seized during the 1930s (with three busts above four kilos), but in the 1940s, the number was eighty-one kilos. In February 1945, police in Tijuana arrested Carlos Aguilar Mora, originally from Sinaloa, for the possession of almost six kilos of marijuana. He was sentenced to four years in prison.[36] In another case, a man was arrested in Tijuana as he picked up two boxes at the post office sent from Ahuacatlán, Nayarit, containing thirty kilos of marijuana. Allegedly, the marijuana was destined for the United States, where the wholesale price per kilo was forty dollars. A letter from the sender mentioned that at the production side one kilo had cost a mere 22.5 pesos.[37] If you didn't get caught you could increase your money nearly eightfold.

The production, transportation, and trafficking of larger quantities of opium and marijuana required more complex levels of organization. And the 1940s witnessed the emergence of a two-tiered system between wholesalers on the one hand and smaller peddlers on the other hand. One network of wholesalers led by José Méndez stood out. Méndez (born in 1916 in La Piedad, Michoacán) married into a Sinaloa family and set up a trafficking network in which he relied on family members and *compadres* from La Piedad and his wife's hometown in the Sierra Madre. Typically, Méndez trusted people to pick up opium in Sinaloa and deliver it to him in Mexicali by plane. Alternatively, he and many others now used the new Sonora–Baja California train link set up in 1938. This traced the Sinaloa coast through Guaymas toward the border, changing at Santa Ana, Sonora, and from there to Puerto Peñasco, and then on to Mexicali.[38] Women usually operated as mules in these operations. For example, in November 1947, a woman associated with Méndez named Guadalupe López González was arrested in Calexico, where she was supposed to mail packages with narcotics destined for handlers in Wyoming, Utah, and Idaho.[39]

Méndez was one of the most well-known traffickers and spent a decade on the wanted list. As early as 1942 the Mexican authorities issued an arrest warrant for Méndez, and he was detained in 1944 but released.[40] In December 1947, a joint operation between Mexican police and U.S. agents (posing as opium buyers) culminated in a gun battle at Méndez's house. Several men who worked for Méndez were arrested, among them his Michoacán compadre Mariano Quintero Aguilar. In the operation, twenty cans of prepared opium were seized, as well as seven ounces of heroin, with an estimated value of fifty thousand dollars in the United States.[41] Méndez remained free but, as we will see, not for long.

The new profits from the border drug trade not only attracted Mexicans, but also figures from U.S. organized crime. The first hint of this was the murder of drug trafficker Enrique Diarte in late 1944. Diarte was a mysterious figure. According to the Mexican policeman who tracked down his killers, he was "from a decent home in Chihuahua, well educated, with an attractive personality, good humoured and a magnificent conversationalist." There were also rumors that he was a cousin of Rodolfo T. Loaiza, the governor of Sinaloa (also murdered, perhaps not coincidentally, in 1944).[42] Such qualities clearly served him well and he moved from a position in the Tijuana police force to become the major linkman between the borderlands opium wholesalers (like Méndez) and U.S. criminals.[43] The latter were led by the equally enigmatic figure of Max Cossman, aka Max Weber, aka John Smith. Cossman had been a relatively small-scale drug dealer in Los Angeles in the 1930s before he was sent down—presumably on the orders of L.A. gangster Bugsy Siegel—to cement a Mexican drug connection in the early 1940s. This he duly did. Diarte was the linkman, Méndez the wholesaler, his Michoacán relatives the heavies, and his relatives in Sinaloa the producers. Then on October 31, 1944, something went wrong. Diarte went missing. The following day his car was discovered, and three days later his decomposing body was found in a ditch.

At first both U.S. and Mexican authorities suspected a Mexican killer, Francisco Orbe, a known heroin dealer who had been seen talking to Diarte in the days leading up to the crime. But soon other associates of Diarte started to come forward, including his supplier, Méndez. These new witnesses claimed that Orbe was involved in processing opium into morphine in a rough-and-ready laboratory on the edge of the city with a mysterious American man called John Smith. It was Smith who met Orbe and Diarte on the day of his death, and according to one of the witnesses it was Smith who shot the bullet that killed Diarte. Asked to pick Smith from a pile of mug shots he pointed to Max Cossman. So did the woman who had rented Smith the shack where he had set up the lab (allegedly to make soap). A few months later the Mexican authorities picked up Cossman trying to change money at a Mexicali bank. He was arrested for the murder but denied the accusation and beat the charges.[44]

The murder revealed the growing links between U.S. organized crime and the Mexican trade, links that would shadow Cossman for the next five years. They would lead to Guadalajara heroin labs run by the former head of the Mexican narcotics police, high-level trysts between Mexican officials and Bugsy Siegel's former lover, and even the collusion of the U.S. ambassador and the Mexican president.[45] (In President Miguel Alemán's personal archive there is a tantalizing card that reads, "Please accept this gift as a tocken [*sic*] of gratitude for your kind consideration of men, Max Cossman").[46] But such drama was still to come. The reasons for the Diarte killing remained opaque. A drug deal gone wrong? Suspicion that Diarte had been compromised? He was certainly being watched by U.S. Customs officers at the time. Or perhaps most intriguingly—as the policeman (and journalist) who investigated the crime hinted—part of a broader conspiracy by Bugsy Siegel and Loaiza's successor as governor of Sinaloa (Pablo Macías Valenzuela) to eliminate Loaiza and his operators from the Sinaloa–Tijuana–Los Angeles opium pipeline for good.[47]

If increasing profits attracted organized crime, it also encouraged a series of crackdowns by both the U.S. and the Mexican authorities. In 1944, the Baja California police rounded up a series of street dealers and, as usual, some innocent Chinese.[48] Three years later, there was a similar attempt to restrict trafficking. In early 1947 Mexican opium poppies had produced a bumper crop, which by spring that year had appeared on the Baja California market. Customs officers in Calexico indicated that drug traffickers were offering narcotics at lower prices, and they launched an undercover investigation with the FBN. U.S. agents and Mexican cops caught one of the smugglers, Jesus Reyna Celaya, alias "the Professor," together with 35 tins of opium. After Reyna was indicted, they moved on to a bigger smuggler, Jesús Demara (El Chihuili).[49] U.S. undercover police posing as "big Hollywood buyers" offered to purchase 138 cans of prepared smoking opium as long as it was taken over to the U.S. side of the border. The date was set for the evening of June 22, 1947, at Woodbine Check, seven miles west of Calexico. The agents approached, three hidden in the back under a blanket and one in the trunk. When the first one leapt out to arrest the smugglers, they opened fire, triggering a gun battle that lasted a full forty-five minutes.[50] One Mexican was arrested, but the rest fled back to Mexicali. Here they took revenge on the local chief of police, Juan Meneses, ambushing and killing him for tipping off the Americans about their operation. In the wake of the assassination, Demara and several other members of his gang were arrested later that month.[51]

The Diarte murder, the Woodbine Check shootout, and the Meneses killing were proof of the rising involvement of organized crime and the use of lethal violence in what had previously been a relatively pacific industry. Similarly, in 1946, two Los Angeles hit men attacked the Tijuana prison with machine guns to liberate two other Americans who had been arrested a month earlier in the possession of twenty-five cans of opium. A prison guard was murdered in the raid.[52]

1950S: THE RETURN TO A LOCAL INDUSTRY

Despite the increasingly hysterical U.S. press coverage of the border drug problem, during the 1950s Baja California's position in the drug trade diminished considerably. FBN head Harry Anslinger pointed to efficient police work.[53] In fact, it was global market forces. Asian heroin returned, predominantly produced by the Chinese nationalists and sent to the West Coast of the United States. So did European heroin. This was manufactured first in Italy and then most famously in Marseilles, where a combination of U.S. mafia and Corsican heavies smuggled over the product to ports like New York and Baltimore. Both products were more refined than the brown Mexican product and were preferred by U.S. addicts.[54]

As new sources returned, the cross-border traffic in Mexican drugs declined sharply. Customs Bureau seizures dropped. The amount of opium fell from six pounds in 1948 and five pounds in 1949 to less than two pounds in 1951 and nothing the following year; marijuana seizures fell from an average of 112 kg per year for 1948 to 1950 to 66 kg a year from 1951 to 1955. Even seizures of heroin—dubbed the California addicts' drug of choice—declined slightly from an average of 1 pound 3 ounces in 1948 to 1950 to just 13.5 ounces during the following four years.[55] In 1955, one agent declared that the Customs Bureau had captured narcotics valued at $428,872 over the past twelve months. Less than $500 worth was seized in California.[56] Five years later, the bureau came to similar conclusions, claiming that seizures along the length of the U.S.-Mexican border only accounted for 4.5 percent of total narcotics seizures.[57] In fact, during the early 1950s drug busts were so minimal, the California Customs Bureau spent more time investigating the smuggling of rare birds than narcotics.[58]

As the market for cross-border smuggling declined, the drug industry in Baja California transformed once more. The days of large-scale wholesalers, like José Méndez, ended. In 1950, his bodyguard was killed in a shootout with a rival peddler.[59] And two years later, the disfigured body of his partner, Mariano Quintero Aguilar, was found buried in a shallow grave just outside Tijuana, and Méndez himself was shot in a restaurant in Culiacán.[60] Instead, they were replaced by an array of smaller-scale sellers. These did not import large quantities of raw opium from Sonora or Sinaloa, they did not seek links with U.S. organized crime organizations, and they dealt in smaller quantities and more varied types of narcotics than their predecessors. The switch was summed up by the commissioner of customs, who argued that border sellers now ran "a localised sellers' market doing a retail trade with addicts and petty peddlers." Gone were the days of extensive farm-to-arm operations. Instead traffickers simply "tr[ied] to meet the insistent demand of the addict colony with any sort of drug available."[61]

The most high-profile of these 1950s sellers was Miguel Barragán Bautista, aka Big Mike. Barragán was born in Zamora, Michoacán, in 1914. During the 1930s, he traveled north to the United States and was briefly incarcerated for armed robbery. When he returned to Mexico in the early 1940s, he fell in with Méndez's gang and became a relatively low-level drug peddler. In 1949, he was arrested for selling a small amount of morphine to an addict at a traveling theater on Tijuana's main tourist drag. Two years later, the police raided his house and found nine small packets of heroin; Barragán claimed that the drugs were for personal use and that he was a long-time addict. Despite these inauspicious beginnings, during the following decade Barragán's fortunes rose. By the 1960s U.S. agents claimed that he owned a large ranch in Tecate, a palatial home in Tijuana's upscale Colonia Independencia, taxicabs, a dog racing track, and the city's largest brothel.[62]

Unlike his former boss, Barragán did not rely on his links to Mexican drug producers. Though he probably got some opiates from Méndez's old connections, in general he sourced narcotics from wherever he could. Marijuana he often grew on his ranch in Tecate; heroin he often acquired via Jorge Moreno Chauvet, the Mexico City–based contact to the French Connection. To sell the drugs, Barragán used two methods. On the one hand, he made links with a handful of Southern California's small-scale heroin pushers. These would go down to Tijuana, buy a few ounces of heroin from one of Barragán's stash houses and then either personally smuggle it over the border or (for a slightly higher price) ask one of Barragán's lieutenants to arrange its transport. In 1955, Oscar Palm, a Los Angeles heroin dealer, explained the system to a Senate subcommittee. He mentioned that he often phoned ahead to make an order. When he arrived at the stash house, one of Barragán's workers handed over the drugs at $400 an ounce if Palm wanted to risk carrying the drugs, or $500 if Barragán organized the smuggling.

On the other hand, Barragán's organization also provided even smaller amounts to local users. In a subsequent subcommittee hearing, the Los Angeles prostitute Bebe Phoenix explained that she often traveled over the border, took a taxi to a four-room stash house, bought a few grains of heroin from one of Barragán's runners, and then smuggled the small bag back into the United States under her bra.[63]

Barragán's organization relied on four essential groups. They reveal certain similarities to the old trafficking organizations but also some innovations. First, there were family members. His brother, Juan, his wife, Imelda Galindo, and his brother-in-law, Al Galindo, were also involved in the drug trade. Second, there were local officials, probably on both the U.S. and the Mexican sides of the border. The drug peddler Oscar Palm declared, "If Mike deals with you, there is no finger. No, neither Mexicans nor Americans arrest you."[64] A few

Highs and Lows

years later, another U.S. informant made a similar claim, stating that a Tijuana police officer would accompany shipments over the border. Third, there were other traffickers in Tijuana. As supplies ran down and competition dropped, violence among drug sellers appeared to decline. There were no high-profile shootouts like the Woodbine Check confrontation or prominent murders like the Diarte case. Unwilling to let fact checking get in the way of a good rumor, Ovid Demaris speculated that Barragán rubbed out suspected informants, had "dumped a lot of people" in a secret burial ground outside Tijuana, and occasionally cremated his victims with gasoline. But there is no evidence for these grotesque punishments. In fact, U.S. agents thought that Barragán often worked together with other relatively small-scale suppliers like Telesforo Parra López and Cruz Macías to source drugs. Finally, Barragán increasingly relied on his contacts in the United States. He appears to have been extremely close to the Hernández brothers, Juan and Roberto, from East Los Angeles, especially after they fled to Tijuana in the late 1950s. According to Los Angeles police chief Parker, he used these contacts to establish a syndicate of drug peddlers in the city by the following decade.[65]

The other major border dealer during the 1950s was Telesforo Parra López, aka Pipas. Parra, like Barragán, was an immigrant to the border. He was born in a small ranch outside Choix in northern Sinaloa around the turn of the century. He started his career working for a sugar cane cooperative in his hometown, but he allegedly stole nearly a thousand pesos from the communal savings and used the money to try to get into the opium business. In an extraordinary letter published in a Los Mochis (Sinaloa) newspaper in 1944, he both explained his move into the business and the way in which the early drug trade worked. He said he had originally bought the opium from relatives in Mocorito, the center of the opium market at the time. He brought the opium to Los Mochis, where he immediately approached the mayor and the chief of police and asked if they wanted to buy it. The mayor contacted a couple of well-known Chinese wholesalers and the deal was made. Parra would leave the 28.6 kilos of opium in a hotel room in Los Mochis; the Chinese would pay four hundred pesos per kilo; and the profits would be split between Parra, the chief of police, and the mayor. But on the day of the deal, the chief of police reneged on the agreement, seized the opium, sold it to the Chinese, arrested Parra, and cut him out of the profits. In what Parra termed a "sham trial" he was exclusively blamed for bringing the drugs into the city. At the trial the chief of police told Parra he was "surprised that I should mingle in affairs such as this knowing how it was prohibited." Unimpressed, Parra replied that "the strangeness of the affair was not so much that I was mingled in it but that the authorities were the magnates of such a dirty business." Parra was fined and ordered to leave Los Mochis.[66]

By 1950 he had come, like many Sinaloans, to Tijuana, where he moved from wholesaling opium to masterminding the border's drugs-for-stolen-cars industry. As early as 1950, the FBN reported that drug addicts were stealing cars in Los Angeles, driving them over the border where they were sold either for cash or heroin. A new car, with titles, would fetch as much as $1,200 or six cans of opium. Many were then driven south to the ports of Santa Rosalia or La Paz where they were transported over to buyers in Sinaloa or Sonora. Three years later, the U.S. authorities eventually broke the ring and arrested a group of car thieves led by Frank H. Tellez, aka El Borrego, of East Los Angeles. The subsequent trial contains heavy racial overtones as the prosecutors described how a group of "Pachuco" criminals led by Parra López, a Mexican "kingpin heroin peddler," had coerced a group of suburban white kids of both sexes into stealing cars and taking heroin.[67]

Beyond Barragán and Parra López, the U.S. authorities also mentioned other relatively small-scale heroin peddlers. Some—like Cruz Macías—came from a similar background as Barragán, were migrants from the center west (Macías came from Tonalá, Jalisco), and had cut their teeth with the Méndez gang in the 1940s. Like Barragán, they valued good connections to the authorities. During the early 1960s, Cruz Macías's son was a best friend of the state's chief prosecutor.[68] Others were more predatory traffickers who used their political influence to arrest traffickers, confiscate drugs, and then sell the drugs to U.S. buyers. The most high-profile example was Salomón Sandez Jr., the nephew of governor Braulio Maldonado. In 1955 the police chief of Baja California confiscated opium from an unnamed trafficker in Tijuana. He handed this over to Salomón Sandez Sr., who owned the Gato Negro club just off the city's main strip. Not content with dealing small amounts out of the club, his son, Sandez Jr., traveled over to Los Angeles, where he was arrested selling the heroin to potential buyers.[69]

Finally, a growing number of smugglers were of Mexican American descent. The most notorious two dealers were the brothers Roberto and Juan Hernández, aka Big and Little Brother. During the early 1950s they were low-level marijuana smugglers who brought over small quantities of the drug to sell in East Los Angeles. After being charged with drug trafficking, they both jumped bail and escaped over to Tijuana, where they took advantage of their dual citizenship to avoid extradition proceedings. Here they teamed up with Miguel Barragán and started to sell heroin to their old U.S. contacts. By the 1960s, they had become Tijuana's most prominent marijuana and heroin dealers.[70]

CONCLUSIONS

The rise and fall of Baja California's drugs trade, the shifts in scale, structure, market, personnel, protection, and levels of violence aptly illustrate how global market forces out of the control of Mexican smugglers and dealers shaped regional narcotics industries. During the 1930s and again during the 1950s, most opiates came from Europe or Asia, and the U.S. market for Mexican marijuana was very narrow.[71] As a result, the Baja California trade was small-scale and limited itself to local sales and light cross-border smuggling. Violence connected to the trade was rare. And though the authorities often imposed protection, they kept squabbles in house. Drugs were just one of many exploitable vices. Alternative profitable shakedowns from bars, brothels, and gambling establishments were available.

During the 1940s, however, the border market grew radically. Tijuana now became the go-to pleasure resort for off-duty San Diego sailors. The local market in both opiates and marijuana increased. As European and Asian sources of opiates vanished, Baja California became one of, if not the, key transhipment route for Mexican opiates grown and processed in the Golden Triangle. A new group of Mexican smugglers and U.S. organized crime figures moved into the trade. As the stakes rose, conflicts between traffickers and between traffickers and the authorities often turned bloody.

Outside the mechanics of the trade, the chapter also demonstrates the disconnection between popular perceptions of the drug trade and on-the-ground realities. For California civil society organizations, politicians, and journalists, 1950s Tijuana was "the Border Hell town," the only city on the continent where "teenagers can step into a saloon and buy drinks, then stroll back to the washrooms and buy marijuana and then wander into a book store and study pornographic books and pictures, then walk along the main street and pick up a prostitute and top off the evening by stopping at an all night pharmacy to buy habit forming drugs over the counter."[72] But the reality was very different. By the 1950s the Tijuana drug trade was really on the slide. It provided for a handful of San Diego addicts and a few partygoing youngsters, but little more.

NOTES

1. For the black legend of the border more generally, see Humberto Felix Berumen, *Tijuana la Horrible: Entre la historia y el mito* (Mexicali: Colegio de la Frontera Norte, 2003); Ramon Eduardo Ruiz, *On the Rim of Mexico: Encounters of the Rich and Poor* (London: Routledge, 2019), chap. 3.

2. Wil G. Pansters and Benjamin T. Smith, "U.S. Moral Panics, Mexican Politics, and the Borderlands Origins of the War on Drugs 1950–1962," *Journal of Contemporary History* 55, no. 2 (2020): 364–87; Keith Monroe, "Tijuana: Border Hell Town," *Coronet*, September 1956, 123–28.

3. Ovid Demaris, *Poso del Mundo: Inside the Mexican-American Border, from Tijuana to Matamoros* (Boston: Little Brown and Company, 1970).

4. Juan Carlos Reyna, *El Extraditado, Benjamín Arellano Félix* (Mexico City: Grijalbo, 2014); Jesús Blancornelas, *El Cartel: Los Arellano Félix: La mafia más poderosa en la historia de América Latina* (Mexico City: Delbolsillo, 2009).

5. James A. Sandos, "Northern Separatism during the Mexican Revolution: An Inquiry into the Role of Drug Trafficking, 1910–1920," *The Americas* 41, no. 2 (1984): 191–214; James A. Sandos, "Prostitution and Drugs: The United States Army on the Mexican-American Border, 1916–1917," *Pacific Historical Review* 49, no. 4 (1980): 621–45; Joseph Richard Werne, "Esteban Cantú y la Soberanía Mexicana en Baja California," *Historia Mexicana* 30, no. 1 (1980): 1–32.

6. José Alfredo Gómez Estrada, *Gobierno y casinos: El origen de la riqueza de Abelardo L. Rodríguez* (Mexico City: Instituto Mora, 2002), 101–45.

7. Eric Schantz, "De la farmacia abierta a la criminalización de los enervantes: la transición al regimen de control de droga en la zona fronteriza de México y Estados Unidos," in *En la encrucijada. Historia, marginalidad y delito en América Latina y los Estados Unidos de Norteamérica (siglos XIX y XX)*, ed. Jorge Alberto Trujillo (Guadalajara: Universidad de Guadalajara, 2010); Eric Schantz, "From the Mexicali Rose to the Tijuana Brass: Vice Tours of the United States-Mexico Border, 1910–1965" (PhD diss., University of California at Los Angeles, 2001).

8. National Archives and Records Administration (NARA), Record Group (RG) 170, box 22, Report of consul Frank Bohr, Feb. 1927.

9. Lawrence A. Herzog, *From Aztec to High Tech: Architecture and Landscape Across the Mexico-United States* (Baltimore: Johns Hopkins University Press, 2010), 61.

10. Ruiz, *On the Rim of Mexico*, 45.

11. Paul Vanderwood, *Juan Soldado, Rapist, Murderer, Martyr, Saint* (Durham, NC: Duke University Press, 2004), 159–62.

12. Lawrence Douglas Taylor Hansen, "La transformación de Baja California en Estado, 1931–1952," *Estudios Fronterizos* 1, no. 1 (2000): 61.

13. This required ending the isolation of Mexico's northwest from the rest of the country's railroad network. Until after the Mexican Revolution the entire railroad

system in Sonora and Sinaloa was U.S.- and British-owned and connected to the U.S. network but not to Mexico's interior railroad system. See Leo E. Zonn, "Los ferrocarriles de Sonora y Sinaloa, México: una geografía histórica," *Clío* 5, no. 2 (1997): 132.

14. Eric Schneider, *Smack, Heroin and the American City* (Philadelphia: University of Pennsylvania Press, 2008), 10–15.

15. NARA, RG59, 1930–1939, roll 33, Consul at Ensenada, Report, 9/4/1935.

16. NARA, RG59, 1930–1939, Evans to Collector of Customs, San Diego, 6/21/1935.

17. *Westways Magazine*, January 1955; U.S. Grant IV, "A Sojourn in Baja California, 1915," *Southern California Quarterly* 45, no. 2 (June 1963): 123–68.

18. NARA, RG59, 1930–1939, roll 33, Smale to Secretary of State, 1/21/1936.

19. Catalina Velázquez Morales, *Los inmigrantes Chinos en Baja California, 1920–1937* (Tijuana: UABC, 2001).

20. NARA, RG59, 1930–1939, roll 33, Commissioner to Customs, 5/10/1940.

21. Archivo de la Casa de la Cultura Júridica de Tijuana (ACCJT), caja 67, exp. 18, 1938, Gom Mem et al.

22. ACCJT, 1930–1939, Delitos contra la salud.

23. NARA, RG59, 1930–1939, Roll 33, District Officer Smith to Anslinger, 4/19/1933.

24. NARA RG170, box 22, Report Joseph Treglia, 4/23/1936.

25. NARA, RG59, 1930–1939, roll 33, Consul of Ensenada Report, 9/4/1935.

26. NARA RG170, box 23, DJCTE2646987 Secret Agent Memorandum, 1/26/1948.

27. NARA, RG59, 1930–1939, roll 33, Consul of Ensenada Report, 5/12/1931, and Consul of Tijuana Report, 12/18/1933; NARA, RG170, box 22, Report Joseph Treglia, 5/23/1936.

28. NARA, RG170, box 22, Report Joseph Treglia, 5/23/1936.

29. NARA RG170, box 23, UN Reports of U.S. regarding Mexico, 1940–1947.

30. See Fernández Velázquez, chapter 8 in this volume.

31. Archivo del Estado de Baja California (AEBC), caja 184, exp. 4, Enrique Rayón Díaz to Gobernador del Territorio, 8/24/1944.

32. ACJJT, 1945, caja 3, expediente 32, Francisco Suárez Buelna, Jesus Meza Ortíz, Venancio López López, Severiano Melendre López, and Enrique Domínguez Galindo.

33. ACJJT, 1943, caja 2, exp. 41.

34. ACJJT, Delitos contra la salud, 1930–1950.

35. NARA RG170, box 22, Sutherland to Anslinger, 8/26/1936.

36. ACJJT, 1945 caja 1, exp. 9, Carlos Aguilar Mora.

37. ACJJT, 1946, caja 1, exp. 21, Luis Rosas.

38. The section between Santa Ana and Puerto Peñasco was only finished in 1948–1949.

39. NARA Riverside, CA, RG36, Vader to Customs supervising agent, 8/10/1948.

40. *El Detective Internacional*, June 20, 1946.

41. NARA RG 170, box 23, Gardner to Commissioner of Customs, 1/8/1948, ACJJT, 1949, caja 7, exp. 143.

42. Joaquín Aguilar Robles, *Frontera Norte: Memorias de un detective* (Mexico City: Costa-Amic SA, 1984); *El Detective Internacional*, April 13, 1946.

43. Archivo Histórico de la Ciudad de México, Departamento del DF, Exp. N/522/7203.

44. Aguilar Robles, *Frontera Norte*; *El Detective Internacional*, June 20, 1946, September 21, 1946, June 8, 1946, April 13, 1946.

45. Juan Alberto Cedillo, *La cosa nostra en México* (1938–1950) (Mexico City: Grijalbo, 2011).

46. Archivo General de la Nación (AGN), Ramo Presidentes, Miguel Alemán Valdés (MAV), 541/178.

47. *El Detective Internacional*, June 20, 1946.

48. AGN, Ramo Presidentes, Manuel Avila Camacho (MAC), 422.1, Juan Felipe Rico to Escudero, 8/18/1945.

49. NARA Riverside RG36, Annual report 1948 of Fourteenth Customs Agency by Frederick H. Gardner, 8/16/1948.

50. AGN, MAV, 606.3/67, Speech of Harry Anslinger to United Nations, 1947.

51. NARA Riverside RG 36, Annual report 1948 of Fourteenth Customs Agency by Frederick H. Gardner, 8/16/1948; Gabriel Trujillo Muñoz, "Juan Meneses Adarga: Un episodio del libro rojo nacional," *Acequias* 54 (2010): 27–31.

52. Eric Schantz, "Surcando un hábito doméstico: La expansión interna del mercado de opiáceos y marihuana en México, 1936–1953," in *Voces y memorias del olvido. Historia, marginalidad y delito en América Latina*, ed. Jorge Alberto Trujillo (Guadalajara: Universidad de Guadalajara, 2014), 217–18.

53. *Los Angeles Times*, February 13, 1953; NARA, RG170, box 160, Rebasa to Anslinger, 9/4/1959; Rebasa to Anslinger, 8/24/1959.

54. Schneider, *Smack*, 76.

55. See the Customs Bureau reports in NARA Riverside, RG36, 1948–1955.

56. *Hearings before the Subcommittee on Improvements in the Federal Criminal Code of the Committee on the Judiciary, United States Senate, Eighty Fourth Congress, First Session on Illicit Narcotics Traffic, June 2, 3, 4, 1955* (Washington DC: Government Printing Office, 1955), 152–53.

57. NARA, RG170, box 161, Ralph Kelly, Commissioner of Customs, to Filmore Fines, 6/24/1960.

58. NARA Riverside, RG36, U.S. Customs Report for San Diego, 1952.

59. *San Diego Union*, February 28, 1950; *San Diego Union*, February 5, 1950.

60. ACJJT, caja 3, expediente 143, Mariano Quintero Aguilar; *San Diego Union*, September 13, 1952; *La Prensa* (San Antonio), August 17, 1951.

61. NARA, RG170, box 161, Ralph Kelly, Commissioner of Customs, to Filmore Fines, 6/24/1960.

62. He is mentioned as one of Méndez's henchmen let out of prison to visit the funeral of Méndez's bodyguard. *San Diego Union*, February 9, 1950. Ovid Demaris claims that he was imprisoned in Puget Sound. The FBN claims that he was imprisoned in San Quentin. Demaris, *Poso del Mundo*, 155; NARA, RG170, box 161, Miguel Barragán Bautista file, 1965; Archivo de la Suprema Corte de Justicia, amparo 5280, Miguel Barragán Bautista, 1951; AEBC, 184.4, Francisco Krauss Morales to Agente del Ministerio Público, 10/18/1949.

63. Barragán even sold as far afield as to Texas traffickers. *Hearings before the Subcommittee on Improvements in the Federal Criminal Code of the Committee on the Judiciary, United States Senate, Eighty-Fourth Congress, First Session Pursuant to S. Res 67, Illicit Narcotics traffic, November 14, 15, 16, 17 and 18, 1955* (Washington DC: Government Printing Office, 1956), 3786, 3588ff, 3696ff; Demaris, *El Poso del Mundo*, 156; NARA RG170, box 161, Miguel Barragán Bautista file, 1965.

64. *Hearings before the Subcommittee on Improvements*, 3786.

65. NARA RG170, box 161, Miguel Barragán Bautista file, 1965; Demaris, *El Poso del Mundo*, 156; *Hearings before the Subcommittee on Improvements*; *Report of the Committee on the Judiciary, United States Senate, Made by its Subcommittee to Investigate Juvenile Delinquency Pursuant to S. Res. 265* (Washington DC: Government Printing Office, 1964), 14.

66. NARA RG84, box 3, Mcmillin to Herbert Bursley, 11/2/1944.

67. NARA RG170, box 161, Telesforo Parrasa [*sic*], aka Pipas file; NARA Riverside, RG36, U.S. Customs Report 1953; *Los Angeles Times*, February 23, 1953; NARA, RG170, box 161, Treasury Dept. San Diego to Supervising Customs Agent, 5/26/1950.

68. E. Castillo, *La Otra Mafia* (Tijuana, n.p., n.d.), 56; NARA, RG170, box 161, Cruz Macias report, c. 1960.

69. U.S. Treasury, Bureau of Narcotics, *Traffic in Opium and Other Dangerous Drugs*, (Washington DC: Government Printing Office, 1964), 56; NARA, RG170, box 161, GW Cunningham to Carlos Sodi, 11/14/1955.

70. NARA Riverside, RG36, Customs Report 1953; NARA, RG170, box 161, Juan and Robert Chavira Hernández reports, 5/20/1965; U.S. Treasury, Bureau of Narcotics, *Traffic in Opium and Other Dangerous Drugs* (Washington DC: Government Printing Office, 1964), 45; *Hearings before the Subcommittee To Investigate Juvenile Delinquency of the Committee on the Judiciary, U.S. Senate, Eighty Seventh Congress, Second Session, Pursuant to S. Res 265, Part II, Narcotics Traffic and Its Effects on Juvenile and Young Adult Criminality, May 9, 17 and 29, 1962* (Washington DC: Government Printing Office, 1963).

71. As Carlos Flores explains in chapter 9 of this volume, most reached the United States through Texas to the East Coast.

72. Monroe, "Tijuana," 123.

7

Policing the Drug Trade
U.S. Narcotic Agents in Mexico, 1936–1963

CARLOS A. PÉREZ RICART

INTRODUCTION

This chapter examines the activities of U.S. narcotic agents in Mexico between 1936 and the early 1960s. It begins in the mid-1930s, a time to which I have traced the first trips of U.S. narcotic agents to Mexico with the purpose of conducting investigations on drug trafficking, and ends in 1963, when the Federal Bureau of Narcotics (FBN) established a permanent office in Mexico City.[1]

The chapter draws on archival sources, police reports, diaries, biographies of former drug agents and traffickers, local newspapers, magazines, police journals, U.S. Congress hearings, and customs records. While all these sources have their own limitations—the most notorious being "the inherently speculative and exaggerated nature" of the documents—they remain an invaluable source of information.[2]

The chapter is divided into four different sections. The first addresses the origins of U.S. concerns about drugs coming from Mexico, and narrates the first drug investigations in Mexico by U.S. narcotics agents. Drawing on the experience of agent Alvin F. Scharff, the chapter illustrates the participation of U.S. Customs agents in the eradication campaigns that took place in Mexico's northwest during the late 1930s. The second part addresses the main differences between FBN and Customs Bureau investigation techniques in Mexico and presents some of the most relevant undercover operations U.S. narcotic agents were involved in during the 1940s and early 1950s. The third part depicts the most representative undercover operations organized by the FBN in Mexico between 1959 and 1963. Finally, the last section analyzes the establishment of an FBN branch office in Mexico, and presents a conclusion.

THE FIRST DRUG INVESTIGATIONS IN MEXICO BY U.S. NARCOTICS AGENTS

Since the mid-1930s, drug trafficking investigations in Mexico have been carried out by agents of two different Treasury Department agencies, the U.S. Customs and the FBN. The former agency enjoyed jurisdiction over narcotics crimes in Mexico, as well as the rest of Latin America (and Europe). Most of their agents, however, had no training in drug investigations and exercised a wide range of activities beyond enforcing drug laws, including collecting tariffs, preventing the smuggling of alcohol, and the trade of Chinese women to the United States. On the other hand, FBN agents had no jurisdiction over narcotic drugs in Mexico, but were better prepared for undertaking drug investigations, as this was their sole mission. As will be shown in this chapter, even though bureaucratic struggles prevented FBN agents from operating in Mexico legally, they did it intermittently since the mid-1930s. Most FBN agents involved in drug investigations in Mexico were attached to the domestic offices the agency had in California, New Mexico, Arizona, and Texas.

Mexican laws did not distinguish between Customs and FBN agents. The entrance to Mexico by agents of both agencies remained illegal for most of the century despite the continuous requests of the Treasury Department to regulate their presence. To some extent, the lack of a regulatory framework was perceived as the reason why the small but vibrant illegal trafficking of opium could not be stopped. An article published in the *New York Times* in 1928 illustrates this argument:

> The fact that there is no arrangement with the Mexican Government for the United States Narcotic Division to maintain its special agents in Mexico prevents tracing the drug gangs down [...] the task of stopping the traffic is well-nigh hopeless unless a way is found for cooperation with Mexico whereby undercover men may set a watch at Mexican ports and work with other undercover men at border transit points.[3]

Paradoxically, the main resistance didn't come from the Mexican government, but from the State Department, which rejected any sort of formalization for the presence of narcotics agents in Mexico. The first drug-enforcement agreement in 1930 between Mexico and the United States addressed the issue of sharing data but did not address the question of U.S. agents' operations across the Mexican border.[4] In 1941, the Mexican narcotics service was prepared to formalize an agreement with a Treasury Department's special representative in Mexico City on the presence of U.S. agents in Mexico. But when the Treasury's representative sought confirmation from Washington, the American Republic Division of the State Department deemed a formal accord unwise.[5] The informal arrangement was preferable. The only requirement was "not to overrun Mexico with its agents."[6] For more than two decades, the matter remained unregulated until it became a major diplomatic problem in the early 1960s, as will be shown later.

The presence of narcotics agents in Mexico in the mid-1930s is well-registered and shows that despite the illegal nature of their enterprise, Mexican authorities were quite flexible with their presence. In 1936, FBN agents Victor D. Carli and Morris Adelson went to Tijuana to interview two informers. They were accompanied by two Mexican officials "connected with the Public Health Department of the Mexican government."[7] The activities of both agents in Tijuana remain a mystery, but they could have participated in an undercover operation, as this was one of their specialties.[8] In 1936, Joseph L. V. Treglia, a special Customs employee, stayed in Mexicali for two weeks investigating alleged narcotics smuggling to the United States.[9] That same year, Leroy T. Sutherland, a federal narcotics agent attached to the FBN office in San Diego, made a trip along the U.S.-Mexican border "from San Diego west to the Arizona line for the purpose of securing information regarding illegal traffic in narcotic drugs."[10] In Mexico he talked to many local and federal authorities, and he visited Mexicali, Tijuana, and even Ensenada, more than a hundred kilometers south of the border.[11] The report he sent to his supervisor in San Diego presents an excellent overview of the small but vibrant market of opium along the border.

In the history of U.S. counternarcotics operations, Alvin Scharff deserves a special place, even if he never attained the formal title of narcotics agent. As Elaine Carey has observed, "Scharff's life story is as infamous as those of the traffickers he tracked."[12] Scharff, a special agent of the Treasury Department, was active in policing activities in Texas since 1917 and maintained a decades-long competition with FBN commissioner Harry Anslinger. He acted as an undercover agent in Europe and constructed a vast network of informants from Shanghai to Marseille in the late 1930s before working as Customs agent in charge in Houston, Texas, until the mid-1950s.[13] In between, he always found time to operate in Mexico in different capacities.

Scharff had "been in and out" of Mexico since about 1912.[14] He operated in Sonora as a special employee of the War Department during the First World War.[15] In 1917 he was appointed inspector of customs in Nogales, Arizona, where he met Harry S. Creighton for the first time, then special agent in charge of the Customs Service and also a key figure in the history of U.S. law enforcement in Mexico.

In January 1934, Creighton sent Scharff to Mexico City to ascertain the true values of legal goods exported from Mexico to the United States.[16] This nonrelated narcotics issue kept Al Scharff busy in Mexico City for almost two years. In 1936, however, he became interested in the issue of production of opium in Mexico. His interest in narcotics led to meetings with José Siurob, minister of public health and in charge of enforcement of the narcotic and drug supervisory laws, as well as with "almost every high official in the Mexican Government."[17]

Scharff's first drug investigation took place in 1936, when he participated in smashing a transnational network of smugglers based in Havana with tentacles in Shanghai, Buenos Aires, Istanbul, and Mexico City. That same group was accused among other transactions of smuggling 400 kg of heroin worth $1,000,000 through Veracruz one year before.[18] His participation in that narcotics case has been narrated by his biographer, Garland Roark, probably in exaggerated terms. According to Roark, Scharff captured the leaders of the trafficking gang in Mexico City himself. According to the same version, Ignacio García Tellez (attorney general), Luis G. Franco (head of the Office of Alcohol and Narcotics), and Siurob assigned a staff of special investigators and policemen to Scharff for these actions.[19] While the case won the attention of the Mexican media, the direct participation of the American agent wasn't mentioned.[20] This would be a common pattern in the relationship with the media: U.S. counternarcotics operations in Mexico would normally not be published by the Mexican media except for the cases in which (mostly local) political motivations had special interests in unmasking the agents. Scharff remained in Mexico City for a few more months before sailing to Paris in January of 1937, where he was meant to organize a system to deter the flow of narcotic drugs destined for the United States from the Far East via Europe. As in Mexico, he served not as a narcotics officer but as acting treasury representative. Scharff's stay in Europe lasted only a few months. In April 1938 he was once again called by the Customs Bureau to help with a new project: a poppy-destruction program in Mexico. Creighton, who assumed some of Scharff's duties while he was in Europe, negotiated with Luis G. Franco regarding the undertaking of this enterprise, as well as the participation of a U.S. agent in it. Due to his previous experience in Mexico and his knowledge of Spanish (an unusual attribute for Treasury agents at the time), Scharff was selected. His official task was simple: to assist the Mexican narcotics law enforcement officers in discovering and eradicating fields of opium poppies in southern Sonora, northern Sinaloa, and Nayarit.[21] The enterprise was (reluctantly) allowed by the State Department with two conditions: to restrain Scharff's function to an "advisory capacity" and to avoid any mention of his name in the press.[22]

In Mexico, the new head of the Public Health Service, Leónides Andreu Almazán, as well as the new head of the Office of Alcohol and Narcotics, Leopoldo Salazar Viniegra, promised Scharff to support his activities in Mexico by assigning him two of their employees. Scharff even gained the support of Cdr. Miguel Hernández Guzmán, then chief of the Fourth Military Zone, who offered to place "soldiers, army trucks, and horses at Señor Scharff's disposal."[23] Scharff headed toward Sinaloa and stayed in the northwest for a few weeks, during which time he directly participated in the destruction of opium poppy fields.[24] This effort was the first in which Public Health Service officials and soldiers worked together in narcotics efforts.[25]

In the biography written by Garland Roark, Scharff is portrayed as the chief of the entire enterprise. As with other narrations on this topic, we lack *Mexican* sources to corroborate or contradict this. It is clear, though, that Scharff's role in the campaign was not limited to an advisory capacity, as the State Department had ordered.[26] To what extent President Lázaro Cárdenas was aware of the presence of Scharff is impossible to know, but it is undisputable that Scharff's activities in the mountains had the approval of high Mexican officials.[27]

Scharff's identity remained unrevealed to the Mexican and U.S. media that reported on the "poppy war" that took place in the Mexican northwest during the spring of 1938.[28] For most of the U.S. media, the campaign was directed by "an unnamed U.S. Treasury operative whose cooperation had been enlisted by Dr. Leopoldo Salazar."[29]

Scharff was probably the first U.S. narcotics agent to operate directly in the mountains, arresting drug traffickers and burning fields of opium poppies. During the late 1930s and 1940s, the campaigns expanded to new territories and were accompanied by U.S. Customs officials of the same agency. Some of their names and reports to their supervisors are well-maintained in the archives: Philip M. Caldwell (lieutenant, U.S. Customs Patrol), T. S. Simpson (customs agent), Salvador Peña (special employee), W. J. Harmon (supervising customs agent), Carl Peterson (patrol inspector), Lake T. Webb (sergeant, U.S. Customs Patrol), and a few others. Their work was undertaken discreetly and was limited to specific regions. They were provided with funds to cover the expenses of the Mexican agents, "as well as for entertainment of officials, purchase of information and extra food for the Mexican soldiers who actually do the work of destroying the poppies."[30] Predictably, State Department officials warned continuously against the "too liberal or open" spending of U.S. Customs funds "because of possible criticism by anti-Government or anti-American newspapers."[31]

As part of their work, the agents attended meetings with high-ranking Mexican officials, negotiated with mayors, local policemen, local attorneys, sanitary department delegates, and military authorities. They made lists of the places where poppies were being grown, estimated the number of acres under cultivation, and followed up the cases of sowers and traffickers arrested during the spring campaigns.[32] What is more, they informally trained Mexican officials, some of whom "worked faithfully with and under the guidance and training" of U.S. agents.[33] One of them even became an "honorary inspector" of the Mexican Department of Control of Narcotics.[34]

Apart from a few exceptions, the agents did not stay in Mexico for more than a few months. Once the campaigns ended, they went back to their posts in one of the multiple offices of the Customs Bureau along the Mexican border. The evaluation and design of the campaigns were left in the hands of the Treasury representative in Mexico City, a permanent position created in 1941 and occupied first by H. S. Creighton. He and his successors (Sidney J. Kennedy, Dolor J. DeLagrave, J. Eugene Couchon, Francis X. DiLucia, and Benjamin S. White) played an active role in the planning of the eradication campaigns.

In general, U.S. Customs agents did not behave much differently than temporal agents (TDY) of the Drug Enforcement Administration (DEA) would behave in the mid-1970s in the Mexican mountains. But while in the early 1940s the campaigns were accompanied by one or two U.S. Customs agents, in the mid-1970s the campaigns were supervised by some twenty-five or thirty DEA agents who stayed in the mountains for more than six months.[35] Notwithstanding, the core functions remained the same.

POLICING THE DRUG TRADE: THE 1940S

While the supervision of the eradication campaigns was mostly a Customs Bureau matter, police and investigative activities in Mexico were conducted by both FBN agents and Customs officials. Even though they cooperated in some cases, their ways of policing the drug trade differed vastly from one another. In the following, I will specify the nature of these differences.

Customs officials generally avoided carrying out *buy-and-bust* operations in Mexico. They preferred the use of *cold convoys*, an investigative technique used when drug traffickers, discovered in the course of an inspection, are allowed to proceed from the border to their intended destination while under the surveillance of law enforcement agents.[36] A variation of this was when informants on the other side of the border alerted Customs inspectors about when and where a drug shipment would cross the border. Unlike the more common investigation technique of *control delivery*, cold convoys ensure that the offender is unaware that the contraband has been discovered. This had the advantage of prompting a larger investigation with the possibility of disrupting an entire trafficking network.

The Customs Bureau devised this technique in the late 1940s for drug shipments coming from Mexico. Customs agents attempted to convince Mexican narcotics officers to work undercover themselves and to encourage or persuade the traffickers to make deliveries of narcotics from Mexico to the United States, "meanwhile informing U.S. Customs officers of the prospective deliveries."[37] The success of this strategy unleashed the anger of Anslinger. Cold convoys meant that Customs officials started doing narcotic investigations also deep inside the United States, a task under the sole authority of the FBN. Anslinger also argued that through their informant network in Mexico, Customs agents were interfering in FBN undercover operations. The conflict escalated to the point that Anslinger "went to court and challenged the legality of convoys and the right of Customs agents to hire informants in Mexico."[38]

Mexican officers had few incentives to collaborate with Customs and engage in cold convoy investigations. Since the arrests took place in the United States, their job was barely recognized, and they had nothing concrete to show to their supervisors. This is why the Customs Bureau had a more urgent need than the FBN to hire paid informants, or *madrinas* as they were known in Mexico, for the purpose of receiving information on drug shipments coming to the border.[39] The Records of the U.S. Customs Service present evidence of a wide (and surprisingly disorganized) network of paid informants that the bureau had in Mexico. *Special employees* or *special endeavors* (SE) were former and active narcotics officers or drug dealers. While some collaborated with the U.S. Customs Bureau for years, others only cooperated for a short period. In most cases their point of contact was a specific agent working on a narcotics case. As soon as this agent was assigned to another office, the contact with the SE was lost. Some were paid on a per diem basis and some on a reward basis. Due to the limited funds, the bureau preferred to pay on a reward basis. As might be expected, the quality of the information provided fluctuated accordingly. While sometimes the data provided was key for finishing a case, on other occasions the information provided was utterly false, sometimes to the point of endangering the lives of the agents involved in the operations.

The approach of the FBN was different. Despite not having jurisdiction over criminal offenses in Mexico, the FBN had the capacity to gather basic biographical information and arrest records of every suspect in the United States and abroad (a capacity only comparable to the one of Interpol). That is, Anslinger and his close circle knew more than the Customs Bureau about the Mexican sources of heroin or marijuana of the criminal networks operating in the United States. This explains why, disregarding the formal authority of the U.S. Customs Bureau in Mexico, FBN agents did not restrain themselves and crossed the border several times. Unlike the Customs Bureau, the FBN preferred to carry out buy-and-bust operations directly in Mexico, an entrapment technique employed by narcotics agents to catch unsuspecting drug dealers.

Even if Mexican courts disputed the legality of buy-and-bust operations as a legitimate method of apprehending criminals, FBN promoted the implementation of this technique by Mexican officials and pursued the legalization of the technique for decades. While it was improbable that buy-and-bust operations would result in bigger cases, they had the advantage of identifying and criminalizing street sellers and addicts. In other words, buy-and-bust techniques were in accord with the FBN's prohibitive and punitive approach toward drugs in the United States.[40] According to Anslinger, the FBN pioneered the development of the technique. But this was not true, as the historiography on criminology has incontrovertibly proven.[41] On some occasions, buy-and-bust operations in Mexico were conducted by the FBN agents themselves. They typically posed as U.S. consumers or retailers ready to pay good prices for drugs. It was nevertheless preferable to leave this kind of work to the Mexicans or some SE. The problem with them was that Mexican officials lacked the training and the SEs were not always reliable.[42]

By the mid-1940s, the so-called 107th Street Mob was probably the best-organized heroin trafficking syndicate in the United States. The headquarters of the organization were in New York. Yet according to the FBN, the tentacles of the mob had reached Mexico as well. According to the agency, large quantities of opium and morphine were trafficked from Mexico into California and then shipped directly for distribution in Los Angeles, San Francisco, Boston, and New York.[43] The immobilization of the mob became an obsession for the Treasury Department, whose agencies sent their officers to Mexico in pursuit of the supply source.

By 1943, the mob's suspected source of supply was identified by the FBN: Enrique Diarte Escobar (probably a fake name), "one of the most flagrant smugglers of narcotic drugs operating out of Mexicali and Tijuana."[44] In October of 1944, the newly appointed inspector general of Baja California's police, Colonel Escudero, developed a plan to arrest Diarte in cooperation with Customs officials. In the framework of a joint operation, it was agreed that R. M. Wadsworth, an officer of the Southwest Customs Patrol, would purchase narcotics directly from Diarte in Mexicali. Wadsworth "spent the evenings of October 26 and 27 in Mexicali, and in his own way and with his command of the Spanish language attempted to meet with Diarte."[45] He failed; some days later Diarte's body was found about seventeen kilometers east of Tijuana. In the same month, Customs agent T. S. Simpson assisted two Mexican officers, Rafael Palomar and Ignacio Mancilla, in the arrest of Arnaldo Mendoza and Sabas Ruacha (both in Ciudad Juárez) and Luciano Quezada (in Nogales), all three probably part of Diarte's criminal network.[46] Palomar and Mancilla were working "secretly in Tijuana" with the Customs Bureau and were paid "3,000 pesos per month, in addition to their normal salaries."[47] Working along the border with U.S. agents was undoubtably profitable for Mexican federal agents; unlike their colleagues in other cities, they were well dressed and equipped with expensive handguns and government automobiles for their investigations.

The other supposed key link for the mob in Mexico was Max Cossman (aka Max Weber) arrested on January 26, 1945, in Mexicali and accused of murdering Diarte. Again, his detention was accomplished through collaboration between the Customs Bureau and Escudero. According to the annual report of the FBN, not only Cossman but also 106 other persons involved in this network were arrested in Mexico in what was allegedly "one of the biggest arrests made in the history of Mexico."[48] As with most FBN claims, this is only half true. The number 106 was obtained from a list of arrests that were indeed made in Baja California between October 1944 and March 1945 but that were unrelated to the mob or any specific organization.[49] Cossman spent a few years in jail and escaped before getting caught again in the early 1950s.[50] During this entire period, Anslinger and his favorite agent, George H. White, engaged with the case to the point that White traveled to Mexico City several times in the late 1940s to follow up on the details of the investigations against Cossman. With little evidence, they tried to convince the Mexicans officials of the existence of a solid relation between Cossman and the mob, as well as the merchant Elias Eliopoulos, the biggest drug baron in Europe at the time.

As Diarte's and Cossman's cases show, U.S. drug agencies constructed their own interpretations of the dynamics of drug trafficking in Mexico. Most of the time, these interpretations were oversimplified and full of stereotypes. As Gingeras has shown for Turkey, "FBN agents tended to highlight the activities of large-scale or major trafficking syndicates at the expense of smaller independent outfits and networks."[51] U.S. narcotics agents portrayed drug smugglers as social actors capable of exerting genuine organizational control over the whole chain of illicit traffic. This interpretation remains a component of modern drug control and has influenced the way drug policing has been executed in Mexico throughout half of the last century.[52]

Throughout the 1940s, U.S. Customs officials, FBN agents, and Mexican authorities set up various operations to detain traffickers. Among the most famous was the investigation into Ignacia Jasso Gonzales, aka La Nacha. In the summer of 1942, narcotic agents Westover and Crook crossed the border to Ciudad Juárez to buy opium and morphine from La Nacha.[53] The operation lasted a few weeks and brought the undercover agents to "the mountains of Guadalajara," where La Nacha managed poppy fields and a morphine lab. La Nacha and her runners and lieutenants were arrested in the following months.[54] This success sparked a new spirit of cooperation between Mexicans and U.S. agents. As a result of this, the Mexican police accomplished the arrest of "eleven Chinese men, four Mexican men and one Mexican woman" in Chihuahua in 1943.[55] The archives also reveal the existence of an unnamed agent of the FBN who used to work undercover in Mexican border cities in the autumn of 1946.[56] A second one (or possibly the same one?) with the signature W. Y. E. traveled to Los Mochis to inquire about the structure of the Chinese bands involved in the transport of opium to the United States that same year. After August

1947, another FBN agent worked along the border in an undercover capacity in the investigation against the Francisco J. and Luis Lavat group, according to Anslinger "the most important criminal organization operating between the United States and Mexico."[57] A successful prosecution against them was brought in Los Angeles in late 1948.

As Smith and Pansters explain, from 1948 to the end of the 1950s, there was a decrease in quantities of narcotics being smuggled across the Mexican border to the United States. Seizures of opium and marijuana dropped and the Customs Bureau's and FBN's focus on Mexico diminished. Over this period, which lasted approximately twelve years, Mexican opium was not a priority and cocaine had not yet appeared as a popular drug in the United States. Moreover, Anslinger's attention now focused on Turkey, Europe, and the Far East.[58] As a result, fewer undercover narcotics operations took place during the early 1950s. FBN records, however, register some buy-and-bust operations in General Terán, Nuevo León, Nuevo Laredo, Tamaulipas, Mocorito, Sinaloa, and Ciudad Juárez, Chihuahua.[59] In most cases the targets were relatively small-scale heroin, amphetamines, and barbiturates smugglers.

THE LATE 1950S AND EARLY 1960S: OUTBREAK OF FBN UNDERCOVER OPERATIONS IN MEXICO

It is possible to identify at least three differences between the antidrug operations that took place in the 1940s and the ones that took place from 1959 onwards. First, while in the 1940s the Customs Bureau acted as the leading entity in law enforcement operations, by the late 1950s this role was assumed by the FBN. The second difference is that Anslinger stopped playing a leading role in planning FBN operations (he retired in 1962 from his role as commissioner of narcotics). Most of the operations carried out from the late 1950s and later were designed by the district supervisors of two regional offices in the Southwest: number 10, which comprised the states of Texas, Louisiana, and Mississippi, with headquarters in Dallas; and number 14, which comprised the states of California, Arizona, and Nevada, with headquarters in San Francisco. Most of the agents that participated in undercover operations in Mexico were attached to either of these two offices. The third difference is the number of operations. While trips to Mexico were sporadic in the 1940s, by May 1960 Henry L. Giordano, deputy commissioner of narcotics, conceded that agents "were almost daily going into Mexico."[60] Agent Howard Chappell admitted in an interview to have undertaken "two dozen of cases" from 1956 to 1961.[61] In a meeting with other law enforcement officials, agent Daniel Casey spoke about forty-seven cases and the arrest of seventy-eight defendants carried out by FBN undercover agents and Mexican federal authorities between 1959 and 1962.[62] The third difference is related to the nature of the drug trafficking, its size, and types of seizures. Cocaine appears as a relevant drug (although not comparable with its later boom in the 1980s) and the raw opium almost disappeared and was replaced by heroin. As cocaine trafficking appeared, airports started to figure as one of the main places for joint operations between FBN officials and Mexican authorities.

Some things remained the same. The agents were not better prepared than before. While some of the agents attached to the regional offices in California and Texas had some knowledge of Mexico and spoke Spanish, most of them had no special training for operating overseas. Joseph Arpaio—the (in)famous Sheriff of Maricopa County, Arizona—remembers how he got to Turkey to work as an FBN undercover agent in the early 1960s: "The bureau sent me. The bureau put me on a plane, dropped me off in Istanbul, and told me to get to work. Good luck, good-bye, keep in touch, and get the job done."[63] As Arpaio recognized, he "wasn't provided with training or equipment or education or contacts."[64] The same holds true for many agents that traveled to Mexico and were expected to engage in undercover operations.

As before, the issue of dealing with the media remained. It was a general practice of the FBN to use magazines and crime publications to promote the success stories of their agents overseas.[65] While the cases against some suspected drug traffickers received favorable comments in the U.S. media, the Mexican federal government was uncomfortable with their promotion. On several occasions, representatives of the Mexican government communicated their concerns to the FBN about the many journalistic reports that "clearly indicated that American agents had actively participated in setting up the cases in Mexico." The interpretation of the FBN was that the Mexican government's desire was to "alleviate criticism by left wing or enthusiastic nationalists."[66]

U.S. agencies tried to be cautious, working only with persons they trusted. As in the 1940s, the presence of U.S. agents was still unregulated: it was neither allowed nor entirely prohibited. Therefore, they depended heavily on unwilling local police forces with little incentives to cooperate with the agents.

Despite all this, an informal arrangement existed, and the FBN made genuine efforts to comply with some minimal unspoken rules: their agents would not venture into the countryside without the presence of local officers; they updated their counterparts about their informants and movements; they were forbidden from carrying firearms (this rule was broken more often than others): and they could not testify in judicial trials. Despite the limited rights to do actual policing, they tried to stretch their scope of activity as much as possible by employing special employees, bribing police officials, and constructing strong links among high-ranking Mexican authorities.

As the following pages will show, the cooperation with specific allies brought good results. In the late 1950s, the FBN benefited from a key contact in northern Mexico: José Antonio Farías, the chief of the Coahuila Judicial Police. Together with him and the state policemen under his command, agents of the FBN office in Texas collaborated in many undercover operations in Piedras Negras and surroundings. The most prominent one took place on December 1, 1959, and was aimed at Emilio Rosas and Adolfo Jiménez, who according to FBN reports were suppliers of 90 percent of the heroin in San Antonio, Texas, over the period from 1957 to 1959.[67] Other cases followed. For instance, on March 7, 1960, Francisco Salinas Domínguez was arrested in Piedras Negras; Salinas was detained while he attempted to deliver twenty-five grams of heroin to an FBN agent and an SE. A third case was the arrest in Saltillo of Alejo Castro Flores on July 1, 1960. According to an internal report, he was arrested when he was about to deliver "approximately" one kilo of heroin to undercover agents. There was also the arrest of Salvador Abraham Pérez and his group on July 31, 1960, as he delivered twenty-five grams of heroin to an undercover agent before getting busted by the Coahuila State Police, and finally there was the arrest of José Hernández Rodríguez, aka "Charly Fernando," in Piedras Negras on January 18, 1961. He was arrested when he was about to deliver twenty grams of heroin to an FBN undercover agent.[68]

On February 4, 1960, in Nuevo Laredo, agents of the Mexican federal police and FBN agents John A. Frost and J. Kelly (both in an undercover capacity) failed in an attempt to arrest Octavio Barberena and El Gordo, his accomplice. Barbarena was a nightclub owner in Nuevo Laredo and was assumed to be an important source for heroin consumed in Houston, Texas. The suspected traffickers escaped and opened fire on the FBN agents. According to FBN accounts, a Mexican officer, Rafael García Tello, was critically wounded while protecting one of the FBN agents.[69] Local newspapers reported the failed arrest but kept quiet about the participation of U.S. agents in the case. The heroism of García Tello was well-rewarded by the U.S. authorities. The Mexican officer was visited at the hospital by U.S. ambassador to Mexico, Robert C. Hill, received an official commendation from H. J. Anslinger, and was invited to have special training at the Treasury Department Training School.[70] He remained a key contact of the FBN in Mexico as he was appointed chief federal narcotics agent in Ciudad Juárez in 1962, where he conducted major seizures of marijuana and opium.[71]

Not all undercover operations took place along the U.S.-Mexican border. FBN agents went as far as to Mexico City to establish cases against major drug traffickers. The most famous operation was the one developed against Jorge Asaf y Bala ("The Al Capone of the Mexican underworld") and Salvador Segundo Escabi in November of 1959, both of them paradigmatic cases of a new class of international cocaine and heroin traffickers who began to use Mexico as a safe house en route to the United States in the late 1950s and early 1960s.[72] Unlike other cases developed by agents attached to FBN offices in California or Texas, this one was set up by Reynaldo Maduro and James Attie, agents attached to different office districts: New York and Chicago.

The investigation started in mid-1959 New York when agent Maduro (of Puerto Rican descent) opened a case against the trafficker Salvador Escabi (also of Puerto Rican descent). According to an informant, Escabi had just arrived in town with a 250-pound supply of marijuana. While working undercover, Maduro met Escabi and offered to buy some of his supply. He was surprised to see that Escabi was not only prepared to sell marijuana, but also cocaine. The delivery of cocaine, however, would have to be made in Mexico City. Thus, in the hope of getting a bigger case, instead of arresting Escabi for trafficking marijuana, Maduro arranged a meeting with Escabi and his source of supply, Jorge Asaf y Bala, a few weeks later in Mexico City. In Mexico City, Maduro learned that his colleague from the FBN Chicago office, James Attie, was also in Mexico working on a pan-American network of cocaine traffickers.[73] Approached by Maduro, Attie became involved in the Escabi-Asaf case. Maduro also secured the collaboration of the director of the Judicial Federal Police, Manuel Suárez Domínguez (years later indicted as a major trafficker), and Óscar Rabasa (Mexican representative at the Commission of Narcotic Drugs). Suárez and Rabasa agreed that due to the "Arabic background" of Attie, "he could be of help to them in marking cases against three persons of Arab extractions."[74] On November 24, 1959, Maduro and Attie made the arrangements for the delivery of three kilograms of heroin (and not cocaine as promised by Escabi in New York) to a room at the Emporio Hotel in Mexico

City, where Asaf y Bala and Escabi were finally arrested by the Mexican federal police. Although the Mexican press covered the arrest of both traffickers, the participation of the U.S. agents was not noted.[75]

Days after the arrest, Maduro and Attie visited Mexican attorney general Óscar Treviño Rios. According to Attie, a grateful Treviño affirmed his desire to work closer with the United States in the fight against narcotics and stated that in case of emergency "there was no need for exchange of official letters [. . .] a telephone call from the Commissioner [Anslinger], or a telegram would be sufficient."[76] As a sign of good will, one of the Mexican officials who had collaborated with Maduro and Attie in the arrest was invited to attend a six-week program at the Treasury Department's Law Enforcement Officer Training School.[77] The case got a twist some weeks later, however, when in January 1960 *Life* magazine published an accurate, if highly stylized, article on the Asaf-Escabi arrest, in which the participation of Maduro and Attie was highlighted.[78]

Asaf y Bala and Escabi were sentenced to serve eight and seven years in prison, but their attorneys appealed the conviction on the grounds of entrapment.[79] A year and a half after the undercover operation in the Hotel Emporio, Asaf and Escabi were let out by a federal judge. The case illustrates how purchases of narcotics by U.S. law enforcement officers were not always rewarded with convictions, as expected by U.S. agencies.

Another case with important repercussions took place in January 1961 when agents of the PJF arrested Baldemar Soto in Mexicali. According to FBN reports, Soto was the "top narcotics pusher" of that city and the principal distributor of heroin manufactured in the laboratory of Telesforo Parra López, a trafficker who, according to an FBN agent, "passed out the word that he will give out any sum of money for any agent that is killed who is attempting to make any purchase from him or trying to make an arrest."[80]

What is more, according to FBN reports, Soto was well-acquainted with Eligio Esquivel Méndez, governor of Baja California. It could have been just one of many cases completed by Mexican authorities in the surroundings of Mexicali at the time, but the case made it into the newspapers of Mexicali and Tijuana when witnesses began to report that U.S. agents accompanied PJF officers in the arrest of Soto. According to most versions, "approximately seven United States agents assisted [. . .] the Mexican Federal Police in the arrest of Soto González and that those agents were observed by Mexican citizens to have been heavily armed."[81] Although the witnesses were unable to tell if the agents were from the FBI, the Customs Bureau, or the FBN, editorials and local politicians began to complain about what they interpreted as a "clear violation of Mexican sovereignty."[82]

The arrest of Baldemar Soto was planned by FBN agents from Districts 14 and 10 in cooperation with Amador Toca Cangas, federal district attorney of the state of Baja California. It was not the first one. After the appointment of Toca Cangas in late 1950s, successful joint operations had been made in the Tijuana-Mexicali area through the cooperative efforts of Toca Cangas, the PJF, and the FBN.[83] In only one month, Toca Cangas led the investigation and arrest of five different (but probably intertwined) smuggling networks in that area. Such records made him "without a doubt the finest Federal Prosecutor" the FBN ever had in Tijuana.[84]

Official records of the FBN only admit the technical assistance of the agency in the investigation. The bureau's reports, however, acknowledge the direct participation of FBN officials under the supervision of agent Howard Chappell as undercover operatives with the purpose of generating arrests. Through their internal correspondence we know, for example, that "the alertness" of FBN agent Kenneth W. Conant restrained Soto "from killing a Mexican agent," that Conant "returned to Los Angeles for a few days rest and recuperation," and that Richard D. Rock, "the only other Spanish-speaking agent" the agency had in Los Angeles, "was sent down to Tijuana to work with Federal Prosecutor Toca."[85] The documents also show that Conant could speak Spanish "well enough" and that "he [could] pass for a Mexican so that no one would realize that an American [was] present at an arrest."[86]

In its official response the FBN only admitted to cooperating with Toca Cangas by providing him with leads and information previously gathered in the United States. But as agent Howard W. Chappell recognized in an internal memo, "This is, of course, a very general description of our participation and one which I am sure the officials at Mexicali would accept without requiring any detail as to the full extent to which we have in the past participated in cases made in Mexico."[87]

Unfortunately for the FBN, the explanation did not satisfy two local politicians, who demanded that the Mexican attorney general (PGR) clarify the presence of U.S. law enforcement agents in Mexico. Governor Esquivel went to the effort of traveling to Mexico City to discuss the issue with Oscar Treviño Ríos, Mexico's deputy attorney general. According to FBN sources, Esquivel demanded to get prosecutor Toca Cangas out of Tijuana and Mexicali.[88] According to another FBN report, the Mexican Immigration Office also complained about the presence of American agents in Mexico with the Mexican Ministry of the Interior (Secretaría de Gobernación).[89] Even Soto's attorney issued a statement to the Mexicali press stating that he was preparing a complaint addressed to Washington DC "concerning the activity of American Officers in Baja California."[90]

The U.S. consul in Mexicali was unaware that Soto had been arrested until a story about it was published in Mexico City newspapers, nor had he been notified of the FBN agent's participation in the operation.[91] The U.S. consul in Tijuana had more information than the one in Mexicali but expressed his concerns about the "large enough" number of local and federal United States law enforcement and investigative officials regularly visiting the area. In the interpretation of the Consulate they were "causing resentment on the part of unreasonably nationalistic Mexican newsmen, who are thereby conditioned to pick up and overplay rash accusations.[92] It was the opinion of the Consulate that the unfavorable publicity was making it difficult "if not impossible" to convince Mexican officials to cooperate with them.[93] The truth is that Soto's case had repercussions for other U.S. agencies as well as for the Mexican attorney general. In the weeks after the arrest, sheriff's officers from Imperial County (across the border from Mexicali) had been turned back at the border and not been permitted to cross. Customs agents also encountered difficulties: they were required to fill out Mexican forms when they attempted to cross into Mexicali, and they were "followed around and observed by Mexican Officials."[94] Simultaneously the Mexican attorney general confessed to the senior Customs representative in Mexico City that they had had no advance notice that an investigation was taking place against Baldemar Soto. According to this version "the case had been made in Mexicali and had been made without the approval of the Attorney General."[95]

For various reasons, then, many actors were displeased with the participation of FBN agents in seizures and arrests of drug traffickers. These actors—Soto's attorney, the Mexican press, the U.S. Customs Bureau, the consulates on the border, the Mexican attorney general, the Mexican Immigration Office, Baja California politicians, and the Mexicali local police—had nothing in common apart from their opposition to the status quo.

To find a solution to a problem that was becoming increasingly important, the Mexican attorney general, Fernando López Arias, flew to Washington DC in May of 1961 to negotiate the terms under which his agents were supposed to work in Mexico with high-ranking Treasury Department officials and representatives of the FBN and the Bureau of Customs. An internal memorandum written by Henry L. Giordano sheds some light about what was agreed in that meeting. According to his account, López Arias reminded the attendees that buy cases were considered entrapment by the Mexican courts. It was agreed that in the future "no buy cases will be made in Mexico," "no U.S. Narcotic agents will be permitted to testify in Mexican Courts," and that "in all cases developed in Mexico in which an undercover agent or an informant negotiates with a trafficker for delivery of narcotics, the trafficker is to be arrested in possession of the narcotics before he can make [the] delivery to the undercover agent or to the informant."[96] A set of guidelines was discussed during the following months by Mexican deputy attorney general Treviño Rios and officials of the Treasury Department. The most important points were the following: U.S. narcotics agents would only be allowed to work in Mexico when their assistance was requested by the attorney general; while working in Mexico, they would have to be under the direction and supervision of the Federal Judicial Police or another federal agency of the government; they would be allowed to work in an undercover capacity, and in such a capacity negotiate the delivery of narcotic drugs from a trafficker, provided that no funds would be advanced to the trafficker and that arrangements would be made for the trafficker to be arrested by Mexican police officers prior to the consummation of the delivery; finally, under no circumstances would U.S. officers leak any information concerning their participation in specific cases developed in Mexico to the newspapers. Even though these guidelines were not published in a final document—neither in the compilation of narcotics agreements signed by the Mexican attorney general nor in the Treasury Department papers—some drafts of a "statement of intent between Mexico and the United States" are to be found in the FBN archive.[97]

The complications caused by the Soto case did not discourage FBN agents from contining to make cases in Mexicali. Only days after the detention of Baldemar Soto in January, FBN agent Jayme R. Licuanan was preparing to participate in an undercover operation against Salomón Sandez "Tutu" and his distributors.[98] He worked on that case at least until March of 1961.[99]

Agent Conant stayed in Mexico as a "non-participating officer" "at least for the record" and was in charge of providing Toca Cangas with money and vehicles.[100] On January 21, 1961, agents Chappell and Conant worked with Toca Cangas in an attempt to apprehend Miguel Barrágan "Big Mike," a heroin trafficker active since the early 1950s in Tijuana and Mexicali.[101] On January 22, Conant provided "a flash roll and vehicles used by the Mexican Federal Authorities in Mexicali to arrest José Luis Chin for the sale of 3 ounces of heroin."[102] On February 26, Conant and another agent called Jackson met Toca Cangas at his Tijuana office to discuss arrangements for a narcotics purchase that same day. The operation was frustrated when a reporter from *El Veredicto*, a small Tijuana newspaper, took pictures of agent Jackson driving a car in the streets of Mexicali after the meeting. Jackson noticed the action of the paparazzo and pursued the reporter until catching him a few blocks further. Irritated by the situation, Jackson "tried to have the man arrested or at least have the film seized."[103] Fortunately, a Mexican agent was there to remind Jackson how unrealistic his idea was. Some days later, a confidential informant (a former state narcotics agent) told Jackson and Conant that he had seen some of the pictures taken by the reporter. He stated that "Jackson was wearing black gloves and dressed in black shirt and pants." What is more, the informant stated that he knew "what model of car, the color of each and the brand of each car driven by the agents" was.[104] The pictures were not published in any newspaper, but that only amplified the fear that the reporter might have sold the pictures to local traffickers. This could have been the reason why from February 24 through March 3 so many undercover operations were unsuccessful in the Tijuana-Mexicali area. That week, they had tried "at least one, sometimes two or three each day with no results."[105] Drawing on these considerations, the person responsible for the collaboration with Toca Cangas, Howard Chappell, decided that Jackson would stay out of Mexico until further notice and that Conant would stay as a liaison agent with the Mexican authorities but would refrain from attempting any undercover purchases along the Mexican-California border.[106] It was better to "slow down [the] investigations a little bit and to catch up on the status of numerous cases already completed," that is, "to determine what action has been taken by Mexican Federal Courts, what sentences have been imposed.[107] As he would find out several months later, most accused traffickers had acquired freedom only months after their arrest. Everyone arrested and classified by the FBN as a major violator had been released.[108] FBN officers in the Dallas office continued working undercover in collaboration with the Coahuila State Police as they had been doing since 1959. In January 1961 they were already initiating a new investigation against two suspected traffickers in Piedras Negras.[109] In the same city, agents of that district worked undercover in the case against Emilio Maldonado Rosas in

February of 1963, and in the case against José Hernández, who was arrested in January of 1962.[110]

THE VICTORY OF THE FEDERAL BUREAU OF NARCOTICS OVER THE CUSTOMS BUREAU

Anslinger and his district supervisors pressured the U.S. Congress to change the balance of power between the Customs Bureau and the FBN in Mexico. In his testimony before a congressional committee in late 1959, George H. White stated that the Mexicans were doing their part of the job, but they were not receiving appropriate assistance from the FBN "because the Bureau of Customs considered it to be their prerogative to work in Latin America." If, White added, "we were able to work in Mexico in the same fashion that we do in Europe and the Middle East the combined efforts of the Mexican and American authorities would, undoubtedly, result in a drastic reduction in the narcotic problem."[111]

It was not easy to convince the U.S. Congress to change the 1934 arrangement that gave the Customs Bureau jurisdiction over narcotics offenses in Mexico. It is true that the FBN had good standing among members of Congress, but the Customs Bureau had even more legislative influence due to the many policy areas in which the bureau was present. As stated recently by a scholar, "Customs simply had more buttons to push."[112]

Despite the Customs Bureau's advantageous position, the FBN triumphed. A first directive issued in January 1960 allowed the FBN to pursue some police cases in Mexico if it seemed that the investigation might result in an important conspiracy.[113] That same year, Anslinger suggested to Óscar Rabasa the assignment of an FBN agent in Mexico City. The role of this agent, as proposed by Anslinger, was to work with Mexican officers in narcotics investigations "through the undercover approach which has proved so successful."[114] In a formal letter addressed to the State Department, Anslinger stated that the agent would be an addition to Customs representatives already working in Mexico and Monterrey.[115] In 1962, the Treasury Department recommended Congress that the FBN should assume responsibility for all narcotics enforcement work in foreign countries, including Mexico.[116]

Some months later, in February of 1963, the FBN inaugurated its District 18 headquarters office with authority over Mexico, Central America, and South America. Located in Mexico City, the official purpose of the office was twofold:

to prevent the traffic of drugs to the United States and to assist local police officials in investigation duties. Two agents were assigned to the Mexico office: William Durkin and Reynaldo Maduro, who had worked on the Asaf y Bala case a few years earlier. The office was assigned an annual budget of $23,000 (including salary and operating expenses). Former Customs officers in Mexico, Steve Minas and Jesus M. Martínez, were offered a job with the FBN, which they rejected, probably as an act of bureaucratic loyalty.[117] As customary for previous Treasury representatives in Mexico City, Durkin assumed administrative and investigative responsibilities. In addition to other responsibilities, he took charge of the day-to-day management of the Narcotic Control Project Mexico, the first package of narcotics assistance to Mexico, through which almost $500,000 was invested in helicopters, light weapons, and grenade launchers.[118] Durkin and Maduro, as well as another agent stationed in Monterrey, Richard D. Rock, also participated in undercover operations in various areas of the country, including Mexico City, Guerrero, Jalisco, and other cities along the border.

In February of 1968, the Johnson administration redefined the field of drug policy in the United States. The administration decided to merge the FBN and the Bureau of Drug Abuse Control (BDAC), an entity created in 1966, into the Bureau of Narcotics and Dangerous Drugs (BNDD). Even though most former FBN agents stayed in the BNDD, they suddenly lost much of their independence and organizational culture. What is more, the State Department took the issue of narcotics more seriously and stopped the "independent and free-wheeling approach towards counter-narcotic operations" with some success.[119] New guidelines were established, and a more centralized approach was imposed. But BNDD narcotics agents—and later DEA ones—remained key actors in the U.S.-Mexican relations with respect to narcotics. The War on Drugs had formally begun.

NOTES

1. In this chapter U.S. narcotics agents will be defined as any U.S. law enforcement official at the local, state, or federal level involved with drug laws, notwithstanding if they had any special training in drug investigations.

2. Paul Gootenberg, "The 'Pre-Colombian' Era of Drug Trafficking in the Americas: Cocaine, 1945–1965," *The Americas* 64, no. 2 (2007): 134. The absence of good archival sources in Mexico for this topic (records of the regional offices of the Federal Mexican Police, records of local and state law enforcement agencies, internal files of the Mexican attorney general, etc.) makes the study of U.S. narcotics agents even more challenging.

3. *New York Times*, February 26, 1928.

4. PGR Relación México-E.U., vol. IV.1, J. Vasquez Schiaffino to U.S. Chargé d'affaires, 2/10/1930.

5. William Walker, *Drug Control in the Americas* (Albuquerque: University of New Mexico Press, 1981), 164.

6. Walker, *Drug Control*, 164.

7. National Archives and Record Administration (NARA), Record Group (RG) 170, box 160, file 1, Joseph A. Manning to Harry J. Anslinger, 4/17/1936.

8. *The Evening News*, April 8, 1937.

9. NARA, RG170, box 22, file 3, Joseph L. V. Treglia to H. N. Gillman, 4/23/1936.

10. NARA, RG170, box 22, file 1, Joseph A. Manning to Harry J. Anslinger, 8/26/1936.

11. NARA, RG170, box 22, file 1, Joseph A. Manning to Harry J. Anslinger, 9/9/1936.

12. Elaine Carey, *Women Drug Traffickers: Mules, Bosses, and Organized Crime* (Albuquerque: University of New Mexico Press, 2014), 82.

13. For a (very narrative) biography of Scharff, see Garland Roark, *The Coin of Contraband: The True History of United States Customs Investigator Al Scharff* (Garden City, NY: Doubleday Company, 1964).

14. *Committee on the Judiciary. Senate Subcommittee on Narcotics, "Illicit Narcotics Traffic. Part 7: Austin, Dallas, Fort Worth, Houston, and San Antonio, Texas (Hearings Published),"* 8/22/1955, 2943, HRG-1955-SJS-0067, Congressional Publications.

15. Roark, *The Coin*, chaps. II, III, and IV.

16. Roark, *The Coin*, 304.

17. Roark, *The Coin*, 323, 329.

18. *Honolulu Star-Bulletin*, February 13, 1937.

19. Roark, *The Coin*, 329.

20. *Weekly News Sheet*, October 16, 1936.

21. NARA, RG170, box 22, file 3, Carroll Gray to Irey, 4/18/1938.

22. Roark, *The Coin*, 351–52.

23. Roark, *The Coin*, 356.

24. NARA, RG170, box 22, file 4, Alvin F. Scharff to Deputy Commissioner of Customs Gorman, 4/19/1938.

25. NARA, RG170, box 22, file 3, Carroll Gray to Irey, 4/18/1938.

26. NARA, RG170, box 22, file 3, Carroll Gray to Irey, 4/18/1938.

27. NARA, RG170, box 22, file 4, Leónides Andreu Almazán to Harry J. Anslinger, 4/21/1938.

28. *El Universal*, April 22, 1938.

29. *North-China Herald and Supreme Court & Consular Gazette* (1870–1941), August 2, 1938.

30. NARA, RG170, box 22, file 6, S. J. Kennedy, 4/3/1944, 4/5/1944.

31. NARA, RG170, box 22, file 6, S. J. Kennedy, 4/3/1944, 4/5/1944.

32. For the account of another agent in 1940, see NARA, RG170, box 22, file 2, Philip M. Caldwell, "Memorandum," 3/27/1940.

33. NARA, RG170, box 22, file 7, Salvador Peña to Commissioner of Customs, 6/18/1945.

34. NARA, RG170, box 22, file 7, Demetrio Mayoral Pardo to the Minister of Health, 4/12/1945.

35. *Hearing before the Subcommittee to Investigate Juvenile Delinquency of the Committee on the Judiciary, United States Senate, Ninety-Fifth Congress, Second Session, February 10, 1978*, testimony of Mathea Falco, director for internal narcotic control (1978), 116.

36. United Nations Office on Drugs and Crime Regional Office for South Asia, *Standard Operating Procedures on Precursor Chemical Control* (Vienna: UNODC, 2010), 40.

37. NARA, RG170, box 22, file 7, J. P. Scheehan to San Francisco California Supervising Customs Agent, 2/25/1946.

38. Douglas Valentine, *The Strength of the Wolf: The Secret History of America's War on Drugs* (New York: Verso Books, 2004), 145.

39. For a discussion on the role of these actors in policing activities, see Gustavo Fondevila, "Controlling the Madrinas: The Police Informer Management and Control System in Mexico," *Police Journal* 86 (2013): 116–42.

40. Rebecca Carroll, "Under the Influence: Harry Anslinger's Role in Shaping America's Drug Policy," in *Federal Drug Control Policy: The Evolution of Policy and Practice*, ed. Jonathan Erlan and Joseph Spillane (New York: Haworth Press, 2004), 61–99.

41. Harry Anslinger and Will Oursler, *The Murderers: The Story of the Narcotic Gangs* (New York: Farrar, Straus and Cudahy, 1962).

42. NARA, RG170, box 160, file 2, Howard W. Chappell to George W. White, 3/6/1961.

43. U.S. Bureau of Narcotics, *Traffic in Opium and Other Dangerous Drugs: For the Year Ended December 31, 1944* (Washington DC: Government Printing Office, 1945), 21–23.

44. U.S. Bureau of Narcotics, *Traffic 1944*, 23.

45. NARA, RG170, box 22, file 6, Rae V. Vader to Supervising Customs Agent, 11/9/1944.

46. NARA, RG170, box 22, file 6, T. S. Simpson to Commissioner of Customs, 10/16/1944.

47. NARA, RG170, box 22, file 7, Earl T. Crain to Ambassador Messersmith, 1/9/1946.

48. U.S. Bureau of Narcotics, *Traffic 1944*, 24.

49. NARA, RG170, box 22, file 7, "Estadística de La Labor Desarrollada," 5/31/1955.

50. Archivo del Distrito Federal, Jefatura de Policía, Servicio Secreto, Expediente N/522/7205, Silvestre Fernández, 301/1952.

51. Ryan Gingeras, *Heroin, Organized Crime, and the Making of Modern Turkey* (Oxford: Oxford University Press, 2014), 181.

52. See also Morris, chapter 13 in this volume. For a critique, see Oswaldo Zavala, *Los Cárteles No Existen: Narcotráfico y Cultura en México* (Mexico City: Malpaso, 2018).

53. Carey, *Women*, 128–29.

54. John J. Cochran, "The Bureau of Narcotics: The Country Has Reason to Appreciate the Outstanding Work of Hon. H. J. Anslinger and His Organization," in *Congressional Record Bound*, 1943, A523–24.

55. NARA, RG170, box 22, file 5, Customs Agent T. S. Simpson to Commissioner of Customs, 11/29/1943.

56. NARA, RG170, box 22, file 7, Terry A. Talent to Harry J. Anslinger, 11/15/1946.

57. Stanford University, Department of Special Collections and University Archives, George White Papers, box 1, file 10, Harry J. Anslinger to Francisco González de la Vega, 11/17/1948.

58. Gingeras, *Heroin*.

59. For Nuevo León, see *Committee on the Judiciary. Senate Subcommittee to Investigate Juvenile Delinquency in the U.S, "Juvenile Delinquency. Part 12: Narcotic and Dangerous Drug Abuse in the State of California (Hearings Published),"* 8/6/1962, 2540, HRG-1962-SJS-0037, Congressional Publications; for Tamualipas, see NARA, RG170, box 161, file 2, Ernest M. Gentry to Harry J. Anslinger, 8/25/1952; for Sinaloa, see NARA, RG161, file 2, T. S. Simpson to The Commissioner of Customs, 1/20/1954; *Subcommittee to Investigate Juvenile Delinquency in the U.S, "Juvenile Delinquency. Part 12: Narcotic and Dangerous Drug Abuse in the State of California (Hearings Published),"* 2536.

60. NARA, RG170, box 161, file 4, Henry L. Giordano to Deputy Commissioner of Customs, 3/5/1960.

61. Valentine, *The Strength*, 205.

62. *Subcommittee To Investigate Juvenile Delinquency in the U.S, "Juvenile Delinquency. Part 12: Narcotic and Dangerous Drug Abuse in the State of California (Hearings Published),"* 2984.

63. Joe Arpaio and Len Sherman, *Joe's Law: America's Toughest Sheriff Takes on Illegal Immigration, Drugs, and Everything Else That Threatens America* (New York: Summit Publishing Group, 1996), 153.

64. Arpaio and Sherman, *Joe's Law*, 153.

65. Matthew R. Pembleton, "The Voice of the Bureau: How Frederic Sondern and the Bureau of Narcotics Crafted a Drug War and Shaped Popular Understanding of Drugs, Addiction, and Organized Crime in the 1950s," *Journal of American Culture* 38, no. 2 (2015): 113–29.

66. NARA, RG170, box 161, file 4, Howard W. Chappell to George H. White, 6/9/1960.

67. NARA, RG170, box 161, file 4, Harry J. Anslinger to Óscar Rabasa, 10/12/1959.

68. For some of this cases, see NARA, RG170, box 160, file 2, Ernest M. Gentry to Harry J. Anslinger, 7/6/1962.

69. U.S. Bureau of Narcotics, *Traffic in Opium and Other Dangerous Drugs: For the Year Ended December 31, 1959* (Washington DC: Government Printing Office, 1960), 20.

70. *Laredo Times*, February 22, 1960, sec. 1.

71. *El Paso Times*, July 31, 1962.

72. Gootenberg, "The 'Pre-Colombian,'" 159–60.

73. NARA, RG170, box 161, file 4, James Attie to George Belk, 12/2/1959.

74. NARA, RG170, box 161, file 4, James Attie to George Belk, 1/12/1959.

75. For example, *El Siglo de Torreón*, November 29, 1959.

76. NARA, RG170, box 161, file 4, James Attie to George Belk, 12/2/1959.

77. NARA, RG170, box 161, file 4, O'Carroll to Héctor Hernández Tello, 16/12/1959.

78. *Life*, January 15, 1960, 87–98.

79. NARA, RG170, box 160, file 2, Benjamin S. White Jr. to The Commissioner of Customs, 4/13/1961.

80. About Soto see NARA, RG170, box 160, file 2, Edgar Hoover to Department of State Office of Security, 1/17/1961; about Parra López, see *Committee on the Judiciary, Senate Subcommittee to Investigate Juvenile Delinquency in the U.S, "Juvenile Delinquency. Part 11: Illegal Narcotics Traffic and Its Effect on Juvenile and Young Adult Criminality,"* 5/9/1962, 2687, HRG-1962-SJS-0036, Congressional Publications.

81. NARA, RG170, box 160, file 2, Edgar Hoover to Department of State Office of Security, 1/17/1961.

82. NARA, RG170, box 160, file 2, Edgar Hoover to Department of State Office of Security, 1/17/1961.

83. NARA, RG170, box 160, file 2, Harry J. Anslinger to Gilmore Flues, 1/16/1961.

84. NARA, RG170, box 160, file 2, Howard W. Chappell, 1/20/1961.

85. NARA, RG170, box 160, file 2, Wayland L. Speer to Harry J. Anslinger, 1/25/1961.

86. Chappell, "Developments in Cooperation with Mexican Federal Officials, Memorandum Report, Bureau of Narcotics, District Num. 14."

87. NARA, RG170, box 160, file 2, Howard W. Chappell to George W. White, 1/27/1961.

88. NARA, RG170, box 161, file 5, Wayland L. Speer to Harry J. Anslinger, "Operation in Mexico: Lower California," 1/18/1961.

89. NARA, RG170, box 160, file 2, Howard W. Chappell, "Status 14-Mex-17," 1/23/1961.

90. NARA, RG170, box 160, file 2, Chappell to White, 1/27/1961.

91. NARA, RG170, box 160, file 2, Benjamin S. White Jr. to the Commissioner of Customs, 1/19/1961.

92. NARA, RG170, box 160, file 2, Joseph A. Cicala to the Department of State, 2/6/1971.

93. NARA, RG170, box 160, file 2, Joseph A. Cicala to the Department of State, 2/6/1971.

94. NARA, RG170, box 160, file 2, Howard W. Chappell, "Status 14-Mex-17," 1/27/1961.

95. NARA, RG170, box 160, file 2, White Jr. to the Commissioner of Customs, 1/19/1961.

96. NARA, RG170, box 161, file 5, Henry L. Giordano to District Supervisors, 5/23/1961.

97. NARA, RG170, box 160, file 2, Edwin F. Rains to Carl DeBaggio, 9/26/1961.

98. Chappell, "Developments in Cooperation with Mexican Federal Officials, Memorandum Report, Bureau of Narcotics, District Num. 14."

99. NARA, RG170, box 160, file 2, Jaiyme R. Licuanan, "Memorandum Report," 3/3/1961.

100. Chappell, "Developments in Cooperation with Mexican Federal Officials, Memorandum Report, Bureau of Narcotics, District Num. 14."

101. *Committee on the Judiciary, Senate Subcommittee on Narcotics, "Illicit Narcotics Traffic. Part 8: San Francisco and Los Angeles, California (Hearings Published),"* 11/14/1955, 3762–63, HRG-1955-SJS-0068, Congressional Publications. See Smith and Pansters, chapter 6 in this volume.

102. NARA, RG170, box 160, file 2, Chappell to White, 1/27/1961.

103. NARA, RG170, box 160, file 2, Kenneth W. Conant, "Memorandum Report."

104. NARA, RG170, box 160, file 2, Kenneth W. Conant, "Memorandum Report."

105. NARA, RG170, box 160, file 2, Kenneth W. Conant, "Memorandum Report."

106. NARA, RG170, box 160, file 2, Howard W. Chappell to George W. White, "Mexican Cooperation," 3/6/1961.

107. NARA, RG170, box 160, file 2, Howard W. Chappell to George W. White, "Mexican Cooperation," 3/6/1961.

108. NARA, RG170, box 160, file 2, John A. Trainor to FBN District Supervisor George H. White, 6/7/1962.

109. NARA, RG170, box 160, file 2, White Jr. to the Commissioner of Customs, 1/19/1961.

110. For both cases, see *Committee on Government Operations, Senate Permanent Subcommittee on Investigations, "Organized Crime and Illicit Traffic in Narcotics, Part 3 (Hearings Published),"* 10/29/1963, HRG-1963-OPS-0033, Congressional Publications.

111. NARA, RG170, box 161, file 4, George H. White to Harry J. Anslinger, 12/2/1959.

112. Tony Payan, *Cops, Soldiers and Diplomats: Explaining Agency Behavior in the War on Drugs* (Lanham, MD: Lexington Books, 2006), 69.

113. NARA, RG170, box 49, file 3, Gilmore Flues, "Investigative Jurisdiction," 1/15/1960.

114. NARA, RG170, box 161, file 4, Harry J. Anslinger to Óscar Rabasa, 3/14/1960.

115. NARA, RG170, box 161, file 4, Harry J. Anslinger to OES Department of State Elwyn F. Chase, 3/14/1960.

116. NARA, RG170, box 49, file 3, James A. Reed, "Consolidation of Treasury Foreign Enforcement Program," 7/13/1962.

117. NARA, RG170, box 49, file 3, Jesús Martínez to C. A. Emerick, 7/1/1962.

118. NARA, RG170, box 160, file 3, Charles Siragusa to William J. Durkin, 2/7/1963; NARA, RG170, box 160, file 3, William J. Durkin to Henry L. Giordano, 3/21/1963.

119. Gingeras, *Heroin*, 184.

8

"Rayando la Bola, Cortando la Rama"
The Production of Opium and Marijuana in Sinaloa, 1940–ca. 1975

JUAN ANTONIO FERNÁNDEZ VELÁZQUEZ

Sinaloa has become synonymous with the drug trade. Now its reputation for narcotics overshadows previous reputations for mining wealth and agricultural production. During the 1970s the state was the birthplace of narcocorridos. And the capital, Culiacán, birthed the world's only shrine to a patron saint of drug traffickers.[1] Now the state has a cartel named after it. Many of Mexico's most notorious traffickers from the Guadalajara Cartel trio of Miguel Angel Félix Gallardo, Rafael Caro Quintero, and Ernesto Fonseca Carrillo to contemporary kingpins like Joaquin "el Chapo" Guzmán Loera and Ismael "el Mayo" Zambada come from the state.[2]

Yet there is more to Sinaloa's drug production than just the headlines and the attention-grabbing culture. The state's inhabitants have been growing, processing, and transporting narcotics in bulk since the early 1940s. To do so they have adapted drug trafficking into the rhythms of everyday life and the structures of social relations. It is these social relations that form the basis of this chapter.

By employing evidence found in oral testimonies, judicial cases, and newspaper reports, it is possible to piece together two interlinking characteristics of these social relations. In many ways, the trades in both opium and marijuana have been organized in a hierarchical fashion. They have aped traditional commercial relations. Traffickers have employed intermediaries to buy bulk narcotics from growers. Profits have been organized accordingly. Traffickers and intermediaries have always earned substantially more than drug growers.

Yet at the same time, drug trafficking in Sinaloa has also relied heavily on horizontal ties. These have pushed growers to cooperate rather than compete to produce the required amounts of narcotics. Links of family, marriage, friendship, *compadrazgo*, and locality have also bound together hierarchical relations. Traffickers have tended to employ intermediaries and growers with whom they have more than just business relationships. Furthermore, such relations have come together to form drug trafficking clans. These were the essential unit of drug trafficking from the 1940s through the 1970s. They allowed the trade to survive and to thrive. And despite the contemporary importance of cartel loyalty, even now such clans remain important units of drug organization.

THE ORIGINS OF DRUG TRAFFICKING IN SINALOA

For more than seventy years, journalists, academics, and local intellectuals have sought to discover the first acts of drug production in Sinaloa. They have sought to discover the Ur-narco, the first peasant to slit a poppy seedpod or the first farmer to cut, package, and sell prime marijuana. Such narratives have weight especially among those keen to "clean" Sinaloa's image. The stories exonerate the locals and lay the blame squarely on Chinese immigrants, American corporations, or the American authorities.[3] In reality, whatever the actual origins of the trades, they have always really been about one thing: American demand. And they have risen and fallen in lockstep with this demand.

The trade in opium arrived in Sinaloa during the late nineteenth century. It came with the Chinese immigrants who started to settle in the state's major cities of Los Mochis, Mazatlán, and Culiacán. By 1919 there were 1,680 in the state.[4] Seven years later there were more than 2,000.[5] Most became merchants or farmers but a few started to produce small amounts of opium poppies. They boiled down the gum and then sold it to the small local market of opium smokers.[6] It worked as pain relief and as a social drug.[7]

Throughout the 1910s and 1920s, Sinophobe groups began to challenge Sinaloa's Chinese community. This culminated in the wake of the Great Crash of 1929. Anti-Chinese mobs scoured the capital looking for the city's Chinese inhabitants. Those they found were arrested, caged, and then loaded onto cattle trains and shipped south to Nayarit. When the Nayarit authorities complained, they were shipped farther south, many of them ending up on the coffee plantations of Chiapas.[8]

The forced exile of Sinaloa's Chinese community effectively put an end to the state's small-scale, local smoking opium trade. It was resurrected, however, in the late 1930s. This time it was about demand. The early rumblings of World War II cut the United States off from Asian sources of smoking opium and European sources of morphine and heroin. This time Sinaloa traffickers joined up with the few remaining Chinese opium experts to fill this new demand. By 1942, the U.S. Customs authorities were discovering bulk amounts of opium and smoking opium being smuggled over the border. Two years later, they were noticing both morphine and heroin being moved north.[9]

Cannabis, on the other hand, was introduced to Mexico in the sixteenth century. It was used to produce hemp, which was then employed to make clothes and ropes. A hardy plant, it escaped the set fields. And by the late eighteenth century indigenous and mestizo healers were using a wild version of the herb for various remedies.[10] In Sinaloa, it seems even by the early twentieth century, use was relatively rare. Manuel Lazcano y Ochoa, the former attorney general of Sinaloa, remarked that during the Revolution, use was "scarce, localized and limited." "The songs don't lie, the cockroach couldn't walk because there wasn't any marijuana to smoke."[11]

Yet during the 1960s the marijuana trade took off. Again, it was a question of demand. While use of other counterculture narcotics like peyote, LSD, and heroin rose and fell, marijuana consumption kept on growing. In 1962, around two million Americans had experimented with marijuana. In the first half of the decade, uptake was gradual. Around half a million per year tried the drug for the first time. But then suddenly use took off. By 1970 three million Americans annually were trying the drug for the first time.[12]

Sinaloa became the center of the marijuana as well as the opium trade. In some ways one led to the other. Opium traffickers already had contacts in the United States, protectors in the local government, and a ready army of peasant growers. Some—like Pedro Aviles Pérez—dabbled in both businesses, wholesaling both heroin and marijuana from his base in San Luis Río Colorado.

But it was also about location. To the south of the state lay Mazatlán. By the mid-1960s, it was the hippie holiday destination of choice. Thousands of partying Americans would come down every year to surf, to drink, and to buy weed. Jerry Kamstra, one of the early smugglers, described the place as "the headquarters for every freak driving down the west of Mexico, a drop zone for dealers and amateur smugglers, a shooting gallery for junkies, a street corner for spare changes and stranded drifters."[13]

The opium and marijuana trades were in different areas of the state. The map below, put together using both judicial records and newspapers reports, reveals quite clearly that most opium poppy fields were to the north of the state in the municipalities of Ahome, El Fuerte, Choix, Sinaloa, and Mocorito. Marijuana growing, however, was focused on the more southern municipalities of San Ignacio, Elota, and Cosalá. Finally the central municipalities of Badiraguato and Culiacán grew both types of narcotic.

Though the drugs were grown in different areas, both trades were organized in fairly similar ways. At the bottom were the peasant cultivators. They sold the produce to intermediaries. These in turn passed the wares on to the traffickers. Where there was a slight difference was in the case of the processors. In the opium trade, traffickers or intermediaries would hand over the opium to processors or chemists to transform the gum into morphine or heroin.

THE STRATIFICATION OF SINALOAN DRUG TRAFFICKING

Cultivators

Cultivating opium poppies is tough work. You need to sow the crop, weed it carefully, and ensure that it gets enough water. Harvesting the opium gum is a matter of care and timing. You need to scrape the seedpod with a sharp blade in late afternoon. Then you collect the gum the following morning.

Most cultivators were highland peasants. Before the opium industry took off in the 1940s, most were dedicated to the production of corn, beans, and other agricultural products. Some also kept a few livestock. A handful—that had lands in the deep valleys—had fruit trees or small sugar cane operations. Even fewer still sorted for gold in the region's streams.[14]

Cooperation was—and still is—key to this work. The first level of this cooperation was the family. Each member of the family did a specific job. Men were usually responsible for setting up the irrigation system, sowing the poppy seeds, and selling the final product. Women and children were usually in charge of weeding the fields and harvesting the gum. Small hands were needed for such delicate work.

> We used to work so that the harvest was good, big and small, we used to know that there we would make money, it was a work like any other, in the sierra, that was how we looked on it. The children and women used to help.

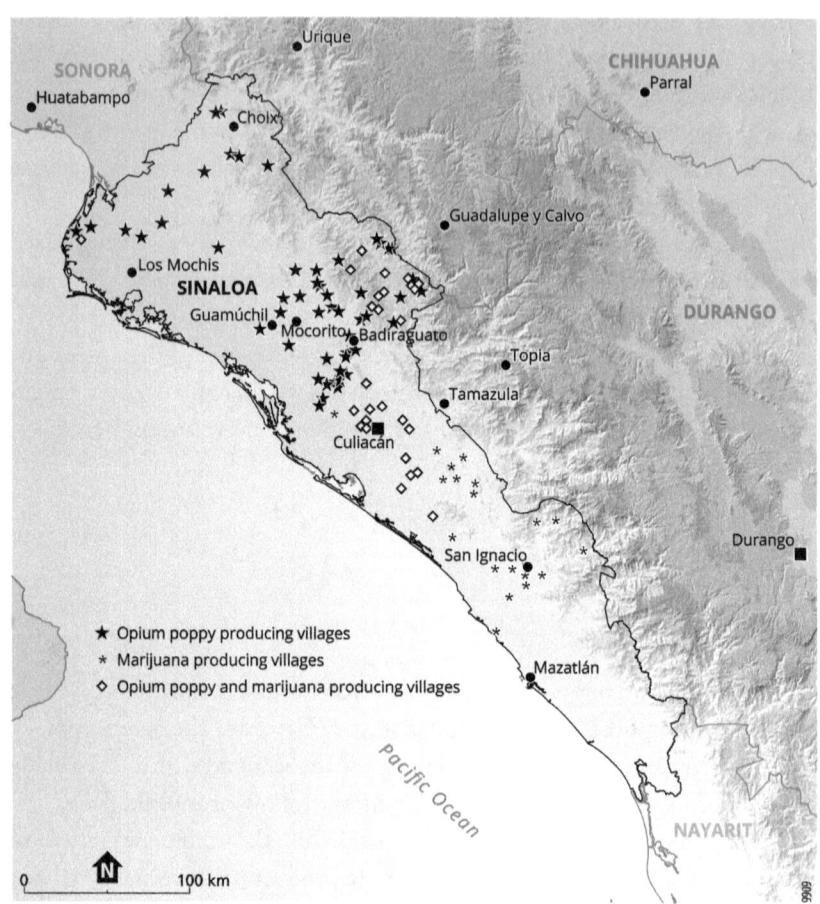

MAP 3 Map of Sinaloa (credits: UU-Geo-C&M–Carto).

Then we looked for someone to sell it to. The men went to Culiacán to sell it or sometimes the buyers came to us. Sometimes they came from Chihuahua or Durango, sometimes gringos even came to look for it.[15]

Yet cooperation extended beyond the nuclear family. Cultivators also employed links of friendship and compadrazgo to fulfill the demands of the opium intermediaries. Groups of cultivators would get together to produce the necessary amount. Then they would split the profits.

On one occasion I had to supply a request of "goma" for Natividad Paez from the Bubunica ranch in Badiraguato about two hours from here. It was twenty

> kilos and he needed it in two weeks. I asked a compadre from La Lapara ranch to help me gather ten kilos. He sold each kilo to me at 100 pesos and I got some profit out if it.[16]

These temporary alliances among cultivators soon hardened into networks of opium suppliers. Certain communities or villages would cooperate every year to fulfill the orders of a particular intermediary. In fact, there were even certain territorial identities created out of the commerce in drugs. Geography, friendship, and commercial interest aligned.

> We had good clients, among them "Nacho" Landell from the La Lapara ranch or a man they called "El Indio" from La Soledad. They bought only from the people of Badiraguato. They used to give the opportunity to sell all the harvest that we brought together. We used to come to an agreement to gather together everything we harvested in October. By the end of the year there was always money.[17]

In the 1940s roving groups of federal policemen regularly came across these joint family operations. In 1947 they discovered a scattering of poppy fields around the village of Tepuche. They found that most were owned by the Diarte brothers, Juan, Jesús, and Ramón. They used to sell most of the produce to their compadres—the Beltrán family—from the nearby village of Santiago de los Caballeros. The gang was even searching for new fields to sow down the mountains in the municipality of Culiacán.[18]

The transition from the cultivation of poppies to that of marijuana in the mid-1960s changed drug-cultivation practices and expanded the area dedicated to drug growing and the number of people dedicated to the trade. Growing the marijuana was much easier than growing opium poppies. Marijuana needed less care and less irrigation. It could be grown at altitude away from streams and rivers: "The parts [of the harvest] were in places that we knew well, over there on top of the hill, hidden in the mountains in the pathways, the higher the cultivation the more difficult for the soldiers to find."[19]

Yet harvesting the marijuana required more effort and was more time-consuming than harvesting opium gum. Peasants had to cut down all the marijuana, divide the plant into the *colas* (or tops), the middle, and the bottom. Then they had to take the harvested marijuana to a nearby patio to let it dry out in the sun. When this was done, it was usually packaged into burlap sacks and taken down the mountain to the intermediary. And most marijuana fields were even smaller than the poppy ones. They were usually measured in square meters rather than fractions of a hectare. The peasants involved in the harvest were usually paid a relatively generous daily wage: "There was a lot of people involved in the cutting. They were paid a daily wage. People from the nearby ranches came down to work the fields of marijuana, 'la motita,' as we called it. We looked forward to harvest time because we knew that it was sure money."[20]

Yet the peasant workers, like the opium harvesters, were also usually linked by friendship or family ties. Parents would initiate their children as young as nine or ten by taking them to the marijuana harvests up in the mountains. Family traditions of cultivating narcotics would emerge. The field owners would employ compadres and neighbors both to ensure the money stayed in the community and to ensure that if they were caught by the police or the army, they would be unlikely to talk. "There was people that contracted you every harvest season, they paid you daily and a little more according to the kilos you harvested, after they had been laid out and dried in the sun and packaged."[21]

The cultivators of the drugs were at the base of the commercial pyramid. An opium peasant—employed to work on someone else's land in the 1950s—would earn between two and three pesos a day, though these payments could fall dramatically in the more remote areas of the sierra.[22] If peasants owned their land they could earn substantially more. Even sold up in the sierra, each kilo of opium could fetch around one hundred pesos. And even a small patch of half a hectare of poppies could produce seven and a half kilos.[23]

Processors

For sale on the border, opium gum needed to be processed into morphine or heroin. To do this you needed chemicals including calcium oxide, ammonium chloride, acetic anhydride, and sodium carbonate. You needed equipment including pots, barrels, pH strips, and evaporators. Finally, and most importantly, you needed knowledge of how much of the chemicals to add, how long to boil them for, and how to extra the morphine base. You also needed patience. In his *El Diario de un Narcotraficante*, A. Nacaveva describes the processing of the opium gum as a time-consuming and exhausting activity, which involves almost a week of stirring up foul-smelling chemical broths.[24]

Opium processors were—as a result—extremely important to the overall trade. Initially, many learned the basics from trained chemists. But by the 1950s, at least, many were taking chemistry and pharmacy courses at the local university, the Universidad Autónoma de Sinaloa. Some started in the business before they finished their degrees. To maximize their profits they also started to traffic.

> I was in my fifth year when I bought myself a Volkswagen; I had never had a car before. This used to take the drugs ... one of the times that I made the journey I handed over three loads to a man ... three loads of $8,000 dollars each! Imagine that! I was going up. The business was to make quality product and take it to the U.S., the business was to cross it.[25]

Some of the labs were up in the sierra in shacks or houses. In fact the first "morphine lab" that federal police discovered in Sinaloa was a small, prefab laboratory consisting of a few pots and pans and around five kilos of crude opium. It was discovered up in the remote hamlet of Bacacoragua, Badiraguato, in April 1947 and was owned by Miguel Urias Uriarte.[26]

Yet increasingly the labs were in the suburbs of Culiacán. Here it was easier to track down and buy the chemicals either wholesale or from individual pharmacies. Again, A. Nacaveva in *El Diario de un Narcotraficante* describes buying small amounts of chemicals at dozens of different pharmacies to avoid detection.[27]

Processors were usually independent operators. They were contracted by a trafficker to produce a certain amount of narcotics. They were handed a certain amount of gum in order to do this. A kilo of gum usually produced around a hundred grams of heroin.[28] The requests were usually made at least a month in advance, especially for big orders. Processors needed the time to source all the chemicals and establish the lab. Payment, especially for big orders, was also usually made in advance. "The big amounts were paid in advance. You needed to prepare everything with a week of anticipation, to buy the chemicals, they brought the gum, you were in charge of the rest."[29]

Payment also depended on the quality of the product produced. Heroin was more expensive and involved more work than morphine. The stronger the heroin, the greater the price.

> We chemists worked with a contract, it was a spoken arrangement. We had to help the trafficker make the heroin. The work depended on how good the opium was that we were given. This was relevant for the production process. Some of the opium we made into morphine, some of the opium we made into heroin. It depended on the activating agents that we used.[30]

The processors, like the cultivators, usually worked together as tight groups. Most groups were composed of family members. Miguel Urias Uriarte, the owner of the morphine lab discovered in 1947, sired a clan of fellow chemists who worked together to produce heroin. In 1971, for example, the police arrested Rosario Rivera Velázquez, Martha Landeros Benítez, Concepción Uriarte, and Abraham Uriarte Rodelo. They were all originally from Bacacoragua and had all been contracted to produce heroin from sixty-four kilos of raw opium. They were asked to do so by another family member, Micaela Uriarte Obeso, who was in Tijuana organizing the sale with her clients.[31]

Another branch of the Urías Uriarte and Uriarte Araujo family formed another processing clan based in Colonia 6 de Enero in Culiacán. Here they established a laboratory where family members or a few trusted neighbors from their village were contracted for the processing of opium.[32]

In the relationship between the trafficker and the processor, trust was extremely important. The traffickers were not only handing over valuable opium they had paid for, they were also risking their own arrest should the processors be caught. As a result, if the trafficker could not find a close relative to act as processor, he usually picked a neighbor, compadre, or close friend. Miguel Angel Peñuelas, from Pericos, Mocorito, remembered the local trafficker was Alejo Cazares. He was a major operator. He had planes and landing strips, and at harvest time he would buy up to five hundred kilos of opium gum. He would then employ Peñuelas's father—a close friend—to process the opium gum into morphine.[33]

Chemists made substantially more than the cultivators despite the money they had to spend on the processing chemicals. During the 1950s and 1960s, they could make between two hundred and five hundred pesos a kilo, depending on the quality and consistency of the product.[34]

Intermediaries

The intermediaries were in charge of collecting the drugs from the cultivators and handing them over to the traffickers. Both intermediaries and traffickers worked for a percentage of the eventual sales. The earnings of the intermediary depended on distance. How far away were the cultivators and where was the collection point? The further the distance, the greater the risk, and the greater the earning for the intermediary. Intermediaries were also responsible for making sure that the local authorities, police patrols, and army squadrons didn't interfere with the trade.

Most intermediaries already had a degree of economic power. They were often village merchants or shopkeepers. Such men already had contacts and influence among peasant growers. They had sufficient capital to front the growers' money. And their stores often doubled as effective stash houses for the opium gum that was collected.

> The intermediary organized the cooperation between the sowers. He had to know the sowers well. And he had a contract for a certain amount with the trafficker. He used to say to us, "This month we have to get together so many kilos" and we dedicated ourselves to sowing it. A lot of times the harvests were paid in advance. It was a verbal contract to hand over what we had promised.[35]

Roberto Mendez, from the small town of Mineral Magistral outside Mocorito, was one of these intermediaries. He owned a shop that catered for the village's miners and farmers. When an undercover FBN agent visited him in March 1947 he boasted that he was "the leader of the people of the village." He was, in effect, the cacique. He offered to show the agent his clients who were growing the opium poppies up in the hills. The FBN agent refused.

Instead Mendez offered to explain to him how his business worked. After collecting the opium he would contact Chinese buyers in the coastal town of Los Mochis. A Chinese hotel owner, who lived in Mocorito, would act as negotiator, checking the quality and setting the price. The opium was then wrapped in cheese, dipped in wax to disguise the smell and sent to the buyers. Interference from the authorities was not an issue. Mendez boasted that one of his cousins was high up in the state police. And the general in charge of the military zone was a good friend. In fact, he had just stayed a couple of nights in Mendez's vast residence in the center of town. Business, he declared, was good.[36]

As Mendez's story suggests, intermediaries also needed political power. Most importantly, they needed to be on good terms with the local authorities. In Badiraguato, Ignacio "Nacho" Landell was one of the principal intermediaries. He was close to Fermín Fernández, the Badiraguato mayor in 1936 and 1937 and again in 1941 and 1942.[37] Fermín used to charge his friend Nacho a fixed rate of ten kilos of opium gum in return for allowing him to sell the substance out of his general store in La Lapara. No doubt, at times this could cause problems. In the early 1940s the state government attempted to take control of the regulation of the opium trade from the local authorities. The head of the Judicial Police of Sinaloa, Alfonso Leyzaola, attempted to collect revenue from the trade instead of having it go to the Badiraguato mayor. Many refused to pay, claiming that they had already paid the mayor, Fernández. The disagreement got so heated that locals eventually killed the interfering police chief.[38]

But most of the time, intermediaries managed to smooth out possible conflicts with interfering political authorities. Also in 1941, an army lieutenant arrived in the highland village of Santiago de los Caballeros. He was there to demand his payoff. He was met by a group of local intermediaries. They corralled their growers to come down the slopes and pay the army lieutenant a percentage of their crop in kind. By the end of the day, the lieutenant walked off with 6.5 kilos of crude opium.[39]

Away from the municipal center, political representatives also played a key role in organizing the cultivation and collecting the resulting gum. In these small communities it was often the *síndico* who played this role. In Los Cortijitos, Badiraguato, this was Antonio Cuén. He owned his own poppy fields, charged other inhabitants a quota for protecting theirs, and also collected the harvest.[40]

The intermediaries were at the center of the highlands' drug-trafficking networks. They were involved in every stage of the process from handing out the seeds through paying the cultivators in advance, collecting the produce, and paying off the authorities to making sure the narcotics got to the producer. In this role the intermediaries often earned a fair amount of the profits from the trade.

Not all these intermediaries—it should be said—were men. Women also played an important role. In fact, in the early 1970s the future Guadalajara kingpin, Ernesto Fonseca, employed a Tierra Blanca women, Rosa Lilia Lara, as a key intermediary. She, in turn, used other women to fan out across the city and buy up opium.[41] Rafael Caro Quintero's aunt, Manuela Caro, was also an important intermediary. She shuttled opium gum between the highlands and potential buyers in Culiacán and up on the border. These included other former residents of Santiago de los Caballeros like Eduardo "Lalo" Fernández Juárez, Gil Caro, and Onofre Landell.[42]

Traffickers

Traffickers were in charge of acquiring the drugs produced in the highland region and then taking them up to the border. Here they would either cross them over the border or they would sell them to Americans coming south. For Sinaloa, the main routes were through Tijuana and Mexicali in Baja California Norte, through Nogales, Agua Prieta, or San Luis Río Colorado in Sonora, or through Ciudad Juárez in Chihuahua.

In general traffickers could have one of two characteristics. Some were from rural backgrounds and had migrated to one of the three principal urban centers in the state (Culiacán, Los Mochis, or Mazatlán). Their aim was to use their rural networks and extend them into the cities, where they often also had family members. Others had urban roots. Their contacts up in the sierra were less likely to be close family members. In fact, they were closer to clients.

Tijuana was probably the most popular trafficking route. Many Sinaloa clans moved up to the border city and established themselves there. They still relied, however, on family members back in their highland hometowns. María Dolores Medina Villa, María Chávez Ortíz, and Hector Gutiérrez were three traffickers from Badiraguato. They had moved to Tijuana in the early 1970s and were in charge of selling the drugs to their North American clients in the La Mesa neighborhood in San Diego. The heroin came from producers back in the sierra. And the product was brought up by a father and son team from Culiacán, Gustavo Alvarado and Gustavo Alvarado Barrón.[43]

During the late 1960s, the small town of San Luis Río Colorado on the Sonora border also became an important trafficking spot. Members of the Urías clan, led by Celia Rivera Urías, established an artisan products store as a front. Relatives brought kilos of crude opium up from the highlands. Rivera Urías and another group of relatives would process the opium into heroin at the back of the shop before selling it.[44]

One of the common strategies employed by the traffickers was to share out the risk by traveling in groups of four or five. Each would carry a small quantity of drugs. The aim was that most of the traffickers got through, but this was not always the case. In 1973, police intercepted Ester Parra Cosío and Ramón Medrano Suárez coming into Tijuana, who were carrying 480 grams of heroin between them. They were also accompanied by José Luis Quiñonez Valenzuela, who was carrying a small quantity of marijuana. He was also the heroin smugglers' contact with the U.S. buyers.[45]

Marijuana was of course much harder to transport in bulk. To make sufficient profit it needed to be transported in kilos and even tons. Packing the marijuana was a tough business. The weed had to be unloaded from burlap sacks, soaked in sugar solution or soda to keep it together, and then pressed into blocks either manually or by a pneumatic press. Big loads could need dozens of workers. And there were entire villages that were dedicated to this work, including Sanalona (Culiacán), Capirato (Mocorito), or Los Limones (Mazatlán). In 1973 the army raided Los Limones and uncovered the entire operation. They found four tons of recently chopped marijuana plants, four hundred kilos packed into one-kilo packages, and another three hundred loose kilos. There were also a couple of hydraulic presses and trucks, which could carry up to twelve tons.[46]

The difficulty in transporting large amounts of marijuana and the increasing vigilance of the federal police led many of the traffickers to use planes. Planes could duck beneath the border radar and could be bought relatively easily from the United States. By the early 1970s, serious traffickers, like Jesús Medina Lugo, the leader of a clan of fifteen or so members, possessed a series of hidden landing strips throughout the sierra. He would collect the product in Tierra Blanca and then move it to these landing strips to move to the United States.[47] So did the traffickers Ramiro Madrid Quintero and Francisco Beltrán Bustamante. They were caught attempting to load 222 kilos of marijuana onto their plane just outside Culiacán. Their idea was to land in Mazatlán, where two other members of the clan waited. These two would be in charge of flying the product up to the United States.[48]

It was the traffickers that earned the major profits from the trade. During the 1950s a gram of heroin cost around 125 pesos in Culiacán. That same gram cost around 2,500 pesos in Tijuana.[49] By the 1970s the profits were even higher. Miguel Angel Peñuelas remembers that a standard 28 gram or 1 ounce load of heroin was around eight thousand dollars in 1975 in Culiacán. That same ounce was worth fourteen thousand dollars by the time it arrived in the United States.[50]

The markup for marijuana was also high, although not as high as that of heroin. Jerry Kamstra, a U.S smuggler who operated in Mexico throughout most of the 1960s, observed how earnings rose and fell in relation to supply and demand. Yet the one constant was the large increase in profits as soon as the weed got over the border. On the other side of the border, earnings were even greater. In 1975 a kilo of marijuana bought at the border for $150 could make you up to $1,000 when sold wholesale in San Francisco.[51]

SINALOA'S DRUG-PRODUCTION CLANS

In some ways, drug production in Sinaloa was a purely commercial venture. And like many capitalist enterprises it was structured vertically. Those at the top made the big money. Those at the bottom made enough to survive, but little more. But the drug business was also different from other extractive and exploitive capitalist enterprises. Because it was high-value and illegal, it demanded that the different tiers of the trade were linked by more than simple commercial interests.

They also needed to be linked by trust and by informal exchanges of favors. As a result, traffickers often reinvested profits back into producing communities and licit businesses. At the same time, the different layers of the business were connected by blood, by compadrazgo, and by neighborhood affiliation. What were essentially businesses also doubled as tightly knit clans.[52]

These clans piggybacked on already existing traditions and commercial interests. Village produce merchants turned to buying up opium. Their former clients turned to growing the crop. And the women in the family mixed their commercial tasks with other household activities. Teresa Leyva Valenzuela, for example, was a young girl when she started to weed and harvest the opium poppies. She mixed it with attending primary school, caring for livestock, and cutting and collecting wood. It was part of her and her mother's household responsibilities. In fact, it was her mother that taught her.[53]

Cooperation extended beyond close family. If cultivators were unable to sate the demands of individual intermediaries or traffickers, they formed cooperatives of neighbors and friends. Again Teresa Leyva Valenzuela remembers that her husband set up one of these organizations.

> Well I was small, and I remember, when I married, I lived in La Lapara, I was 17 years old, my husband was 47, and he had sowed gum. He formed a cooperative with the other neighbors. It was his job to collect all the gum together. Everyone who sowed it brought it to him. He then waited until it was time to sell it all to Nacho Landell.[54]

Such cooperatives not only made sure that intermediaries didn't go elsewhere for their supplies, but they also meant that the wealth from the opium crop was divided relatively evenly among the peasant farmers.

Sinaloa's drug-trafficking clans, however, were not simply highland organizations. They spanned the city and the countryside. The Rafael Buelna market in Culiacán was key. "Gomeros" would visit the market during the opium harvest. They would bring down their gum, sell it, and then spend their money in the adjoining bars and cantinas. Here they would establish links with other opium farmers but also with city traffickers, processors, and intermediaries.[55]

This relationship between the inhabitants of the highland communities and those of the city was solidified by a constant flow of people and commerce between the two places. They traveled to and from the mountains by mule, horse, and increasingly by bus or truck. "I remember that during these years, in the 1950s, people brought gum on the trams from Culiacán to the Rafael Buelna market as well as Tierra Blanca in milk churns in black balls, that was the gum, it was seen as something normal."[56]

The city was also the place where intermediaries met and firmed up arrangements with the larger traffickers. Miguel Angel Peñuelas, an intermediary from Pericos, Mocorito, would bring the opium gum to Doña Porfiria Caro, who lived in El Vallado in the south of Culiacán. She employed a lot of people like Peñuelas and would combine their different loads to make cargoes of fifty or a hundred kilos of gum.[57]

Culiacán was also the place where these networks came together to solve some of the more technical problems of trafficking, for example how to store the opium. They decided on the cans usually used to store and distribute pork fat. The attorney general of Sinaloa remembers coming across one of these small workshops. "We found a tin workshop, small but complete. There were very malleable sheets of everything there, with which they made small jars, which were filled with exact ounces of drugs. In that workshop they canned the product they had previously brought from Badiraguato [...] they explained that they were taking it to a very famous party on May 5 in Tucson, Arizona.[58]

The trafficking of opium was done so openly, particularly in the Tierra Blanca neighborhood, that the inhabitants used to talk openly about the supposed "adventures" of the traffickers. They referred to the wealthy members of Culiacán society who often financially backed their investments. It was well-known that local elites didn't discriminate against those involved in the industry.[59]

> In the first place, the zones where poppies were grown are perfectly known by the authorities. And not only by them, but by an infinity of persons including many working people. Especially the women that have been contracted to go to the plantations to collect the gum, just like they used to go to pick tomatoes. The names of small and large traffickers are passed around. They

are well known and they wear suits of linen or cashmere, whether they are walking in the street or driving a luxurious car.[60]

One of the major opium clans of the 1950s was led by Leonardo Gastélum. He was originally from Mocorito and had contacts in Culiacán but also up at the border at Nogales. His growers predominantly came from the villages of La Vainilla, Pericos, Paredones, Capirito, and Chicorato. Miguel Angel Peñuelas remembers them well. "In Capirito the relatives of Enrique Cazares sowed poppies. There were the Andanas and the Valdéz in Chicorato and in La Vainilla, it was the Olguins that were dedicated to sowing and selling the gum."[61] These cultivators sold their crops to two intermediaries from the Payán family, the brothers Jesús and Refugio "Cuco." They then passed the gum to their compadre, Leonardo Gastélum.[62]

There were similar clans of marijuana traffickers like the Monzón-Terrazas gang. As early as 1963 the police caught three members of the gang—María del Rosario Monzón, María López Esparza, and Pedro López—with two and a half tons of marijuana in a suburb of Culiacán. They were all related and originally from Badiraguato. They revealed that they were working with four Terrazas brothers: Domingo, Francisco, Manuel, and José María Terrazas. These were their neighbors from Badiraguato and were discovered with another load nearby.[63]

Another example of these trafficking clans was that operated by Eduardo "Lalo" Fernández Juárez. The nephew of the mayor of Badiraguato, Fermín Fernandez, Lalo had started as a processor of heroin before moving on to trafficking the product. His network was a classic mixture of family and compadres. Two of his key employees who actually moved the drugs to the United States were Enrique and Fermín Fernández Morales (cousins). Two of his intermediaries who brought the drugs from the highlands were Fermín Fernández Salazar (uncle) and Ignacio Landell Monzón (compadre). And two of the main cultivators of the opium gum were Ricardo and Manuel Fernández Salazar (uncles).

CONCLUSIONS

During the 1940s, drug trafficking shifted from being a marginal activity practiced only by a handful of mostly Chinese opium growers to a relatively central activity. It became normalized and even institutionalized. It became a daily activity for many highland peasants. Though many commentators have tended to focus on the stories of important leaders and powerful *capos*, this is misleading. The real story is of thousands of peasant cultivators forced to work marijuana and opium fields because of limited options.

Commentators have also focused on the destructive force of drug trafficking on relationships and communities. Guillermo Valdés Castellanos claims that violence is "in the DNA" of Mexican drug trafficking.[64] But for the first thirty years, drug trafficking overlaid and imbricated with Sinaloa's cooperative traditions. Family and community members cooperated to bring in the harvest of opium gum. And family members, compadres, and neighbors collaborated to process the gum into heroin and take it over the border. In fact, at least initially the drug industry probably strengthened rather than weakened community ties.

Finally this focus on drug-trafficking clans also reveals the reality behind what even now are often described in much of the security literature as cartels. Even now, as Anabel Hernández's recent book has demonstrated, the Sinaloa Cartel is more a convenient elision of drug-trafficking clans than a price-fixing cartel or even a mafia in the traditional sense.

NOTES

1. Nery Cordova, *La Narcocultura: Simbologia de la Transgresión, el Poder y la Muerte: Sinaloa y su leyenda negra* (Culiacán: UAS, 2011); Jorge Alan Sánchez Godoy, "Procesos de institucionalización de la narcocultura en Sinaloa," *Frontera Norte* 21, no. 41 (2009): 77–103.

2. Diego Osorno, *El Cartel de Sinaloa: Una historia del uso político del narco* (Mexico City: Grijalbo, 2020).

3. Froylán Vladimir Enciso Higuera, "The Origins of Contemporary Drug Contraband: A Global Interpretation from Sinaloa" (Diss., Stony Brook University, 2015); José María Figueroa, Gilberto López Alanis, *Encuentros con la Historia, Badiraguato, Tomo I* (Culiacán: Once Rios, 2002); Froylán Vladimir Enciso Higuera, "El origen del narco, según la glosa popular sinaloense," *Arenas. Revista sinaloense de ciencias sociales* 36 (2014): 10–33; Hector Olea, *Badiraguato: Vision Panorámica de su historia* (Culiacán: 1988).

4. Mayra Vidales Quintero, "Los comerciantes chinos en Culiacán 1900–1920," *Revista Clío* (1993): 36.

5. Carlos Resa Nestares, Narco-Mex S. A. *Economía política y administración de empresa en la industria Mexicana de las drogas ilegales* (N.p., 2005), 474.

6. Luis Astorga, *El Siglo de Drogas. El narcotráfico, del Porfiriato al nuevo milenio*

(Mexico City: Plaza y Janés, 2005), 66; Archivo de la Casa de la Cultura Júridica de Mazatlán (ACCJM), Ramo Penal, 1933, exp. 5, Francisco Wong et al.

7. ACCJM, Ramo Penal, 1933, exp. 14, Luis Fon.

8. Manuel Lazcano Ochoa, *Una vida en la vida de un sinaloense* (Los Mochis: Universidad de Occidente, 1992), 40.

9. Pansters and Smith, chapter 1 in this volume.

10. Isaac Campos, *Home Grown: Marijuana and the Origins of Mexico's War on Drugs* (Chapel Hill: University of North Carolina Press, 2014), 39–66.

11. Lazcano Ochoa, *Una vida en la vida*, 205.

12. Guillermo Valdés Castellanos, *Historia del Narcotráfico en México* (Mexico City: Aguilar, 2013), 290.

13. Jerry Kamstra, *Weed: Adventures of a Dope Smuggler* (New York: Harper & Row, 1974), 65.

14. Mario de la Parra Valle, *Informe Sanitario y Breve Estudio de la Disenteria Amibiana en el Municipio de Badiraguato, Sinaloa* (Mexico City, 1948), 4–7.

15. Venancio Leyva, interview, Badiraguato, Sinaloa, May 11, 2014.

16. Ramón Leyva, interview, Culiacán, February 6, 2014.

17. David Laija Serrano, interview, La Lapara, Badiraguato, Sinaloa, May 9, 2014.

18. ACCJM, Ramo Penal, 1947, exp. 31, fojas 16 y ss. *El Informador*, Guadalajara, January 29, 1944, 1; *El Informador*, October 18, 1943, 1, 6.

19. Teresa Leyva Valenzuela, interview, Badiraguato, May 9, 2014.

20. Venancio Leyva, interview, Badiraguato, May 11, 2014.

21. Teresa Leyva Valenzuela, interview, Badiraguato, May 9, 2014.

22. Martin Lozoya, interview, Culiacán, June 14, 2015.

23. National Archives and Records Administration (NARA), Record Group (RG) 170, Salvador Peña report, 15/06/1944.

24. A. Nacaveva, *El diario de un narcotraficante* (Mexico City: B. Costa Amic, 1967), 62–80.

25. Miguel Ángel Peñuelas, interview, in Pericos, Mocorito, February 26, 2014.

26. Archivo del Tribunal Superior de Justicia, Amparos, Miguel Urias Uriarte. 1947.

27. Nacaveva, *El Diario*, 52.

28. Miguel Angel Peñuelas, interview, Pericos, Mocorito, February 24, 2014.

29. Miguel Angel Peñuelas, interview, Pericos, Mocorito, February 24, 2014.

30. Miguel Angel Peñuelas, interview, Pericos, Mocorito, February 24, 2014.

31. *El Universal*, July 4, 1971, 1.

32. *El Nacional*, August 24, 1971, 1, *Excélsior*, August 27, 1971, 26.

33. Miguel Angel Peñuelas, interview, Pericos, Mocorito, February 24, 2014.

34. Miguel Angel Peñuelas, interview, Pericos, Mocorito, February 24, 2014.

35. José Payán, interview, Badiraguato, May 18, 2014.

36. NARA, RG170, box 23, Anon to Terry Talent, 3/16/1947; Terry Talent to Commissioner of Customs, 3/11/1947.

37. "Presidentes municipales de Badiraguato," in *Badiraguato Encuentros con la historia* (Culiacán: Gobierno del Estado de Sinaloa y Academia Cultural "Roberto Hernández Rodríguez" A. C., 2002), 22–23.

38. Oscar Lara Salazar, *La Carraca* (Culiacán: Instituto Sinaloense de la Cultura, 2010); Teresa Leyva Valenzuela, interview, Badiraguato, May 9, 2014.

39. AGN, Ramo Presidentes, Manuel Avila Camacho, 422/2 Rodolfo Loaiza to President Avila Camacho, 14/04/1941.

40. ACCJM, Ramo Penal, 1947, exp. 31, fojas 16 y ss.

41. *El Nacional*, August 4, 1971, 1.

42. Anonymous source, interview, July 28, 2020.

43. *El Heraldo*, January 17, 1973, 5.

44. Archivo General de la Nación (AGN), Secretaria de Gobernación, Expediente s/n, 3/2/1974, foja 2.

45. *La Prensa*, May 28, 1972, 1.

46. *El Crucero*, March 20, 1973, 5.

47. *Excélsior*, March 4, 1972, 1.

48. *El Día*, August 10, 1972, 10.

49. Astorga, *El Siglo*, 92.

50. Miguel Ángel Peñuelas, interview, Pericos, Mocorito, February 24, 2014.

51. Kamstra, *Weed*, 326.

52. Sarmiento Luis Fernando y Ciro Krauthausen, *Cocaína y Co. Un mercado ilegal por dentro* (Bogotá: Universidad Nacional de Colombia, 1993), 38–45.

53. Teresa Leyva Valenzuela, interview, Badiraguato, May 9, 2014.

54. Teresa Leyva Valenzuela, interview, Badiraguato, May 9, 2014.

55. Herberto Sinagawa Montoya and Luis Antonio García, *Después de todo, fue muy divertido: relatos autobiográficos de Herberto Sinagawa Montoya* (Culiacán: H. Ayuntamiento de Culiacán, 2005), 53.

56. Teresa Leyva Valenzuela, interview, Badiraguato, May 9, 2014.

57. Miguel Angel Peñuelas, interview, Pericos, Mocorito, February 24, 2014.

58. Lazcano Ochoa, *Una vida en la vida*, 200

59. *La Voz de Sinaloa*, June 20, 1947, 2.

60. *La Voz de Sinaloa*, September 2, 1947, 1.

61. Miguel Angel Peñuelas, interview, Pericos, Mocorito, February 24, 2014.

62. *El Diario de Culiacán*, June 20, 1951, 1.

63. *El Diario de Culiacán*, December 30, 1963, 1.

64. Valdés Castellanos, *Historia*, 130.

9

With a Little Help from His Friends
Juan N. Guerra, Smuggling, and Drug Trafficking in Tamaulipas and Nuevo León, 1940s–1960s

CARLOS ANTONIO FLORES PÉREZ

INTRODUCTION

In official speech—governmental and sometimes the media as well—the phenomenon of illicit narcotics trafficking tends to be portrayed as the result of ethereal forces or, at best, the underlying responsibility for its unbridled development is attributed to the ingenuity of a few emblematic criminal figures. The historical evidence available, however, reveals a distinct perspective: these actors are simply links in much broader, though shrouded, social networks that encompass political, institutional, and entrepreneurial actors with the common goal of obtaining enormous profits by promoting and protecting illicit practices. These actors share the historical responsibility for the growth of narcotics trafficking, while the hegemony they maintain over diverse institutions gives them stability in a sphere of action that by its very nature is volatile. The objective of this chapter is to demonstrate this situation in the case of northeastern Mexico by focusing on the state of Tamaulipas, which is one of the main platforms for exporting drugs to the United States. Tamaulipas is a border state that directly abuts Texas and Nuevo León, the main pole of economic development in the region. The analysis centers on the figure of Juan Nepomuceno Guerra Cárdenas, a smuggler and drug trafficker who founded the criminal network that came to be known as the Gulf Cartel (Cártel del Golfo). As will be seen, aside from certain personal qualities that Guerra may have possessed, his long criminal trajectory and the continuing participation of many of his relatives as key characters in contraband activities seem to be tightly linked to a broad network of political and institutional benefactors with whom he was associated and who ensured him impunity. With this goal in mind, I begin by providing readers with the contextual information needed to better understand the process and relations elucidated herein.

NORTHEAST MEXICO: LATE NINETEENTH CENTURY TO THE EARLY 1940S

Tamaulipas sits in the far northeast corner of Mexico. It borders the U.S. state of Texas as well as the Mexican states of Veracruz, Nuevo León, and San Luis Potosí. It also shares many similarities with the two states to the west, Nuevo León and Coahuila. In all three states, economically powerful families have developed overlapping business interests in a variety of worlds, including smuggling. The first large-scale smuggling operations involved liquor. Monterrey, the capital of Nuevo León, had been a major manufacturing hub since the nineteenth century, and one of its major industries was beer production. By the second decade of the twentieth century, the Cervecería Cuauhtémoc was producing eight hundred thousand barrels a year. This upsurge in production coincided with the 1920 Volstead Act, the legislation that ushered in the Prohibition Era and, as a consequence, the large-scale smuggling of alcohol from Mexico into the United States. As Alex Saragoza argues, some of that alcohol surely came from the vast legal production of the Monterrey factory.[1]

While there were smugglers engaged in more rudimentary smuggling activities, the more sophisticated alcohol contraband appeared to be managed by actors well-connected to the local political and business elite. Members of the military who were later identified as protectors of alcohol contraband were also involved in smuggling arms from the United States into Mexico to support possible subversive actions sponsored by the owners of the Cuauhtémoc brewery at the end of the 1930s. Years later, they continued to protect the regional smugglers, and together with some of the latter's most successful and conspicuous protégés (Juan N. Guerra and his brother), these military men became the exclusive distributors of beer from the Cuauhtémoc brewery in several parts of Tamaulipas. These networks of smugglers were the predecessors of the drug traffickers of later decades.

After Volstead was repealed in 1933, many of those smugglers turned to moving narcotics, for this was an easy way to continue using the established contacts and knowhow acquired in the liquor-smuggling days. This can be observed in the case of Germán Barrera González, from the border town of Mier, Tamaulipas, who originally acquired his wealth through smuggling and who would become the patriarch of a family that enjoyed political and economic pre-eminence in this part of the border region and maintained close ties with smugglers and future drug traffickers, such as Juan N. Guerra. In his autobiography, he recalls that the ratification of the so-called "U.S. dry laws" were "highly-important to him," since he made big money from liquor smuggling until he was captured by Mexican troops and imprisoned in Monterrey.[2] But his stay in prison was brief because the military zone commander intervened in his favor. After that he would no longer run into problems. Later on, his criminal record proved not to be a drawback for further business success, as he used the money from smuggling to become a major gasoline distributor, first for the U.S. company El Águila, then for the state company Pemex. In 1947, he even got permission, with other family members, to set up a branch of the Banco Mercantil del Norte in the border town of Miguel Alemán. Old habits, however, die hard, so in the 1960s and 1970s the owners of the bank and other members of the Barrera González family were repeatedly flagged by the DFS as drug traffickers and smugglers.

But it was not only aspiring entrepreneurs who sought to take advantage of Tamaulipas's location, for politicians and soldiers soon got involved in this lucrative trade. First among these was a lieutenant colonel named Tiburcio Garza Zamora, who was based in Reynosa from the late 1920s to the early 1940s. Despite his paltry army salary, Garza rose to become a big border businessman. In 1946 he even purchased and ran Reynosa's large electrical company. The source of his wealth was, of course, smuggling. According to government spies who arrived in the city in 1940, he "controlled" the "persons that lived from smuggling... in the villages on the Río Bravo," though by that time they recognized that his control was slipping.[3]

In the midst of the political tensions surrounding the 1940 presidential elections, Garza Zamora smuggled arms into the country to prepare for an eventual rebellion headed by presidential contender Juan Andreu Almazán, who enjoyed the support of the Nuevo León bourgeoisie, including the owners of the Cuauhtémoc brewery. Even though circumstances changed after Almazán's defeat, the federal government feared that Garza Zamora's connections to contraband might harm its interests and favor those of its political enemies. In this context the federal government sought to bring the smuggling networks under its de facto control through the new governor of Nuevo León, Bonifacio Salinas Leal, who appeared keen to crack down on Garza's businesses. In the end, though, President Cárdenas's intent to terminate Almazán's control over smuggling in the area through the replacement of Garza Zamora wasn't effective, as the latter and Salinas Leal would eventually join forces in a political and military camarilla that continued to protect smuggling in Tamaulipas and Nuevo León.

JUAN N. GUERRA, SMUGGLING AND THE ARRIVAL OF *ALEMANISMO* IN TAMAULIPAS

In January 1941, after a series of failed political maneuvers, Tiburcio Garza Zamora was appointed police inspector in Nuevo León during Bonifacio Salinas Leal's term as governor, a position that allowed him to strengthen relationships with certain superiors that would prove to be of vital importance.[4] In late 1946, the commander of the 8th Military Zone in Tampico, Tamaulipas, was Gen. Anacleto Guerrero, a former governor of Nuevo León. In December of that year, the local press stated that the general would be replaced by Gen. Bonifacio Salinas Leal, a man who, according to reports from the Office of Political and Social Information, had protected smuggling operations.[5] Salinas Leal was appointed commander of the military zone on December 15, 1946, by the recently elected president, Miguel Alemán Valdés, who had assumed office on December 1 of that year.[6] Just a few months later, new political and illicit events shook Tamaulipas. Around April 1947, Miguel Alemán and a clique allied with him in that state maneuvered politically to depose governor Hugo Pedro González—who was linked to former president Emilio Portes Gil—and replace him with General Raúl Gárate Legleu, who at the time was the undersecretary of national defense.[7] General Gárate had the de facto support of Bonifacio Salinas Leal, the commander of the 8th Military Zone, and Tiburcio Garza Zamora. In fact, in 1949, Gárate and Salinas Leal tried to convince Alemán that the former should inherit the governorship at the end of Salinas's term. Though their bid was unsuccessful, General Salinas did ensure that Garza Zamora was endorsed by the president to take command of the garrison in Reynosa.[8]

In 1947, Portes Gil's formerly influential political faction was ousted by a group of army officers and politicians allied with President Alemán. Smuggling activities soon intensified as men linked to the new power group were appointed to key administrative positions and Customs posts. Historical

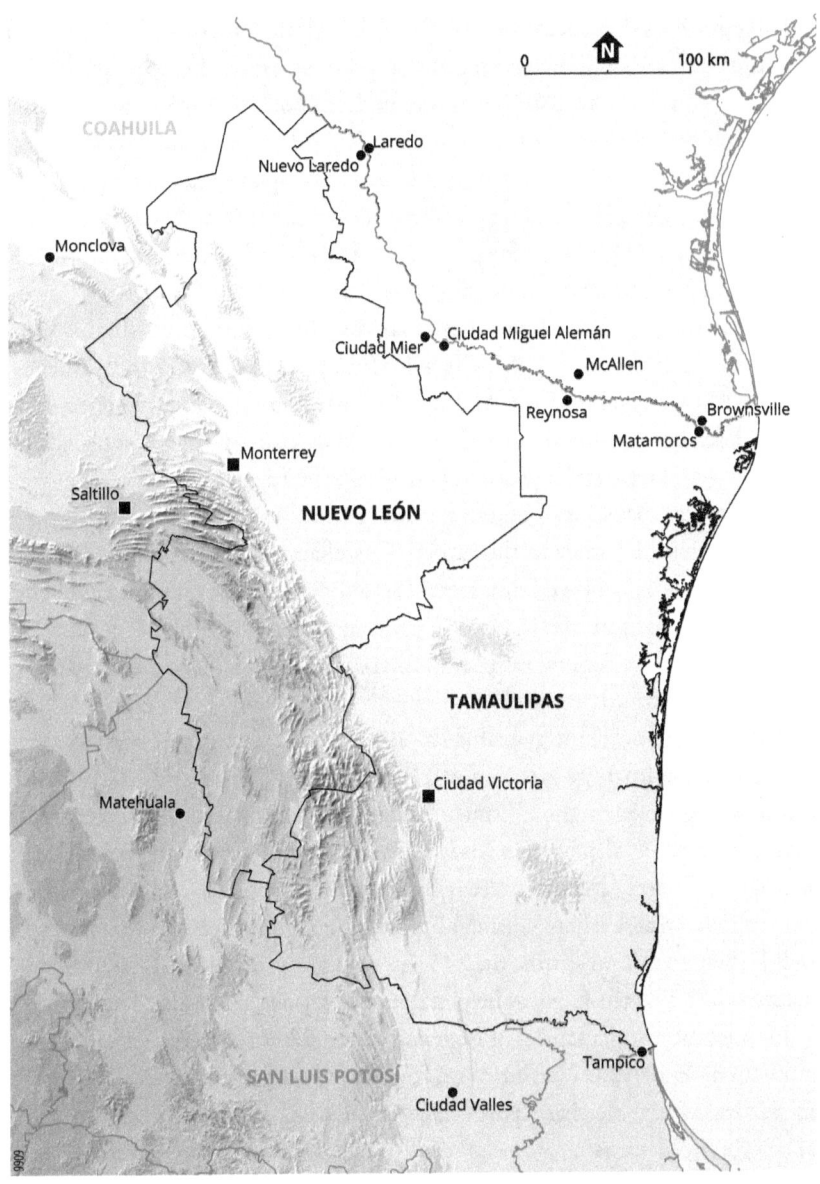

MAP 4 Map of Tamaulipas and Nuevo León (credits: UU-Geo-C&M–Carto).

documents show that Alemán participated directly in designating high-ranking Customs officials, which was an unusual practice for the head of state.[9] The president's direct intervention was revealed in a reply to Aarón Sáenz Garza, who supported the request that Benjamín R. Hill—son of the revolutionary general Benjamín Hill—had sent to Alemán to be appointed head of the Federal Treasury Office in Tijuana. Through his private aide, the secretary of the treasury informed Hill that the president had personally appointed someone else to that post, so it was impossible to satisfy his wishes.[10]

In Matamoros, Tamaulipas, these maneuverings resulted in Miguel Solís Alemán—a relative of the president—becoming head of the Customs Agency (Resguardo Aduanal).[11] The Customs administrator was Cristo Lapierre, who would later be appointed general customs inspector—a higher supervisory position—and replaced by Francisco Castellanos Tuexi, a former state governor and general prosecutor of justice of the Federal District.[12] During his time in the prosecutor's office in the capital, Castellanos had surrounded himself with a group who followed him from Tamaulipas to perform ministerial and political functions in Mexico City. His team included Juan N. Guerra, who was an agent of the Federal District's Judicial Police from 1943 to 1944, during Castellanos's administration.[13]

According to available genealogical information, Guerra was born in Matamoros, Tamaulipas, in 1915, son of Plácido Guerra Lerma and María Eloísa Cárdenas, and lived on the El Tahuachal ranch.[14] Although these records show that his father was also born in Matamoros, in an interview with an American journalist, Guerra later stated that his father was actually a native of Mier, Tamaulipas, an area where Germán Barrera González (born 1901) was already well-known to military authorities for his smuggling activities. It seems likely, in retrospect, that the Guerras helped Barrera consolidate his illicit activities.[15]

In 1947, the municipalities of Reynosa and Matamoros were neighbors (the municipalities of Valle Hermoso and Río Bravo had not yet been established), so it is inconceivable that figures like Tiburcio Garza Zamora, commander of the Reynosa garrison, Bonifacio Salinas Leal, commander of the military zone, and his ally, Francisco Castellanos, the former prosecutor of the Federal District and former governor of Tamaulipas, could have been unaware of Guerra's participation in smuggling. The first two had firsthand knowledge of contraband operations in Tamaulipas and Nuevo León; in fact, existing documentation shows that they protected those activities. Castellanos, meanwhile, had been their boss in the prosecutor's office in Mexico City.[16]

The fact is that when Guerra assassinated his wife, Gloria Landeros, during a conjugal dispute in 1947, he was by no means unknown in Public Security and Customs circles in the state. Indeed, his "dreadful record [for] he has always lived outside the law and the substantial capital that he possesses has been obtained through contraband of all kinds" was already a matter of public record.[17] Missives sent to the president, and eight-column headers in local newspapers that scooped the murder and followed the case closely, revealed the many irregularities that occurred during the judicial process Guerra faced. Among other things, it emerged that his father made death threats against the deceased's parents, that Plácido Guerra and the official entrusted with investigating the case were *compadres*, and that attempts were made to appoint Guerra's attorney as the official in charge.[18] Despite the murderer's well-documented criminal record and pleas to support the victim's family sent to President Alemán—who supported the recently established powers in the state—these judicial irregularities allowed Guerra's foul deed to go unpunished. He was only detained briefly. The structure of institutional, political, judicial, and military power allowed Guerra to continue to manage his illegal activities. In 1956, his family celebrated the wedding of one of its members with a party that was widely reported on the social pages of newspapers in Matamoros. Attendees included a judge, Venustiano Guerra, whom governor Raúl Gárate had considered a prime candidate to become his senior government official (Oficial Mayor) and who would later become leader of the Partido Revolucionario Institucional's (PRI) Organizing Committee in Tamaulipas.[19]

Also in that year, a lawyer had set up offices on the top floor of a building where Juan N. Guerra had established a bar called Piedras Negras. He was Raúl Morales Farías, who would later serve as Guerra's head attorney.[20] Morales Farías was the father of Raúl Morales Cadena, a future state attorney general during Manuel Cavazos Lerma's administration (1993–1999) and later a judge on the state's Supreme Court.[21]

A year later, *El Porvenir*, a newspaper in Nuevo León, published a report with photographs of the birthday party of Gen. Anacleto Guerrero Guajardo, the former governor of Nuevo León and commander of the military zone of Tamaulipas. His friends from both states attended the festivity, representing the region's most conspicuous political, security, and business networks. Also present were the state's senior government official, Manuel Flores; the mayor of Monterrey, José Luis Lozano; federal congressman Ángel Lozano; and the former general secretary of government, Ramiro Tamez, among other figures of Nuevo León politics, as well as Gen. Domingo Martínez, the commander of the 7th Military Zone. The state of Tamaulipas, meanwhile, was also well-represented by Brig. Gen. Tiburcio Garza Zamora; the chief customs inspector, Francisco Yarritou; the head of the Federal Treasury Office in Reynosa, Guillermo García González; and Juan N. Guerra, from Matamoros.[22]

POWER NETWORKS AND ILLICIT SMUGGLING IN TAMAULIPAS IN THE 1960S

In 1960, during the administration of President Adolfo López Mateos, recurring acts of violence in Tamaulipas evidenced the consolidation of a network made up of politicians, security officials, and criminals devoted to smuggling and drug trafficking. In April, a bloody incident occurred in Matamoros that attracted the attention of authorities and media alike. On the 14th, the commander of Customs Surveillance in Reynosa, Lt. Col. Octavio Villa Coss, was murdered in an altercation with the smuggler Juan N. Guerra in his Piedras Negras bar.[23] Villa Coss was a soldier, former substitute federal congressman, and son of the renowned revolutionary leader Francisco Villa. Local authorities ordered the arrest of the alleged perpetrators and even detained eyewitnesses to the crime, including a waiter named Manuel Duarte Araujo; army officer and Customs Inspection commander in Reynosa, Felipe García Segovia; the head of the Customs Office in Matamoros, Zeferino Vega Cantú; and Carlos García, aka La Máquina, who was Guerra's driver. Duarte Araujo and Vega Cantú were defended by none other than Raúl Morales Farías, Guerra's attorney.[24] Guerra himself fled after the murder.

The statements given by the various witnesses were plagued with contradictions, so they were tried for obstruction of justice.[25] Duarte stated that the killer was the driver, Carlos García, who was apprehended days later and confessed, even though his mother and wife declared that he had been at home, nowhere near Guerra's bar on the night of the murder. During the trial, he was even asked if he had received money from Guerra to confess to the crime.[26] Forensic evidence contradicted his confession, for autopsy results showed that the trajectory of the bullets that ended Villa Coss's life pointed to Guerra as the gunman.[27] Not surprisingly, the driver was also defended by attorney Morales Farías.[28] The local press alleged that Villa Coss and Guerra had had some kind of disagreement, and that Reynosa customs commander Garcia Segovia had insisted that Villa Coss go to Guerra's bar to patch things up. In addition, newspaper articles suggested that customs officers had attempted to extort the band of Matamoros smugglers.[29] The press further alleged that Villa Coss had gone to Matamoros to speak with Guerra after meeting with Gen. Tiburcio Garza Zamora in Reynosa while target shooting just a few hours before the murder. "If the lieutenant colonel had had the intention to use his gun, he failed to recall that [it] had only one bullet left because the rest of the ammo had been spent target shooting at General and congressman Tiburcio Garza Zamora's ranch."[30] Because of the victim's ancestry, the case captured the attention of national authorities and the media. Villa Coss's brothers—also military men—were brought into the investigation, and the federal attorney general (PGR), the Federal Directorate of Security (DFS), and even members of the presidential military detail (*estado mayor presidencial*) were entrusted with investigating the case. At the local level, this task fell to the state attorney general's office.[31]

As time passed, new information about the case surfaced in the press, which intimated that the murder had occurred due to differences between Guerra and Customs officers over contraband merchandise that was transported in a truck belonging to Roberto Guerra Cárdenas, Juan's brother. The vehicle, which had been confiscated by the Customs office in the city of Miguel Alemán, Tamaulipas, was used to deliver Carta Blanca beer, a business in which, according to information published earlier in the press, the Guerra Cárdenas brothers were also involved.[32] Carta Blanca was the emblematic product of the Cuauhtémoc brewing company, a company previously linked to transborder smuggling of alcohol and weapons. According to an undated memo from the DFS, Gen. Tiburcio Garza Zamora was the exclusive dealer of Carta Blanca beer in the area.[33]

Newspapers in Nuevo León, meanwhile, reported aspects of the case that did not appear in the press in Tamaulipas:

> At two a.m., Lieutenant-Colonel Octavio Villa Coss, son of the guerrillero Francisco Villa, was killed by four shots in the Piedras Negras bar after a heated argument with Zeferino Vega Cantú and Juan N. Guerra, owner of the locale; Villa was the regional commander of Customs Surveillance, and Vega Cantú the head of Customs Services in this city [Matamoros]. The crime is believed to be related to drug trafficking and contraband."[34]

A few days later, the same newspaper printed again that "The regional commander of Customs Surveillance was murdered. Lieutenant-Colonel Villa Coss was carrying out special investigations into coffee and drug smuggling that signaled Juan N. Guerra as the perpetrator."[35] According to that report, the Customs commander Zeferino Vega himself participated in those activities, along with Guerra. Once again, reports pointed out Guerra's criminal record and links:

> This crime, in which the owner of the establishment, Juan N. Guerra, sadly infamous for five [previous] murders, and Commander Vega Cantú were identified as participants in this death [...] In addition, information from Matamoros indicates that Lieutenant-Colonel Villa Coss did not drink, so his presence in the Piedras Negras bar must have been due to orders to arrest Juan N. Guerra, who was identified as a coffee smuggler with ample links to drug traffickers.[36]

According to this report, Villa Coss and Guerra had entered into a heated discussion. The latter had offered Coss 250,000 pesos in exchange for his freedom, but when Coss rejected the offer he was shot and killed. The note also confirmed that Villa Coss had attended a party held at the Hualala ranch near San Fernando just a few hours before his death.

On April 24, 1960, an anonymous "Customs officer" wrote to President López Mateos with information on Villa Coss's murder and the dynamics of cross-border smuggling in Tamaulipas. His goal was to convince the president to send someone trustworthy to verify his affirmations. He stated that the intellectual author of the homicide was Gen. Tiburcio Garza Zamora, who ran border smuggling in Tamaulipas with Juan N. Guerra as his protégé. He further stated that Guerra was hiding on the Hualala ranch, property of Garza Zamora, who provided him with information on the evolution of the case and related judicial inquiries.[37]

Aside from these declarations in the media, however, the federal investigation was limited or, at least, its final results were. After the initial police investigations and after the victim's brothers had been appointed to key positions in Customs offices, the federal secretary of the treasury and public credit, Antonio Ortiz Mena, promptly removed the latter from their posts.[38] Although there was talk of a "clean-up" of the local Customs administration, men involved in smuggling, like Zeferino Vega Cantú, who was in charge of Customs surveillance in Matamoros, were ratified in their posts, while others who apparently had no such links were removed.[39] Eduardo Garduño, undersecretary of the treasury, whose responsibilities included administrating

Customs offices throughout the country, and his father-in-law, Col. Enrique Carrola Antuna—who coordinated the alternate structure of Customs surveillance in which the deceased Villa Coss had worked—also found themselves abruptly separated from the service.[40]

A month earlier, in August, members of the president's security detail, in coordination with the secretary of the treasury and public credit and the Presidency of the republic itself, launched a disarmament campaign in the area, while concurrently inquiring into the dynamics of contraband along the Tamaulipas border. This group was commanded by Maj. Óscar González Sánchez and Capt. Alfonso Solís Bolaños, who ordered that checkpoints be set up to inspect vehicles for illegal firearms owned by residents of Matamoros.[41] The campaign lasted about a month, but the results were meager at best, for the "special group" collected only twenty-two guns of different calibers, a 16-caliber shotgun, and three 22-caliber carbines.[42] They also made a list of known smugglers, but it included only men who were already in prison.[43]

On September 20th, Juan N. Guerra appeared before Leopoldo Tapia, Óscar González Sánchez, and Jorge Antonio Bielba, military officers of the special group of the president's security detail, accompanied by former governor Francisco Castellanos Tuexi, who had been his boss in the General Prosecutor's Office in Mexico City and who had been head of Customs in Matamoros between 1952 and 1958. Guerra had obtained an amparo from the Third Circuit judge of the Unitary Tribunal in Monterrey, Nuevo León, that prevented his apprehension.[44] The magistrate in charge of that tribunal was Ramón Palacios Vargas, who in 1967 was named general prosecutor of justice for Nuevo León and, in 1970, supernumerary magistrate of the Supreme Court of Justice of the Nation.[45]

In the interview held in the Ritz Hotel, which lasted no more than half an hour, Francisco Castellanos told the officers that Guerra wished "to stay out of illicit acts." The latter responded that they were not responsible for analyzing past situations already resolved by law and stated that their concern was to maintain the tranquility of the town. The officers also suggested that Guerra should abstain from carrying arms and that if he did not then they would proceed against him.

A memo from the head of the DFS, Col. Manuel Rangel Escamilla, dated October 11, 1960, informed an undisclosed superior about the political, economic, and social situation that prevailed in Matamoros, Tamaulipas. His report revealed unambiguously that:

In the North of the Republic, Roberto and Juan N. Guerra are considered the largest smugglers of firearms, commercial merchandise and narcotics. In the past, they were involved in terrorism and the intellectual authors of many crimes, among them that [involving] mayor Ernesto Elizondo, as well as the aforementioned murder of Lt. Col. Octavio Villa Coss, killed inside a local bar; a crime that remains unpunished today because the attorney Raúl Morales Farías, legal adviser to the Guerra brothers, managed through trickery to have Juan N. Guerra's driver accept responsibility for the murder, reducing [Guerra's] role to that of participating in a cover-up.[46]

Colonel Rangel Escamilla underscored the network's political maneuverings, which were supported by Gen. Tiburcio Garza Zamora, who along with Lauro Villalón, promoted Raúl Morales Farías's candidacy for municipal president of Matamoros.[47] On this point, the colonel wrote:

> His profession as a defense attorney is exercised mostly in cases of smugglers, criminals and drug traffickers, all of whom are notorious in the region. He is the lead lawyer of a business owned by Roberto and Juan N. Guerra, whom he supports in opening bars, centers of vice and others that operate in the locality under the protection of Roberto Guerra.[48]

and added:

> The aforementioned Morales Farías, in addition to enjoying the support of portesgilista officials, receives economic support from Roberto and Juan N. Guerra, distributors of Carta Blanca beer in Matamoros, known smugglers and promoters of vices. Likewise, the National Revolutionary Coalition—whose finances in the municipality are handled by Roberto Guerra—backs him up.[49]

The people that Colonel Rangel Escamilla wrongly identified as *portesgilistas* were in reality members of the camarilla of politicians and military officers who, as mentioned before, had joined forces with Miguel Alemán Valdés to reconfigure the distribution of power in the state in 1947 by deposing Governor Hugo Pedro González and replacing him with Gen. Raúl Gárate Legleu. All this was corroborated by a confidential report of the DFS, which talked about the political machinations carried out by some of those military officers to support Gen. Bonifacio Salinas Leal as a possible PRI precandidate for the

Presidency of the Republic. This report further pointed out that this group was "led by Generals Raul Gárate, Anacleto Guerrero, Tiburcio Garza Zamora and other prominent military officers."[50]

The Dimensions of Trafficking

It is extremely difficult to precisely determine the volume of drugs that was being smuggled through the Tamaulipas corridor. Because so much of Mexico's opium was produced in the Golden Triangle region, much of the raw opium, smoking opium, and heroin was transported over border crossings in Baja California and Sonora. But not all drugs came from the Golden Triangle, and it seems that the Tamaulipas route played a growing role in trafficking drugs from different sources in the 1950s and 1960s.

Marijuana especially was grown throughout Mexico and increasingly, it seems, in Nuevo León. Moreover, in the 1950s and 1960s much of the heroin came from Europe, especially French Connection white heroin that arrived at ports on Mexico's eastern coast. Tamaulipas was an easy avenue along which those drugs could reach markets on the U.S. East Coast. Disaggregated lists of drug arrests bear out the region's growing importance. In 1963–1964, 1,089 Mexicans were arrested on drug charges. Tamaulipas was behind only Mexico City and Baja California in the numbers of arrests, accounting for 127 charges. There were also 71 arrests in the neighboring state of Nuevo León. In the same year, more than two tons of marijuana were captured in Nuevo León alone. Together they accounted for around a third of all marijuana seizures in Mexico.[51] Finally, Manuel Suárez Domínguez, once the head of the Federal Judicial Police, attempted to smuggle 45 kg of high-grade European heroin across the Tamaulipas-Texas border in 1970.[52]

GUERRA'S NETWORK IN MIER, MIGUEL ALEMÁN, AND MONTERREY
The network devoted to trafficking illicit substances that had Juan N. Guerra as one of its most powerful figures operated not only in the strategic municipalities of Matamoros and Reynosa but also in the cities of Mier and Miguel Alemán in Tamaulipas. As discussed above, its members maintained close ties to important figures in the region's spheres of economic and political power. On April 23, 1960, the press reported that a formal order had been issued in Miguel Alemán for the arrest of a group of coffee smugglers. That city, founded in 1950, was separated from Mier on the initiative of Raúl Gárate and local

politicians, including relatives of Germán Barrera González, the smuggler who for decades exerted control over local politics.[53] Those indicted were Albino García, Leonel Salinas, Donato Elizondo, and Manuel López.[54] The reader will recall that a truck distributing Carta Blanca beer, property of Roberto Guerra Cárdenas, had been detained there in an event that eventually led to the murder of Octavio Villa Coss. It seems quite possible, then, that this Albino García was Albino García Cárdenas, a cousin of the Guerra Cárdenas brothers and father of Juan García Abrego, who became a prominent drug trafficker with his own criminal network in the 1980s and 1990s.[55] This hypothesis is supported by additional data that show that the Guerra family also smuggled illicit substances in this area of the border with the consent and protection—perhaps even active participation—of political and business actors. According to the report on the warrant for the arrest of Albino García and the other traffickers detained, investigations ultimately led to a man named Rogelio Garza, the presumed owner of the smuggled goods.[56]

Because Garza's maternal surname is not mentioned in the report, it is difficult to be sure, but two men with the same name—Rogelio Garza—were on the regional scene of illicit trafficking around that time. The first was once the head of the secret arm of the municipal police in Reynosa. According to the local press, he protected smugglers and traffickers in a zone controlled, as mentioned above, by Gen. Tiburcio Garza Zamora, a native and resident of that locality.[57] The second figure, however, may be the more logical choice due to the following connections. On September 29, 1960, the society sections of newspapers in Nuevo Leon reported the marriage of Katia Canavati and Alfredo Esper.[58] Katia was the daughter of the late Tafich Canavati and niece of Anuar Canavati and Pedro Canavati, two influential Lebanese businessmen. The wedding was attended by many family members and friends, including Rogelio Garza Cortés, Yolanda Canavati's husband.[59] In May 1974, Garza Cortés was arrested by the Federal Judicial Police in the patio of a Salinas y Rocha store in Monterrey carrying half a kilogram of cocaine. After he identified his dealer, agents seized a total of 2.5 kg of that drug.[60]

The Canavati family had achieved a notorious economic bonanza and social recognition by establishing numerous textile and commercial businesses. In addition to his entrepreneurial activities, Anuar acquired a reputation as a philanthropist and sports promoter by collaborating, for example, with the businessman Jorge Pasquel (who also had links to President Alemán and smuggling) to develop baseball in Mexico.⁶¹ They had meshed smoothly into Nuevo León's business circles, and their descendants participated in emblematic businesses in Monterrey. In 1960, for instance, Jorge Canavati Jr.—an engineer and son of Pedro Canavati—served as the public relations manager of the Cuauhtémoc brewery, while in 1953 the family inaugurated one of the most famous hotels in Monterrey—the Ambassador—whose construction was supervised by Espiridión Canavati. The Ambassador was praised in the press as the "pride of the city" due to its size and luxurious installations. Anuar's brother Pedro, one of the family's patriarchs, was the lawyer for the hotel managers, most of whom were relatives.⁶²

But the Canavati clan also had a shady side. Just a few months earlier, in June 1953, the local press reported that two Syrian-Lebanese millionaires—Jorge Talgie and Jesús Canavati—had been arrested for the large-scale smuggling of nylon clothing after a truck carrying contraband was seized by Customs authorities on the Mexico City–Laredo highway. Canavati was detained when he went to pick up the goods at a trucking firm called Central de Líneas.⁶³

Interestingly, already since 1937 newspapers in Monterrey had reported on the amparos that the federal justice system had granted Pedro Canavati after the Second District Judge in Nuevo Laredo issued the formal warrant for his imprisonment for contraband.⁶⁴ In that same year, the Casa Canavati—a clothing store in Nuevo Laredo owned by Pedro Canavati—offered its employees an end-of-year Christmas party (*posada*). Attendees included Pablo Peña, the mayor, and Gen. Leopoldo Dorantes, commander of the local garrison and another future supporter of the candidacy of Juan Andreu Almazán, along with Tiburcio Garza Zamora and the cream of Laredo's society on both sides of the border.⁶⁵

In 1959, Alfredo Gómez Urcaza, in a letter to President López Mateos, denounced that,

> The main smuggler is the foreigner Pedro Canavati of Monterrey N.L., currently living at Apeninos #2725 Col. Jardín, and with businesses at Padre Mier #361-PT and Modesto Arreola #540 Pte., together with his sons, Jesús P. Canavati, resident in Laredo, Texas, Jorge, who lives in Monterrey at Río Guadalquivir #211-Ote., Col. Del Valle, and Nicolás P. Canavati, whose known address is Río Danubio #215, Col. Del Valle. These individuals have amassed a fortune above 100 million pesos only through smuggling, but no

one has ever bothered them because they wield powerful influence, especially over the previous customs director, Lic. Jesús Arizmendi Marquina, who was paid huge amounts to allow them to continue operating unpunished [sic].[66]

The letter continued:

The men in charge of moving the goods along the river, before transferring it to trucks or planes, were the smugglers Ramiro and Octavio Barrera, Juan González, also known as Juan el Chapeado, Santiago Guerra and Ramón Rodríguez, the latter living in Los Guerra, Tamaulipas. All the merchandise passes through [his] ranch, located in that town and [is then] transported in trucks, because this ranch offers the advantage of sitting near the river to Roma, Texas. Merchandise is usually moved at night or in the early morning with the support of the commander of the Customs office, Alejandro Bernal Garza [sic].[67]

According to a 1974 report by the DFS, Ramiro Barrera, Juan González, and Santiago Guerra were well-known smugglers of various goods, including firearms and drugs, who belonged to the organized crime network that trafficked under the protection of the region's Customs and security authorities. The report also identified Juan N. Guerra as a principal figure.[68] This shows that those men had been participating in such illicit activities since the 1950s and had links with important businessmen. In 1963, Raúl Pérez Gil also wrote to President López Mateos on this matter. In addition to confirming the participation of Pedro, Nicolás P., Jorge, and Jesús Canavati in smuggling, he revealed that:

The person in charge of moving the merchandise both in Monterrey and Mexico City was Juan González, El Chapeado, who lives at Tulancingo #1548, Col. Las Mitras Monterrey, N.L. Almost all goods cross the border at Piedras Negras, Coah., or Cd. Miguel Alemán, Tamps. The way they smuggle the goods is they send [them] through Piedras Negras, Coah., to Mexico, while merchandise destined for their clients in Monterrey, N.L., goes through Cd. Miguel Alemán, Tamps.
[...] In Monterrey, N.L., they're protected by the chief of the First Zone, Guillermo Ortiz Rubio, first commander Antonio Guerrero Velázquez, Rodolfo González and Antonio Sánchez Flores, all loyal supporters of Canavati, who receive payments from these smugglers.[69]

Juan González, "El Chapeado," was not only a smuggler, but also a savvy real estate investor. As early as 1957 he and his wife had created a front company called Fincas Nuevo León, a company that built residences throughout the city. To protect themselves, they registered the company under their sons' names.[70]

What may have appeared as a lengthy digression from the main topic of this article is actually far from that, for one of the most important smugglers, also linked to Juan N. Guerra, was this Juan *el Chapeado* González.[71] His real name was Juan Manuel González Garza and he was born in Aguaeguas, Nuevo León, on August 24th, 1911.[72] In 1960, a newspaper in Nuevo León reported that:

> Scared of having his freedom taken away (by fiscal agents), Juan González Garza filed for an amparo in the District Court and was granted a provisional suspension. He said that various agents, apparently of the Federal Fiscal police, looked for him at his home, perhaps intending to arrest him and take him to Mexico City, due to his alleged involvement in activities related to smuggling.[73]

In August 1973, the society section of a Nuevo Leon newspaper reported on another gala event: the marriage of Homero Juan González Herrera, son of Juan Manuel González Garza, to Rosa María García Fuentes. This couple's godparents were a man from Aguaeguas, Nuevo León, and his wife: Carlos Salinas Lozano and Cora G. de Salinas.[74] Carlos Salinas was the brother of Raúl Salinas Lozano, who served as secretary of industry and commerce from 1958 to 1964, and a brother-in-law of Antonio Ortiz Mena, the secretary of the treasury and public credit in the same period. These were precisely the two governmental agencies whose functions included, first, issuing the importation and exportation permits required to conduct international trade, and, second, combating contraband activities. The Salinas brothers were the father and uncle, respectively, of future Mexican president Carlos Salinas de Gortari. Judicial documents from courts in the United States suggest links between Raúl Salinas Lozano and Juan N. Guerra and his nephew, Juan García Abrego, in cocaine trafficking from the late 1980s to the mid-1990s.[75]

Once again, but now moving ahead to the 1960s, another wedding was the occasion for a reunion of this network of powerful actors and businessmen who constantly appeared to have links to key figures involved in diverse trafficking activities. Later, those men would create the organized crime group known as the Gulf Cartel. On May 25, 1969, the head of the Molinos Azteca company, former governors Bonifacio Salinas Leal, Eduardo A. Elizondo, and

Eduardo Livas Villareal, as well as Gen. Tiburcio Garza Zamora, Raúl Salinas Lozano, and teacher-politician Carlos Hank González, all got together to celebrate the marriage of the daughter of another businessman, Roberto González Barrera.[76] Many of these men were directly linked to trafficking in the region where Juan N. Guerra was the predominant figure in those years. Additional historical evidence later revealed that other actors recently incorporated into this network would participate in these activities in later decades.[77]

CONCLUSION

Setting aside official state and media imaginaries, the criminal networks that operated diverse trafficking activities along Mexico's northeastern border have been made up of actors and personalities quite distinct from the individuals entrusted with handling the operative dynamics and logistics of those illicit activities. The figure of Juan N. Guerra Cárdenas appears in the media, and in several expressions of collective memory, as a man well-versed in criminal knowledge with exceptional delinquent capacities. While not pretending to look down on Guerra's astuteness, it is clear that the main factor that allowed him to sustain his criminal career, and then develop and expand the criminal network in which he was the dominant figure, was the protection by numerous powerful actors and, in some cases, their active participation in criminal activities. To give an idea of the dimensions of Guerra's operating capacities, consider for example that the 1996 U.S. trial of Juan García Abrego—Guerra's nephew and leader of the Gulf Cartel during the 1980s and 1990s—established that around 1990 his dealers were able to introduce forty tons of cocaine into the United States in one sole shipment, and that the tentacles of the cartel reached all the way to New York City, where regular shipments were received. Trial documents also reveal that the network operated with the support of many institutional protectors, just as it had during the early years, and that the main criminal network that managed trafficking in the region included leading players in the political, security, and commercial domains.[78] It is clear that there is no other way to explain the continued operations of a criminal actor so evidently identified as a smuggler and drug trafficker by diverse government institutions in Mexico that, in fact, had the means to indict him and put him on trial on multiple occasions. Years later, Juan N. Guerra boasted that he was "a product of fate."[79] Perhaps, in light of everything we have seen, it would be more accurate to say that he became what he was thanks to a little help from his friends, that is, from the ongoing support of his partners in the highest tiers of political and economic power, which allowed them to accumulate their own ill-gotten fortunes. These examples may help us understand, much more accurately, the scale, evolution, and composition of organized crime groups devoted to drug trafficking in Mexico.

NOTES

1. Alex Saragoza, *La élite de Monterrey y el Estado mexicano 1880–1940* (Monterrey: Fondo Editorial de Nuevo León, 2008), 172.
2. Germán Barrera González, *Breves apuntes de mi vida* (Cd. Miguel Alemán, n.p., 1972), 13.
3. Archivo General de la Nación (AGN), Dirección General de Investigaciones Políticas y Sociales (DGIPS), caja 127, exp. 30, Inspector PS-1 to Jefe de la Oficina de Información Política y Social, 5/19/1940.
4. *Valley Sunday Star Monitor Herald*, January 26, 1941, 3.
5. *El Norte*, December 9, 1946; AGN/DGIPS, caja 127, exp. 30, Inspector PS-1 to office of Información Política y Social, 5/19/1940.
6. *El Norte*, January 1, 1947, 5.
7. Arturo Alvarado Mendoza, *El portesgilismo en Tamaulipas. Estudio sobre la constitución de la autoridad pública en el México posrevolucionario* (Mexico City: El Colegio de México, 2005), 76–77; Carlos Flores Pérez, *Historias de polvo y sangre. Génesis y evolución del tráfico de drogas en el estado de Tamaulipas* (Mexico City: CIESAS, 2013), 115–22. Participants included Col. Carlos I. Serrano, a senator linked to Alemán who is recognized as the planner and real power behind the Federal Directorate of Public Security (DFS). According to a document from the CIA penned in 1951, Serrano was involved in drug trafficking. Cited in Stephen Niblo, *Mexico in the 1940s. Modernity, Politics and Corruption* (Wilmington, DE: Scholarly Resources, 2001), 178.
8. Ciro De la Garza Treviño, *La Revolución Mexicana en el estado de Tamaulipas* (Mexico City: Librería de Manuel Porrúa, 1971), 737–41.
9. Flores Pérez, *Historias de polvo*, 136–37.
10. AGN, Ramo Presidentes, Miguel Alemán Valdés (MAV), 710.1/57, María Teresa Muro to Benjamín R. Hill, 1/17/1947; Aarón Sáenz Garza to Miguel Alemán, 3/7/1947.
11. *La Voz de la Frontera*, July 21, 1950.
12. Flores Pérez, *Historias de polvo*, 138.
13. Flores Pérez, *Historias de polvo*, 140. In 2011, a request was filed with the general prosecutor of justice of the Federal District to obtain the public version of the dossier on Juan N. Guerra Cárdenas, which is on file in the General Directorate of Politics and Criminal Statistics, through the Institute of Access to Public Information of the Federal District. The number of the request is rr. 1190/2011.

14. The search for these data was conducted on the *Family Search* website at https://familysearch.org/pal:/MM9.1.1/MQ86-HFJ.

15. *Brownsville Herald*, January 26, 1996.

16. AGN/DGIPS, caja 127, exp. 30, Inspector PS-1 to Jefe de la Oficina de Información Política y Social, 6/19/1940.

17. *Noticiero*, July 25, 1947, 1.

18. Flores Pérez, *Historias de polvo*, 144–46.

19. De la Garza, *La Revolución Mexicana*, 734; *Noticiero Diario de la Tarde*, April 9, 1956, 5. On the partisan accusation by Judge Guerra, see De la Garza, *La Revolución Mexicana*, 1025.

20. *Noticiero Diario de la Tarde*, April 7, 1956, 1, 4.

21. Flores Pérez, *Historias de polvo*, 153. On the quality of the magistrate Morales Cadena, see *Noticentro Tamaulipas*, February 11, 2015, online at: http://noticentro.mx/2015/02/11/propone-gobernador-ratificacion-del-magistrado-raul-morales-cadena/, accessed March 31, 2017.

22. *El Porvenir*, July 14, 1957, 2.

23. *Noticiero Diario de la Tarde*, April 16, 1960, 1–2.

24. *Noticiero Diario de la Tarde*, April 16, 1960, 1–2.

25. *El Regional de Matamoros*, April 17, 1960.

26. *El Regional de Matamoros*, April 20, 1960; *Noticiero Diario de la Tarde*, April 21, 1960, 1–4; *El Regional de Matamoros*, April 21, 1960, 1, and police news page.

27. *El Regional de Matamoros*, June 11, 1960, police news page.

28. *El Regional de Matamoros*, April 19, 1960, 1, and police news page.

29. *Noticiero Diario de la Tarde*, April 16, 1960, 1–2.

30. *Noticiero Diario de la Tarde*, April 16, 1960, 1–2.

31. *Noticiero Diario de la Tarde*, April 26, 1960, 1, 3.

32. *Noticiero Diario de la Tarde*, May 14, 1960, 1, 3. On the participation of the Guerra Cárdenas brothers in distributing Carta Blanca beer, see *El Bravo de Matamoros*, March 21, 1957, 3.

33. AGN/DFS, Versión Pública Tiburcio Garza Zamora, f. 49. Undated document from the DFS on the municipality of Reynosa.

34. *El Porvenir*, April 15, 1960, 2.

35. *El Porvenir*, April 16, 1960, 8.

36. *El Porvenir*, April 18, 1960, 8.

37. AGN, Ramo Presidentes, Adolfo López Mateos (ALM), 541/248, Customs Supervisor to Adolfo López Mateos, 4/24/1960. The informant places the Hualala ranch in Reynosa, but it is actually in the municipality of San Fernando. In 1960, the municipality of Río Bravo had not yet been created, so the municipalities of Reynosa and San Fernando abutted. In any case, this ranch was not in the boundary area at the time.

38. *Noticiero Diario de la Tarde*, May 24, 1960, 1, 2.

39. *Noticiero Diario de la Tarde*, September 2, 1960, 1, 4.
40. *Noticiero Diario de la Tarde*, September 29, 1960, 1, 4.
41. *Noticiero Diario de la Tarde*, August 12, 1960, 1, 4.
42. *Noticiero Diario de la Tarde*, August 22, 1960, 1.
43. *Noticiero Diario de la Tarde*, September 19, 1960, 4.
44. *Noticiero Diario de la Tarde*, August 22, 1960, 4.
45. Procuraduría General de Justicia del Estado de Nuevo León, *Procuradores de Justicia en Nuevo León. Una retrospectiva a su vida y origen desde 1917 en honor al valor y la justicia* (Monterrey: Procuraduría General de Justicia del Estado de Nuevo León, n.d.), 45.
46. AGN/DFS, Versión Pública Octavio Villa Coss, Memo from Colonel Manuel Rangel Escamilla, 10/11/1960, 12.
47. AGN/DFS, Versión Pública Octavio Villa Coss, Memo from Colonel Manuel Rangel Escamilla, 10/11/1960, 12.
48. AGN/DFS, Versión Pública Octavio Villa Coss, Memo from Colonel Manuel Rangel Escamilla, 10/11/1960, 13.
49. AGN/DFS, Versión Pública Octavio Villa Coss, Memo from Colonel Manuel Rangel Escamilla, 10/11/1960, 16.
50. (S.A.) *Informe Confidencial*, 8/27/1957, Versión Pública, Raúl Gárate Legleu, DFS, AGN, 7. Raúl Morales Farías's relation with General Gárate was also reported in the press. For example, in October 1952, various friends of Gárate organized a lunch for the former governor while he was a senator. The first person to speak publicly and congratulate him was, precisely, Raúl Morales Farías. Another attendee was Gen. Tiburcio Garza Zamora. See *El Heraldo de Brownsville*, October 21, 1952, 1.
51. Procuraduría General de la República, *Memoria de la Procuraduría General de la República 1963–1964* (Mexico City: PGR, 1964), 220–22.
52. Luis Rodríguez Manzanera, *Los estupefacientes y el Estado mexicano*, 2nd ed. (Mexico City: Ediciones Botas, 1974), 61.
53. De la Garza, *La Revolución Mexicana*, 754–55. In 1962, a DGIPS report on Advento Guerra Barrera—a figure in local politics—revealed a certain public disgust with the permanence of these families in public office. AGN/DGIPS, Versión Pública Advento Guerra Barrera, 1–2. Of the twenty mayors elected between 1950 and 2007, twelve had one or both of these surnames.
54. *El Porvenir*, April 24, 1960, 8.
55. Yolanda Figueroa, *El Capo del Golfo. Vida y captura de Juan García Abrego* (Mexico City: Grijalbo, 1996), 20.
56. *El Porvenir*, April 24, 1960, 8.
57. *Noticiero Diario de la Tarde*, March 8, 1960, 1, 4.
58. *El Porvenir*, September 29, 1960, 1, 5, society section.
59. *El Porvenir*, September 29, 1960.
60. *Excélsior*, May 3, 1974, 22.

61. On the relationship between Anuar Canavati and Jorge Pasquel, see *Tiempo Real*, April 25, 2015. On Pasquel's relationship with Alemán and smuggling, see Niblo, *Mexico in the 1940s*, 212–15 and 344–47. Niblo reported information suggesting that Pasquel was apparently one of Alemán's *prestanombres*. He also includes information from primary sources that links Pasquel to drug trafficking.

62. *El Porvenir*, November 30, 1960, 10. See also *El Porvenir*, December 4, 1953, 23, 25.

63. *El Porvenir*, June 3, 1953, 1.

64. *El Porvenir*, January 15, 1937, 4.

65. On this party, see *El Tiempo de Laredo*, December 24, 1937, 1. On General Dorantes's relationship with Almazán and Tiburcio Garza Zamora, see Juan Andreu Almazán, *Memorias, informes y documentos sobre la campaña política de 1940* (Mexico City: Quintanar Impresor, 1941), 105.

66. AGN/ALM, 564.3/7, Alfredo Gómez Urcaza to Adolfo López Mateos, 8/5/1959.

67. AGN/ALM, 564.3/7, Alfredo Gómez Urcaza to Adolfo López Mateos, 8/5/1959.

68. AGN/DFS, Versión Pública, Francisco Guerra, 1.

69. AGN/ALM, 564.3/7, Raúl Pérez Gil to Adolfo López Mateos, undated but received 7/9/1963.

70. Instituto Registral y Catastral del Estado de Nuevo León, Notaría Pública N° 10, Escritura Pública Número 1907, 5/24/1971.

71. *El Norte*, June 7, 1995.

72. Archivo del Registro Civil de Agualeguas, Nuevo León, Acta de Nacimiento no. 78, Año 1911, Nacimientos, Años 1911–1920. Available online at: https://familysearch.org/ark:/61903/3:1:33SQ-G5PY-ZYR?mode=g&i=48&wc=M6ST-16D%3A203524101%2C203705401&cc=1916238, accessed April 21, 2017.

73. *El Porvenir*, January 27, 1960, 2.

74. *El Porvenir*, August 3, 1973, 7. This publication included a photograph of the groom with his relatives, including Juan Manuel González Garza.

75. United States of America v. $9,041,598.68, H-95-3182, 6/15/1995, document 125, 4–8, United States District Court, Southern District of Texas, Houston Division. This document was sealed by the court but was filtered to the Mexican press. The reporter, Carlos Marín, published it in an article in the magazine *Proceso*, February 17, 1997. See Flores Pérez, *Historias de polvo*, 273–76.

76. *El Porvenir*, May 25, 1969, 1, 7, society section.

77. See Flores Pérez, *Historias de polvo*, chaps. 4 and 5.

78. United States v. Juan García Abrego, CR. No. H-93.167-SS, Appendix A, 6, 29–30 and 33, United States District Court for the Southern District of Texas, Houston Division.

79. *Brownsville Herald*, January 26, 1996, http://www.brownsvilleherald.com/news/matamoros-28819—mexican-garcia.html, accessed April 21, 2017.

PART III

Drug Trafficking, the Drug War, the Dirty War, and the Unintended Consequences

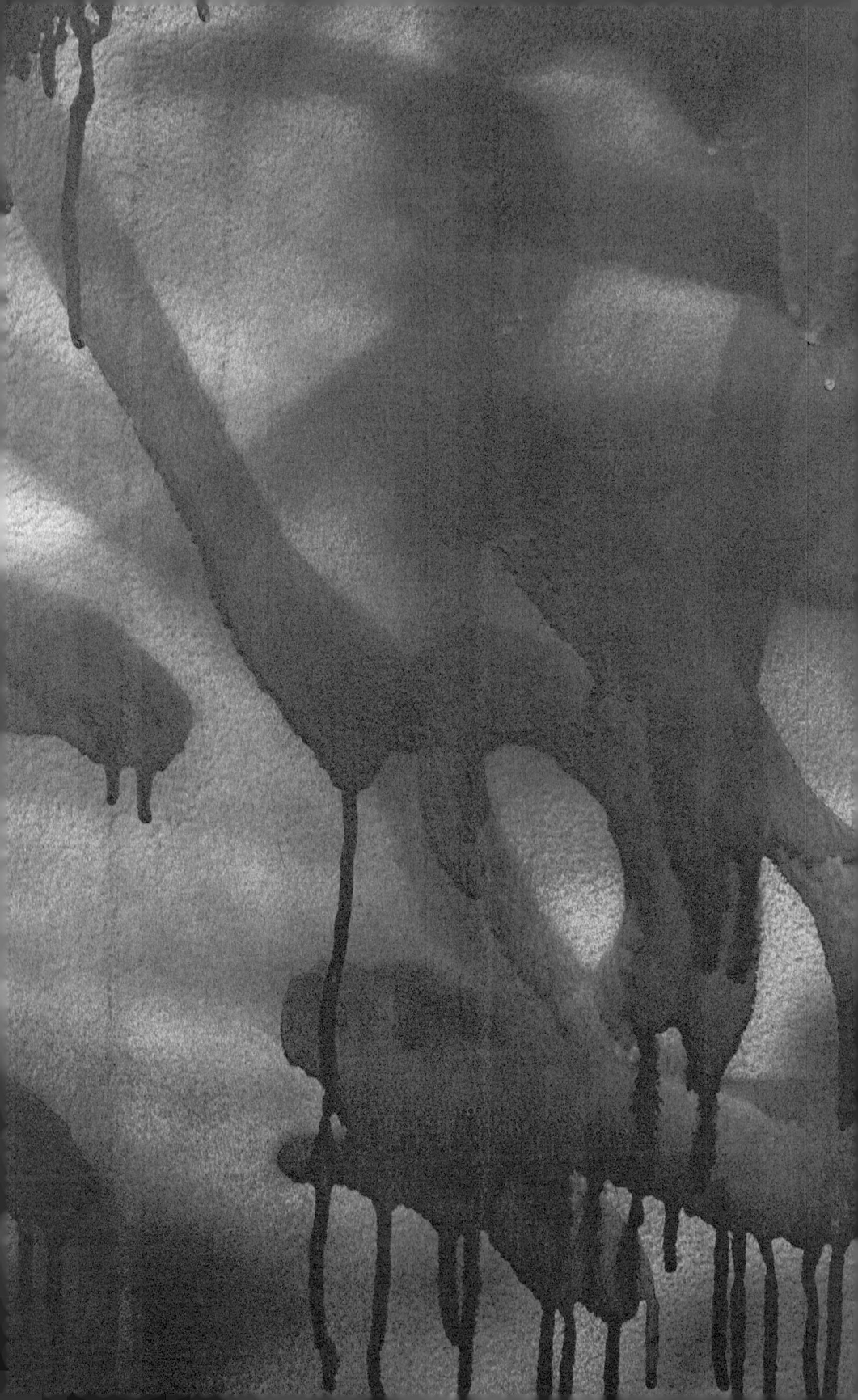

10

Caciques, Traffickers, and Soldiers
Drug Trafficking in the *Cardenista* Territory of Michoacán, 1960–1970

SALVADOR MALDONADO ARANDA

INTRODUCTION

Since the early decades of the twentieth century, the state of Michoacán has been one of the most prominent Mexican states in the geography of drug trafficking in the country, but it also has been the subject of a long history of diplomatic discussions of the "drug problem" between the governments of Mexico and the United States.[1] Indeed, Michoacán stands out because of recurring federal interventions to combat trafficking and the violence that accompanied them. Parallel to this, the national government has long shown interest in the state's history of local *caciquismo*, that is, local territorial domains controlled by political "bosses" where poppies and marijuana were often cultivated.[2] In the same period, regional political leaders engaged in dramatic political-ideological confrontations with the federal state that generated broad fissures between the federation and Michoacán.[3] Later, in 1962, the army repressed a clandestine *sinarquista* movement operating from the mountains—shrouded by drug plantations—that fought to defend its churches.[4] These are but some of the episodes that form part of the history of Michoacán in which, without doubt, drug trafficking played a significant role.

Early in 1958, recently elected president Adolfo López Mateos ordered one of the first military campaigns against drugs and delinquency in Michoacán in response to international pressures to eradicate illicit narcotics cultivation and trafficking and, at the same time, take advantage of incursions by the army to impose limits on caciques (local bosses) in the state. Later, the fight against drug trafficking extended to other missions, even penetrating into what some authors call the *cardenista* fiefdom, which was constituted around the Cárdenas family (Lázaro and Dámaso) and also consisted of small local cacicazgos that, according to Veledíaz, protected trafficking operations.[5] It is against this background that this chapter addresses the following questions: What was the nature of the fight against trafficking? What role did the army play in it? What were its results and consequences? And what can this case teach us about the role of the Mexican state in relation to the War on Drugs?[6]

BRIEF NOTES ON THE NATIONAL AND INTERNATIONAL CONTEXT

Exhaustive documentation on the agenda of bilateral relations between México and the United States in the early twentieth century provides a fascinating account of the complexity of the geography of Mexican trafficking and of the roles played by Mexican authorities and the traffickers themselves.[7] During numerous meetings of representatives of the two nations to align the bilateral agenda for combating drugs, Mexico's delegation emphasized that since 1947 the federal government had initiated "permanent national campaigns" to convince growers to "voluntarily" destroy illegal crops.[8] Mexico's representative added that authorities were conducting "educational programs for peasants to motivate them to produce legal crops and aerial surveillance to detect prohibited plantations. He noted that the persecution of drug growers in the northwest had had the effect of displacing them further south, towards Michoacán and Jalisco."[9] U.S. pressure to control drugs had not eased at all since that time. In the 1950s the U.S. Senate subcommittee that investigated juvenile delinquency began to focus attention on the flow of illicit drugs from Mexico into Southern California.[10] Its conclusions—delivered directly to the president—included the finding that because the international border was the main entry point for drugs, stanching the flow would be impossible. It therefore recommended a strategy of destroying illegal plantations in Mexico, after it had concluded that despite a series of bilateral accords, U.S. policy had not been "sufficiently aggressive" and had failed to sustain "sufficient pressure" on Mexican authorities.[11] In 1962, in the aftermath of this report, and as military action against drugs in Mexico commenced, presidents Adolfo López Mateos and John F. Kennedy confirmed that they needed to collaborate to resolve the drug problem.

This was the setting for the first anti-drug-trafficking campaigns in Michoacán. Efforts to eradicate illicit plantations and the violence they generated turned out to be much more complex than anyone had expected. It also became clear that multiple problematics, aside from the drug trade, needed to be addressed on the ground: illegal timber markets, cattle rustling, livestock ranching, and armed groups, to name but a few.[12] Also, Michoacán was experiencing a prolonged period of caciquismo, among which the one led by Dámaso Cárdenas, the brother of former president Lázaro Cárdenas, was the most important.[13] In 1949, despite his brother's opposition, Dámaso Cárdenas was nominated as candidate to govern his home state and subsequently triumphed in the election. Dámaso's ambition reflected his intense desire to wield power, fed by his failure to win the governorship in previous years. Thus he maintained his hold on power during the following six-year term, because his successor (David Franco Rodríguez) was tied to him politically. Franco Rodríguez's close links to Dámaso's regional political power explain how the former was first elected as federal congressman in 1949 and, in 1952, as senator.[14] At that time, former president Lázaro Cárdenas was directing a national-level project in southern Michoacán to promote regional agricultural, mining, metallurgic, and infrastructure development.[15] This huge development project was carried out in the center of a region where drug cultivation was expanding, vendetta violence, cattle rustling, and the use of firearms were all rampant, and where long-standing cacique politics with its common use of violence and clientelism was deeply entrenched.[16] It was in this area of southern Michoacán that General Cárdenas spent most of his time, managing perhaps the most ambitious economic project in the Republic, amidst caciques, traffickers, corrupt social and political leaders, and avaricious businessmen but also, at the other end of the political spectrum, amidst oppositional groups and leaders who had found there a fertile space for ideological work and political mobilizations.[17]

So it was that in 1958 the federal government launched its first attack on drugs in Michoacán under tremendous international pressure to eradicate the scourge of illegal narcotics. But that year was also significant because it brought the triumph of the Cuban Revolution, whose main leaders, including Fidel Castro, had received Lázaro Cárdenas's support to remain in Mexico and avoid deportation during the repression of the Batista government.[18] Benítez has pointed out that Cárdenas contributed to "saving" Cuba's revolutionary movement by interceding with President Adolfo Ruiz Cortines (1952–1958) to allow Castro to stay in Mexico. During the succeeding López Mateos presidency, however, the Mexican government became increasingly uneasy regarding Cárdenas's political clout.[19] In his book *Apuntes*, Cárdenas suggests that the political excesses committed by the governing class were due to its economic dependence on foreign countries through signing agreements for the exploitation of Mexico's national resources.[20] Those circumstances spurred General Cárdenas to participate openly in politics, once again, by establishing a firm position to the left of the government.[21] These developments began to concern President López Mateos, especially when the federal government obtained information that at least one shipment of arms from the United States had been discovered in the city of Morelia, and that some Cubans in the city of Uruapan were recruiting people to go to the island. The army knew that Cárdenas was aware of those situations and, allegedly, had evidence that implicated him in them. It seems clear that López Mateos viewed all these events with great concern; in fact, in mid-December 1959, he instructed his secretary of national defense (SEDENA), Agustín Olachea, to infiltrate the cardenista fiefdom.[22]

The political role of the Cárdenas family and its power networks based on local caciques, together with U.S. pressure to expand the War on Drugs, forged a political panorama that seemed to convince López Mateos that he had no choice but to authorize a military campaign against drugs and violence in Michoacán. So in 1959 the 49th Infantry Battalion was deployed to the city of Apatzingán under the orders of Cdr. Salvador Rangel Medina.[23] There, the battalion, the state police, and an agency of the Secret Service were instructed to "impose a little order" by administering an "ongoing whipping" effectuated by military units deployed in twenty-seven strategic points in southern Michoacán. Our research suggests that the military intervention against narcotics in the cardenista sanctuary, while clearly a response to international antidrug pressures, also sheds considerable light on how the fight against drugs was utilized as a means of constructing state hegemony in regions where caciques were—to at least some extent—sufficiently powerful to demonstrate their insubordination to national power.[24] Upon evaluating these military operations in Michoacán, and subsequent federal interventions,[25] the first element that emerges is that antidrug policies were transformed into an early extension of power struggles between regional and national interests that could well have turned the bilateral agenda on drugs on its head and opened the way for those policies to become resources for constructing the dominance of the federal state.[26]

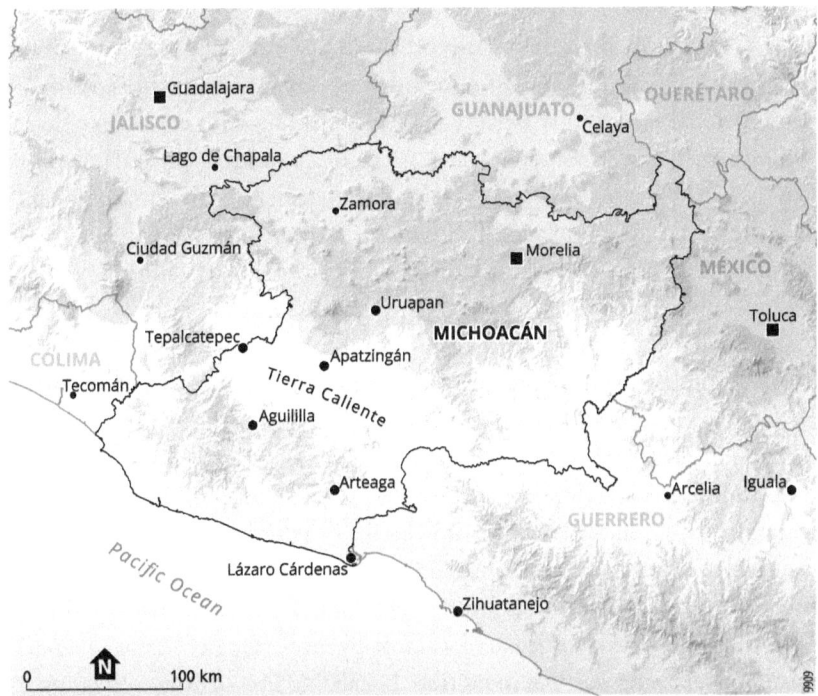

MAP 5 Map of Michoacán (credits: UU-Geo-C&M–Carto).

PREPARING THE GROUND FOR INTERVENTIONS

The secretary of national defense instructed Commander Rangel Medina to take certain precautions in military operations against drug trafficking in Michoacán. He was authorized to act independently of the 21st Military Zone in Morelia, which at the time was commanded by Félix Ireta, an ex-governor, military officer, and personal friend of Lázaro Cárdenas. General Olachea suggested doing reconnaissance before deploying the battalion. When Rangel Medina returned from those rounds, as he recalled years later in a conversation with journalist Veledíaz, he had understood that "the leaves of the trees don't move" without first consulting ex-president Cárdenas. Upon assuming control of the garrison in Apatzingán, and after a press conference at which he was questioned about his real objectives, Commander Rangel took advantage of his independence from the military based in Michoacán to prohibit the establishment of brothels around the army base and ask the mayor to regulate nightclubs and alcohol sales, among other things. In response to these measures, various armed groups shot up the military installations around dawn one day. Undeterred, Rangel decreed that the members of *defensas rurales* (rural defense forces) that "strutted" around bearing arms could only do so while on active duty, another measure that caused bewilderment and provoked new assaults.[27] Protests against the battalion continued in the ensuing weeks, and a soldier accused the leader of the unit assigned to the municipality of Aguililla of sending his men into private homes to steal everything they could and of selling firearms elsewhere. Despite strictly punishing those involved, Commander Rangel was unable to control acts of corruption.

After completing his reconnaissance of the terrain, Rangel implemented a strategy of gathering information from local authorities, muleteers, and merchants in order to better assess the prevailing situation. Military bulletins from those years clearly show that narcotics were Rangel's primary concern, which included not only the identification of trafficking, but also the location and size of production sites, forms of cultivation and processing, and transportation and commercialization networks. Once his men had gathered what they considered sufficient "local intelligence" (*inteligencia pueblerina*), the first operations were put in motion. Localizing sites of drug cultivation in those years, however, was no easy task for the army. In fact, a military bulletin issued by the 49th Battalion states that:

> Before its transfer to Michoacán, the campaign to combat poppy-growers and opium-traffickers occupied an important place in the missions assigned to the Battalion three years ago (1959). Inexplicably these [illicit] activities had become normal work in some regions in southern Michoacán. Many people affirm that the plantations and freedom that growers enjoyed had reached such extremes that poppy gum often replaced money in commercial transactions [...]
>
> [Regarding] the activities performed to discover and destroy fields and persecute growers and traffickers [...] it is no exaggeration to say that Aguililla and parts of Coalcomán, Tumbiscatío, and Aquila are making history as municipalities where illegal crops flourish [...] Regular surveillance there, pursuing known individuals to discover the location of gum produced in previous years that has not yet been sold, and the unalterable posture of never compromising with traffickers, will suffice to maintain the successes obtained to date.[28]

According to Rangel, the drugs were "of the best quality used for export," and the fields were "gigantic, well-fertilized, irrigated and fumigated, like a special gift for millionaires and people with exclusive tastes."[29] Apparently, the main destination of the drugs produced in Michoacán was the United States, and the transport routes commonly ran through cities and towns where local leaders or caciques protected operations in the territories they controlled. These bulletins identify some caciques on the coast and in the Tierra Caliente, political leaders in Morelia, and, above all, officials in charge of public order in indigenous communities and villages in the sierra who protected trafficking. In fact, the fight against narcotics often led to open or covert combat with local authorities who were henchmen of the caciques who protected traffickers. The bulletin also narrates that:

> [Our] mate Quintero [...] just carried out a raid that could have been successful, for all preparations had been made to destroy a marijuana field of over a thousand square meters. But success soon turned to failure, [because] the official in charge of public order was informed in time, so when our [operatives] arrived, they found only stalks, for all the branches had been removed. They could only gather a few kilos as a sample, a bit of seed, and remains of the plants that had been harvested.[30]

A second bulletin, dated October 1962, said, "some audacious men there still strive, at all costs, to maintain Aguililla as a center for traffickers and gum-suppliers."[31] Despite this cold reality, in December 1962 the commander wrote:

> Well friends, we're approaching the end of our third year in these lands that have become infamous in other areas of the country; its poor fame due to the more-or-less unfit character of many of its inhabitants. Comparing the work performed over the past twelve months with the activities of previous years, we conclude that this year gives no cause for complaint about what was accomplished since, as usual, we have just returned from an operation called Terrenate. [...] The year that ends may well be remembered as one of successful missions in all we proposed to do in all respects. Regarding narcotics, fresh [in our minds] are the names Estopila, Marcelino, Chupamirto, Changunga, Comanche, Amistad and Cardoso, operations conducted in the sierra that, compensating for the terror, privations and fatigues [suffered], succeeded in destroying one hundred and fifty-seven hectares of poppy and twenty-one marijuana fields, plus the ones gutted by the growers themselves

before we could get there, or in response to calls by the 49th [Battalion]. Over forty traffickers were arrested [...] we had the good fortune to operate under the orders of General Higuera in the Ahuijullo operation, with troops from the 8th Dragons Regiment and the 25th Infantry.

We also advanced in [seizing] drugs [...] over twelve kilos of gum and a raid by Quintero that confiscated more than three kilos of that drug while it was being weighed. Other investigations led us to lay our hands on several "little angels" here in Apatzingán and Uruapan, sometimes on our own initiative, but more recently on instructions from the National Defense.

Regarding villains, those affected have no reason to complain [...] no matter where they were sent to rest [and] enjoy a well-deserved repose, from Nueva Italia to the sea, on the coast, and from Coahuayana to Melchor Ocampo. They were many, but we see that the list hasn't ended. Our efforts to control cattle rustling failed in some areas and were only half-successful in others.

Regarding internal security, we conducted two operations: Cananea and Terrenate. The former entailed many sacrifices and privations for the personnel [...] while on the second [...] there's no more to say [but] we failed to find any leaders (gallos de estaca) [...].[32]

According to these military bulletins, only a few years after arriving in Michoacán, the army had successfully investigated many aspects of the region, including its geography and political, economic, and social problems. Likewise, it had come to partially comprehend the protection networks that intertwined traffickers with local authorities, strategies for concealing cultivation sites, and the perils that soldiers faced in armed skirmishes or while on routine reconnaissance. They also had a clearer understanding of their own limitations in terms of dismantling trafficking operations in areas where de facto sovereignties were firmly entrenched. Conducting military operations required sending patrols to scout the lands between sierra and coast looking for fields and traffickers for weeks or even months. Locating fields was complicated and risky. Testimony Carlos Flores gathered from a commander who led a military unit as part of operation *Pulpo* in Michoacán at the end of the 1960s highlights the adverse conditions entailed in the struggle against drug trafficking:

We couldn't enter many places for they were totally inaccessible and, in reality, our forces were too few to penetrate such areas. Places like Aguililla, for example, part of Michoacán, around Caleta de Campos, have no roads

[but] were full of marijuana. You could easily spot the plantations, but couldn't go in; there weren't enough troops, and we weren't all that eager [...] The zone commander knew where the fields were [but] rarely acted because he didn't have the ways or means.[33]

The difficulties the army faced in eradicating drugs included inaccessible terrain, protection networks in collusion with local authorities, armed skirmishes under unequal circumstances, and questionable military discipline. In fact, it was virtually impossible to eliminate trafficking because, as the bulletins show, ringleaders were friendly with politicians in the state capital of Morelia. The commander's many inquiries led him to uncover significant networks connecting public officials to the drug world and to confirm that several local bosses (*cabecillas*) enjoyed—directly or indirectly—the support of General Cárdenas, who, as is well-known, had established a short-lived, state-run morphine program during his presidency, though he soon bowed to international pressure and closed it down. According to Commander Rangel, "Every day, the information patrols compiled on the ground with peasants made it clearer that those involved in the trafficking business had friendships in Morelia and with the Executive of the Tepalcatepec project" [i.e., General Cárdenas]. Surprisingly, he acknowledged that his subordinates had informed him of an episode in which the battalion's subcommander and second-in-command—taking advantage of Rangel's absence—granted permits in his name to bear arms and gave some traffickers permits to plant drugs.[34] But the most surprising fact is that Rangel, whom the army considered a straight arrow (*recto*) and strict leader (*cabrón*), seemed incapable of doing anything substantive to curb the godfathers of the drug trade. Even so, on November 6, 1964, he made this pompous statement to the media: "*Drug trafficking has now ended in the tierra caliente* [...] Having eliminated the main traffickers, now conspicuous by their absence, peons and former growers are devoted to honourable work; local residents no longer flee upon seeing soldiers and, according to reports we've gathered, planting drugs is a thing of the past."[35]

In January 1965, however, the commander complained of the trivial cooperation by state agencies to limit the freedoms enjoyed by traffickers and other criminals. In his words, "This comment is relevant because lately we have seen cases of people who, availing themselves of legalistic tricks or the most varied resources, escape the punishment they deserve. [This] just occurred with a pair of traffickers and a man with many prior arrests who, after long pursuit, were apprehended [but] obtained their freedom in much less time than it took to transfer and consign them."³⁶ During this lament he added:

> Apart from negating the troops' efforts to maintain the rule of law so as to ensure the peace of mind of good people [...] the real danger for citizens of letting such delinquents walk free is that they aided in detaining them, so when the accused are back on the streets feeling like they have impunity, they not only carry on with greater bravado, but immediately seek revenge on those who, directly or indirectly, tipped off the soldiers so they could perform their duty. In several cases, people who acted as guides have been murdered, or who, running similar risks, facilitated the arrest of delinquents, paid for their devotion to justice with their lives once the criminals were freed. Safety in the region as the basis for its integral development; the success of classic antidrugs military campaigns and other activities, and the work of convincing people we began a while ago so that residents would come to trust the law when problems arise that are of the exclusive competence of judicial officials, risk failing as long as officials apply procedures that do not reflect reality. Hence, placing the common good above all else, we call on the authorities to apply the Penal Code with well-defined, practical criteria.³⁷

THE IRREGULAR WAR ON DRUG TRAFFICKING

A review of the battalion's bulletins makes it clear that drug cultivation and trafficking in Michoacán had spread to many regions; that this expansion occurred within a complex context that combined geography, dispersed population centers, and protection networks or tolerance; and that eradicating this system did not depend exclusively on the capacity to use force, but rather on a whole constellation of local and regional powers that were perfectly capable of frustrating all kinds of military operations. In fact, more than fifty soldiers and a lieutenant were killed by traffickers or caciques during military operations. For example, in the March 1963 bulletin, the commander wrote, "According to reports received, on the first of this month a highly distinguished officer of the battalion was shot in the back in Melchor Ocampo. This was none other than our friend Refugio Ruíz Prado, a valiant and peaceful man who [was] the leader of the corps in Arteaga [...] The killer is a cacique from the coast [who] is held in jail in Ocampo."³⁸ Faced with these adverse conditions, the army came to conclude that the protocols dictated for military action were limited compared to the scale of violence. In the November 1962 bulletin we read that:

> According to the current missions entrusted to the battalions and regiments, reality shows that the prosecution of criminals, the fight to control cattle rustling, the antinarcotics campaigns, and the general disarmament program itself, which at first sight promised to be quite simple, require the constant application of procedures more related to irregular warfare than to the norms established for organically structured units, as the battalion has proven during its three years of deployment in Michoacán's tierra caliente.[39]

Applying procedures of irregular warfare—as during the Cold War—meant doing espionage in towns and villages, open or selective military combat, interrogating civilians without judicial orders and regardless of any criminal record—or lack thereof—and disarmament. Schemes of irregular warfare opened the door to other military strategies, such as creating civil (paramilitary) defense patrols by recruiting local inhabitants, training them in self-defense and the use of firearms, and then sending them back home to fight drug traffickers. Authorizing strategies of irregular warfare broadened the army's powers to interfere with local order. At that point, Commander Rangel told his subordinates:

> The Ministry of National Defense has dictated a disposition that outlines the cases in which troops can intervene in affairs related to effectuating resolutions of the Agrarian Department. That disposition stipulates that interventions may only occur after a petition has been channeled through the Ministry of the Interior to the Ministry of National Defense, so the [National] Defense itself shall dictate the ensuing orders. At the same time, the Ministry reminds you that federal forces must not intervene in the holding of ejidal assemblies, not even on the pretext of maintaining order. Finally, the disposition leaves it to the criteria of the zone's military commander whether to order his troops to intervene in cases where order has been disrupted [and] to support the police when they are insufficient, whatever the circumstances, under the guiding principle that the constitutional mission of our Armed Institution can best be fulfilled by preventing alterations of public order.[40]

This bulletin concludes with this observation: "As the intervention of many outstanding services had become a custom in cases like those anticipated in the disposition, company and unit commanders [shall] take note that these shall not be repeated henceforth, except for those ordered by the Command of the 21st Military Zone."[41] This clearly indicates that army patrols had routinely intervened in meetings of civil society on the pretext of imposing order in the region. It is hardly surprising, of course, to learn that these orders were not always respected. The documents reviewed reveal that the army continued to intervene in ejidal meetings, disputes, and public demonstrations. In fact, the battalion's commander stated that the army would never "waste its time in useless discussions as to whether or not it should perform the tasks that pertain to soldiers or gendarmes."[42] The monthly bulletins thus allow us to infer that the new orders sent to the armed forces only formalized and legitimized their acts during ejidal or neighborhood assemblies, in executing judicial sentences, in periodically inspecting civilians, and in evicting ejidatarios who invaded lands or held demonstrations. As mentioned above, the Tierra Caliente was the region where General Cárdenas directed the most important agricultural development project in the state. But the implementation of agrarian reform and fomenting the region's agricultural development had allowed neo-latifundios and caciquismo to expand, a situation Cárdenas openly criticized. This situation had led to the emergence of peasant and neighborhood organizations and the Union of Public Service Users, many of which had connections with the Central Campesina Independiente (CCI) or the Movimiento de Liberación National (MNL). According to Nava, "The Cárdenas who returned to politics stood clearly to the left of the national political system. When [. . .] he was informed of the neo-latifundios formed around Apatzingán by the North American Jenkins, he declared that 'México is not safe from a revolution because when monopolies are allowed to develop they cause social unrest, which always translates into movements of social evolution.'"[43] Our research on the role of the Tepalcatepec and Balsas Commission in southern Michoacán provides sufficient historical evidence of the agrarian, political, and social problems in which the army openly intervened.[44]

The army's new marching orders gave it more freedom to broaden its scope of activity. In the aforementioned Terrenate security operation, a group of heavily armed men raided, disarmed, and captured members of the rural defense forces of Los Anonillos (a small village in Tepalcatepec) after they had set up camp in the sierra in open rebellion against the federal government. Commander Rangel pointed out that

> Upon investigating the case, it turned out that this version was correct that there were numerous groups and uprisings among the Defense Forces in the area. It involved sinarquistas who defended their churches (and priests) from the threat of destruction. Informants reported they had fled into the mountains to fight the government and communists, with many of our boys going back to the days of wearing sandals and white cotton pants (calzón) [...] of signal codes, of wearing, or shaving, off beards and mustaches, of concealing carabines in the folds of their loose clothing and, as one might well suppose, of bus terminals being invaded by peasants with military-like haircuts [...] The raid went well, and in less time than it takes a rooster to crow, three of the main leaders were apprehended and, of course, taken to Morelia."[45]

A total of forty-one men surrendered.[46]

Understandably, the military strategies to eradicate trafficking and violence in the study area produced assaults on civilians by "commanders for whom contact with civil society and the attentions they receive make them lose their head so that they begin to suppose that such attentions are the least that their imaginary merits deserve, so instead of serving impartially and striving to make rich and poor alike see their units as symbols of law and order, they seek personal benefit and so become veritable vultures that molest and abuse the humblest and poorest."[47]

FROM IRREGULAR WAR TO SOCIAL SURVEILLANCE

Shifting the army's antitrafficking operations toward diffusing agrarian conflicts and controlling crime-related violence had become a common practice simply because growing and transporting drugs was deeply entrenched in so many rural communities.[48] Those activities had long been under military surveillance, but the severity of these situations magnified as daily violence among local civilians expanded and the municipal police proved incapable of doing much about it. In one of many letters sent to the state attorney general—this one dated October 3, 1962—a man named Telésforo denounced the death of his son at the hands of the rural defense forces: "I didn't bother to inform the local authorities because I'm sure the municipal police aren't in any condition to combat these delinquents, simply because they're so heavily armed and the police have only nightsticks and one or two pretty useless rifles. Therefore, I ask the federal forces to take charge and proceed to disarm the rural defense forces."[49] Missives with similar messages were often sent to the attorney general or the command of the 21st Military Zone. In one dated September 10, 1965, petitioners for lands in Coalcomán denounced to the governor that they were victims of landowners "by virtue of the fact that they [control] the Rural Defense's arms."[50] Meanwhile, the town leader (*jefe de tenencia*) of Cenobio Moreno, municipality of Apatzingán, beseeched the mayor time and again to send the municipal police on campaigns against alcoholism, gambling and prostitution, among other vices, "[but] was always denied under the pretext that members of the police force had been assigned to other, more important, activities."[51]

Other files contain letters from neighborhood representatives in Apatzingán who pleaded with officials to send forces that could "impose a bit of order" on the operations of brothels, "disguised as saloons or restaurants." Moreover, the society of heads of families of a primary school near one of many brothels in the area petitioned state authorities to close a saloon where brawls occurred "due to the presence of 'ladies of the evening' that local authorities choose to ignore."[52] Well-known nightclubs, like the Cadillac, El 33, and El Taxi, paradoxically, were actually visited frequently by municipal police, soldiers, businessmen, and common folk. In response to this deluge of accusations, the state attorney general commissioned the head of the Secret Service to investigate. That official entrusted the mission to two of his agents, who filed the following report: "All the brothels, saloons and restaurants operate selling alcoholic drinks on Saturdays and Sundays. The proprietors of the establishments pay what they call 'simulations' to the Municipal Treasury."[53] Upon receiving this news, the state government ordered the army to secretly investigate murders in saloons and brothels. A printed report included in a confidential letter to the minister of the interior stated that inspections of saloons and brothels revealed that they operated day and night with the tacit approval of the police inspector, circumstances that generated the inconformity of other saloonkeepers.[54]

Scenarios like these obliged the armed forces to deal with situations that were much more complex than simply apprehending traffickers. On December 31, 1962, the commander of the corps deployed in Coahuayana reported the death of an ejidatario and several confrontations with so-called delinquents, with whom an agent in the Federal Public Attorney's office was found to be colluding. Similarly, the secretary of a Regional Peasant Committee, Everardo Mendoza, denounced the "grave situation" that civilians in Aquila faced after two gunmen called Guillén murdered eleven people. They requested that the army intervene.[55] In the town of Chapula, municipality of Aguililla, a commission of peasants formally petitioned the governor to provide individual guarantees so they could go out and cultivate their fields, because seven ejidatarios had been murdered by "evildoers" on May 4, 1969. In fact, they asked the military zone to give them escorts.[56] Meanwhile, on February 7, 1966, in La Palma (Apatzingán), several residents who had been victimized by attacks perpetrated by a group of federal agents also complained to the governor, while the delegate from the community of El Pilón, municipality of Buenavista, informed the governor that the military unit in Los Reyes,

> failing to present any order or give information on their mission in the community, had entered ejidatarios' homes on the pretext of searching for firearms. As a result, on the night of 21 January 1968, the unit fired on a group of peasants and children that were walking along the street, killing one ejidatario and injuring a young man. The following Monday, troops under the command of officials who apparently pertained to the Military Zone of Zamora arrived to investigate, but only humiliated ejidatarios and treated one and all like criminals and murderers."

The aforementioned committee reported that "numerous groups of ejidatarios" from Chiquihuitillo and La Nopalera (Apatzingán) manifested that their town was living in a state of agitation and fear because of the constant comings and goings of unknown groups bearing arms; hence they implored the mayor to ask the commander of the 51st Battalion to "carry out permanent search missions."[57]

Turning to acts by the Secret Service, we find that on April 8, 1969, Eloisa Sánchez complained that her husband had been arrested for robbery by the head of that agency.[58] Months later, an inmate of the Apatzingán penitentiary detained for robbery denounced a similar act by the Secret Service.[59] Shortly after that, the prison became a source of accusations of illegal activity, including those of several inmates who said they were still in jail even though they had been absolved judicially. Another case involved the leader of an organization pertaining to the Confederación de Trabajadores Mexicanos union (CTM) in a person's death in which two Secret Service agents were also implicated.[60]

The extraordinary aspect of that case was that it revealed how, in certain milieus, secret agents had become so "popular" with residents that there was no longer anything "secret" about them. In fact, people in Apatzingán wrote to the state government asking it to authorize their participation: "since there are no authorities here, nor commanders to defend residents, we ask the Attorney General to kindly order the Head of the Secret Service of this city to come and investigate, and disarm all those who have become scandalous."[61]

CIVIC-SANITARY MILITARY CAMPAIGNS

By 1962, the military operations against marijuana and poppy cultivation were complemented by new orders that supported social and civic interventions conceived to forge closer relations with citizens. Initiatives of this type, however, were only put into practice after periods of open combat against traffickers, rural violence, and public demonstrations. Commander Rangel described them as attempts to "smooth over" differences with populations that had once been objects of suspicion and repression. According to the leader of the military zone, "The Battalion that patrols the Michoacán *tierra caliente* had been unable to initiate a formal campaign of cooperation with civil authorities in any matter that did not involve taking down villains, pursuing traffickers and cattle rustlers, or carrying out disarmament. [But] conditions have changed, so without abandoning surveillance or slacking off in the combat unit's fundamental missions, the first steps have been taken in a new facet of activities to serve the region." Eight months after writing those notes, in the August 1963 bulletin he noted that "A sanitary and civic crusade has just ended involving inhabitants of indigenous communities. The results could hardly be more encouraging: some 2,283 people were vaccinated; another 1,685 received check-ups and medical attention [and] 254 received dental care."[62] That sanitary and civic program was called operation Cornila. In the area of civic education, campaigns were designed to "explain the Revolution to all indigenous people, what the revolutionary governments have done to benefit peasants and the indigenous, [and] the works that the current government has undertaken. To ensure that nothing was omitted, the operators went to great lengths to explain the role the indigenous themselves can play in the government's projects, their duties towards their communities, and their rights as Mexicans."[63] In two similar operations—Jeringa and Huizontla—the army continued its efforts to achieve rapprochement with local communities, especially those where it had met resistance, like Pómaro, Coire, Aquila, Estopila, and Coalcomán, five localities embedded in drug-producing zones. The goal of those missions was to establish more amicable relations, once some semblance of order had been restored. After some sanitary and civic operations, Rangel believed they "*had won the friendship of those who a year ago were our enemies, weapons in hand*; we hope they have understood the solutions given to the problems of young men of military age."[64]

FROM MICHOACÁN TO GUERRERO

In August 1965, the 49th Battalion received orders to relocate to Iguala in the neighboring state of Guerrero.[65] The 21st Military Zone of Michoacán remained under the command of former governor General Ireta, but he had moderated his opposition to federal intervention. Once the 49th was installed in Iguala, Commander Rangel recalled that the work carried out in Michoacán had allowed the battalion to "acquire valuable professional experience that will be useful in the future, especially when it comes to mobilizing aggressively against villains and drug cultivators or bandits (*cuatreros*)."[66] In fact, before leaving Apatzingán the unit continued to send out military patrols to search for drugs and capture known felons. According to Rangel, there were only pending cases such as "the guy who directed the killing in Salitre of the *rurales* and our soldiers deployed in Coire, and the one who murdered private Arrencaño and soldier Segrero in Piedras Blancas."[67]

In Guerrero, the 49th Battalion began to implement the same strategy, that is, patrolling and scrutinizing trails across the Guerrero landscape, where they found similar problems: cattle rustlers, men with arms, traffickers, and common criminals, among others. But the region now under the battalion's jurisdiction included the area where a guerrilla movement had begun to form. Rangel Medina had been an adviser to the past three presidents, was highly regarded in military and political circles, and had become well-versed in combat tactics through his experience in southern Michoacán.[68] There were considerable similarities between Michoacán's Tierra Caliente and the Costa Grande area of Guerrero in terms of geography, poverty, boss rule (caciquismo), and the involvement of various law enforcement agencies in protecting drug cultivation and trafficking, "[which was] a normal activity in those areas due to the high yields produced."[69]

After his assignments in various military zones, Rangel was named commander of the Military Zone of Guerrero in November 1973 after a private interview with President Echeverría on the recent creation of the Brigada de Ajusticiamiento de los Pobres guerrilla organization in Guerrero. With Rangel Medina's appointment, the army became increasingly involved in combating the guerrilla forces of Lucio Cabañas and Genaro Vázquez, for that was the task he was entrusted with.[70] Upon his arrival in Guerrero, his close friend, Gen. Marcelino García Barragán, said, "now I believe Guerrero will be pacified," adding that he would never forget "the influence that Michoacán has had on the so-called guerrillas of Guerrero."[71]

CONCLUSIONS

At the beginning of this chapter I asked what the case of Michoacán teaches us about the role of the state in drug trafficking in Mexico in the 1960s and 1970s. The historical and anthropological research conducted over more than fifteen years in southern Michoacán, where trafficking flourished with such force and violence, leads me to affirm a number of things. First, the expansion of marijuana and poppy cultivation arose from a changing combination of international antidrug policies and national policies of eradication or tolerance. Second, the struggle against drug trafficking undertaken by the Mexican state revealed a whole series of political and social problems, including the entrenchment of trafficking in rural communities. Various rural caciques exercised territorial control over entire regions or municipalities in collusion with armed groups like rural defense forces or simple gunmen, and it was in those areas where drug cultivation expanded. Those conditions, in turn, gave rise to a type of political, armed, and social protection that made it impossible for state security agencies to completely eradicate trafficking. Third, the Mexican state utilized the fight against trafficking as a strategy for constructing federal control over regions where powerful caciques—like the Cárdenas family—and local cacique-based networks of power could protect, tolerate, or simply turn a blind eye to the expansion of trafficking in their respective territorial domains. It is highly significant that the 49th Infantry Battalion, authorized by President López Mateos to infiltrate the cardenista fiefdom, was commissioned not only to eradicate drug cultivation and apprehend traffickers, but also to act on the margins of a military zone controlled indirectly by General Cárdenas. But when the general and former president

Lázaro Cárdenas began to question the course the country was taking and generate strong political opposition—as in southern Michoacán, where he led a large-scale regional development project—the antitrafficking strategy was broadened to the sphere of public security through interventions in ejido life, bar fights, and violence in rural towns. Finally, we can say that the fight against drug trafficking in Michoacán by the Mexican state would not be a matter of such concern were it not for the international pressure applied by the United States to eradicate cultivation and trafficking, but it certainly was a matter of concern for the substantial political opposition to the national regime that emerged in subnational entities like Michoacán during the 1960s. Therefore, although this antitrafficking strategy was implemented in Michoacán, at the level of the national government the connections between politicians and traffickers seem not to have been taken particularly seriously, despite Commander Rangel's insistence on the need to improve the administration of justice. The connivance among caciques, traffickers, and politicians had built up enormous obstacles to the army's efforts to eradicate cultivation and transport. What certainly was a key concern at the national level and deemed capable of interfering with the construction of the tentative hegemony of the federal Mexican state was growing political opposition. The fight against drug trafficking was adapted to combat the latter.[72]

NOTES

1. Luis Astorga, *Drogas sin fronteras* (Mexico City: Debolsillo, 2005); Salvador Maldonado, *Los márgenes del estado mexicano. Territorios ilegales, desarrollo y violencia en Michoacán* (Zamora: El Colegio de Michoacán, 2010).

2. Enrique Guerra, *Caciquismo y orden público en Michoacán, 1920–1940* (Mexico City: El Colegio de México, 2002); Veronika Oikón, *Los hombres del poder en Michoacán. 1924–1962* (Zamora, El Colegio de Michoacán/UNMSH, 2004); Pablo Vargas, *Lealtades de la sumisión. Caciquismo: poder local y regional en la Ciénega de Chapala, Michoacán* (Zamora: El Colegio de Michoacán, 1993).

3. Paul Friedrich, *Los príncipes de naranja. Un ensayo de método antropohistórico* (Mexico City: Grijalbo, 1991).

4. In December 1962, a military operation called Terrenate was launched against a group of peasants, who, "invoking imaginary religious persecution," rose up in arms. According to the commander, "After investigating the case, that version turned out to be true, signaling numerous groups and the uprisings of various Rural Defenses in the area. These were *sinarquistas* who defended their churches and priests from

the threat of destruction; according to informants, they fled to the hills to fight the government." See Maldonado, *Los márgenes*, 312–15.

5. Juan Veledíaz, *El general sin memoria. Una crónica de los silencios del ejército mexicano* (Mexico City: Debate, 2010); V. A. Equihua, *Lázaro Cárdenas; su feudo y la política nacional*, (Mexico City: Editorial Eréndira, 1951).

6. The chapter is based primarily on research in the Archivo Histórico del Poder Ejecutivo del Estado de Michoacán (AHPEEM), the Registro Agrario Nacional (RAN), and newspaper sources. I examined the Ramo Municipal, a category that covers municipalities like Apatzingán, Aguililla, Tepalcatepec, Buenavista, and Coalcomán. This study uncovered sixteen military bulletins written or dictated by Commander Rangel from his garrison in Apatzingán between 1959 and 1965, and innumerable missives, memos, etc. on the role of the army and the state government in the fight against trafficking and delinquency. Each bulletin has twenty-five to thirty typed pages that narrate official orders from the SEDENA, military operations, punishments, captures, and the destruction of plantations, etc. They end with civic lessons and announcements for soldiers.

7. Astorga, *Las Drogas*; see also Pérez Montfort, chapter 3 in this volume.

8. Astorga, *Las Drogas*, 448.

9. Astorga, *Las Drogas*, 448, 449.

10. Smith and Pansters, chapter 6 in this volume.

11. Astorga, *Las Drogas*, 468.

12. Hubert Cochet, *Alambradas en la sierra* (Mexico City: CEMCA/El Colegio de Michoacán/Orstom, 1991).

13. Guerra, *Caciquismo*; Oikón, *Los hombres*; Vargas, *Lealtades*; Luis González y González, *La Querencia* (Mexico City: Hexágono, 1991).

14. Oikón, *Los hombres*, 385, 442.

15. David Barkin et al., *Desarrollo Económico Regional: enfoque por cuencas hidrológicas de México* (Mexico City: Siglo XXI, 1979); Juan M. Durán Juárez and Alain Bustin, *Revolución agrícola en la Tierra Caliente de Michoacán* (Zamora: El Colegio de Michoacán, 1983).

16. Maldonado, *Los margénes*; Guerra, *Caciquismo*.

17. González y González, *La Querencia*; Maldonado, *Los margénes*.

18. Fernando Benítez, *Lázaro Cárdenas y la Revolución Mexicana* (Mexico City: Fondo de Cultura Económica, 1986).

19. Elisa Servín, "Algunas ramas de un árbol frondoso. El cardenismo a mediados del siglo XX," *Historias* 69 (2008): 81–96.

20. Lázaro Cárdenas, *Lázaro Cárdenas: Apuntes. Una selección* (Mexico City: UNAM-Centro de Estudios de la Revolución Mexicana Lázaro Cárdenas, A.C., 2003).

21. Benítez, *Lázaro Cárdenas*; Servín, "Algunas ramas."

22. Veledíaz, *El general*, 185, 143.

23. Commander Rangel's military experience in Michoacán was key to his 1973

appointment as commander of the Military Zone of the state of Guerrero, where he was tasked with fighting the guerrilla led by Lucio Cabañas.

24. Jeffrey W. Rubin, *Decentering the Regime. Ethnicity, Radicalism, and Democracy in Juchitán, Mexico* (Durham, NC: Duke University Press, 1997).

25. In the 1980s, the army began an antitrafficking campaign amidst broad postelectoral mobilizations in reaction to the 1988 election. Later, in 2014, in the face of the domination by the Caballeros Templarios Cartel, another federal intervention was launched, but this one first suppressed state and local power.

26. As Foucault points out, punishment is a way of administrating illegalities, of tracing limits of tolerance, and of allowing a certain range of freedom to some while pressuring others. The differential handling of illegal acts by mediating punishment forms part of the mechanisms of domination. Michel Foucault, *Vigilar y Castigar* (Mexico City: Siglo XXI, 1989), 277–78.

27. Veledíaz, *El general*, 146, 153.

28. AHPEEM, Ramo Municipios: Apatzingán, caja 4, exp. 5. *Boletín mensual*, October 1962, year V, no. 10, 4–5.

29. Ibid., 4.

30. Ibid., 7.

31. Ibid., 7.

32. AHPEEM, Ramo Municipios: Apatzingán, caja 4, exp. 5. *Boletín mensual*, October 1962, year V, no. 12, 2–3.

33. Carlos Flores Pérez, *El Estado en Crisis: Crimen Organizado y Política. Desafíos para la consolidación democrática* (Mexico City: Publicaciones de la Casa Chata, CIESAS, 2010), 173.

34. Veledíaz, *El general*, 156, 170.

35. *La Voz de Michoacán*, November 6, 1964, emphasis added.

36. AHPEEM, Ramo Municipios: Apatzingán, caja 4, exp. 5. *Boletín mensual*, January 1965, year 8, no. 1, 1.

37. Ibid., 1.

38. AHPEEM, Ramo Municipios: Apatzingán, caja 4, exp. 5. *Boletín mensual*, March 1965, 9.

39. AHPEEM, Ramo Municipios: Apatzingán, caja 4, exp. 5. *Boletín mensual*, November 1962, year 5, no. 11.

40. Ibid., 3–4.

41. Ibid., 2–4.

42. Ibid., 4.

43. Eduardo Nava, "El Cardenismo en Michoacán (1910–1990)" (Tesis de Doctorado en Ciencia Política, UNAM, 2004), 369.

44. Maldonado, *Los margénes*.

45. AHPEEM, Ramo Municipios: Apatzingán, caja 4, exp. 5. *Boletín mensual*, November 1962, year 5, no. 11, 4.

46. Ibid., 7.
47. AHPEEM, Ramo Municipios: Apatzingán, caja 4, exp. 5. *Boletín mensual*, January 1965, year 8, no. 1, 2.
48. AHPEEM, Ramo Gobernación, Serie Elecciones, exp. 19, n/d.
49. AHPEEM, Ramo Municipios: Apatzingán, caja 4, exp. 6.
50. Ibid.
51. Ibid.
52. An official report identified a total of around 1,300 prostitutes working in bars. The report was compiled at the request of state authorities with the support of the municipal government, which maintained more-or-less clear control due to the quotas it paid to the municipal police. AHPEEM, Ramo Municipios: Apatzingán, caja 4, exp. 6.
53. AHPEEM, Ramo Municipios: Apatzingán, caja 4, exp. 5.
54. Ibid.
55. *Oficio del Secretario General del Comité Regional Campesino* to the Secretary of Government of Michoacán, who forwarded it to the state prosecutor. Unfortunately, there was no follow-up on the situation denounced. AHPEEM, Ramo Municipios: Apatzingán, caja 4, exp. 3.
56. AHPEEM, Ramo Municipios: Apatzingán, caja 4, exp. 3.
57. AHPEEM, Ramo Municipios: Apatzingán, caja 12, exp. 4.
58. AHPEEM, Ramo Municipios: Apatzingán, caja 15, exp. 4. Some army bulletins mention a soldier surnamed Baldomero, who may be the same person, since some soldiers dressed as civilians in attempts to obtain confidential information.
59. AHPEEM, Ramo Municipios: Apatzingán, caja 16, exp. 2.
60. AHPEEM, Ramo Municipios: Apatzingán, caja 1, exp. 1 and caja 10, exp. 2.
61. AHPEEM, Ramo Municipios: Apatzingán, caja 10, exp. 1.
62. AHPEEM, Ramo Municipios: Apatzingán, caja 4, exp. 5. *Boletín mensual*, August 1963, 3.
63. Ibid., 3.
64. Ibid., 3. Emphasis added.
65. According to the file published on the Internet by the *Instituto de Acceso a la Información* (*Ley de Transparencia*), the general left his post in the 49th Battalion on March 15, 1966.
66. AHPEEM, Ramo Municipios: Apatzingán, caja 4, exp. 5. *Boletín mensual*, August 1965, 3.
67. Ibid., 5.
68. He had also taken courses in counterinsurgency in the United States.
69. Veledíaz, *El general*, 291.
70. See Aviña, chapter 12 in this volume.
71. Veledíaz, *El general*, 289. As an anecdote, Veledíaz writes that before the 49th Battalion moved to Iguala, Lázaro Cárdenas called Rangel Medina. In what was a

friendly chat, Cárdenas reminded him of some cards he had written years before and addressed to President López Mateos regarding Cárdenas's actions in Michoacán [but] that he held no grudge, for he understood what his obligations were. To avoid future doubts, however, they destroyed the cards together in a show of friendship. It is said that Rangel Medina was left in shock.

72. Salvador Maldonado, "Drogas, violencia y militarización en el México rural. El caso de Michoacán," *Revista Mexicana de Sociología* 74, no. 1 (Jan.–March 2012): 5–39.

11

The War on Drugs, Counterinsurgency, and the State of Siege in the Golden Triangle, 1977–1982
ADELA CEDILLO

The surge in demand for Mexican heroin and marijuana in the United States in the late 1960s, caused by the interruption of the so-called French Connection that supplied heroin from Turkey to the United States, marked a watershed in the binational relationship. The Nixon administration coerced Mexico to change its antidrug strategy through Operation Intercept (1969), which required a thorough inspection of all vehicles at the U.S.-Mexico border during a time when unregulated air traffic and sea routes were turning into the primary ways of drug smuggling. While this coup de force came as a surprise to the Mexican government, the economic impact of the border shutdown compelled the Díaz Ordaz administration to accept key aspects of the so-called "War on Drugs" by means of Operation Cooperation (1969). This chapter explores how what started as a U.S. war on Mexican soil gradually evolved until it became an instrument of the ruling Institutional Revolutionary Party (PRI) to reassert its hegemony in both the political arena and the criminal world. There is no direct evidence that U.S. agents encouraged the PRI's utilization of the War on Drugs to suppress leftist dissenters, but they clearly did not oppose it because it was in tune with the U.S. global war on communism.

As Luis Astorga has shown, the drug trade was ingrained in the state's power structures, hence the major paradox of the Mexican antidrugs policies is that the same security apparatus that benefited from the drug industry was in charge of its disruption.[1] While Operation Cooperation and its successor, Operation Canador (1970–1975), represented weak attempts to respond to the U.S. antinarcotics agenda, the Mexican government reached a point of total compliance through operations Trizo (1975–1976) and Condor (1977–1987). Operation Condor was not only the longest and most ambitious antidrug campaign of Cold War Mexico, but also the first spearheaded by the Drug Enforcement Administration (DEA). Although the DEA only played a leading role from 1977 to 1978, it established the standards the Mexican security apparatus should meet, especially concerning the implementation of a cutting-edge aerial defoliation program.

The scholarship on the Mexican antidrug efforts has typically characterized Operation Condor as another failed campaign, but a closer analysis shows that it represented a turning point in the militarization, modernization, and centralization of the antidrug policies. The first stage of Operation Condor developed in the Golden Triangle—the intersection of the states of Sinaloa, Durango, and Chihuahua—a region with minimal state presence, the largest production of marijuana and poppy nationwide, and the setting of antidrug campaigns since the 1940s. One major aspect of the operation was the creation of the Task Force "Condor" (FTC), a detachment that periodically entered drug production areas to help eradicate plants in conjunction with the aerial defoliation program.

This chapter argues that Operation Condor seized upon the counterinsurgency framework forged during the Dirty War on guerrilla movements (1964–1982) to secure social control over drug growers and traffickers.[2] The national security apparatus also broadened the concept of "internal enemy" to include all peasant communities from the Golden Triangle, and it imposed a de facto state of siege on them in order to prevent turmoil. In addition, with U.S. financial and technical support for the antidrug campaign, the Mexican government enlarged its counterinsurgency infrastructure to suppress political unrest, especially in Sinaloa and Chihuahua. Guerrillas, peasants, and rank-and-file drug traffickers were treated with the same harshness, although for different reasons. The administrations of Echeverría and López Portillo embraced the U.S. antidrug agenda as part of their efforts to foster the PRI's hegemony in the aftermath of the Tlatelolco massacre that had shattered the social consensus around the ruling party.[3] As Aileen Teague points out, Mexico "was not the only country supplying drugs to the United States, but it was the first one to import the U.S. War on Drugs framework on such a scale and, in doing so, used the antidrug campaign to reconcile its own political and social challenges."⁴ This chapter contributes to nuancing the "U.S. pressure–Mexican response" model of the evolvement of antidrug policies as proposed in the introduction to this volume.⁵

This chapter shows that the campaign's dramatic measures did not aim to eliminate the illegal drug trade or to terminate the gang wars, but to enforce the political-military control of the population and do away with independent local powers. Operation Condor attacked traditional drug clans to reorganize the drug industry and advance its decentralization from the northwest. It served as a strategy to curb the participation of local police agencies in the drug trade, namely the Sinaloa Judicial Police (PJS), the Chihuahua Judicial Police (PJC), and the Municipal Police. At the same time, the government allowed federal agencies, like the Federal Security Directorate (DFS), the Federal Judicial Police (PJF), and the military to take over the drug trade networks to limit the power of drug lords and subject them to the *priísta* clientelist regime.⁶ Although there is no compelling evidence to demonstrate that the president's or the PRI's leadership designed such plan, archival documents reveal the disputes between local and federal agencies over the control of the drug industry. The DFS sent a copy of its daily reports to the presidency, thus it is safe to assume that presidents approved the role of federal agencies in the drug war.⁷

This chapter provides examples of the implementation of Operation Condor in Sinaloa and the Golden Triangle spanning from the first to the ninth task forces (1977–1983). From 1983 to January 1988 there were eight task forces more, but unlike his predecessor, President Miguel de la Madrid managed the antidrug campaign with a low profile. During the first years, the DEA's aerial defoliation program accomplished the temporary destruction of the only cash crops in the highlands and wreaked havoc on the local economy, while the FTC wielded extreme violence against dozens of hamlets. In the meantime, the authorities kept announcing the detention of drug traffickers and the seizures of tons of drugs, and routinely invited journalists to watch agents burn narcotics.⁸

It would be far-fetched to depict Operation Condor as a half-real, half-simulated campaign to terrorize the population to ensure the ruling party's dominion not only in the political field but also in what Alfred McCoy coined the "covert netherworld," an autonomous clandestine realm where organized crime, the secret services, and other elements of the ruling elite compete for economic power and sovereignty.⁹ Violence mediated the relations between the Mexican state and organized crime in the twentieth century, but the antidrug policies guaranteed that drug lords played under the nonwritten rules of the PRI.

THE BEGINNING OF A U.S. WAR ON MEXICAN SOIL

In September 1969, the U.S. government launched Operation Intercept to force Mexico into more effective drug law enforcement.[10] The Díaz Ordaz administration was determined to maintain a sovereign antidrug policy, but after Operation Intercept wreaked havoc on the border economy, it had to accept larger U.S. intervention in domestic affairs. By mid-October 1969, both countries announced Operation Cooperation as a joint strategy to reduce the production and smuggling of narcotics. The Mexican government code-named it Operation Canador (a shorthand for Cannabis-Adormidera), which was its official name until 1975.[11] The Ministry of National Defense (SEDENA) deployed around five thousand soldiers in drug cultivation zones. Canador intensified the traditional manual eradication campaign, and, for the first time, U.S. law enforcement monitored the Mexican troops.[12]

Nonetheless, Díaz Ordaz was reluctant to accept the technicalization of the War on Drugs that the U.S. government advocated, which included the use of remote sensing equipment and aircraft to spread herbicides, the destruction of laboratories and warehouses, and the utilization of enforcement personnel to expand undercover operations and conspiracy-type investigations.[13] Conversely, during the last years of his administration, Luis Echeverría (1970–1976) became the first president to apply the U.S. national security doctrine to the antidrug policy as his administration bore witness to a major shift in the drug industry. While in 1965 Mexico's opium production was minuscule, by 1975 the country was supplying up to 87 percent of the heroin entering the United States.[14]

In 1975, the Mexican government dealt with considerable pressure to eradicate the opium production. President Gerald Ford had expressed on various occasions that the illegal export of opium to the United States would be considered a national security threat.[15] Thus, for the first time, the Mexican government agreed on the aggressive source control of aerial defoliation coordinated by the DEA, the new U.S. antidrug agency founded in 1973. Edward Heath was appointed to run the DEA office in Mexico.

The Joint Opium Poppy Eradication-Interdiction Campaign known as

Trizo (Tri-zone) was inaugurated on November 15, 1975. It comprised the three major drug-production zones in the country. Zone I encompassed Sonora, Chihuahua, Sinaloa, and Durango; Zone II Jalisco, Nayarit, Colima, Zacatecas, and Michoacán; and Zone III Guerrero, Oaxaca, and Morelos. Alejandro Gertz Manero was appointed senior official (*oficial mayor*) of the Attorney General's Office (PGR) and the overall campaign coordinator. The DEA sent to Mexico several agents and Evergreen Corporation contract pilots who had prior experience in Vietnam and the Southeast Asian Golden Triangle.[16] It also provided financial and technical assistance to the PGR-PJF and helped with gathering intelligence.[17]

Trizo used Bell-206 and Bell-212 helicopters to airlift Mexican troops to destroy illegal crops and apprehend growers, but its most significant innovation was spraying herbicidal solutions like paraquat and 2.4-D.[18] Both contract and local pilots carried out the spraying missions and the DEA agents/pilots focused on reconnaissance flights to evaluate the success of the campaign.[19] The campaign's phase I came to an end on April 15, 1976, and phase II ran from early September to late November 1976. While previous antidrug efforts with a dual civil-military command were actually led by the military, Trizo contributed to strengthening the leadership of the PGR. Thus Trizo might have been the reason the military sought to retake the control of the campaign by increasing the military personnel and expanding their functions.[20]

In the last months of their respective terms, Echeverría and Ford agreed on an ambitious binational operation that continued with the permanent aerial defoliation and manual eradication as well as the military's control of the drug grower communities. The DEA continued to refer to it as Trizo, but in Mexico the operation was code-named Condor.[21] The operation dismissed the trizone division and established thirteen zones instead. It began by launching an all-out attack against the Golden Triangle, or Zone VI, the region where more than twenty thousand highlanders allegedly produced 70 percent of the narcotics in Mexico.[22]

STATE COLLUSION WITH DRUG TRAFFICKING ON THE EVE OF OPERATION CONDOR

The extreme U.S. pressure against Mexico to intensify its antidrug policy contradicted the security forces' drive to continue benefiting from the generalized practice of extorting drug traffickers. In addition, in 1976, Mexico underwent its worst economic crisis since 1954, which entailed a drastic devaluation of the peso against the U.S. dollar. The Mexican government did not have real grounds to prevent the massive wealth of drug sales in the United States from entering the country. The Mexican government solved the conundrum in a cunning way, one that proved satisfactory for the United States and allowed for the advancement of the PRI's political agenda. Given that the northwestern narco-elite was the major profit maker, security forces diminished its power by decentralizing the drug industry from the Golden Triangle for it to flourish in other regions under the control of the Federal Judicial Police (PJF), the Federal Security Directorate (DFS), and sectors of the military in charge of counterinsurgency campaigns. Journalist José Luis García Cabrera maintained that Operation Condor resulted from a decision by the López Portillo administration to increase its participation in the drug trade.[23] While archival evidence only involves the security forces in the design of the antidrug strategy, the prevalent mechanisms of one-party rule made it highly unlikely that the presidency or the PRI leadership did not take part in the decision-making process of any overt or covert domestic policy.

By 1977, media outlets reported that the clans that controlled the heroin trade in Sinaloa, Chihuahua, and Durango were the Favela, Macías, Herrera, Valenzuela, Avilés-Quintero, Romero, and Sicilia Falcón families, and to a lesser extent the Leyva, Aispuro, Alvarado, Jasso, and Hernández families.[24] A couple of years later, only a few of those families were still of any importance in the drug trade.[25] It seems that Mexico's federal agencies sought to regulate the competition among drug clans by eliminating the weakest links in the production chain, while at the same time protecting the most successful entrepreneurs.

The reorganization of the drug industry did not affect the interests of members of the PRI's elite who were narco-caciques (bosses), like the former governor of Sinaloa, Leopoldo Sánchez Celis (1963–1968).[26] Several top politicians involved in the drug industry even rose to prominent positions in the López Portillo administration (1977–1982). Javier García Paniagua, whose involvement in the criminal networks is well-documented, became head of the DFS, a position that enabled him to surveil allies and rivals alike.[27] According to the DFS, the governor of Chihuahua between 1968 and 1974, Oscar Flores Sánchez, protected a group from Hidalgo del Parral, which controlled the state's opium industry. While the DFS had reservations about Flores's personal involvement in the drug trade, it emphasized that senior members of his administration like the state attorney general, Antonio Quezada

Fornelli, were directly connected to it.[28] Other DFS reports show that authorities had detailed knowledge of the drug-trafficking networks that went from the Golden Triangle to the U.S.-Mexico border.

In late 1976, Flores became the new attorney general of Mexico and appointed his former collaborator, the controversial general Raúl Mendiolea Cerecero, as chief of the PJF, and Quezada Fornelli as deputy of the PGR in Chihuahua. Flores also boosted the career of the Carlos Aguilar Garza, from Tamaulipas, by appointing him as coordinator of the Public Prosecutor's Office in the northwest. The DFS identified both Mendiolea and Aguilar Garza as protectors of drug traffickers.[29] Nevertheless, these officials would have leading roles in Operation Condor. It seems that the Mexican government sought to reach new agreements with illegal actors through top officials already acquainted with drug-trafficking networks.

The federalization of the narcotics trade was ridden with interagency conflicts, contradictions, and unpredictable situations that raised questions about whether military power was above the civilian rule. Furthermore, Operation Condor was not only directed against drug traffickers; its general tactics of population control also served to contain the agrarian, guerrilla, and human rights movements taking place in the northwest during the 1970s.

OPERATION CONDOR: BATTLEFIELD BETWEEN SECURITY AGENCIES

In 1976, Culiacán, which had around 250,000 inhabitants, experienced an unprecedented number of 543 homicides after drug clans began to fight each other for their share in the market.[30] The local population was upset by the state government's passiveness toward the wave of violence, which was the result of its widely known links to drug traffickers.[31] The so-called *gente de bien*—organized in business, merchant, farmers, and other professional associations—pressured the government to call in the military to protect public security because they did not trust the corrupt Sinaloa Judicial Police (PJS), whose chiefs either used their position to become drug traffickers themselves or to protect particular drug lords.[32] On December 7, 1976, the Sinaloa state congress demanded that the federal state intervene with the military and the federal police (PJF) in the state. The Sinaloa government then announced Operation Condor as its alleged empathetic response to society's claims.[33] Mexican media did not mention the DEA's role in the operation at all.

Operation Condor went into effect in Culiacán on January 16, 1977, only a month and a half after President López Portillo took office. It began with a military parade led by Lt. Gen. José Francisco Hernández Toledo, the general coordinator of the Task Force "Condor" (FTC), symbolizing the recapturing of the territory by the Mexican state.[34] Sinaloa governor Alfonso G. Calderón and Maj. Gen. Ricardo Cervantes, commander of the 9th Military Zone headquartered in Culiacán, along with other high-level authorities, also attended the event.

Operation Condor had both a civil and a military command. Gertz Manero continued as the national campaign coordinator, while Aguilar Garza and Cruz López were respectively the PGR coordinator and deputy coordinator in the northwest.[35] The military component, however, overshadowed the aerial defoliation program controlled by the PGR. Also, the military authority superseded the public prosecutor's law enforcement duties and became the actual sovereign power by imposing a de facto state of siege in the Golden Triangle.

During the first phase of the operation 1,200 regular troops and paratroopers constituted the FTC.[36] Troops served six months on a rotational basis, while the Parachute Fusiliers Brigade (BFP), the elite counterinsurgency unit in the countryside, participated in the campaign from time to time at the request of the high command. The FTC set up its military base in Badiraguato—where drug lords largely controlled the territory—and had jurisdiction over other municipalities, including Choix, Sinaloa de Leyva, and Culiacán in Sinaloa, Guadalupe y Calvo, Morelos, and Batopilas in Chihuahua, and Tamazula and Canelas in Durango, spanning an area of approximately eighty thousand square kilometers.[37]

From 1977 to 1987, the FTC operated with nineteen commanders.[38] Significantly, commanders like Hernández Toledo, Euroza Delgado, Heine Rangel, Díaz Escobar Figueroa, Gómez Ruiz, and Careaga Estrambasaguas had prior field experience in counterinsurgency campaigns across Mexico, from the 1968 Tlatelolco massacre to the extermination of rural guerrillas in Chihuahua and Guerrero (see also Aviña, chapter 12 in this volume).[39] The background of these top officers foreshadowed the counterinsurgency tactics against peasant communities.[40]

On February 9, 1977, Hernández Toledo claimed that in the highlands there were enough weapons to make a "little revolution," yet the military had eradicated 720 illegal crops and seized 121 tons of marijuana, thus anticipating the success of Operation Condor within the next three months.[41] Throughout

1977, authorities repeatedly affirmed that the problem was nearly solved. The DEA reached the same conclusion, given its faith in the aerial defoliation program. Initially, mainstream public opinion backed Condor, but after months of systematic abuses they became disappointed with its outcomes.[42]

From January 1977 onward, troops of the 9th Military Zone patrolled the streets of Culiacán and its surroundings, established random checkpoints, and carried out disarmament campaigns. As early as April 1977, though, the authorities realized that bank robbery, kidnapping, schoolgirl rape, car theft, and assault on tourists had increased as a result of Condor.[43] Besides social violence, the state of siege brought about gross human rights abuses. In 1977 alone, there were more than four hundred complaints against troops by peasants, cattle ranchers, and professionals.[44] In the highlands, several mass killings took place but went unreported in media outlets. For instance, on October 31, 1977, thirteen alleged drug traffickers and one soldier died in Las Juntas, La Noria, Mazatlán.[45] No investigation was ever carried out to determine whether the FTC had shot the civilians or whether they were combat deaths.

While the FTC had territorial control over the Sinaloa highlands, the intricate dynamics of violence in the Culiacán Valley resulted from the participation of several agencies: Municipal Police, PJS, PGR-PJF, DFS, White Brigade (a secret death squad), and the 9th Military Zone. The FTC, the 9th Military Zone, and the judicial forces experienced regular commander turnovers, allegedly to prevent corruption. In fact, that practice made it difficult to reach long-lasting agreements among actors and added to the growing political instability. Furthermore, the DEA agents headquartered in Culiacán ended up favoring the PGR-PJF, while the DFS had a closer relationship with the CIA. In some cases, the lack of cooperation among agencies and internecine strife impeded any institutional functioning.

Despite the astounding number of security agents in the streets of Culiacán, there were several high-profile killings and jailbreaks. On March 3, 1977, the PJS subchief, Alfredo Reyes Curiel, was shot for extorting drug traffickers.[46] At the end of that month, Maj. Gustavo Sámano, a military advisor for the FTC, was assassinated allegedly for pointing out police officers linked to drug traffickers as well as drug-cultivation areas.[47] Sámano, however, was not an untarnished officer. On November 10, 1975, when Sámano was head of the prison guards at the infamous Social Rehabilitation Institute of Sinaloa (IRSS), one of the most important heroin traffickers of southern Sinaloa, Manuel Salcido Uzeta, alias El Cochiloco ("Crazy Pig"), and six of his men spectacularly escaped. Sámano was removed from his position but managed to evade a PJF investigation.[48] El Cochiloco became one of the most important drug lords in the 1980s.

The state attorney suspended the investigation of Sámano's case, but the military accused the PJS of being the perpetrator. Prior to Sámano's execution, the relationship between the 9th Military Zone and the PJS was strained because the military carried out law enforcement functions while the local police took part in the drug trade and smuggled weapons.[49] As soon as Condor began, the military disarmed the PJS agents. Major General Cervantes then handled Sámano's death as a personal matter, exerting a ruthless revenge against the PJS. On May 1, 1977, he called Governor Calderón into his office in the 9th Military Zone to force him to listen to the recorded interrogation of a PJS agent who confessed that his unit killed Sámano.[50] After the meeting, the military detained Calderón's seven PJS security guards and escorted Calderón to the Government Palace to ensure that he would formally dismiss the culprits. The military tortured and disappeared the security guards.[51] Cervantes humiliated Calderón and sent a terrifying message to the PJS: no one was above the military. Shortly afterwards, Gral. Alberto Quintanar replaced Cervantes, even though the latter had only been in the position for five months. The message from the presidency was clear: no one was above the PRI's civilian elite.[52] The DFS in Sinaloa assumed the role of protecting that elite.

On February 13, 1978, Roberto Martínez Montenegro, a journalist for the local *Noroeste* newspaper and correspondent for the national newspaper *Excélsior*, who had written news reports on the relationship between PJS agents and drug traffickers in Sinaloa, was shot dead in Culiacán. Unlike other killed journalists, Montenegro's case incited national uproar and galvanized several media outlets from different states to demand justice and protection for freedom of expression, an unusual demand in the largely state-controlled media landscape.[53]

The DGIPS reported that the PJF had killed Montenegro because he had planned to write about its widespread practice of extorting drug traffickers.[54] The execution marked a turning point in the relationship between the PGR-PJF and Sinaloa's authorities. The DFS subchief, Miguel Nazar Haro, traveled to Sinaloa to investigate the case and back the governor, a maneuver that infuriated the PJF. Then the PJF tortured several PJS agents and forced them to self-incriminate for Montenegro's homicide.[55] Jaime Alcalá, along with Gral. Alberto Quintanar, went one step further and detained the commander of the State Government's Special Group (GEGS), Víctor Gómez Vidal, for his involvement with the DFS. Quintanar's troops were also on the verge of assaulting the PJS headquarters.[56]

The PJF took advantage of the situation to crack down on another of its traditional enemies: Sinaloa's Bar Association "Eustaquio Buelna" (CAEB), the only NGO that spoke out against the massive human rights abuses carried out by both the police and the military. On April 14, 1978, the CAEB vice president, Jesús Michel Jacobo, was detained and tortured during four days as part of a ploy to bring charges against Calderón and Nazar Haro for Montenegro's execution.[57]

The DFS prevented the PJF from making a public statement accusing the GEGS of Montenegro's killing, while Calderón and Sánchez Celis went to Mexico City to negotiate with the federal government.[58] The terms of those conversations remain secret, but the balance of power favored the DFS. The GEGS agents were released on April 18, while the PJS agents remained in jail. The next day, Nazar Haro declared that Montenegro was a PJF *madrina* (informant) and that other madrinas had him killed over a dispute about money. The murder was never clarified.

On September 15, 1978, PJF agents seemingly ambushed and killed the major heroin trafficker in Baja California and Sonora, Pedro Avilés, alias "El licenciado," and his seven companions in Loma de Rodriguera, Sinaloa.[59] Notwithstanding that Carlos Aguilar and Jaime Alcalá received bribes from the Avilés clan, the PJF followed orders from a top authority that deemed the veteran drug lord disposable.[60] Aguilar and Alcalá were later sent to Tijuana and Cruz López assumed the position of PGR coordinator in the northwest. Whether Avilés's execution was intended to favor other drug traffickers or to serve as a state performance to prove the efficacy of the antidrug campaign is hard to determine. Chief drug traffickers associated with Avilés and other Golden Triangle's kingpins, however, survived the first stage of Operation Condor and increased their power.[61] The removal of Avilés brought about the reorganization of criminal networks, and from late 1978 to 1982 it was not so clear which organization would hegemonize the narcotics field in the region.

The recurring high-profile assassinations during this period make evident the lack of governance and the difficulties of the many actors to reach long-lasting agreements over the management of the drug trade. The government reports of Governor Calderón and President López Portillo contained triumphalist statements about drug eradication but silenced the social cost of Operation

Condor and the clashes between security agencies.[62] The 1977 elections in Sinaloa had the lowest turnout in the history of the state.[63] In the northwest, violence rather than consensus buttressed the regime.

THE STATE OF SIEGE IN THE SIERRA MADRE OCCIDENTAL

Journalist Francisco Ortiz Pinchetti, one of the first to conduct investigative journalism on Operation Condor, defined Sinaloa as a "transplant of South America," where state-terror regimes prevailed.[64] Ortiz disregarded the fact that the counterinsurgency campaigns had ravaged the Sierra Tarahumara pursuing guerrillas since the mid-1960s. Thus, although Operation Condor in South America began in 1975, the Mexican Condor fitted an older local tradition. The worst human rights abuses of the Mexican war on drugs occurred during the Carter administration, who expressed his concern about the atrocities committed by the Argentinian dictatorship but showed little interest in the Mexican case. Richard B. Craig summarized the most significant human rights charges against Operation Condor: (1) the use of dangerous herbicides; (2) the failure or inability to protect those who attacked drug-related corruption; (3) the abuse of fundamental rights during arrest, detention, and imprisonment for narcotics violations; and (4) the disregard of *campesino* rights during drug-related maneuvers in the countryside.[65]

In the Golden Triangle, the military had enough intelligence to direct their assaults against drug clans, but they targeted peasant families and innocent civilians indiscriminately. The FTC committed systematic illegal detentions, executions, forced disappearances, acts of torture, rape, pillage, and extortion. By following a scorched earth policy, the troops destroyed both illicit and livelihood crops, plundered stored harvests, and burned the homes of poor peasants. In consequence, the regional economy was devastated, and thousands of *serranos* had to flee the region.[66] The municipalities that stand out in the sources as the most affected were Badiraguato, Guadalupe y Calvo, Tamazula, Morelos, Urique, Batopilas, Topia, Canelas, and Guanaceví. A key source to understanding the dimensions of Operation Condor are files declassified by the SEDENA, which include a series of complaints by serranos from 1977 to 1986 against the FTC and show that the high command rarely recognized the abuses.

In 1978, the NGO "Eustaquio Buelna" conducted a survey of 457 out of 1,300 prisoners in the IRSS; 85 percent of them were poor peasants and laborers and the remaining 15 percent were predominantly urban youth. The report states that both the PJF and troops based in Sinaloa carried out all detentions and illegally deprived a person of freedom in 90 percent of the cases, because detainees were not caught in flagrante delicto nor did they have an arrest warrant. In all cases, the arrests were performed with excessive violence and were followed by intense torture sessions even though detainees, unarmed and compliant, lacked any relevant information to confess. The agents also sacked the belongings of the victims as spoils of war.[67] Families were not notified about the whereabouts of the detainees and had to travel to town to search for them.[68] Massive detentions only served the purpose of simulating the success of Operation Condor.

The protracted terror policy caused a massive exodus from Badiraguato, Guadalupe y Calvo, and Tamazula to Culiacán and to the United States. The Sierra Madre Occidental had a low population density before Condor, with hamlets or *rancherías* from twenty to one hundred inhabitants. Oscar Loza Ochoa, one of the oldest human rights activists in Sinaloa, estimates that in the wake of the operation up to two thousand hamlets were abandoned.[69] In any case, the demographic statistics of the Golden Triangle municipalities significantly differ from the exponential demographic growth in the rest of the country during the 1970s.[70] The available sources do not suggest that there was a deliberate plan to depopulate the Golden Triangle, yet they show that the government was totally insensitive about the forced displacement of thousands of rural residents.

THE SPECTER OF AN ECOCIDE

During the initial year of Operation Condor, U.S. researchers expressed concern over the paraquat contamination of up to a quarter of the Mexican marijuana that entered the United States and the health damage it caused.[71] Conspiracy theorists then accused the U.S. government of deliberately poisoning marijuana plants to discourage its consumption. In Mexico, researchers warned that the herbicide could contaminate food crops as well as poison water. Journalists observed the paradox of the government's damage to health in the name of public health.[72]

Given the secrecy of the aerial defoliation program, the exact concentration of paraquat and other herbicides sprayed on crops was unknown, unleashing speculation about permanent soil damage. In an interview with the author, however, the authorities of Badiraguato claimed they had never heard about ecological damage or land that had become useless as a result of aerial defoliation.[73]

An anonymous PGR-PJF informer interviewed by journalist Anabel Hernández asserted that when drug growers paid informal "taxes" to security forces, they were allowed to put colored flags in their crops, depending on the arrangement. Thus when helicopters flew over the fields, instead of defoliating they sprayed them with water.[74] The evidence regarding the massive extortion of peasants backs the claim that drug growers who met the authorities' demands had their crops untouched.

According to Heath, 1977 was the most effective year for the eradication campaign.[75] Despite this alleged success, the Mexican government called off the participation of the DEA in 1978 purportedly to reduce social upheaval, even though the state of siege curbed the possibility of a backlash.[76] Pyes suggested that the State Department squeezed the DEA out of its supervisory role because it was alarmed that DEA investigations of high Mexican officials would jeopardize the cooperation of the Mexican government.[77]

After the DEA quit, the amount of opium poppy hectares destroyed fell from 9,311 hectares in 1977 to 1,819, an 80.4 percent decrease.[78] Heath observed that the fall was also due to the fact that drug traffickers switched from heroin to cocaine, but he did not bring into question the success of the aerial defoliation program. On the contrary, he asserted that a private firm from the United States operating under a U.S.-Mexican contract monitored the effectiveness of the program. The company, Aviation Associates International (AAI), which had also worked in Southeast Asia, was in charge of the surveillance flights after April 1978. Nevertheless, if Mexican pilots knew what crops they should spray with water, the Mexican government could easily circumvent the certification. It seems that the entrenched corruption of Mexican authorities prevented the Golden Triangle from experiencing an ecocide.

According to the DEA's official version, the defoliation program was a major success because by 1979 it had lessened the demand for Mexican heroin in the United States.[79] There was a dramatic drop in heroin's purity as well as a decrease in U.S. heroin-related deaths, which went from 1,455 in 1974 to 471 in 1978. The Mexican government also promoted its program as the most successful eradication effort in the world.[80] Heath acknowledged, however, that major drug lords responded to the scarcity of opium by switching to cocaine.

As early as 1977, up to 30 percent of Peru's annual production of thirty-two tons of pure cocaine were smuggled into the United States through Mexico.[81]

Pyes's investigation found out that U.S. authorities acknowledged that Mexican federal narcotics agents used access to comprehensive intelligence data, including what U.S. law enforcement supplied, to run a sophisticated protection racket based on "selective enforcement," arresting only traffickers who would not pay the extortion.[82] But there is no evidence to suggest that the U.S. government aimed to punish the Mexican government for its bogus antidrug policy.[83] On the contrary, in 1983 the House Select Committee on Narcotics Abuse and Control praised the Mexican government for its success in building "the world's finest aerial crop-eradication program. Its size, professionalism, competence, performance, and experience make it the world leader in this technique."[84] Marshall alleges that such assessments represented one of the greatest coverups in the history of U.S. drug enforcement, given that the U.S. officials knew that Operation Condor was a sham but hid this fact from the public, allegedly for a combination of diplomatic and propagandistic reasons.[85]

THE OUTCOMES OF OPERATION CONDOR

SEDENA's final figures about Operation Condor from 1977 to 1987 indicate that 224,252 illegal crops were destroyed and that 2,019 presumed criminals were indicted. In addition, twenty-seven civilians and nineteen soldiers died.[86] The PGR also reported the loss of thirty-four agents, pilots, and mechanics from 1977 to 1979.[87] But other reports hint that the death toll was much higher. Heath mentioned two DEA agents and fifty-eight Mexican officials killed in the course of the eradication program up to 1980.[88] Furthermore, the DEA claimed that four thousand members of illegal drug organizations had been arrested by 1979.[89] In its report of activities concerning the López Portillo administration, the PGR stated that from 1976 to 1980 it had promoted the withdrawal from prosecution in more than two thousand drug-related cases.[90]

In any case, official figures do not reflect the significance of Operation Condor. It not only reinforced the PRI's hegemony in the political arena but also in what McCoy coined as the "covert netherworld."[91] Operation Condor consolidated the intermingling of federal security forces, the political elite, and the organized crime. A considerable number of officers who participated in both the Dirty War and the War on Drugs became involved in drug trafficking or controlled other illegal businesses.[92]

State agents in charge of Operation Condor used the campaign's resources to increase their power and expand their criminal networks. Jaime Alcalá sold protection to drug traffickers in Jalisco until 1979, when El Cochiloco killed him in Guadalajara in revenge for his participation in the Avilés execution.[93] Authorities detained Aguilar Garza for drug-related activities, first in Tamaulipas in 1984 and later in Texas in 1989; he was killed in 1993 in a settling of accounts.[94]

The most widespread interpretation about the outcomes of Operation Condor maintains that the partial destruction of the Golden Triangle provoked the increase of drug production in other Mexican states and caused a "cockroach effect," whereby criminals spread and then regrouped in other regions. This view neglects that the DFS played a key role in the final arrangements between drug lords and the Mexican government. Kingpins like Félix Gallardo, Caro Quintero, and Fonseca Carrillo moved to Guadalajara because of their close relationship with the DFS chiefs García Paniagua and Nazar Haro.[95] Given that Condor favored the removal of less successful drug clans and placed the control of the drug market in fewer hands, those drug lords were able to form a centralized crime syndicate that the DEA dubbed the Guadalajara Cartel.

In a paradoxical way, the removal of the Sinaloan drug lords from their base and their relocation to Jalisco signaled the triumph of the federal government over independent local powers. As Watt and Zepeda showed, the PRI accomplished the subjection of drug lords to its clientelist regime.[96] Rather than a façade to please the U.S. government as many have suggested, Operation Condor instead was a counterinsurgency war whose ultimate payoff was the consolidation of a narco-clientelist regime.

CONCLUSIONS

The antidrug operations of the late 1970s in Mexico were based on the use of cutting-edge technology for the aerial defoliation programs and the application of a counterinsurgency framework to overpower traditional drug clans. Operation Condor served an array of purposes that were beneficial for both the U.S. and the Mexican governments. On the U.S. side, it fostered the perception that the U.S. government had obliged Mexicans to take stronger action against the illegal drug trade by welcoming the DEA leadership and the full-fledged militarization of the drug-producing zones. In Mexico, Condor served to establish a state of siege in the countryside to prevent the emergence of independent actors, either political or criminal. The Mexican government used the Golden Triangle as a showcase of the alleged success of the joint drug-eradication campaign, concealing the destruction of thousands of peasant communities. Finally, the DFS consolidated its power by becoming the protector of the political elite and the mediator between the ruling party and the most powerful drug kingpins, who created the Guadalajara Cartel, the most nefarious legacy of Operation Condor.

NOTES

1. Luis Astorga, "Drug Trafficking in Mexico: A First General Assessment," Management of Social Transformation, Discussion paper no. 36: http://unesdoc.unesco.org/images/0011/001176/117644Eo.pdf, accessed February 10, 2017.

2. For a comparative perspective on how state territorial control, insurgent movements, and antidrug policies overlap, see Daniel Weimer, *Seeing Drugs: Modernization, Counterinsurgency, and U.S. Narcotics Control in the Third World, 1969–1976* (Kent, OH: Kent State University Press, 2011).

3. For the aftermath of the Tlatelolco massacre see Louise Walker, *Waking from the Dream: Mexico's Middle Class After 1968* (Stanford, CA: Stanford University Press, 2015).

4. Aileen Teague, "Mexico's Dirty War on Drugs: Source Control and Dissidence in Drug Enforcement," *Social History of Alcohol and Drugs* 33, no. 1 (March 2019): 65. Teague looks at how the PRI used the U.S. drug war as part of its efforts at domestic repression, but disregards the local dynamics of the drug war in the countryside.

5. See also the chapters by Campos (chapter 2), Pérez Montfort (chapter 3), and Pérez Ricart (chapter 7) in this volume.

6. The PRI's clientelism was a system where patrons provided benefits to their clients including protection, support in the struggles with rivals, and opportunities for political ascendancy or economic prosperity. In exchange, clients gave loyalty, money, or useful services to the government. Benjamin Smith, "The Rise and Fall of Narcopopulism: Drugs, Politics, and Society in Sinaloa 1930–1980," *Journal for the Study of Radicalism* 7, no. 2 (Fall 2013): 129–32.

7. In 2005, Vicente Capello, a former DFS archivist who was also in charge of the DFS archive in the National Archive (AGN), explained to the author in an informal conversation the institutional distribution of the DFS reports' copies. I collected most evidence for this chapter from the AGN, especially the DFS and the DGIPS sections, although the official censorship and limited access to original documents made it impossible to have a complete picture of the archive's contents.

8. As several DFS documents related to drug distribution show, authorities burned a small part of narcotics and stored the rest in unsafe facilities where corrupted civil

servants stole them in order to sell them to drug gangs. AGN/DFS, Public Version, Narcotráfico, 1954–1985, 3 volumes.

9. Alfred McCoy, "Covert Netherworld: Clandestine Services and Criminal Syndicates in Shaping the Philippine State," in *Government of the shadows*, ed. Eric Wilson (London: Pluto Press, 2009), 228.

10. Kate Doyle, "Operation Intercept: The Perils of Unilateralism," April 13, 2013, http://nsarchive.gwu.edu/NSAEBB/NSAEBB86/, accessed January 26, 2017; Richard B. Craig, "Operation Intercept: The International Politics of Pressure," *Review of Politics* 42, no. 4 (October 1980): 556–80.

11. In 1975, during the peak of antiguerrilla operations, the military developed a plan that explicitly merged Canador with a counterinsurgency strategy called Joint Plan DN-PR-1 or Plan Tecpan. AGN, SEDENA, box 101, file 301, 1-153, "Plan Conjunto, Plan Tecpan DN-PR-1," 1975. The United States also launched eradication programs with their own brands, like the Special Enforcement Activity in Mexico (SEAM, 1974) and SEAM CLEARVIEW (1975). See Carlos Pérez Ricart, "Las agencias antinarcóticos de los Estados Unidos y la construcción trasnacional de la guerra contra las drogas en México" (PhD diss., Freie Universität Berlin, 2016), 375–80.

12. Edward Heath explained how the military only cut down the larger poppy plants while leaving the budding crops, thus allowing farmers to salvage part of their crops. Edward Heath, "Mexican Opium Eradication Campaign" (MA thesis, California State University, 1981), 23.

13. "Task Force Report, Narcotics, Marijuana, and Dangerous Drugs. Findings and Recommendations," 6/6/1969, http://nsarchive.gwu.edu/NSAEBB/NSAEBB86/intercept01.pdf.

14. Heath, "Mexican Opium," 5.

15. Heath, "Mexican Opium," 30.

16. Evergreen International Aviation was closely related to the CIA and in 1975 put George Doole—head of CIA air operations until 1971—on its board of directors. Jonathan Marshall, "CIA Assets and the Rise of the Guadalajara Connection," *Crime, Law and Social Change* 16, no. 1 (1991): 90.

17. Heath, "Mexican Opium," 41. The DEA was authorized to interrogate farmers and financiers arrested by the PJF. Given that the PJF used torture as a standard investigative method, the DEA agents bore witness to that practice and might have occasionally intervened in the sessions. Craig Pyes, "Legal Murders," *Village Voice*, June 4, 1979, 11–15.

18. Gertz Manero responded to criticism in media outlets regarding the use of herbicides by claiming that paraquat (gramoxone) was inoffensive to the environment. Other cables by the Department of State reveal the efforts by the Mexican government to conceal or deny the extent of the U.S. involvement in the narcotics campaign. "Press Conference on Herbicides," January 9, 1976. https://wikileaks.org/plusd/cables/1976STATE005410_b.html; "Excelsior Story on Vance/Ojeda Agree-

ment," January 16, 1976, https://wikileaks.org/plusd/cables/1976MEXICO00608_b.html; and "Attorney General's Ground Rules for MOPPS," August 17, 1976, https://wikileaks.org/plusd/cables/1976MEXICO10555_b.html, accessed April 10, 2018.

19. For the depiction of the remote sensing technology and the type of helicopters employed by Trizo, see Pérez Ricart, "Las agencias antinarcóticas," 362–85. Despite Trizo's alleged accomplishments, in 1975 Mexico sent 6.5 tons of pure heroin to the United States, which in that year recorded 1,789 heroin-related deaths. Heath, "Mexican Opium," 31.

20. Richard B. Craig, "La Campaña Permanente: Mexico's Antidrug Campaign," *Journal of Interamerican Studies and World Affairs* 20, no. 2 (May 1978): 117–18.

21. "Condor" seems to be a code-name for military operations that are conducted in mountains or rugged terrain. It has been used for operations by different armies around the world, including the famous yet unrelated Operation Condor from South America.

22. Richard Craig, "Operation Condor: Mexico's Antidrug Campaign Enters a New Era," *Journal of Interamerican Studies and World Affairs* 22, no. 3 (August 1980): 352.

23. José Luis García Cabrera, *El Pastel! 1920–2000*, vol. 1 (Bloomington, IN: Palibrio, 2012), kindle edition.

24. "12 clanes Mexicanos en el tráfico de heroína," *Proceso*, June 12, 1977.

25. Sicilia Falcón, the Herrera family, and Jorge Favela Escobar were overtly targeted and forced out of business. Celia Toro, *Mexico's War on Drugs: Causes and Consequences* (Boulder, CO: Lynne Rienner, 1995), 27.

26. AGN, DFS, public version, "Leopoldo Sánchez Celis," files 1 (1952–1966) and 2 (1966–1985). Sánchez Celis became partner of Miguel Angel Félix Gallardo, who was a member of his personal guard when he was governor. Félix Gallardo would become one of the most powerful kingpins in the 1980s.

27. Juan Veledíaz, *Jinetes de Tlatelolco. Marcelino García Barragán y otros relatos del ejército mexicano* (Mexico City: Proceso, 2017), 190–92.

28. AGN, DFS, public version, "Narcotráfico," August 1978, 64. The DEA was also aware of Flores Sánchez's connections to class one drug traffickers. Pyes, "Legal Murders," 12.

29. Mendiolea was subchief of the Preventive Police of Mexico City, one of the agencies that suppressed the 1968 student movement. Carlos Flores Pérez, *Historias de Polvo y Sangre. Génesis y Evolución del Tráfico de Drogas en el Estado de Tamaulipas* (Mexico City: CIESAS, 2013), 215–16.

30. *El Sol de México*, December 21, 1976, 1.

31. AGN, DGIPS, box 1707 B, file 8, 145–49, "Estado de Sinaloa," 11/12/1976.

32. AGN, DGIPS, box 1711-C, file 12, 107–8, "Estado de Sinaloa," 4/7/1976 and 5/25/1976, 125; *El Heraldo de México*, February 23, 1978, 7; AGN, DGIPS, box 1711-C, file 12, 31–34, "Estado de Sinaloa," 6/16/1975.

33. AGN, DGIPS, box 1711-C, file 10, 185, "Estado de Sinaloa," 11/10/1972.

34. AGN, DGIPS, box 1711-C, file 12, 258, "Estado de Sinaloa," 1/16/1976.

35. At least 250 PGR agents participated in Operation Condor, most of them in the northwest. Craig, "Operation Condor," 348.

36. Heath, "Mexican Opium," 35. Roughly ten thousand troops participated in the FTC overall.

37. The FTC would expand to other municipalities in the three-state zone. Tomás Guevara, "Operación Condor. Compilación de artículos del *Noroeste*," *Culiacán*, January–December 1977, 1–5.

38. "Comandantes de la Fuerza de Tarea Cóndor," SEDENA, http://www.sedena.gob.mx/leytrans/petic/2005/may/20052005a3.html, accessed February 10, 2017.

39. Rafael Rodríguez Castañeda, *El policía: la guerra sucia no se olvida* (Barcelona: Grijalbo, 2013); Julio Scherer and Carlos Monsiváis, *Parte de Guerra. Tlatelolco 1968* (Mexico City: Nuevo Siglo/Aguilar, 1999); Roderic Ai Camp, *Generals in the Palacio: The Military in Modern Mexico* (New York: Oxford University Press, 1992); Juan Veledíaz, *El General sin memoria: una crónica de los silencios del ejército mexicano* (Mexico City: Debate, 2010); and Veledíaz, *Jinetes de Tlaltelolco*.

40. In 1979, Infantry Captain Salvador Cienfuegos spent one week with the FTC IV in Badiraguato, as chief of international affairs and crime of the subsection of intelligence from the National Defense Staff. As national defense secretary (2012–2018), Cienfuegos was involved in cases related to both counterinsurgency and the drug war, seconding a long military tradition. "Salvador Cienfuegos Zepeda's Service Record," public version, https://www.gob.mx/cms/uploads/attachment/file/606752/ANEXO_06_EXPEDIENTE_GENERAL_VIRGILIO_MENDEZ_TI_FINAL_NEGRO_-__Parte_04_.pdf, accessed January 21, 2021.

41. *Noroeste*, February 10, 1977, 1; AGN, DGIPS, box 1711-C, file 12, "Estado de Sinaloa," 2/9/1977.

42. AGN, DGIPS, box 1711-C, file 13, 24, "Estado de Sinaloa," 3/15/1977.

43. When drug sales were disrupted, gangs switched to alternative criminal activities. AGN, DFS, box 1711-C, file 13, 56, "Estado de Sinaloa," 5/12/1977.

44. Governor Calderón admitted that the military was perpetrating abuses against innocent civilians, but the 9th Military Zone did not receive his criticism well. AGN, DGIPS, box 1711-C, file 14, [Penitenciaría del Estado de Sinaloa, 11/18/1977, and Instituto de Readaptación Social del Estado de Sinaloa, 12/19/1977], 127–37.

45. AGN, DGIPS, box 1711-C, file 13, 176, "Estado de Sinaloa," October 31, 1977. There are also several reports of massacres in the highlands during the antidrug campaigns of previous years.

46. Reyes was one of several officers from both the PJS and the Municipal Police who were killed during the Condor years for drug-related issues. AGN, DGIPS, box 1711-C, file 13, 20, "Estado de Sinaloa," 3/3/1977.

47. AGN, DGIPS, box 1711-C, file 13, 45, "Estado de Sinaloa," 3/25/1977.

48. AGN, DGIPS, box 1711-C, file 12, 73–74. "Estado de Sinaloa," 11/10/1975.

49. AGN, DGIPS, box 1707-B, file 9, 6, "Estado de Sinaloa," 2/23/1977; AGN, DGIPS, box 1711-C, file 13, 48–49, "Estado de Sinaloa," 3/31/1977.

50. The state attorney, the chief of the PJS, and the director of government spent one night in the 9th military camp. "Elenco Político," *Proceso,* June 4, 1977.

51. AGN, DGIPS, box 1711-C, file 13, 70, "Estado de Sinaloa," 5/6/1977.

52. AGN, DGIPS, box 1711-C, file 13, 78, "Estado de Sinaloa," 5/31/1977.

53. AGN, DGIPS, box 1711-C, file 13, 240–80 [assassination of Roberto Martínez Montenegro], February and March 1977.

54. AGN, DGIPS, box 1711-C, file 14, 37–38, "Estado de Sinaloa," 5/13/1978. Pyes also collected this version, specifying that Montenegro would charge Alcalá and other agents with extorting millions of pesos from narcotics suspects through the use of torture. Pyes, "Legal Murders," 12.

55. AGN, DGIPS, box 1711-C, file 14, 247, "Estado de Sinaloa," 2/14/1978.

56. PJF agents tortured Gómez in front of Gral. Mendiolea. Gómez's pregnant wife and his three-year old son were tortured next to him. AGN, DGIPS, box 1711-C, file 14, 42–44, "Estado de Sinaloa," 5/15/1978; Pyes, "Legal Murders," 13–15.

57. AGN, DFS, public version, 2–4, "Colegio de Abogados 'Eustaquio Buelna.'"

58. AGN, DGIPS, box 1711-C, file 14, 64, 68, "Estado de Sinaloa," 4/17/1978.

59. The official version stated that Avilés was killed by accident because he did not stop his car in a PJF checkpoint, but this was a blatant cover-up. AGN, DFS, public versión, 14, "Pedro Avilés Pérez," 9/16/1978.

60. Juan Veledíaz, "La muerte de 'El León de la Sierra,' el primer Padrino del narco," http://laparednoticias.com/la-muerte-de-el-leon-de-la-sierra-el-primer-padrino-del-narco/, accessed March 12, 2017.

61. Jaime Herrera Nevarez, the most powerful heroin kingpin according to the DEA, was detained in 1978, but unlike Avilés, the DEA and the PJF gave him the opportunity to negotiate his surrender. Eduardo Fernández, the drug lord who helped introduce the cocaine trade to Sinaloa, fled untroubled to Puebla. Pedro Avilés worked with most of the drug traffickers that would dominate the drug scene during the early 1980s: Ernesto Fonseca, Rafael Caro Quintero, Miguel Ángel Félix Gallardo, El Cochiloco, Juan José Esparragoza, Javier Barba, Amado Carrillo Fuentes, and the brothers Rafael and Juan Quintero Payán. Juan Carlos Reyna suggests that during the 1976 gang wars, some drug traffickers had become independent from Pedro Avilés and made new arrangements with the PJF, among them Ernesto Fonseca and Rafael Caro Quintero. Juan Carlos Reyna and Farrah Fresnedo, *El Extraditado* (Barcelona: Grijalbo, 2014), kindle edition.

62. "Informes de Gobierno del Presidente Constitucional de los Estados Unidos Mexicanos José López Portillo," http://www.diputados.gob.mx/sedia/sia/re/RE-ISS-09-06-15.pdf, accessed March 10, 2017; "Tercer Informe que rinde al H. Congreso del Estado el C. Gobernador Constitucional de Sinaloa, Alfonso G. Calderón," December 1, 1977.

63. AGN, DGIPS, box 1707-B, file 9, 104–6, "Estado de Sinaloa," 11/6/1977.
64. Francisco Ortiz Pinchetti, ed., *La Operación Cóndor* (Mexico City: Proceso, 1991), 13.
65. Richard B. Craig, "Human Rights and Mexico's Antidrug Campaign," *Social Science Quarterly* 60, no. 4 (March 1980): 691–701.
66. Ortiz, *La Operación Cóndor*, 68; AGN, DGIPS, box 1711-C, file 13, "Estado de Sinaloa," 13; Pyes, "Legal Murders," 11–15.
67. AGN, DFS, public version of the "Colegio de Abogados 'Eustaquio Buelna,'" 18, 5/13/1978, (hereafter CAEB report). According to Pyes, the CAEB published a second report containing 110 more prisoners' testimonials, and one of them included an eyewitness account of a crucifixion. Pyes, "Legal Murders," 11.
68. AGN, SEDENA, Fuerza de Tarea Cóndor: quejas, box 44, file 1012–1979, 31, "Para informar a la superioridad," 6/1/1979.
69. Oscar Loza Ochoa, interview with the author, Culiacán, Sinaloa, May 2, 2017.
70. Censos y conteos del Instituto Nacional de Estadística y Geografía, http://www.beta.inegi.org.mx/proyectos/ccpv/cpvsh/default.html, accessed March 13, 2018. From 1970 to 1980 Badiraguato went from 29,252 inhabitants to 23,742, Guadalupe y Calvo from 29,053 to 30,023, and Tamazula, Durango, from 18,315 to 20,647.
71. Jeffrey Smith, "Spraying Herbicides on Mexican Marijuana Backfires on U.S.," *New Series* 199, no. 4331 (February 24, 1978): 861–64; "Paraquat Contamination of Marijuana," *Morbidity and Mortality Weekly Report* 28, no. 8 (March 2, 1979): 93–94; L. Garmon, "Pot-Smokers May Be Imperiled by Paraquat-Spraying Program, *Science News* 124, no. 4 (July 23, 1983), 55.
72. Ortiz, *La Operación Condor*, 48.
73. Discussion of the author with the authorities of the Badiraguato City Hall, Badiraguato, Sinaloa, May 10, 2017.
74. Anabel Hernández, *Los señores del narco* (Mexico City: Random House Mondadori, 2010), 120.
75. Heath, "Mexican Opium," 41.
76. "Drug Enforcement Administration, 1975–1980." https://www.dea.gov/about/history/1975-1980.pdf, accessed November 10, 2017. For a quantitative analysis of the results of Trizo, see James Michael Van Wert, "Government of Mexico Herbicidal Opium Poppy Eradication Program: A Summative Evaluation" (PhD diss., University of Southern California, 1982).
77. Pyes, "Legal Murders," 11.
78. In 1980 less than nine hundred opium poppy hectares were destroyed. Heath, "Mexican Opium," 37, 67.
79. DEA officials stuck to a narrative of success to justify their expenses, even though they internally acknowledged the program's shortcomings. Marshall, "CIA Assets," 90.
80. Heath, "Mexican Opium," 76.

81. Heath, "Mexican Opium," 36.

82. Pyes, "Legal Murders," 11–15.

83. Pérez Ricart, "Las agencias antinarcóticos," 442.

84. Cited by Marshall, "CIA Assets," 89.

85. Marshall, "CIA Assets."

86. "Resultados de la Fuerza de Tarea Cóndor": http://www.sedena.gob.mx/leytrans/petic/2005/may/20052005a4.html, accessed March 20, 2018.

87. "Periodo del presidente José López Portillo," PGR, http://pgr.gob.mx/que-es-la-pgr/Documents/XIV.pdf, accessed March 15, 2018.

88. Heath, "Mexican Opium," iii.

89. "Drug Enforcement Administration History, 1975–1980." https://www.dea.gov/sites/default/files/2018-07/1975–1980%20p%2039–49.pdf, accessed November 10, 2017. The constant detention and release of prisoners make it difficult to have a record of all drug-related cases, but the figures regarding the prosecution of 2,019 cases fall short considering the ten years of Condor activity. Moreover, Craig claims that by mid-1977 there were around six hundred U.S. inmates in Mexican prisons, 85 percent of them for drug-related charges. Craig, "La Campaña Permanente," 125.

90. "Periodo del presidente José López Portillo," http://pgr.gob.mx/que-es-la-pgr/Documents/XIV.pdf, accessed March 15, 2018.

91. McCoy, "Covert Netherworld," 228.

92. I have consulted FOIA documents from both the FBI and the CIA at the National Security Archive (NSA) related to the cases of Nazar Haro, García Paniagua, Mario Arturo Acosta Chaparro, Francisco Quirós Hermosillo, Manlio Fabio Beltrones, and other Mexican officers and officials involved in the drug industry and other illegal activities.

93. Reyna and Fresnedo, *El Extraditado*, kindle edition.

94. Luis Astorga, *El Siglo de Drogas, el narcotráfico, del Porfiriato al nuevo milenio* (Mexico City: Plaza y Janés, 2005), 119.

95. Guillermo Valdés Castellanos, *Historia del Narcotráfico en México* (Mexico City: Aguilar, 2013), 175–76.

96. Peter Watt and Roberto Zepeda, *Drug War Mexico: Politics, Neoliberalism and Violence in the New Narcoeconomy* (London: Zed Books, 2012), 58.

12

Grupo Sangre
Drugs, Death Squads, and the Dirty War Origins of Mexico's Drug Wars

ALEXANDER AVIÑA

"En plan de pleito va a haber sangre."
—José Francisco Ruiz Massieu, July 1988[1]

A DEATH SQUAD APPEARS

Amidst an expanding guerrilla presence and an undeclared military state of siege in early 1974, the Acapulco newspaper *La Verdad* published a chilling letter. "We chose the state of Guerrero because it represents one of the main cradles of subversion," the anonymous authors wrote. "Bandit leaders and pseudo-guerrillas will be executed [*ajusticiados*], even though we know we'll be persecuted for taking the law into our own hands." The authors, self-identified as the Group of Annihilation "Blood," announced their first target and revealed a counterinsurgent purpose: "we will begin with the 'cabañistas' and provide information to the Government."[2] Soon after, charred, bullet-ridden bodies began to appear in the port city and surrounding coastal communities. Local residents, a spy report dated June 24, 1974 stated, wondered whether the victims "were connected to the criminal underworld or drug trafficking."[3] In reality, information obtained through "discreet means" revealed that the "bodies belonged to individuals connected to Lucio Cabañas and his people." Captured after coming down from the mountains that sheltered Party of the Poor [PDLP] guerrillas in search of supplies or to relay messages, Grupo

Sangre tortured these individuals to obtain intelligence. They then forced their captives to drink gasoline and set them on fire.[4]

The appearance of Grupo Sangre in 1974, and the terrorism its members practiced, form part of a broader history of political authoritarianism and counterinsurgent state terror that occurred in the southwestern Mexican state of Guerrero during the 1960s and 1970s. In response to a series of consequential social movements and popular mobilizations that began in the late 1950s, and the eventual development of peasant guerrilla movements by the late 1960s, the Institutional Revolutionary Party (PRI) waged a manifold Dirty War that stretched across two decades. This war ebbed and flowed in intensity according to local exigencies and national responses; involved some combination of military battalions, infamous cacique gunslingers, federal and state police (*judiciales*), and agents from the now-extinct Dirección Federal de Seguridad (DFS); and disappeared hundreds of *guerrerenses* while torturing thousands more. If local infighting between rival caciques and political *camarillas* (cliques) represented a key explanatory factor for the sort of political violence that characterized Guerrero in the 1940s and 1950s,[5] the Dirty War of the 1960s and 1970s exhibited a PRI attempt "to centralize control over an arsenal of repressive instruments and tactics" honed in the previous decades.[6] The tens of thousands of soldiers and police used in the violent counterinsurgent campaigns from 1967 to 1980 against guerrilla organizations like the National Revolutionary Civic Association (ACNR) and the PDLP testify to such centralizing efforts. Grupo Sangre, as a military-police death squad that tortured and killed suspected guerrillas and their supporters, formed one Dirty War modality.

The Dirty War encompassed an additional understudied but constitutive dimension to this story, one that comprises the focus of this chapter: the emergence of a transnational narcotics economy in Guerrero fostered, facilitated, and protected by the same individuals and institutions who waged counterinsurgency. Enmeshed in this messy history of state terror and political violence is the relatively rapid development of the southern state's highlands as a prime site of export-oriented marijuana and opium poppy production beginning in the early 1960s. By the late 1960s and early 1970s, as U.S. psychedelic rock bands like The Rainy Daze and New Riders of the Purple Sage sang about "Acapulco Gold," marijuana and opium poppy production took off in response to American demand and shifts in the global narcotics economy. Counterinsurgency operations in Guerrero thus began as counternarcotic, anticrime campaigns (with a dose of "armed social work"), the latter providing public cover and explanation for the covert former.[7] PRI officials and high-ranking military officers publicly portrayed antiguerrilla efforts in the state as "campaigns against *amapoleros* [poppy farmers]" and "bandits," thereby seeking to delegitimize the political-ideological dimensions of the guerrillas by casting them as armed criminals protecting narco-traffickers and producers.[8] Indeed, high-ranking officials like Gen. Hermenegildo Cuenca Díaz, head of the Mexican military during Luis Echeverría's presidential *sexenio* (1970–1976), blamed guerrillas for the commercial expansion of drug production.

Yet the opaque private transcripts of the state suggest a different history, revealing one foundational moment of what we can polemically refer to as the contemporary Mexican narco-state. Grupo Sangre serves as a sort of historical pivot, connecting the counterinsurgent aspect of the Dirty War with the emergence of the "counternarcotic narco," that is, the antiguerrilla, antinarcotics military and police agents who became narcos themselves. Uncovering the history of Grupo Sangre using truth commission reports, declassified spy and military documents, and oral histories collected by journalists partially reveals how prominent counterinsurgent agents would become key players in a developing regional drug economy after defeating the guerrillas in late 1974. This Mexican death squad, like the urban-based "White Brigade" and "Jaguar Group," helped lay the structural foundations for the 1980s rise of more centralized, cocaine-enriched drug-trafficking organizations that fundamentally depended on intimate local collaboration and negotiation between traffickers and a constellation of state agents: federal and state judicial police, military zone commanders and officials, DFS agents, and politicians.[9] Such collaboration, described by historian Alan Knight as a long-standing "staple, structural feature of a flourishing narco-economy," involved a rent-seeking Mexican state that acted like a mafia in the selling of protection, *plazas* (dealerships), and political power to drug traffickers.[10] The Dirty War origins of the drug economy in Guerrero also suggests that in addition to rent seeking, certain military counterinsurgent experts allegedly engaged in the actual production and circulation of drugs. The use of military Arava planes in the mid-1970s to both dump detained persons into the Pacific Ocean and transport marijuana from Guerrero to the U.S.-Mexico border illustrates this point.[11]

After providing a selective history of drug production in Guerrero up to the 1960s, this chapter will shed light on the 1970s as the Dirty War against the guerrillas, and a boom in opium poppy and marijuana production, intensified.

MAP 6   Map of Guerrero (credits: UU-Geo-C&M–Carto).

Outlining the history of Grupo Sangre—its purpose, practices, members, and allied groups—demonstrates how the contemporary history of drugs in Mexico is intimately intertwined with state efforts to crush popular protest and armed resistance. Guerrero served as a laboratory of sorts. Counterinsurgency epistemologies honed in the struggle against PDLP and ACNR guerrillas subsequently informed and shaped the Mexican government's highly publicized militarized drug interdiction campaigns of the late 1970s and early 1980s.[12] The use of torture, extrajudicial executions, disappearance, and displacement of entire *campesino* communities in "the heart of Mexico's opium citadel"[13] (the highland border region where Sinaloa, Durango, and Chihuahua intersect) during Operation Condor I (1976–1978) echoed previous "pacification" efforts in Guerrero.[14] For counterinsurgency and counternarcotics efforts of the 1970s possessed a similar ontology at their core as "instruments of political control" practiced in the Mexican countryside.[15] In the words of a declassified 1983 CIA report: "the [Mexican] army will also take advantage of the eradication campaign to uncover any arms trafficking and guerrilla activities. . . . *Army eradication forces may devote as much effort to internal security as eradication* [emphasis added]."[16]

BEFORE ACAPULCO GOLD
AND MEXICAN MUD, 1760-1950S

Marijuana's career began in colonial-era Guerrero as hemp cultivated for making industrial fiber. In his pioneering study on the history of marijuana in Mexico, historian Isaac Campos notes the modest success of hemp production in the Costa Chica region of southern Guerrero by the end of the eighteenth century, part of a broader Bourbon effort to encourage hemp production throughout New Spain. But if cannabis had first arrived "as an industrial fiber symbolizing imperial expansion and might," it gradually "developed a reputation as an indigenous drug plant capable of provoking disorder and madness" by the twilight of the colonial era.[17] Campos traces that shift to the 1760s, when Catholic priest and scientist José Antonio Alzate researched indigenous consumption of cannabis, *pipiltzintzintlis*, near Mexico City for religious, divinatory purposes. Though the word *pipiltzintzintlis* disappeared after the eighteenth century, cannabis—or its consumption as a drug—did not. It became *Rosa María* or *mariguana*, mentioned in published sources beginning in 1846 as smoked mostly in Mexico City neighborhoods or along the Pacific Coast stretching from Acapulco north to Puerto Vallarta.[18] Five years after the creation of Guerrero as a federal state in 1849, a Mexico City newspaper reported that "mariguana... in lost hours... has filled with delight the Indians of Chilpancingo."[19]

The opium poppy arrived later in Guerrero, most likely preceded by its opium derivative, as part of a dynamic, late-colonial-era and nineteenth-century trans-Pacific economic network. British and U.S. imperial expansion—in the form of the First Opium War (1839–1842) and Mexican-American War (1846–1848), respectively—facilitated this expanding network, as did the onset of the California Gold Rush (1849).[20] As early as 1809, the royal Spanish interdiction of opium trafficking provided an early instance of state officials participating in the drug business: officials arrested a colonial militia officer and placed him under criminal investigation for allegedly moving opium into Oaxaca.[21] Yet the proliferation of opium poppies in the Mexican highlands—at least as recorded in state sources—likely occurred toward the end of the 1800s, closely intertwined with the first arrival of Chinese immigrants to Sinaloa in 1886.[22] Though one well-traveled scientist included the poppy as part of "the [narcotics] of Mexico" in an 1801 address, official geographic and statistical studies first noted the proliferation of the bright flowers in Sinaloa in 1886. By

Grupo Sangre 267

1892, eight years after the Porfirio Díaz government began subsidizing Pacific steamship trade routes that linked Hong Kong to Acapulco (via Honolulu and Yokohama), those same studies included Guerrero's mountains as home to the poppy.[23]

As in Sinaloa, the flowers found a hospitable topography in the mountains of the Sierra Madre del Sur that traverse the state and continue into Oaxaca. Guerrero remained a marginal producer of opium poppies in the early twentieth century. In contrast, marijuana production surged, leading to its measurement in tons by the mid-1930s in historically peripheral growing areas like Guerrero, Tlaxcala, and Puebla. The rural areas surrounding the city of Iguala in 1935 alone produced nearly ten tons in "less than two months."[24] By the 1940s, marijuana production continued to outpace that of opium poppies in the southern state as wartime disruptions in the global narcotics economy helped make the northern "Golden Triangle" region—Sinaloa, Chihuahua, and Durango—the main center of poppy cultivation and opium production.

But if northern *goma* [opium gum] helped mediate rural social conflicts and forge a temporary "narcopopulist regime," as historian Ben Smith argues for post-1940 Sinaloa, the same did not occur in conflict-ridden Guerrero. The low-intensity warfare that began in 1920, pitting *agrarista* peasants against "shifting coalitions of landowners, *licenciados*, violent entrepreneurs, and the (generally despised) 'professional politicians,'" continued into the 1940s, as did the struggle to win and hold the levers of municipal and state political power by representatives of each side.[25] Add crushing poverty, competing cacique networks, the inability of governors to finish their terms, a lack of state financial resources, political assassinations, and powerful military zone commanders all too willing to violently engage with local political conflicts, and Guerrero—particularly from the perspective of national and state political elites—became "ungovernable"; a land constantly alternating between an insurgent "state of anarchy" and the feudal manor of recalcitrant cacique barons; and a useful stereotype that could (and did) justify either federal political intervention or counterinsurgency as the only ways to rule Guerrero *bronco*.[26] "Laws are for normal people, human begins who can distinguish right from wrong," a military zone commander stationed in Guerrero during the 1970s told journalist Ricardo Garibay, "not for people with impulsive, animalistic tendencies, or worse than animals, incapable of distinguishing the difference between giving someone a hug or stoning them to death."[27]

In reality, the 1940s witnessed the gradual centralization of PRI political power over the state, particularly during the governorship of Baltasar Leyva Mancilla (1945–1951), at the same time that narcotics production began to concern the ruling party. The military search-and-destroy raids that characterized La Gran Campaña, a national drug interdiction campaign launched in 1948 aimed mostly at the Golden Triangle states, extended into Guerrero by the late 1940s and early 1950s.[28] These military units encountered a politically pacified state, "completely dominated by the PRI" by 1952 in the words of a DFS agent, with two main regional *cacicazgos* that generally followed the PRI line and a state economy changed by an Acapulco-centered boom that brought in foreign and national capital.[29] Throughout the 1950s, the commercialization of copra and coffee production along the Pacific coast and highlands, and federal efforts to stimulate agroindustry (sesame seed) in the Tierra Caliente valleys through transportation and irrigation construction projects, occurred in the very regions that produced most of the marijuana and opium poppies.[30] It seems that the narcotics economy in 1950s Guerrero depended not on the absence of the state but in its active, expanding presence. Did inequitable, inconsistent rural modernization programs, and the constant presence of politically consequential military units at the local level, unintentionally help lay the groundwork for a vibrant marijuana and opium poppy export economy that emerged in the 1960s? Historian Lina Britto posits a similar argument for the "Colombian Caribbean" in the 1970s, as do anthropologists Salvador Maldonado and Victoria Malkin for the Michoacán hotlands.[31] Guerrero similarly suggests the argument that posits a causal link between "lawless" lands and surging narcotics production requires critical examination in light of recent "new drug history" studies.[32]

THE DRUG REVOLUTION, 1950–1969

The midcentury political pacification of the state forged by Levya Mancilla proved ephemeral, but the governor's achievement in the form of an expanded and more effective state government (at least in coercive terms) persisted. Generally failing to appease both cacique interests or campesinos, subsequent governors faced intense social conflict and popular mobilization. Agrarian conflicts deepened, sparked not by land tenure demands voiced by landless campesinos (with the exception of Acapulco, where tourism development led to the violent dispossession of ejido lands), but by the monopolization of regional markets, access to credit, processing plants, and transportation networks by rural caciques. Campesino communities living along the coasts and in the adjoining highlands generally kept their small plots of land, but they faced caciques—often backed by locally stationed military units and private gunslingers—who acted as loan sharks and cornered copra and coffee harvests. Beneath these struggles, narcotics production continued on a small scale, though interdiction campaigns in Sinaloa possibly dispersed and increased poppy production southward to states like Michoacán, Jalisco, Nayarit, and Guerrero.[33] Criminal underworld activities in Acapulco briefly surfaced in the form of two well-publicized gangland murders in 1952 and 1959: that of Dr. Ignacio Barajas Lozano and Richard McGovern, respectively. McGovern, a dealer who worked with a transnational heroin ring based in New York City and Montreal, was killed in April for "having introduced a narcotics agent into the organization," his "body found in a ditch in Acapulco."[34]

A few months before authorities discovered McGovern's body, a brave Acapulco newspaper editor sent a telegram to minister of the interior, Gustavo Díaz Ordaz, claiming that state police forces under the command of Governor General Raúl Caballero Aburto (1957–1961) had killed more than a thousand people.[35] Ruled by this violent and nepotistic governor, Guerrero began the 1960s—the decade of the "drug revolution" to quote former marijuana smuggler Jerry Kamstra—in the midst of a popular civic rebellion.[36] While a multiclass civic movement taking to the streets would succeed in removing the general from power (it would take a military-perpetrated massacre in December 1960) and subsequently attempted to create a meaningful social democracy via the ballot box, the massification of U.S. demand for Mexican marijuana exponentially increased production in the highland communities. The increase occurred during the governorship of Raymundo Abarca Alarcón (1963–1969), a military doctor from Iguala who took office under suspicion of electoral fraud and after yet another massacre of protesters in December 1962. Buoyed by the thousands of soldiers sent into the state in 1963 that terrorized opposition political party, militants, and independent campesino unions, the doctor ruled violently in alliance with the state's cacique networks.[37] As DFS agents investigated the existence of "communist" guerrilla cells and soldiers persecuted social activists and organizers, marijuana production surged in the mountains.[38]

An array of northern Mexican and U.S. entrepreneurs began to arrive in the mid- to late 1960s, providing willing campesinos with more potent marijuana seeds (and opium poppy seeds), loans, weaponry, irrigation equipment, and even fertilizer.[39] In some instances, smugglers negotiated directly with local

Guerrero smugglers who organized and led small networks of marijuana-growing campesinos. For instance, an American and Mexican American smuggling duo in 1968 worked with "Jesús," an administrator of more than forty farmers that grew marijuana for him in the mountains of Guerrero and Michoacán.[40] Production occurred on small plots of land, with marijuana plots distributed within a broader patchwork of cornstalks and bean fields. After campesinos planted the seeds in May or June before the start of the rainy season (with a second, irrigation-assisted planting in October), they harvested the plants an estimated five to six months later. Following an intricate process of cutting, separating, and drying, farmers placed the marijuana in burlap sacks and transported them down mountains and into clandestine warehouses distributed throughout major Mexican cities. To get the drugs out, entrepreneurs and smugglers also began to use hastily built clandestine airstrips, or they transported the goods to port cities like Acapulco, where they used private yachts and small boats for smuggling.[41] "*Goma*" [gum] cultivated from opium poppies followed a similar path, moving down mountains to warehouses before arriving at heroin-processing laboratories usually located in cities like Guadalajara and Culiacán.[42] As early as 1964, the name "Acapulco Gold," began to appear on American streets. On September 14, 1965, Mexican federal *judiciales* and U.S. antinarcotics agents made one of the largest marijuana seizures to that date: 3.5 tons, captured in central Guerrero.[43]

These types of production and transportation operations fundamentally depended upon the collaboration of locally stationed military and police units. When Gen. Salvador Rangel Medina began conducting antidrug campaigns in the Michoacán Tierra Caliente in the late 1950s and early 1960s, he confronted a constellation of corrupt forces that protected drug farmers and smugglers, one that he also discovered later in Guerrero; military zone commanders, local politicians, cacique families, and even a number of his own soldiers, "traffickers wearing military uniforms," all participated in the drug business.[44] After his stint in Michoacán, Rangel Medina arrived in Iguala in late 1965 with his 49th Infantry Battalion to discover that "everyone talked about the drug fields in the Costa Grande ... and that the *defensas rurales* in Arcelia and Teloloapan [Tierra Caliente] cultivated marijuana."[45] The narco-constellation encountered by the general facilitated the expansion of drug production to industrial proportions by the late 1960s, concentrated mainly in the highlands of the Costa Grande, Tierra Caliente, North (Iguala) and Central (Chilpancingo) regions.[46] In the Tierra Caliente municipality of Teloloapan,

Grupo Sangre 271

for instance, journalists claimed that local PRI politicians and the Salgado cacicazgo linked to Governor Caritino Maldonado (1969–1971)—including the municipal president Filiberto Martínez Salgado—engaged in the growing and trafficking of marijuana and opium gum (along with theft of ejido lands and livestock rustling).[47] A portion of that cultivation allegedly took place on soldier-protected lands owned by Horacio Román Arellano, an army official who enjoyed legal protection from the federal attorney general's office.[48] A similar arrangement existed in nearby Arcelia, where local politician Celia Espinosa de Olea, agents from the local attorney general's office, and military personnel shielded cattle-rustlers-turned-marijuana-growers.[49]

Some long-established caciques thus seemingly engaged in drug production during the 1960s using the same sort of political and military connections that allowed them to reproduce their local boss control. In the coffee-producing highlands of the Costa Grande, coffee caciques like Jorge Bautista and Saturnino Sánchez from El Paraíso sparked campesino resistance from nearby communities when they decided to plant and cultivate opium poppies in the late 1960s. Locally known for mistreating day laborers, violently persecuting political dissidents, ejido theft, and cornering coffee harvests, both Bautista and Sánchez became "opium poppy pioneers" with the help of the military unit stationed in El Paraíso. The "well-known and feared bandits" who worked for Sánchez allegedly received weapons and ammunition from local military personnel on the condition that they help the soldiers "locate [guerrilla leader] Genaro Vázquez."[50] Similarly, when residents from the nearby community of El Molote accused Bautista of drug production to legal authorities, the cacique in turn alleged that his denouncers fed and protected Vázquez, a claim that would lead to tragic results.[51] Elsewhere in the Costa Grande highlands, campesino communities that had long defended their forests against illegal logging operations led by Melchor Ortega recalled a similar narco-cacique-military alliance by the late 1960s and early 1970s.[52] A campesino from Santa Lucía remembered "that they [military] bought drugs, that during the time of Lucio's uprising, they protected the big marijuana narco-traffickers who came to the region trying to convince campesinos to grow it."[53]

The year 1967 was a key year. As marijuana production entered an unprecedented boom phase,[54] the massacres of the parents of schoolchildren and copra campesinos in Atoyac de Álvarez and Acapulco, respectively, shook the state.[55] As predicted years earlier by General Rangel Medina, the coalitions of judicial authorities, police, cacique gunslingers, livestock ranchers, and "*militares* transformed into servants of caciques" that allotted injustice and humiliation to campesinos provoked popular protest.⁵⁶ Campesino demands for vengeance materialized in the form of armed self-defense and guerrilla warfare. Schoolteacher Lucio Cabañas survived the massacre in Atoyac perpetrated by state judiciales and fled to the mountains to launch the most consequential rural guerrilla movement in Cold War Mexico. A year later, longtime activist and organizer Genaro Vázquez escaped prison and formed a separate revolutionary group. In response, the PRI started waging Dirty War. A regional counterinsurgency began to take shape, using militarized counternarcotics and "depistolization" (disarmament) operations and public discourse as cover to locate and annihilate emerging armed struggles, as the example from El Molote demonstrates. The Dirty War claimed its first disappeared victim, rural schoolteacher Epifanio Avilés Rojas, on May 19, 1969, when military units under the command of Maj. Antonio López Rivera detained the rural schoolteacher in the Tierra Caliente town of Coyuca de Catalán, the capital of a municipality full of mountains covered with marijuana and opium poppies.⁵⁷ Several months later in El Molote, in the midst of the dispute between campesinos and Bautista, Alejandro Simbras disappeared. A member of the 1st Reserva Rural, Simbras and several fellow reservists traveled to the military base in El Paraíso to answer the cacique's accusations that his community had fed the Vázquez-led guerrillas. Simbras never made it home on November 8, 1969, murdered and buried in a clandestine grave by unknown persons.⁵⁸

GRUPO SANGRE

"El marihuanero, digo, no había bronca;
pero al guerrillero sí había que romperle la madre."
—Anonymous Informant⁵⁹

In an April 1970 communiqué sent to Enrique Ramírez y Ramírez, newspaper editor of Mexico City daily *El Día*, PDLP guerrillas addressed their revolutionary cause and deeds to a national audience. Taking the opportunity to correct inaccurate reports that portrayed them as killers and cattle thieves, the authors cast their struggle within a historical lineage that included "Juárez, Villa and Zapata" waged against the rich and the "new Porfirians." After listing recent actions and clarifying their politico-military autonomy from the Vázquez-led armed movement, they described four campaigns launched by the federal government: first, "a health campaign" during which soldiers provided health care and medicine to campesino communities in exchange for intelligence; and, most recently, a fake "campaign against amapoleros" that in reality tortured, robbed, and imprisoned campesinos in order to obtain information on the "armed group we formed." The guerrilla signers of the communiqué, thirty-five in total, described one particularly heinous torture method used by soldiers, one that became the calling card of Grupo Sangre later on: the use of gasoline to burn campesinos' chests.[60]

At first, the counterinsurgency campaigns of the late 1960s, publicly cast as counternarcotic and anticrime, were not supposed to tactically depend on gasoline, torture, and disappearances. Armed "social labor," in the form of free health care, medicine, clothing, and food entered Costa Grande, Costa Chica, and Tierra Caliente highland communities beginning in late 1968 and 1969 intended to undermine campesino support for Cabañas and Vázquez.[61] In an April 1969 meeting with military officials of the 27th (Acapulco) and 35th (Chilpancingo) Military Zones, Gen. Marcelino García Barragán, secretary of national defense, suggested the use of "medical campaigns" to recapture campesino "confidence and affection" for the military; the "total" restructuring of Defensas Rurales and charging them with "eliminating" bandits; and the "extremely discreet" (paramilitary) arming of caciques, like the Torreblanca clan, that historically feuded with the Cabañas family. Ultimately, the general argued, the Mexican Revolution "constituted the only vaccine against the viruses of communism and the clergy."[62] A month later the PDLP sardonically responded to the "500 soldiers dressed like doctors" health campaign in a communiqué: "it seems that if we form armed groups throughout the country, we'll win free medical care for the entire Republic."[63]

The general's last suggestion regarding the secret arming of cacique gun-slingers inaugurated an infradimension of the Dirty War in Guerrero, one to which Grupo Sangre belongs: the use of paramilitaries in a counterinsurgent capacity to violently disarticulate the guerrillas' popular base of support. By design, paramilitaries acted beyond an official capacity, leaving an almost nonexistent "paper trail" as they waged perhaps the dirtiest part of the Dirty War. Military reports sent to Mexico City in November 1969 indicated collaboration between newly arrived military units searching for guerrillas and local narco-traffickers in El Paraíso. State police forces, defensas rurales, and "gunmen [*gavilleros*]," like the criminal group headed by Bulmaro González Chavando in Teloloapan, also formed part of such alliances.[64] In the Costa

Chica region, military officials organized "groups of athletes who later appeared armed and in uniform."[65] This process of paramilitarization resulted in more violence, more conflicts between counterinsurgent forces and civilian communities, and an increase in the number of human rights violations.

By the end of 1969, as the Ministry of National Defense announced an "intensification" of the counternarcotics campaign as a response to Operation Intercept, dozens of campesinos had been tortured or killed in the pursuit of guerrillas.[66] The tally of campesino casualties, imprisonment, and protests, IPS agents reported, mounted in 1970 and 1971.[67] Those numbers spiked when the military launched Operation Friendship (July–August 1970 in the Costa Chica) and Operation Spider Web (spring–summer 1971 in the Costa Grande), campaigns publicly described as counternarcotic and antibandit in design.[68] Declassified documents and subsequent military actions revealed the actual primary target: the guerrilla groups that kidnapped and killed locally hated caciques.[69] Newspapers widely publicized the secondary goals throughout 1971 and early 1972: the seizure-destruction of tons of narcotics and "social labor" campaigns in the form of "health brigades."[70] Local newspapers also published messages from an antecedent to Grupo Sangre in early 1971: ominous letters threatening violence against "subversives" signed by an "anticommunist" organization named "Justicia Anónima de Guerrero."[71] In an April 1971 guerrilla communiqué directed at "The People of Mexico," Vázquez accused the military of collaborating with "killers on the payroll of caciques," a "Mexican version of Brazilian death squads" that included "Justicia Anónima de Guerrero," all responsible for numerous atrocities committed against campesino communities.[72]

The turning point that made Grupo Sangre a counterinsurgent necessity from the perspective of military and political leaders occurred in the summer of 1972, when PDLP guerrillas launched two successful ambushes against military convoys near highland communities north of Acapulco. In between the second ambush of August 1972 and the death squad's public appearance in January 1974, ten to twenty thousand soldiers, federal judiciales, state judiciales "recruited in large part from groups of thieves and murders,"[73] and allied narcos[74] and paramilitaries[75] failed to prevent the PDLP from growing militarily and politically. The brutally heavy-handed military response against campesino communities believed to support the guerrillas—and internal conflicts over strategy within the military—undermined federal efforts to "win hearts and minds" via massive state investment to modernize agricultural production and displace caciques, build new infrastructure, and provide potable water and electricity.[76] All the while, the production of marijuana and opium poppies continued increasing to unprecedented levels, in part due to (not in spite of) the widespread counterinsurgent presence of military and police, as General Rangel Medina signaled in an internal memo in late 1973.[77] The real struggle was against the guerrillas and their supporters. As a military informant who participated in these campaigns told political scientist Carlos Antonio Flores Pérez, "we had a mentality that we didn't have beef with the marijuana growers; but we had to fuck up the guerrillas."[78]

By 1974, especially after PDLP guerrillas kidnapped cacique and future state governor Rubén Figueroa in June, Grupo Sangre became an unofficial part of a broader military plan to comprehensively "destroy the criminals [*maleantes*]" by exercising effective control over the civilian population "in critical areas"; controlling civilian access to and distribution of food and medicine; and waging a "permanent psychological campaign" to undermine popular support for the guerrillas.[79] Officers with specialized counterinsurgency training like Mario Acosta Chaparro, Roberto Heine Rangel, and Enrique Cervantes Aguirre (all future generals) exercised more control over military operations on the ground while secretary of national defense Gen. Hermenegildo Cuenca Díaz directly commanded from Mexico City.[80] Grupo Sangre's letter to *La Verdad* in January 1974 seemingly formed part of the plan's psychological component: a shadowy group with a fear-inducing name that promised to exterminate "cabañistas" and signed off with "for a peaceful world we will shed blood to fully cleanse it."[81] The next time (and last time in 1974 to my knowledge) the death squad appeared in declassified state documents, the DFS agent described the trail of bodies disfigured by gasoline and bullet wounds mentioned previously in this chapter's introduction. A group made up of "retired police officers and military personnel," Grupo Sangre allegedly took its orders from military zone commander Gen. Salvador Rangel Medina and then Lt. Col. Francisco Quirós Hermosillo, another experienced counterguerrilla official and head of the 2nd Military Police battalion. Local campesinos blamed Quirós Hermosillo for the killings.[82]

The Dirty War continued in Guerrero after soldiers killed Cabañas in December 1974. For instance, a new terror tactic became more systematic in the following year: the use of "death flights" to dump individuals into the Pacific Ocean from military planes and helicopters.[83] The "undeclared state of war,"[84] as some teachers and professors characterized life in 1975 Guerrero, continued for several reasons: the increased military presence remained in the state and newly elected governor Rubén Figueroa (1975–1981) ruled in revanchist style, persecuting remaining PDLP militants, other armed organizations in Acapulco, and organized expressions of social dissidence. Internal military documents in early 1975 discussed a rapid shift from counterinsurgent to counternarcotic operations, taking advantage of military checkpoints and patrols organized "during recent operations ... (rescue of Senator [Rubén] Figueroa)," in the attempt to undermine an increased level of narcotics production that positioned Mexico as the main supplier of heroin and marijuana to the United States.[85] U.S. congressional reports estimated that 90 percent of all heroin seized in 1975 originated from their southern neighbor.[86] Mexican political and military officials publicly (and internally) placed the blame on an alleged narco-guerrilla alliance that "industrialized the narco-trafficking business."[87]

Another related reason for the permanence of the Dirty War was Figueroa's decision to select military counterinsurgency officials linked to the most violent antiguerrilla episodes to lead Guerrero's expanded and paramilitarized police bodies.[88] In the struggle against the PDLP, state and municipal police forces that coordinated with the military practiced a brutal counterinsurgent praxis, one that continued under the leadership of Acosta Chaparro and Quirós Hermosillo during Figueroa's governorship. Torture, extrajudicial executions, disappearances, death flights, clandestine prisons, and torture centers marked this period. By 1977 Acosta Chaparro would command all of Guerrero's police forces while recently ascended General Quirós Hermosillo led the infamous "White Brigade" (along with DFS agent Miguel Nazar Haro), charged with the annihilation of urban guerrillas belonging to Communist League 23 of September.[89]

A new iteration of Grupo Sangre re-emerges within this constellation of repression in declassified documents produced in May 1976. Continuing its work as a military-police death squad with thirty members "who previously formed part of Grupo Sangre," it operated as "a repressive group that worked to avenge criticism voiced against the Governor, or target individuals who have had problems with the Army ... the majority of the detained are disappeared." It operated autonomously, providing operation information only to the governor "or on occasion to the Military Zone Commander in Acapulco." There was an apparent novelty in whom the group additionally targeted: "narco-traffickers (in order to come to an agreement)."[90] Under the leadership of Capt. Francisco Barquín Alonso, a military policeman closely linked to Quirós

Hermosillo, Grupo Sangre 2.0 extorted narco-traffickers and disappeared those who refused to cooperate, even as the military conducted large-scale drug interdiction campaigns in the form of Operations Trizo and Condor in 1976 and 1977 respectively. A separate DFS memo from August 7, 1976, echoed the earlier report on Barquín Alonso's group. For "more than year" a group of "30 individuals" has detained "civilians without informing them of the motivations ... most of whom are not heard from again." On some occasions "they detain persons involved in the trafficking of drugs (marijuana) whom they extort; the whereabouts of these people are unknown."[91] By the late 1970s, Barquín Alonso had moved on from extorting small-time drug dealers. In 1979, allegedly under orders from Quirós Hermosillo, he oversaw the shipment of narcotics aboard Mexican Air Force planes from Acapulco to Laredo, Texas.[92]

CONCLUSION: NARCO-GENERALS

Decades later, in 2002, a protected witness, a former military and police official who worked under Acosta Chaparro in Guerrero, testified in military court that both Quirós Hermosillo and his former boss "began narco-trafficking activities" during the 1970s while simultaneously waging the Dirty War in the form of extrajudicial executions, disappearances, and death flights. The trial, lasting from 2000 to 2002, revealed that both generals had faced investigations for allegedly engaging in narco-trafficking since at least 1988, when Quirós Hermosillo allegedly smuggled 1.5 tons of cocaine. Cocaine bricks bore the general's last name. Another protected witness, former director of the Federal Judicial Police Adrián Carrera Fuentes, admitted that in 1994 he directly connected both Acosta Chaparro and Quirós Hermosillo to Amado Carrillo Fuentes, head of the Ciudad Juárez Cartel during the mid-1990s. The generals, themselves benefiting from their close friendship with the head of the Mexican military General Enrique Cervantes Aguirre (1994–2000) that stretched back to their time in 1970s Guerrero, worked to protect the cartel. In addition to allegedly creating an "intelligence network" to aid the narcos, the "narco-generals" provided the necessary connections with police and naval officials to guarantee the safe passage of Colombian cocaine to the U.S.-Mexico border. At times, they used satellite technology "similar to one used by the Mexican military" and assigned trusted former judicial police officers to serve as bodyguards for the Carrillo Fuentes family. One such police officer, Capt. Francisco Tornez Castro, worked under Acosta Chaparro in 1975 before joining Quirós Hermosillo and the "White Brigade."[93] The trial revealed another more personal relationship that linked Acosta Chaparro to the "Lord of the Skies" Amado Carrillo Fuentes. The head of security for the Ciudad Juárez Cartel, Arturo Hernández González, "El Chaky," grew up in 1970s Acapulco, the son of a *comerciante ambulante* and the godson of Acosta Chaparro.[94]

In Guerrero, the drug war, a self-defeating effort that paradoxically increased drug production and violence, thus began as a counterinsurgency. The recent history of this region from the late 1970s to the present oscillates from drug war to counterinsurgency, from counterinsurgency to drug war. Guerrillas did not go away and neither did the drugs, or the expanded military presence. In a 2009 interview with journalist John Gibler, ERPI guerrilla leader "Ramiro" explained how the Sinaloa Cartel and the "government work together to both eliminate the competition (such as the dreaded Zetas of the Gulf Cartel) and carry out counterinsurgency operations against the guerrillas."[95] As this chapter has outlined, archival traces of such collaboration date back at least to the 1960s. If transnational changes in the global economy of drugs helped stimulate narcotics production in Guerrero beginning in the 1960s, it would take a military-led Dirty War that crushed peaceful and armed expressions of popular protest in the 1970s to become one of Mexico's largest marijuana and opium poppy production zones.[96] By the time "Ramiro" gave his interview, the state was the country's largest producer of opium poppies, feeding a rapidly growing opioid addiction in the United States.

Tracing the subsequent careers of military officers linked to Grupo Sangre further illustrates the connection between drugs and Dirty War. Acosta Chaparro, Quirós Hermosillo, and Barquín Alonso all eventually received prison sentences for protecting the Ciudad Juárez Cartel throughout the 1990s, but not for their violent Dirty War actions committed during the 1970s. A *gomero* guerrerense told journalist Humberto Padgett that Acosta Chaparro owned marijuana and opium poppy fields in the Tierra Caliente region and bought tons of narcotics wholesale "when people already talked about the famous Lord of the Skies."[97] The history of these officers and the death squads they led seemingly evince one of the conclusions reached by a coauthor of a recent Guerrero Truth Commission report. When asked to historically contextualize the 2014 disappearance of forty-three Ayotzinapa students, Enrique González Ruiz responded: "Grupo Sangre was a sinister group and now Guerreros Unidos are the sinister ones, they are the same. Organized crime and the military in Guerrero are not antagonistic forces."[98]

NOTES

1. Armando Bartra, "Sur Profundo," in *Crónicas del sur: utopías campesinas en Guerrero*, ed. Armando Bartra (Mexico City: Era, 2000), 49. Translation: "When in a fight, there will be blood."

2. Archivo General de la Nación (hereafter AGN), Dirección General de Investigaciones Políticas y Sociales (hereafter IPS), caja 1067, exp. 3, 19, 1/9/1974.

3. AGN, Direccíon Federal de Seguridad (hereafter DFS), 100-10-16-4-74, exp. 9, 244, reproduced in Hilda Navarrete Gorjón et al., Comisión de la Verdad del Estado de Guerrero [hereafter COMVERDAD], *Informe Final de Actividades* (October 2014), 24–25.

4. Ibid.

5. Not to mention continued agrarian violence, electoral struggles over municipal and state offices, and even a short-lived rebellion in northern Guerrero prompted by federal efforts to vaccinate livestock. For an incisive work on 1940s and 1950s Guerrero, see Paul Gillingham, "Baltasar Levya Mancilla of Guerrero: Learning Hegemony," in *State Governors in the Mexican Revolution, 1910–1952: Portraits in Conflict, Courage, and Corruption*, ed. Jurgen Buchenau and William Beezley (Lanham, MD: Rowman and Littlefield, 2009), 77–195.

6. Gladys McCormick, *The Logic of Compromise in Mexico: How the Countryside was Key to the Emergence of Authoritarianism* (Chapel Hill: University of North Carolina Press, 2016), 211.

7. I borrow the term "armed social work"—or "social labor" as the Mexican military termed it—from Patricia Owens, *Economy of Force: Counterinsurgency and the Historical Rise of the Social* (Cambridge: Cambridge University Press, 2015).

8. AGN/DFS 100-10-16-4, exp. 1, 12.

9. The White Brigade, or "the Special Brigade," was officially formed in 1976 by military, military police, judiciales, and DFS agents for the purpose of annihilating the urban guerrilla group, the Communist League 23rd of September (some sources cite 1972 as an unofficial foundation date). An elite unit within the Dirección de Investigaciones para la Prevención de la Delincuencia (DIPD), the "Jaguar Group" at times collaborated with the White Brigade and committed a series of human rights violations (including the alleged massacre of twelve Colombians in 1982).

10. Alan Knight, "Narco-Violence and the State in Modern Mexico," in *Violence, Coercion, and State-Making in Twentieth-Century Mexico: The Other Half of the Centaur*, ed. Wil G. Pansters (Stanford, CA: Stanford University Press, 2012), 123–24.

11. Alexander Aviña, "Mexico's Long Dirty War," *NACLA Report on the Americas* 48, no. 2 (July 2016): 144–49.

12. Roderic Ai Camp, *Generals in the Palace: The Military in Modern Mexico* (New York: Oxford University Press, 1991), 91–92.

13. Richard B. Craig, "Operation Condor: Mexico's Antidrug Campaign Enters

a New Era," *Journal of Interamerican Studies and World Affairs* 22, no. 3 (1980): 350. See especially Cedillo, chapter 11 in this volume.

14. The novelty of counternarcotics operations like Canador (1975–1976) and Condor I (1977–1978)—the aerial spraying of defoliant chemicals on marijuana and poppy fields—appeared first in Guerrero and Oaxaca in the early 1970s. See Carlos Pérez Ricart, "U.S. Pressure and Mexican Anti-Drugs Efforts from 1940–1980: Importing the War on Drugs?," in *Beyond the Drug War in Mexico: Human Rights, the Public Sphere and Justice*, ed. Wil G. Pansters, Benjamin T. Smith, and Peter Watt (London: Routledge, 2017), 45.

15. Pérez Ricart, "U.S. Pressure," 46.

16. Pérez Ricart, "U.S. Pressure," 46.

17. Isaac Campos, *Home Grown: Marijuana and the Origins of Mexico's War on Drugs* (Chapel Hill: University of North Carolina Press, 2012), 56.

18. Campos, *Home Grown*, 82.

19. Campos, *Home Grown*, 67.

20. Froylan Enciso, "The Origin of Contemporary Drug Contraband: A Global Interpretation from Sinaloa" (PhD diss., Stony Brook University, 2015), 23–26; Ander Permanyer-Ugartemendia, "Opium after the Manila Galleon: The Spanish Involvement in the Opium Economy in East Asia (1815–1830)," *Investigaciones de Historia Económica—Economic History Research* 10 (2014): 155–64.

21. AGN, Indiferente Virreinal, caja 4080/9159/29.

22. Enciso, "The Origin," 25.

23. Campos, *Home Grown*, 70; Alfonso Luis Velasco, *Geografía y Estadistica de la República Mexicana, X—Estado de Guerrero* (Mexico City: Oficina de la Secretaría de Fomento, 1892), 25, 30; Grace Delgado, *Making the Chinese Mexican: Global Migration, Localism, and Exclusion in the U.S.-Mexico Borderlands* (Stanford, CA: Stanford University Press, 2012), 32–35.

24. Luis Astorga, *El siglo de las drogas: el narcotráfico, del Porfiriato al nuevo milenio* (Mexico City: Plaza Janés, 2005), 48.

25. Gillingham, "Baltasar Leyva," 179.

26. Gillingham, "Baltasar Leyva," 179–81, 83; Thomas Rath, *Myths of Demilitarization in Postrevolutionary Mexico, 1920–1960* (Chapel Hill: University of North Carolina Press, 2013), 142; AGN/DFS 100-10-1, exp. 7, 104–5.

27. Ricardo Garibay, *Acapulco* (Mexico City: Oceano, 2002 [1978]), 132.

28. Richard Craig, "La Campaña Permanente: Mexico's Antidrug Campaign," *Journal of Interamerican Studies and World Affairs* 20, no. 2 (1978): 108.

29. Paul Gillingham, "Force and Consent in Mexican Provincial Politics: Guerrero and Veracruz, 1945–1953" (PhD diss., Oxford University, 2005), 84; Stephen Niblo and Diane Niblo, "Acapulco in Dreams and Reality," *Mexican Studies/Estudios Mexicanos* 24, no. 1 (Winter 2008): 31–51.

30. Tomás Bustamante Alvarez, Arturo León López, and Beatriz Terrazas Mata,

Migración y Agroindustria en Tierra Caliente, Guerrero (Mexico City: Plaza y Valdés, 2000), 73–76.

31. Lina Britto, "The Marihuana Axis: A Regional History of Colombia's First Narcotics Boom, 1935–1985" (PhD diss., New York University, 2013); Salvador Maldonado, "Stories of Drug Trafficking in Rural Mexico: Territories, Drugs and Cartels in Michoacán," *European Review of Latin American and Caribbean Studies* 94 (2013): 48; Victoria Malkin, "Narcotrafficking, Migration and Modernity in Rural Mexico," *Latin American Perspectives* 28, no. 4 (July 2001): 101–28.

32. Paul Gootenberg and Isaac Campos, "Toward a New Drug History of Latin America: A Research Frontier at the Center of Debates," *Hispanic American Historical Review* 95, no. 1 (2015): 1–35.

33. Astorga, *El siglo*, 90.

34. "Organized Crime and Illicit Traffic in Narcotics," *Hearings before the Permanent Subcommittee on Investigations of the Committee on Government Operations, United States Senate, Part 4* (July 30, 1964), 924. McGovern worked with the Carmine Galante and Giuseppe Cotroni heroin ring (involving important members of the Genovese and Lucchese organizations). Throughout the 1950s and early 1960s, Mexico served mainly as a transit point for European heroin entering the United States. According to U.S. law enforcement, 80 percent of the heroin entering the United States from Mexico in 1964 came from French sources. See "Organized Crime and Illicit Traffic in Narcotics," 903–4.

35. Ignacio de la Hoya, cited in Salvador Román Román, *Revuelta cívica en Guerrero (1957–1960): La democracia imposible* (Mexico City: Instituto Nacional de Estudios Históricos de la Revolución Mexicana, 2003), 181.

36. Jerry Kamstra, *Weed: Adventures of a Dope Smuggler* (New York: Bantam Books, 1974), 52. I thank Ben Smith for bringing this book, and Kamstra's 1970 article "Tales of Mexico and Marijuana," to my attention.

37. AGN/DFS 100-10-1-63, exp. 14, 350; "Terror en Guerrero," *Política*, May 15, 1963, quoted in Armando Bartra, *Guerrero bronco: campesinos, ciudadanos y guerrilleros en la Costa Grande* (Mexico City: Era, 2000), 99–100.

38. AGN/DFS, 100-10-16-2, exp. 2, 10–14.

39. *Novedades de Acapulco*, November 5, 1971, in AGN/IPS, caja 1028, exp. 1, 18. Opium poppy growers detained after a shootout with soldiers admitted that "subjects with norteño accents were the ones that provided seeds and money." An opium poppy grower told Humberto Padgett that the Sinaloa seeds arrived in his region in 1973. Humberto Padgett, *Guerrero: Los hombres de verde y la dama de rojo: Crónica de la Nación Gomera* (Mexico City: Urano, 2015), 16. See also AGN/IPS, caja 1028, exp. 1, 1.

40. Kamstra, *Weed*, 101. Jesús also traveled regularly to the U.S.-Mexico border, transporting marijuana to drug traffickers and organizations in Texas using two planes and a "large fleet of trucks." He made his early money as a farmer by growing maguey plants.

41. *New York Times*, September 17, 1969; Kamstra ("Roger Tichborne"), "Tales of Mexico and Marijuana," *Scanlan's Monthly* 1, no. 6 (1970): 8–20; Kamstra, *Weed*, 143–47; Ioan Grillo, *El Narco: The Bloody Rise of Mexican Drug Cartels* (London: Bloomsbury, 2011), 38–43; AGN/IPS, caja 1028, exp. 1, 12; U.S. House of Representatives, Committee on Foreign Affairs, Report 93-125, "The World Narcotics Problem: The Latin American Perspective (April 1973)" (Washington: U.S. Government Printing Office, 1978), 20.

42. A 1977 diplomatic cable claimed that opium farmers in Guerrero could harvest the gum three times a year (two seems like a more realistic number). U.S. Embassy in Mexico, Letter to Secretary of State, "CODEL Slack: Narcotics Discussion with GOM," 2/11/1977, 1977MEXICO02141_c, Wikileaks PlusD, Kissinger Cables; Report of the Comptroller General of the United States, "Opium Eradication Efforts in Mexico: Cautious Optimism Advised [Confidential]," 2/18/1977, GGD-77-6.

43. U.S. Treasury Department, Federal Bureau of Narcotics, "Traffic in Opium and other Dangerous Drugs: A Report for the Year Ended 31 December 1965," 1966, 24.

44. Juan Veledíaz, *El General sin Memoria. Una crónica de los silencios del Ejército mexicano* (Mexico City: Debate, 2010), 143–70, 223–30. General Rangel was sent to Iguala in 1965 to replicate the success of his antidrug programs in Michoacán, which even took him to Fort Bragg in 1966 to discuss such programs and his "winning hearts and minds" approach to armed "social labor." See Maldonado, chapter 10 in this volume for Rangel's antidrugs campaign in Michoacán.

45. Veledíaz, *El general*, 227–28.

46. AGN, Secretaría de la Defensa Nacional [hereafter AGN/SDN], caja 99, exp. 297. This file contains dozens of reports of military operations against cattle rustlers, drug farmers, and smugglers in late 1966. Most of these operations occurred in the Costa Grande and Tierra Caliente highlands.

47. Caritino Maldonado, originally from Coyuca de Catalán, was allegedly also linked to caciques and narcos in his home municipality. COMVERDAD, *Informe Final*, 157–58.

48. Marco Antonio Vargas, "En Guerrero la muerte de un periodista," *¿Por Qué?*, November 13, 1969; "Cartas," *¿Por Qué?*, December 9, 1971. I thank Ben Smith for providing these newspaper articles.

49. Diego Osorno, *El Cartel de Sinaloa: Una historia del uso político del narco* (Mexico City: Grijalbo, 2020), 76.

50. *El Sur de Acapulco*, May 4, 2015. The agrarian disputes in these communities began as early as 1966, when campesinos belonging to the Central Campesina Independiente (CCI) began mobilizing to recover plundered ejido lands. Ejidatarios accused the local military unit of intimidating and interrupting ejido assemblies. AGN/SDN, caja 81, exp. 244, 29–31; AGN/SDN, caja 76, exp. 231, 429.

51. Victor Cardona Galindo, "Páginas de Atoyac: El Paraíso (Séptima Parte)," *El Sur de Acapulco*, May 4, 2015.

52. A personal friend of ex-president Miguel Alemán, Ortega had terrorized these communities since the early 1960s, when ejidatarios voted to cancel the logging contract previously negotiated with the cacique's company. See Alex Aviña, *Specters of Revolution: Peasant Guerrillas in the Cold War Mexican Countryside* (New York: Oxford University Press, 2014), 93.

53. Francisco Gómezjara, *Bonapartismo y lucha campesina en la Costa Grande de Guerrero* (Mexico City: Editorial Posada, 1979), 170.

54. Grillo, *El Narco*, 38–43; Carlos Antonio Flores Pérez, *El estado en crisis: crimen organizado y política. Desafíos para la consolidación democrática* (Mexico City: CIESAS/Casa Chata, 2009), 169; Kamstra, *Weed*, 68.

55. Other lesser-known massacres that occurred in 1960s Guerrero include the killing of civilians and municipal authorities by soldiers in Copola (in southern coastal Guerrero) in September 1961 and the 1965 massacre of eighteen campesinos committed by gunslingers working for caciques in the Tierra Caliente region. Baloy Mayo, *La guerrilla de Genaro y Lucio: Análisis y Resultados* (Mexico City: Grupo Jaguar, 2006 [1980]), 51.

56. Mayo, *La guerrilla*, 226–27. For reports on similar power arrangements elsewhere in the state during the mid-1960s, see AGN/SDN, caja 74, exp. 229, 388–90; AGN/SDN, caja 81, exp. 244, 114–15; DFS 100-10-1-67, exp. 23, 304–6.

57. Aviña, *Specters of Revolution*, 120. Human rights organizations like Comité Eureka list the schoolteacher as the first official Dirty War *desaparecido*.

58. Cardona Galindo, "El Paraíso"; "Crímines de lesa humanidad," Special Prosecutor for Social and Political Movements of the Past [hereafter FEMOSPP Filtrado] (February 2006), 29. The FEMOSPP investigation lists Simbras as the first victim of extrajudicial execution in the Guerrero Dirty War.

59. Flores Pérez, *El estado*, 175.

60. AGN/DFS 100-10-16-4-70, exp. 1, 12.

61. Later "social labor" campaigns in 1971 included the participation of shoe cobblers, dentists, and barbers. AGN/IPS, caja 1195B, exp. 3, 92–93, 254–55.

62. AGN/IPS, caja 549, exp. 3, "28 Abril de 1969, Estado de Guerrero, Informacíon de Acapulco." Jorge Luis Sierra traces internal military discussions on "social labor" and the restructuring of *defensas rurales* to 1964 and 1966, respectively, amidst a professionalization of the Mexican military motivated by rural unrest (especially the Chihuahua guerrilla movement of 1964–1965) and growing social movements. Jorge Luis Sierra, *El enemigo interno: contrainsurgencia y fuerzas armadas en México* (Mexico City: Plaza y Valdés, 2003), 42–49.

63. AGN/IPS, caja 549, exp. 3, "Información de Atoyac de Álvarez," 5/21/1969.

64. "La Guerra Sucia en Guerrero," FEMOSPP Filtrado, 50; AGN/IPS, caja 1182A, exp. 1, 443–44; Osorno, *El Cartel de Sinaloa*, 76–78.

65. Sierra, *El enemigo*, 60–61.

66. AGN/IPS, caja 550, exp. 1, "Estado de Guerrero" 10/21/1969; AGN/IPS, caja 550, exp. 1, "Estado de Guerrero" 12/23/1969; AGN/AGN/SDN, caja 76, exp. 231, 429;

"La Guerra Sucia," FEMOSPP Filtrado, 50–51; Patrick Timmons, "Trump's Wall at Nixon's Border," *NACLA Report on the Americas* 49, no. 1 (2017), 15–24.

67. AGN/IPS, caja 1195B, exp. 3, 430–31.

68. For Operation Spider Web as an antinarcotics campaign, see AGN/SDN, caja 374, exp. 1249, 249, 2; caja 93, exp. 279, 26–31; caja 97, exp. 286, 7–8, 12; caja 91, exp. 276, 86, 176.

69. For Operation Friendship, see AGN AGN/SDN, caja 77, exp. 232, 87, 90–92, 95–96; SND, caja 93, exp. 278, 147–48, 152, 154, 181–82. For Operation Spider Web, see AGN/SDN caja 93, exp. 279, 26–31, 49–50; AGN/SDN caja 97, exp. 286, 3, 7–8, 12, 40–43, 49–50, 65, 84, 90, 96–97.

70. AGN/IPS, caja 550, exp. 1; IPS, caja 1195B, exp. 3, 92–93, 254–55, 491–93.

71. Rafael Aréstegui Ruiz, "Movimientos sociales y violencia en Guerrero," in *Guerrero Indómito*, ed. Juan José Russo (Mexico City: Centro de Estudios Sociales y de Opinión Pública/Juan Pablos Editor, 2013), 86.

72. Antonio Aranda, *Los cívicos guerrerenses* (Mexico City: Luysil, 1979), 161–65.

73. Velediáz, *El general*, 371.

74. AGN/IPS, caja 1182A, exp. 1, 443–44; Velediáz, *El general*, 370–77.

75. Velediáz, *El general*, 384.

76. Velediáz, *El general*, 289–321; Roderic Ai Camp, *Generals in the Palacio: The Military in Modern Mexico* (New York: Oxford University Press, 1992), 45.

77. Velediáz, *El general*, 370–71, 377.

78. Flores Pérez, *El estado*, 175.

79. AGN/SDN, caja 100 exp. 299, 159–68, "7/2/1974: Para Atención de la Superioridad." This plan of action was signed by Gen. Alberto Sánchez López, head of the presidential military staff (Estado Mayor). See also AGN/IPS, caja 1066, exp. 2, 111–14, 126–29.

80. Juan Velediáz, "Los antiguerrilleros," *Proceso*, October 6, 2002; Velediáz, *El general*, 319–21, 351–52. Rangel Medina argued that he was simply a "ceremonial" commander of the 27th Military Zone (Acapulco) from December 1973 to August 1974; Cuenca Díaz directly controlled operations. Acosta Chaparro and Heine Rangel became the pre-eminent counterinsurgency experts in the Mexican military and authored separate books on the subject. Cervantes Aguirre served as secretary of national defense under President Ernesto Zedillo (1994–2000).

81. AGN/IPS, caja 1067, exp. 3, 19.

82. "La Guerra Sucia en Guerrero," FEMOSPP Filtrado, 86; Navarrete Gorjón et al., COMVERDAD, *Informe Final*, 24–25.

83. The FEMOSSP report states that most of the death flights occurred between 1975 and 1979. The COMVERDAD report lists one such flight as early as 1969. Other sources that argue for a pre-1975 usage include Ascención Rosas Mesino, interview with the author, Atoyac de Álvarez, Guerrero, May 16, 2007; Simón Hipólito Castro, *Guerrero, amnistía y represión* (Mexico City: Grijalbo, 1982), 159–64.

84. AGN/IPS, caja 2795, exp. 1, 709.

85. AGN/SDN, caja 101, exp. 301, 9–14.

86. U.S. House of Representatives, Committee on International Relations, "The Shifting Pattern of Narcotics Trafficking: Latin America" (Washington DC: U.S. Government Printing Office, 1976), 1–13.

87. AGN/SDN, caja 101, exp. 301, 34, 37–39; AGN/IPS, caja 1066, exp. 2, 51–55; AGN/IPS, caja 1747B, exp. 6, 17; *Chicago Defender*, June 21, 1975.

88. AGN/IPS, caja 1181, exp. 1, 663–64.

89. AGN/DFS, Versión Pública [hereafter VP], "Mario Acosta Chaparro," exp. 1, 19; AGN/DFS, VP, "Francisco Quirós Hermosillo," exp. 1, 13.

90. AGN/DFS, VP, "Mario Acosta Chaparro," exp. 1, 8; AGN/DFS VP, "Rubén Figueroa Figueroa," exp. 2, 166. An earlier DFS report from August 28, 1975, lists Barquín Alonso as the "Jefe de los Servicios Especiales del Gobierno Local," accused of "arbitrary detentions." AGN/DFS, VP, "Francisco Javier Alonso Barquín," 1–3.

91. AGN/DFS, VP, "Francisco Javier Alonso Barquín," exp. 1, 14.

92. "Tarín Chávez, una historia terrorífica," *Proceso*, November 3, 2002.

93. Edwin Arreola Rueda, "Milicia, narcotráfico, guerrilla y política," Revista electrónica, *Razón Cínica*, May 1, 2004; Veledíaz, *El general*, 21–29; Juan Veledíaz, "Acosta Chaparro: las duedas de una boina verde," *Animal Político*, April 21, 2012; Humberto Padgett, "La gran traición: la inteligencia en manos del narco," *Sinembargo*, October 5, 2013.

94. Humberto Padgett, *Guerrero: Los hombres de verde y la dama de rojo: Crónica de la Nación Gomera* (Mexico City: Urano, 2015), 30; *El Universal*, March 5, 2006.

95. John Gibler, "The Hidden Side of Mexico's Drug War," *Z Magazine* (October 2009). ERPI stands for the Insurgent People's Revolutionary Army, a group whose genealogy traces back to the PDLP.

96. Padgett, *Guerrero*, 37.

97. Padgett, *Guerrero*, 17–18, 23–29, 34. In 2009, WikiLeaks revealed the existence of Cayman Islands–based financial funds held by Swiss Bank Julius Baer for Acosta Chaparro and his wife to the tune of "several million dollars." For the documents see: https://wikileaks.org/wiki/Bank_Julius_Baer_millions_of_U.S.D_in_trust_for_Mexican_mass_murderer_and_drug_trafficker_Arturo_Acosta_Chapparo,_1998.

98. Laura Castellanos, "Guerra Sucia: Ejército la Ordenó," *El Universal*, January 26, 2015. Guerreros Unidos are a violent narco-trafficking organization in the Iguala region.

13

Heroin, the Herreras, and the "Chicago Connection"
The Drug Trade in Durango, 1950–1985

NATHANIEL MORRIS

The crackdown on Mexican drug traffickers that followed the murder of DEA agent Enrique Camarena is often seen as focusing on the Sinaloan-born *capos* of the so-called "Guadalajara Cartel." But as dawn broke on July 23, 1985, just a few months after Camarena's body was found, nearly five hundred federal agents began raids on U.S. properties associated not with Sinaloans, but rather the "Herrera Organization" of Durango. By the end of the day 120 people had been arrested in towns and cities throughout Illinois, Indiana, Texas, Colorado, California, and New York "on charges of conspiring to distribute large amounts of heroin, cocaine and marijuana brought into the United States from Mexico."[1] The raids were the culmination of a two-year investigation into the Herrera trafficking ring, which was regarded by U.S. authorities, in particular the Drug Enforcement Agency (DEA), as the "largest single heroin supplier organization in Mexico, [with] profits [of] $100,000,000 a year. Such net profit would place the Herrera group about 116th in the Fortune magazine listing of America's most profitable corporations, and ninth, just behind Safeway Stores, in profit earned by U.S. retailers."[2]

Since the DEA's founding in 1973 its agents had been chasing the Herreras, but this operation was the largest yet: the culmination of a two-year investigation involving wiretaps, electronic surveillance of banking transactions, undercover operations in U.S. cities, on-the-ground investigations in Mexico, and targeted leaks of information to the media in both countries. It was carried out in coordination with multiple different institutions, from the Mexican military to the cops of northwestern Indiana (whose investigation "focused on a reputed den for cock-fighting, gambling and drug dealing" and was inevitably baptized "Operation Fowl Play").[3]

The raids targeted eight separate distribution rings, and among those arrested were high-ranking capos including Alfredo Herrera Nevárez in El Paso and Jesús Herrera Díaz in Chicago.[4] The arrests followed the detention in Mexico a few weeks before of Jaime Herrera Herrera, a businessman described in a regional newspaper as the "owner of gas stations, restaurants, dancehalls, discotheques, construction companies—which take on drainage and road construction contracts from the state government—bars, mansions, ranches and airlines." Herrera Herrera was the son of the organization's founder, Jaime Herrera Nevárez, "Mexico's heroin tsar and the largest supplier of that drug to Chicago."[5]

According to government press releases and news splashes in the United States and Mexico from the mid-1970s—which have informed both "true crime" narratives and scholarly analyses[6]—the Herrera organization was one of Mexico's biggest, most profitable Mexican trafficking rings: a 5,000-person "farm-to-arm" business led by a family that "so dominated the plaza and so extended their interrelated familial ties and influence, that they controlled entire regions and states."[7] Most of the organization's members hailed from Herrera Nevárez's birthplace in Durango—the imaginatively named town of "Los Herrera"—and a handful of neighboring villages. By the late 1960s, these men—and not a few women—were scattered across Mexico and the United States, from the deserts of Chihuahua and the American Southwest to California, the Midwest, and the Great Lakes. Working together under the direction of Herrera Nevárez, his brothers, and their numerous sons, they were responsible for smuggling and distributing hundreds of tons of Mexican heroin across this vast region and beyond, from New York to Puerto Rico.[8]

Images of the Herrera clan as the all-powerful bosses of a cross-border "narco-empire" have done much to inform popular perceptions of the Mexican drug trade.[9] These tend to view the Mexican state "as static, unified, and corporatist, with clear and unchanging lines of command from the president and the party through local governors, down to peasant commissars."[10] Cartels led by "drug lords" like the Herreras are seen as horizontally inserting themselves into these hierarchies and gaining control of all the rungs of authority below them. The cartels' ability to penetrate deep into state structures is presented as the result of their financial power, itself the product of their total control of all aspects of the drug trade; thus the Herreras are often described as enjoying "complete dominion and control over every stage of heroin production: the cultivation of poppies, the extraction of opium, its refinement into heroin, and its transportation to the principal centers of its consumption."[11] More "popular" trafficking narratives also play to romantic ideas of the "drug trafficker as social bandit," a legitimizing trope naturally promoted by traffickers themselves.[12] Thus the Herreras are often lauded as humble farmers-turned-capos "who distinguished themselves by never recurring to violence against their opponents in the bloody business of narcotics trafficking."[13]

More recent scholarship, however, has challenged once-standard narratives.[14] Instead of a late-twentieth-century tale of cops, criminals, and corruption, historians and social scientists increasingly see the history of the drug trade in the Americas as a more complex *longue durée*, one that provides "a window for looking afresh at some of the biggest questions in Latin American history ... [including] state formation, the rise of modernist biomedical sciences, and, most recently, the impacts of Cold War developmentalism, agrarian change, social violence, authoritarian regimes, and neoliberal globalization."[15] By employing models that "transcend the artificial or politically-imposed distinctions between legitimate legal goods and flows and now illicit ones,"[16] academics have questioned even the most basic aspects of popular drug trade narratives, including the idea of traffickers as constituting shadowy organizations whose influence has penetrated previously honest government authorities.[17] Instead, historians such as Astorga have shown that in many countries, including Mexico, "the drug trade developed 'from within the power structure'" itself.[18]

This chapter uses insights gleaned from the work of these scholars, in combination with other historians' work on the regional aspects of Mexican state formation and a range of archival documents and published sources, to reconstruct the rise of the Herreras and the development of the legends surrounding them and to assess the accuracy of these legends and the Herreras' real impact on the U.S.-Mexico drug trade. In so doing, I shed light on an important but today largely forgotten chapter in the history of Mexican heroin production and trafficking; suggest that the emergence and development of this trade, in Durango at least, was less an expression of criminal genius and more one of rural middle-class entrepreneurialism; show that illicit drug economies and regional Mexican power structures have always been completely intertwined; and, ultimately, argue that post–World War II infrastructure projects—particularly local road-building programs that linked rural poppy growing hotspots with regional commercial centers, and the construction of international highways linking the main cities of Mexico and the United States—were key to the emergence of the "Durango-Chicago" heroin connection, and with it, the birth of the modern "War on Drugs."[19]

A PREHISTORY OF THE DRUG TRADE IN DURANGO, 1920-1950

The state of Durango is the fourth largest of Mexico's thirty-two federal entities, but it has always been sparsely inhabited and is today ranked second-to-last in terms of population density. The state is roughly split into three zones: a heavily forested, mountainous strip in the west, bordering Sinaloa and Chihuahua; a temperate, fertile region in the center, where the state capital, Durango, is located; and vast, arid plains in the east, abutting Zacatecas and Coahuila. Between 1910 and 1940, the state was devastated by the armed Revolution, the Cristero Rebellion, and smaller uprisings led by regional caciques, which paralyzed most of the state's key industries, including mining and large-scale cattle ranching.

Although in 1925 a couple of Chinese-origin individuals living in the mountainous northwestern municipality of Tamazula were accused of cultivating opium poppies,[20] throughout the 1920s most of the opium, morphine, and heroin occasionally reported as being consumed in Durango arrived from the Gómez Palacio-Torreón conurbation,[21] which spanned both sides of the Durango-Coahuila border. Gómez Palacio-Torreón had long been an important railhead and agro-industrial center and was also home to several important traffickers with close links to municipal and state government figures in both Coahuila and Durango.[22] In the early 1930s, however, reports of opium production in Tamazula and the neighboring municipalities of Topia and Canelas, on Durango's border with Sinaloa, became more frequent. This region had been especially battered by the recent revolutionary upheaval, which devastated the local mining industry. Many former miners, living in an area relatively free of state control and in which poppies were easily cultivated, turned to opium as an alternative source of income. This shift was encouraged by growers and traffickers from nearby Sinaloa, where opium production had become an increasingly profitable activity for rural "artisans, ranchers, mid-size farmers, merchants, and miners."[23] As the Sinaloan town of Badiraguato—home both to poppy fields and opium-processing laboratories[24]—and Sinaloa's

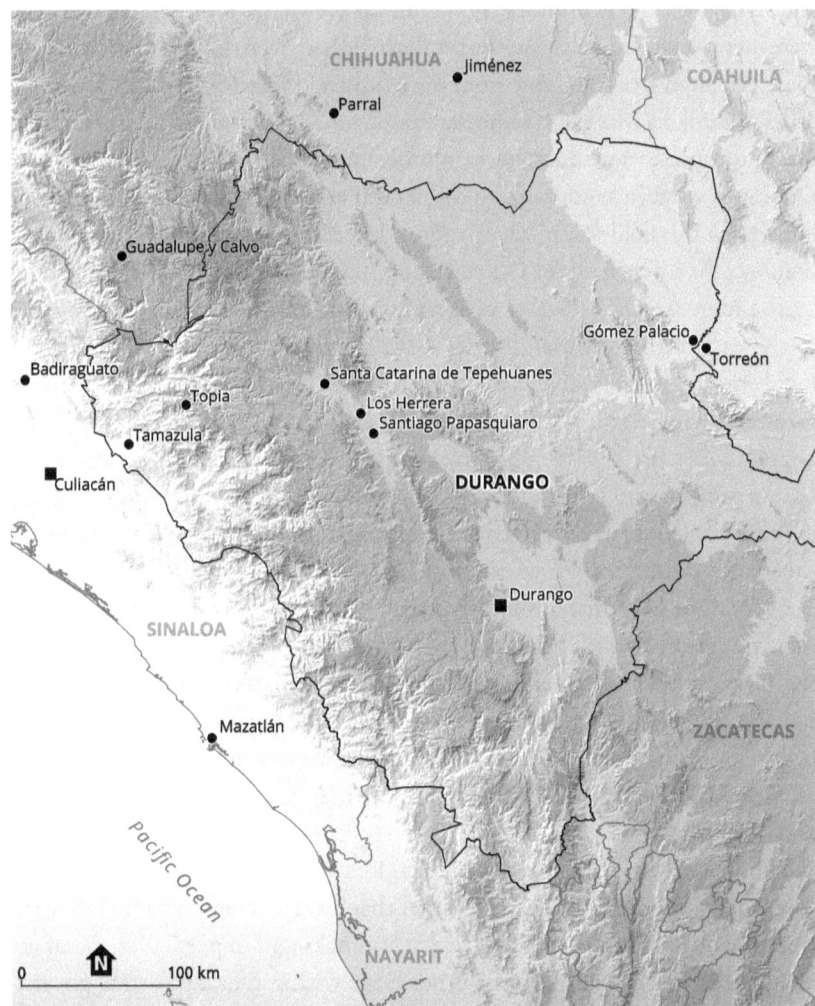

MAP 7 Map of Durango (credits: UU-Geo-C&M–Carto).

state capital, Culiacán—the most important marketplace for Mexican-grown opium and heroin—were closer to northwestern Durango than either Torreón or Durango City, Sinaloan traffickers bought most of Durango's home-grown opium.[25] From Sinaloa, the product was then taken up by road, sea, or rail to Baja California and smuggled across the U.S. border.

During the 1940s, opium production expanded eastward across Durango's mountains,[26] but it remained strongly tied to Sinaloan markets.[27] But municipal and state government authorities in Durango, as well as local military officers, were increasingly interested in the profits to be had from this illicit cash crop. In 1944, Mexican troops, agents from the Ministry of Health, and U.S. Customs officials raided a massive, 232-hectare poppy field, irrigated by a two-kilometer-long concrete aqueduct, in the municipality of Tepehuanes, which linked Durango's western mountains to the central valleys. They conservatively estimated that this field would have produced at least four and a half tons of crude opium,[28] then worth around $2 million (today equivalent to $28 million).[29]

The huge size and distinct geographical location of this plantation—far to the east of the Sinaloan border—are highly significant. So too was the involvement of U.S. officials and U.S. funding in putting together the raid, foreshadowing the leading role they would play in later programs.[30] The Tepehuanes bust also provides clear evidence of collusion between local opium growers and mid-ranking military officials. The soldiers escorting the expedition deliberately delayed their departure for more than a day, allowing the opium producers to harvest most of their crops before disappearing into the hills. One U.S. official suggested that even *before* the Ministry of Health officials set off from Durango City, military or political officials based in the state capital had tipped off the plantation's owners.[31] By 1944, then, the opium trade in Durango, just as in Sinaloa, had become a major concern and begun to assume "a distinct hierarchy, comprising in ascending order 'peasants, pickers, and seasonal workers, intermediaries, capos, political contacts, and protectors.'"[32]

Subsequent expeditions revealed that Durango's traffickers had not so much "corrupted" the government, but rather that local and regional officials were, from the outset, deeply involved in drug trafficking.[33] In particular, members of the de la Rocha clan, who held positions within Durango's state government, the State Judicial Police, and municipal government and police forces, were key players in the local opium trade and effectively sabotaged further eradication expeditions in the mountains of Durango, where opium production became increasingly widespread.[34] By the early 1950s, the de la Rochas had been displaced by Tamazula's Chávez León brothers, who similarly "held posts as the local judge, the head of the local branch of the state police, and a policeman."[35] Given the power of these traffickers-turned-policemen, and the resistance of the growers who enjoyed their protection—which extended to killing the soldiers and police officers threatening their crops—official eradication efforts did little to curb Durango's burgeoning opium industry.[36]

HIGHWAYS, MIGRANTS, AND THE ORIGINS OF THE HERRERA ORGANIZATION

Although Sinaloan traffickers would remain the most important players in Mexico's drug trade for most of the twentieth century,[37] during the 1950s the axis of Durango's opium-smuggling routes began to shift away from Sinaloa and toward Chihuahua. Initially, this was linked to a drug-trafficking boom in the Chihuahuan border city of Ciudad Juárez.[38] As increasing numbers of immigrants from Durango settled there, more of the drugs seized in the city were reported to have originated in that state's opium-production zones.[39] The completion, with significant U.S. assistance, of Pan-American Highway 45 in the mid-1940s, which connected Ciudad Juárez to Parral, Torreón, and Durango City, along with the construction of numerous smaller roads in the state of Durango itself, exacerbated this shift by linking Durango's opium growing hotspots to Juárez and the U.S. market more directly than the old regional railways had done.

The construction of these roads also facilitated the movement of thousands of immigrants from across Durango to the United States, either as contracted guest workers, known as "braceros," or as more normal, migrant workers, both legal and illegal. Many eventually settled in Chicago—the Midwest's most important industrial center—where they joined other Mexicans from across the country.[40] But instead of mixing together as in most other U.S. cities, in Chicago the Mexican immigrants tended to settle together with others from the same state, or even municipality, with each group dominating a different South Side neighborhood.[41] Fierce rivalries quickly developed between the different state-based cliques, which in turn increased each group's internal solidarity.[42]

Some of those who made the journey from Durango to Chicago hailed from the village of Los Herrera, in Santiago Papasquiaro, a large, oddly shaped municipality that, like neighboring Tepehuanes, lay half within Durango's western Sierras, half in Durango's central plains. Although American policemen and DEA agents often described it, for dramatic effect, as an isolated "mountain top village,"[43] Los Herrera was actually a relatively prosperous little place in a gentle valley some fifteen kilometers north of Santiago Papasquiaro and thirty kilometers south of Tepehuanes, along a newly built road that connected Durango City to the state's main opium production zones. The thousand or so inhabitants of Los Herrera—most of them also surnamed Herrera—were small-scale farmers, ranchers, and part-time traveling merchants, or *arrieros*. They were described, in 1938, as "active and industrious workers, who depend above all on agriculture and muleteering for their livelihoods, with the latter occupation very productive for them, as when they are not caring for their crops they dedicate themselves to extracting the products of the settlements in the center of the sierra, such as potatoes, cane, raw sugar, fruits and minerals."[44]

Of course, by the mid-1950s—when Jaime Herrera Nevárez, a young rancher from Los Herrera, was informed by relatives in Chicago of the demand for heroin in that city[45]—the aforementioned "products of the sierra" also included raw opium.

Jaime was born in 1927 or 1928,[46] to a family that had grown wealthy through ranching and logging.[47] Far from being "social bandits," the Herreras, like their Sinaloan counterparts, belonged to the village elite, and their priorities lay in "maintaining the status quo";[48] thus Jaime's father, Miguel Herrera Herrera, was a leading member of a faction that in 1937 opposed the creation of an ejido in the village.[49] Both the extended Herrera and Nevárez clans, as well as the interrelated Corral family (from the village of "Corrales," just across the municipal boundary with Tepehuanes), were well-connected in both Santiago Papasquiaro and Tepehuanes.[50] A Manuel Herrera Nevárez became municipal president of Tepehuanes in 1961;[51] a Juan José Nevárez Nevárez was president of Santiago Papasquiaro from 1980 to 1983;[52] and Carlos Herrera Araluce, who was born in Los Herrera in 1936 but moved to Gómez Palacio as a child, rose from being a local PRI militant and small-scale milk merchant to a cheese-manufacturing magnate and, between 1974 and 1977, Gómez Palacio's municipal president.[53]

Many different accounts exist as to when Jaime Herrera Nevárez began trafficking heroin. José Luis García Cabrera, a journalist with a taste for the sensational, writes that Herrera's father was a poor peasant who, after the military offered him protection, began working with his sons to "cultivate marihuana, and to a lesser extent, opium poppy."[54] Meanwhile, Charles Bowden breathlessly asserts that Herrera Nevárez himself "set up heroin labs ... Starting right after Word War II."[55] But both of these tales are difficult to take seriously, as the Herreras were members of the rural elite, and perhaps already local caciques, rather than hardscrabble peasants, while Herrera Nevárez would have still been a teenager at the end of the war in 1945.

Other, more realistic versions of Herrera Nevárez's early life, based on DEA information, locate his origins as a trafficker between 1957 and 1962.[56] What is certain is that Herrera Nevárez, like many major players in the Mexican drug trade past and present,[57] started out as both a trafficker and a police officer.[58] The DEA put the frequent collaboration between traffickers and Mexican law enforcement down to the latter's precarious working conditions: "Job security, hospitalization, and retirement are not provided for by a civil service system. Therefore, the police have need for additional funds, which must be obtained from other sources [including] prostitution, contraband smuggling, and in some cases, narcotic trafficking.... It is 'the opinion of the sources of information that most of these agents are involved with minor narcotic traffickers.'"[59]

Such economic factors probably motivated Herrera Nevárez to begin trafficking heroin, especially as, during the mid-to late 1960s, he worked as an officer of the State Judicial Police on the Durango City–Gómez Palacio highway, an important corridor for Durango-grown drugs on their way north to Juárez. As a young policeman it would have been hard to avoid occasional contact with the traffickers using this route,[60] not least because, having grown up in Los Herrera, he would have been well aware of the burgeoning opium industry in neighboring Tepehuanes and probably knew some growers, buyers, and traffickers himself.[61] While the DEA noted that most police officers "will not deal with major traffickers for fear of being identified or dismissed,"[62] it would seem Herrera Nevárez took advantage of his growing clout as a police officer, his strategic posting on an important drug-transport corridor, and his close connection to Los Herrera and, from there, to Durango's main opium-production zones to gain a foothold in the regional Mexican drug trade.[63]

Herrera Nevárez's subsequent ascent from small-time trafficker—probably reselling opium confiscated on the highways—to a major player in the international heroin trade was tied to his rise through the ranks of Durango's Judicial Police. This force shouldn't be confused with the Federal Judicial Police (PJF), a branch of the federal Ministry of the Interior. The force to which Herrera Nevárez belonged was rather a state-level investigative police force controlled directly by an appointee of Durango's governor. From the late 1960s onwards, the force's leaders gained notoriety as "the scourges of businessmen, ranchers, traders, and farmers, many of whom they kidnapped, extorted and abused,"[64] which generated "general discontent among the campesinos" and worried federal investigators.[65] It is perhaps significant that in the early 1970s, the force's chief, Arturo González Anguiano, was deposed by Durango's state governor and went straight to work for Carlos Herrera

Araluce, the long-running cacique of Gómez Palacio, suspected drug runner and rumored ally (or even cousin) of Herrera Nevárez.[66] With men like these as serving as his superiors, it is hardly surprising that Herrera Nevárez, who by 1968 had become commander of the Second Section of Durango's Judicial Police,[67] had also worked his way up the regional trafficking ladder far enough to attract the attention of Mexico's central intelligence service—the Dirección Federal de Seguridad (DFS)—which, until the mid-1980s, held a controlling stake in the national drug trade and also kept a keen eye on the activities, licit and illicit, of state police forces around the country. By the mid-1970s, it was rumored that like many of Mexico's other top narco-entrepreneurs, he was not the target of, but rather a badge-carrying *member* of, this powerful and much-feared organization, helping him to further cement his position as the king of Durango's opium trade.[68]

The Herrera 'Empire,' 1970–1978

Although he was obviously highly entrepreneurial, the real success of Herrera Nevárez's trafficking operation lay in the way in which it built on—rather than overturned—well-established local structures and practices. He enjoyed strong links with his home village's elite, Durango's state police force, and the federal security services, all long-standing players in the regional drug trade, with whom any prospective trafficker would have to forge alliances.[69] Herrera Nevárez's success also depended on a diaspora that linked central Durango to Parral, Chihuahua, Ciudad Juárez, and the American Midwest. Journalists and law-enforcement officers have often exaggerated the cohesiveness of the Herrera organization and the strength of the family ties between its members.[70] But a very real, and expansive, network of men and women, linked through blood, marriage, friendship, localist loyalties, and, not least, by money, was still essential to ensuring that the products of the poppy fields of Tamazula and Tepehuanes made it smoothly to Chicago, along a road network that became known in the United States as "the Heroin Highway."[71]

Another "traditional" practice key to the Herreras' business model was the long-standing tendency of Durango's highland peasants to mix the cultivation of commercial crops with subsistence farming. From the 1940s onwards, such commercial crops included poppies. At each harvest (of which there were normally two or even three a year, if the land could be irrigated), a peasant—together with his children and other members of his extended family, according to rural Mexican traditions of *la faena*, or reciprocal collective labor—could extract an estimated twenty to forty kilos of raw opium gum from his hectare of poppies. Thus peasants could supplement average annual (licit) incomes of around US$400 with between US$2,000 and US$4,000 per hectare of illicit cash crop.[72]

The peasants of Tamazula, Topia, and Tepehuanes, however, could only profit from their illicit crops if they could get them to market, traditionally via roving lowland arrieros who worked under the protection of regional caciques. In the case of the opium trade, poppy farmers would leave their produce in a designated spot, where it would be collected by a middleman connected by blood, marriage, or geography to the Herrera clan,[73] in what was a necessarily more secretive version of older, licit trade arrangements between mountain peasants and lowland merchants.[74] The middleman then took the opium to a laboratory, where it was processed into "black tar" heroin at a ratio of ten to one.[75] Initially, the Herrera organization depended on labs operated by the well-established trafficking organizations of Sinaloa, and so the raw opium had to be taken back across the mountains, via Durango and Mazatlán, to Culiacán,[76] significantly eating into Herrera profits.

From 1972, when the "French Connection" linking Turkish opium producers to U.S. heroin users was dismantled, the U.S. market increasingly opened up to Mexican heroin.[77] Between 1972 and 1975, "Mexican heroin increased from 40 to 90 percent of the U.S. market," and by 1976, "cash from drug exports [had] increased sixfold" compared to the profits earned by traffickers during the 1960s.[78] As their business boomed, by 1977 the Herreras had made an important innovation to older practices: they cut out Sinaloan middlemen by establishing their own opium-processing facilities in Durango, in the process assuming cacical control of the local drugs trade and cementing their dominant economic and social positions within the wider region. Jaime's cousins Arnoldo and Manuel Herrera Herrera set up laboratories in Los Herrera and Tepehuanes (the latter a seasonal operation operated by an anonymous chemist who came up from Culiacán for a few weeks at harvest time), while his close associate Enrique Díaz-García constructed another laboratory in Durango itself.[79]

Some of the heroin produced in these labs was smuggled into the United States hidden in wheels of locally produced cheese,[80] or was packed into metal tubes that were fed to cows and shipped north to a slaughterhouse that a member of the Herrera family owned in Chicago.[81] The preferred transport method, however, was to hide the heroin in cars driven by mules—often accompanied by their families—from Durango to Chicago, a fifty-hour drive along a route well-traveled by two generations of local immigrants. The heroin was packed into specially partitioned gas tanks or was hidden in a metal sleeve surrounding the vehicle's driveshaft, which was impossible to spot after picking up a little travel grime and became known as a "Durango drive-shaft."

The first stop for the Herreras' mules after Gómez Palacio was Parral, in southern Chihuahua. As "the most important commercial center of a zone split between the states of Chihuahua and Durango . . . where opium poppy is intensively cultivated," since the 1950s, the city had been "one of the principal centers of processing and trading in heroin."[82] According to the DEA, one of Jaime Herrera Nevárez's cousins served in Parral's police force and helped to "facilitate Herrera interests from there."[83] But even in the absence of such family ties, the Herrera organization could easily afford to keep low-paid regional and national police on their payroll.[84]

According to a report put together by the DFS—of which Jaime Herrera Nevárez was himself rumored to be a member—the Herrera clan's ties to Parral's establishment went much higher still. The DFS believed Herrera Nevárez was connected, "through direct or indirect ties," to a local clique aligned with Chihuahua's political strongman Oscar Flores Sánchez, who was state governor from 1968 to 1974 and Mexico's attorney general from 1976 until 1982. Since the late 1940s, when he played a leading role in the joint U.S.-Mexican campaign against foot-and-mouth disease, Flores Sánchez had been regarded by American agencies including U.S. Customs and the DEA as a close ally. But by 1978 the DFS was convinced that he and his close friend and associate Gen. Raúl Mendiolea, commander of the Federal Judicial Police (PJF), were helping "the main heroin producers in [Parral] region . . . and the distributors of the same in the border region, mainly in Ciudad Juárez . . . [resume] with more vigor and impunity their illicit activities."[85] The DEA at this point still believed, however, that Mendiolea's PJF were "less corrupted than DFS or the State police agencies,"[86] and they ignored the rumors of a connection between two of their most important Mexican collaborators and Herrera Nevárez, by now one of the country's top traffickers.[87]

The Herreras' alleged ties to Mexican officials were complemented by the active collaboration, or simple inadequacy, of immigration and customs officials on both sides of the border. U.S. Customs estimated it was "only able to interdict some two percent of the heroin crossing the Southwest border."[88] The

Herreras' own intelligence service also responded quickly to the emergence of new threats to their operations on the border: "When Mexican authorities started a road-block campaign last year, for instance, Durango traffickers switched within hours to aircraft instead of cars and trucks."[89]

Once the Herreras' mules arrived in Chicago, they dropped off their cargo at a designated meeting point,[90] and then, after receiving payment—typically around US$3,000—headed back to Durango, either flying or driving back via a different border crossing.[91] The heroin was passed on to one of Chicago's various Herrera cells—each based in a different neighborhood—for wholesale distribution to buyers ranging from Mexican and Afro-American street gangs in Chicago itself,[92] to Puerto Rican mafia groups in New York, and other Herrera associates in Denver, Detroit, Dallas, Oklahoma City, and Los Angeles.[93] According to DEA reports, Chicago's Herrera-aligned cells were "content to sell a kilo for $27,500, even though they could work for higher prices." Given their costs, they earned US$21,000 profit per kilo, of which the Chicago Police Department estimated they sent back to Durango, using mules and cash transfer services, about US$17,000.[94]

In Durango, Jaime Herrera Nevárez and his associates invested their profits in "land, ranches, dairies, apartments, resort developments, and financial institutions."[95] They also used the proceeds of both the drug trade, and the profitable licit investments that these in turn supported, to maintain and expand the local patronage networks upon which the power of any Mexican cacique always ultimately depended.[96] Herrera money coursed through the village of Los Herrera, transforming it into a "town of wealthy people, [who] gave work to the men of the other settlements of Santiago [Papasquiaro], and supplied Santiago's boutiques, which were full of clothes from Fifth Avenue."[97] Unlike their flashier Sinaloan counterparts, and more in line with forms of charismatic *serrano* caciquismo that had particularly deep roots in rural Durango,[98] they remained fully embedded in their rough-and-ready home communities by maintaining relatively low profiles, even declining to join the local country club.[99] In Chicago they lived more modestly still, blending easily into South Side neighborhoods dominated by "plain houses and apartment buildings, back alleys and garages, and working-class Latinos."[100] A DEA agent summed it up when he observed that "Most Herreras looked like auto mechanics," with one member of the organization driving "a car so worn-out that it burned oil and left a smoke cloud behind."[101]

The DEA and the Development of the "Herrera Legend"

Exaggerated official briefings and sensationalist media coverage have long colored portrayals of the Herrera organization. The legends that have grown up around them constitute a good example of the "comfortable symbiosis of objectives between law enforcement and the mass media. The first institution shows a propensity to hype the target both to enhance self-esteem and to coax more power and money from governments. The second needs to cater to a public in search of vicarious thrills."[102]

As the preceding sections of this chapter have made clear, the organization founded by Jaime Herrera Nevárez and his relatives owed much of its success to its adaption of venerable local structures and practices to the international heroin business. And its activities remained difficult to disrupt not only because of its protectors within the Mexican government, but also because, far from being a monolithic entity, the Herrera "cartel" was a network of allied but autonomous cells that shared the work of buying raw opium from peasant smallholders, processing it into heroin, transporting it across Mexico and the United States, and distributing it in Chicago.[103] Almost from the first, however, the U.S. authorities, more used to dealing with tight-knit New York mafia families, and frustrated at their inability to penetrate the more diffuse Herreras, played up the size and cohesiveness of what they portrayed as a complete "farm-to-arm" operation, as well as the "tight links between their members, absolute loyalty to their patriarch,"[104] and their leaders' status as "untouchables."[105]

Members of the Herrera family were first identified as traffickers in the early 1970s, when Illinois police named two Mexican bars in Chicago—Noche y Día, owned by Asunción Herrera-Chávez, and El Alacrán, run by Jaime Herrera Nevárez's brother Reyes and his three sons—as "major trafficking headquarters."[106] At this early stage, U.S. law enforcement could do little to disrupt their operation, even after the recently founded DEA shut down investigations into the local cocaine trade to devote more resources to the Herreras.[107] Both institutions lacked native Mexican Spanish speakers, obstructing their attempts to infiltrate an organization dominated by individuals from one small corner of Durango. Eventually, a Mexican American DEA agent, Gustavo Díaz, took to sitting for days on end in the local immigration lockup in rustic dress, allowing him to win the trust of Duranguense peasants who shed some light on the inner workings of the Herrera network.[108] This led to the successful arrests of thirty-eight members of the organization, including Reyes Herrera Nevárez, although charges against him and most of the others were soon dropped for lack of evidence.[109]

Despite these arrests, and that in late 1973 "top DEA and Mexican Government officials met and agreed to establish procedure for exchanging information,"[110] the Mexican authorities remained blissfully "unaware" of any wrongdoing on the part of the leading members of the Herrera family in Durango. A few lower-level Herreras were arrested on drugs charges in Mexico—perhaps accidentally—in 1973,[111] but Attorney General Pedro Ojeda Paullada claimed he had been unaware of the Herrera network's existence until 1974, only learning of it during "a briefing by drug officers in Chicago that he attended while visiting the city to celebrate the anniversary of Mexican independence."[112]

From 1975, President Echeverría, under pressure from U.S. authorities, intensified operations against Mexican marijuana and opium producers.[113] It thus became more difficult for Mexican law enforcement to ignore the Herreras, especially as operations against them in the United States continued apace, leading to the jailing of high-ranking Herrera associates Javier Jaime and Pedro Díaz in Chicago in 1974, following a raid "that netted the DEA 14 pounds of heroin."[114] The agents also found $4,000 in cash and promissory notes from customers amounting to $60,000, together with a notebook containing a "home address and unlisted telephone number for Jaime Herrera Nevárez in Durango."[115] Over the following year, another twenty-nine Chicago Herreras were arrested and a dozen more went into hiding in the United States or Mexico.

The Mexican authorities followed suit by arresting various Herreras in Ciudad Juárez,[116] and in September 1975 Ojeda Paullada even vowed to "crush the Herrera operation within a month,"[117] ordering "repeated Federale [*sic*] raids on suspected labs in the ... Tepehuanes area." But the ongoing collusion of other Mexican officials with the Herreras limited the damage caused by these shows of force: Ojeda's raids, for example, "uncovered nothing, presumably because the Herreras somehow always receive warning and dismantle the labs before the police move in."[118] Meanwhile, despite the efforts of the Chicago Police Force, sixteen members of the Herrera organization continued to operate in Chicago, and the DEA "had little success making those arrested talk about the ring or implicate higher-ups."[119]

Frustrated by the apparent ineffectiveness of their efforts against the Herreras, the DEA increased the pressure on the Mexican government—and won more funding from the U.S. government for itself—by leaking exaggerated information to U.S. newspapers regarding the scale of the Herreras' activities and their alleged corruption of Mexican officials. One such leak involved a DEA investigation into the Herreras' use of wire transfer services. The DEA claimed it had traced US$1,878,323 of Herrera money sent from Chicago to Durango between 1976 and 1977, which it estimated was "about one percent of the total." Thus U.S. newspapers announced the Herreras made US$200 million a year from their Chicago operations alone.[120] Scholarly analysis cast doubt on such figures, determining instead that the Herreras could not have sent back more than US$100 million a year at this point.[121]

Likewise, the DEA estimated that the Herreras imported "0.37 tons (746 lbs.) of pure heroin into the United States each year,"[122] but in briefings to journalists DEA sources preferred to talk about "8.14 tons" of heroin, which was their estimate of the amount of street-level, 5-percent-purity heroin that 0.37 tons of pure heroin would yield. The pronouncements of the Chicago Police Department, also widely reported in the media, were wilder still: they estimated that eleven tons of heroin arrived in Chicago each year, half of it supplied by the Herreras, who therefore stood to make around a billion dollars a year through their wholesale operations.[123]

Similarly, although the Herrera network was a fairly loose association of growers, merchants, chemists, mules, wholesalers, and "protectors"—the relations between all of whom were rooted in long-standing social, political, and economic practices within their home region, and which didn't even control its own heroin laboratories until around 1977—the DEA and its media allies portrayed the Herreras as a centralized, top-down organization that tightly controlled the entire process of producing and trafficking heroin from Durango to Chicago.[124] And although the DEA privately believed that the Herreras controlled only one-third of Chicago's heroin market, both the DEA and Chicago Police Department sources publicly implied that the Midwest's entire heroin trade was under the near-absolute control of Jaime Herrera Nevárez and a handful of his closest relatives.[125]

DEA sources leaked information designed to embarrass the Mexican government. This included the suggestion that the Herreras' "illicit entrepreneurship" provided direct employment to up to 7,460 farm laborers and even allowed the Herreras to invest in their own private airline, providing a "tremendous, if illicit, boon to the Mexican economy."[126] The DEA also claimed the Herreras had become "chiefs of police at the town and municipal levels, directors of state police, mayors and police agents in every law-enforcement agency.... Jaime Herrera himself is said to encourage bright young men to pursue political careers."[127]

By 1978, the DEA's media onslaught meant the publicity-shy Herrera organization was now popularly regarded as an all-powerful group that "controlled the City of Durango in the same manner that American corporations have controlled company towns in the United States."[128] This helped to boost the DEA's own profile and the budget allocated to its Mexican operations (which in 1975 had been only US$1 million),[129] while encouraging Mexico's new president, José López Portillo, to launch a massive new antidrug crusade, dubbed Operation Condor, in the mountains of Durango, Chihuahua, and Sinaloa,[130] and to issue arrest warrants for Herrera Nevárez and his brothers.

In August 1978, the PJF arrested Jaime Herrera Nevárez's brother Rodolfo, who was accused of being the organization's main money launderer, and he confessed to "his personal involvement in the shipment to Chicago of 21 kilograms of heroin ... [and] reluctantly admitted to a conservative figure of approximately 15 million dollars proceeds from shipment of narcotics to Chicago since 1973 related to approximately 30 independent shipments of heroin."[131]

Although this was only a fraction of the quantities of money, and heroin, that the DEA and U.S. newspapers accused the Herreras of dealing in, Rodolfo's arrest was highly significant for the DEA, which hoped his information would lead them to Jaime Herrera Nevárez himself. But even though the head of the PJF, Gen. Raúl Mendiolea, announced that "there was sufficient incriminating evidence for the defendant to be consigned and prosecuted," his close associate and immediate superior, Attorney General Flores Sánchez, quickly ordered Rodolfo's release, claiming that "once before a Mexican judge the defendant would be set free only by stating that the declarations made to the [PJF] were not true and were made under duress."[132]

U.S. officials were "deeply concerned and puzzled by the sudden release of Herrera," which they argued raised "serious doubts about the integrity of cooperative Mexico-U.S. efforts against narcotics traffickers [and] the firmness of Mexico's commitment to interdiction."[133] Such doubts were briefly assuaged a few weeks later, when the supposedly "untouchable" Sinaloan trafficker Pedro Avilés Pérez was killed by the PJF "while resisting arrest at a roadblock ... established for the sole purpose of serving the outstanding warrant for his arrest."[134] Although the DEA was convinced that "special relationships between violators and police officials at all levels of the traffic continue to exist," the agency hoped that the death of Avilés, preceded as it was "by sustained U.S. government pressure, may indicate that traffickers can no longer assume that such arrangements provide continued security under all circumstances."[135]

As if to prove that this was indeed the case, a few weeks later, on October 10, 1978, Jaime Herrera Nevárez surrendered personally to General Mendiolea.[136] The DEA triumphantly announced that "DEA/Mexico enforcement cooperation, particularly during the past two months, has resulted in unprecedented successes in the campaign against the principal organizers and managers of the narcotics traffic in Mexico."[137] But then, despite being charged with "possession, supply and manufacture of the narcotic known as heroin," Flores Sánchez also ordered Herrera Nevárez's release. Embarrassingly for the DEA, it soon became apparent that Herrera had only surrendered for "reasons of security." The DEA's top official in Mexico, Ed Heath, later put this down to problems within the Herrera organization itself.[138] In light of widespread rumors that Pedro Avilés's killing had actually been orchestrated by his own former associates to clear the way for their forming the "Guadalajara Cartel" with members of the DFS,[139] it is also possible that Herrera Nevárez, fearing similar threats if he also refused to join the new organization, turned for protection to his old allies Mendiolea and Flores Sánchez (who were also, helpfully, long-standing rivals of the DFS).

The DEA and U.S. embassy officials in Mexico were incensed by Herrera Nevárez's discharge.[140] The DEA's assistant regional director brought the issue up with Flores Sánchez, whom he reported appeared "uncomfortable about the subject. There was a marked difference in his demeanor during discussion of the Herrera case than in other parts of the meeting . . . it is the opinion of the MRCO supervisory personnel that Herrera was released because of other than legal considerations."[141] The DEA therefore broke with Flores Sánchez and Mendiolea, deciding that the attorney general's office and the PJF "appeared as actively involved in corruption as the DFS."[142] Several DEA agents who had worked closely with the PJF were accused of corruption and purged from the organization,[143] and the DEA launched a new offensive against the Herreras in the media, through official political channels, and on the ground in Mexico and the United States.

Diversification, Decline, and the Fall of 'Los Jaimes'

After his brief spell in jail, Herrera Nevárez returned to his *cacicazgo* in Durango, where he lived "the life of a *padrone*, giving to the poor, befriending the rich, and playing godfather at weddings and baptisms."[144] But the pressure on Herrera and his associates was building, as elements of the Mexican military, working directly with the DEA, stepped up their eradication program in the country's main drug-growing zones, including northern Durango. Attacks on opium producers in Mexico and distribution networks in the United States disrupted the Herreras' Durango-Chicago connection,[145] which, combined with changes in the U.S. market, encouraged Herrera Nevárez's son Jaime Jr. to forge closer links with both Sinaloan and Colombian trafficking groups, allowing the Herreras to begin producing white powder heroin and trafficking cocaine.[146]

But after the murder of DEA agent Enrique Camarena and his pilot Alfredo Zavala in February 1985, and in the additional context of intense internal political and economic pressures caused by the plummeting value of the Mexican peso, President Miguel de la Madrid agreed to unprecedented cooperation with the DEA in order to reassure U.S. officials that it was genuinely committed to the "War on Drugs" and to secure Washington's continued political support and economic assistance. Guadalajara capos Rafael Caro Quintero and Ernesto Fonseca were arrested, the DFS was dissolved, and in June, Jaime Herrera Nevárez's son, Jaime Herrera Herrera, was arrested along with twenty-seven other suspected members of the organization, including federal police chiefs, the commander of the pilots assigned to the attorney general's office in Culiacán, and, most important of all, Hector Quintanilla González, regional coordinator of the government's "Permanent Campaign Against Drug Trafficking" in Yucatán and Durango. It transpired that in Yucatán, Quintanilla had been coordinating shipments of Colombian cocaine to the Herreras, and in Durango earned $40,000 for every hectare of opium he allowed them to harvest.[147] A few weeks later, the U.S. authorities pounced on the Chicago side of the operation, as detailed at the beginning of this chapter.

The Herreras, contrary to their reputed reluctance to use violence, retaliated by assassinating Durango's state security chief "as he stepped from his car in front of his home," in an attack that also killed his son, two of his bodyguards, and the wife of the president of Durango's Tribunal Superior de Justicia.[148] The message evidently found its mark, as a regional judge ordered Jaime Herrera

Herrera's release on a "technicality" soon after. The lawyer who brokered the deal promptly died in "mysterious" circumstances, holding up subsequent investigations and allowing Jaime to escape to Colombia, where he took direct control of the cocaine-distribution arm of the Herrera organization.[149]

To head off local and international criticism in the wake of these suspicious events—and perhaps also to draw attention away from the continuing currency crisis and the government's blatantly corrupt and much-maligned response to the earthquake that struck Mexico City in September—the de la Madrid administration announced, with great fanfare, an "All-Out War Against Drugs!" in Durango. As usual, however, "the regrettable thing was that the real 'big fish' who financed the [marijuana and poppy] plantations were nowhere to be found, as it is well-known that they never show their faces."[150] Still, the Herrera organization's production, smuggling, and distribution networks were undoubtedly shaken by the arrests of high-ranking members on both sides of the border and by the declining influence of their former protectors within the DFS and the PJF.

Two years later, in August 1987, the Mexican judicial police received word that Jaime Herrera Herrera had secretly returned to Mexico on a "business trip," and they arrested him in Torreón after a gunfight that killed two of his associates.[151] Worse still was that he was trailed by government agents "from one house to another, in one of which they also managed to apprehend his associate and father, Jaime Herrera Nevárez."[152] Neither Jaime Jr.—described in the newspapers as "the King of Cocaine"[153] and as "much more important in this business and even more dangerous than [Caro Quintero] and Ernesto Fonseca"[154]—nor Don Jaime himself, the so-called "Tsar of heroin in Mexico,"[155] could buy their way out of prison this time. The latter was extradited to the United States, where he received a life sentence,[156] while Jaime Jr. was handed thirteen years and six months in Mexican jail.[157]

CONCLUSIONS

Ultimately, images of the Herreras as "untouchable" drug lords who controlled much of northern Mexico along with Chicago's heroin trade, are the product of exaggerated official briefings and sensationalist news reports. But this does not mean that the network put together by Jaime Herrera Nevárez and his family was not a powerful one, which, in collaboration with elements of the Mexican state itself, smuggled huge quantities of heroin, and later cocaine, across the

Mexican border and into the American heartland. The arrests of Herrera Nevárez and Jaime Jr. was therefore a genuine victory for the DEA, as well as a powerful statement of purpose by a Mexican government seeking to repair its damaged ties with U.S. authorities in the wake of the Camarena scandal.

Contrary to the hopes of both U.S. and Mexican law enforcement agencies, however, the arrest and imprisonment of the "Two Jaimes" did not spell the end for the Herrera organization. Just as targeting the leaders of the Guadalajara Cartel made good headlines but ultimately did little to curb the power of Sinaloan trafficking rings, neither could this approach halt the flow of heroin and cocaine from Durango to Chicago. The fact that the Herrera organization was less a top-down, monolithic entity, and more a conglomeration of autonomous cells spread across northern Mexico and the United States, enabled it to survive the disruption caused by the arrests of high-ranking members. Thus within a year or two, "those who had been convicted and those who were fugitives had been replaced, [and] Herrera Family operations in cocaine surged."[158]

Indeed, perhaps the most important consequence of the crackdown on the Herreras from the mid-1970s onwards was that it pushed them to build ever-stronger links with Sinaloan traffickers like Caro Quintero and Amado Carrillo Fuentes. After so much initial success in separating the processing, transport, and distribution of Durango-grown heroin from the drug trade in neighboring Sinaloa, the Herrera organization became closely associated with the Guadalajara Cartel bosses who controlled the rest of the Golden Triangle, and the Sinaloan faction that became known as the Juárez Cartel, which controlled the primary crossing-point for Herrera heroin and cocaine into the United States.[159]

But the Herreras' Durango-Chicago trafficking routes remained central to the organization's operations; thus the expansion of illicit supply lines from Mexico to the United States from the old Culiacán-Tijuana railway line up the Pacific Coast to encompass the center-north of the country was an important, lasting change that can be credited to the "narco-arrieros" of Durango. The rise of the Herreras is therefore testament to the paramount importance of efficient smuggling routes (and methods), rather than control of production in the sierra or of distribution in the United States, to the successful emergence and continued success of Mexican drug cartels and their operations.

The case of the Herreras also demonstrates the way such organizations are an inherently curious mix of the microlocal and the multinational: village or family-level enterprises that concurrently span regional and national borders, or even continents, returning the kinds of profits that would make a conglomerate proud, on the back of an "artisanal" product created by a few thousand hardscrabble peasants and rural merchants in the most marginalized regions of the Global South. From the early 1940s through to the peak of the Herrera "empire" in the late 1970s, Durango's growers, chemists, traffickers, and distributors flourished thanks to their intimate links with Mexican institutions, from municipal governments to the state and federal police and the DFS intelligence service, while their activities, at least until the 1980s, have been hit hardest not by the Mexican police or the armed forces, but rather by U.S. officials operating on both sides of the border, aided by their allies in the media.

NOTES

1. Etheleen Rene Shipp, "134 Indicted in Nationwide Drug Distribution Case," *New York Times*, July 24, 1985.

2. Peter A. Lupsha and Kip Schlegel, "The Political Economy of Drug Trafficking: The Herrera Organization (Mexico and the United States)," working paper, University of New Mexico Latin American Institute, 1980, 6.

3. Maurice Possley and John O'Brien, "Midwest Drug Roundup Nets 120 Dealer Suspects," *Brownsville Herald*, July 25, 1985.

4. Shipp, "134 Indicted."

5. "Jaime Herrera y otros prominentes empresarios de Durango, involucrados," *Siglo de Torreón*, June 30, 1985.

6. George Grayson, *Mexico: Narco-Violence and a Failed State?* (New Brunswick, NJ: Transaction Publishers), 34; Charles Bowden, *Down by the River: Drugs, Money, Murder, and Family* (New York: Simon & Schuster, 2002), 169–70; James Mills, *The Underground Empire: Where Crime and Governments Embrace* (New York: Doubleday, 1986), 694–95.

7. Peter A. Lupsha, "Drug Lords and Narco-Corruption: The Players Change But the Game Continues," *Crime, Law and Social Change* 16, no. 41 (1991): 44; cf. Benjamin T. Smith, "The Rise and Fall of Narcopopulism: Drugs, Politics, and Society in Sinaloa, 1930–1980," *Journal for the Study of Radicalism* 7, no. 2 (2013): 126–27.

8. "Testimony of Mary Hohler, Intelligence Analyst," Hearings before Select Committee on Narcotics Abuse and Control (Washington, DC: U.S. Government Printing Office, 1978), 277.

9. Smith, "Rise and Fall," 156 note 8.

10. Ibid., 126–27.

11. José Luis García Cabrera, *¡El Pastel! Parte Uno: 1920–2000* (Mexico: Palibrio, 2012), 44.

12. Mark C. Edberg, "Drug Traffickers as Social Bandits: Culture and Drug Trafficking in Northern Mexico and the Border Region," *Journal of Contemporary Criminal Justice* 17, no. 3 (2001).

13. García Cabrera, *¡El Pastel!*, 43.

14. Smith, "Rise and Fall," 126–27.

15. Paul Gootenberg and Isaac Campos, "Toward a New Drug History of Latin America: A Research Frontier at the Center of Debates," *Hispanic American Historical Review* 95, no. 1 (2015): 4.

16. Paul Gootenberg, "More and More Scholars on Drugs," *Qualitative Sociology* 31, no. 4 (2008): 426.

17. R. T. Naylor, *Wages of Crime: Black Markets, Illegal Finance, and the Underworld Economy* (Ithaca, NY: Cornell University Press, 2002), 28.

18. Smith, "Rise and Fall," 142, citing Luis Astorga, "Drug Trafficking in Mexico: A First General Assessment," *Management of Social Transformation*, discussion paper no. 36.

19. Cf. Gootenberg and Campos, "Toward a New Drug History," 10–13.

20. "Los Chinos Siguen Comerciando Drogas Nocivas," *Siglo de Torreón*, April 16, 1925.

21. Archivo Histórico del Servicio de Salud/Salubridad Pública/Servicio Juridico (AHSS/SP/SJ), C4/E12, Jesús Farías, "Informe," 5/10/1927; AHSS/SP/SJ, C4/E12, Jesús Farías to Secretaria de Salud, 2/2/1931; AHSS/SP/SJ, C4/E12, Medici de Byrón to De la Vega, 3/20/1931.

22. AHSS/SP/SJ, C28/E6, Inspector Juan Requena, to Jefe del Departamento de Salubridad Pública, 7/21/1931.

23. Smith, "Rise and Fall," 134–35.

24. Ibid., 136.

25. Multiple documents taken from the Casa de la Cultura Jurídica de Sinaloa (Mazatlán) (CCJS), and the Casa de la Cultura Jurídica de Baja California Norte (Tijuana) (CCJBCN).

26. Casa de la Cultura Jurídica de Durango (CCJD), Penales/E.38, Juan Francisco Curiel, Miguel Calderon, "Informe," 5/29/1944.

27. NARA/RG170, box 22, Salvador Peña to U.S. Treasury, 5/16/1944.

28. *Siglo de Torreón*, June 13, 1944.

29. CCJD/Penales/E.38, Juan Francisco Curiel, Miguel O. Calderon, "Informe," 5/29/1944.

30. NARA/RG170, box 22, Salvador Peña to U.S. Treasury, 5/16/1944.

31. NARA/RG59/1940-4.1, U.S. Consul Durango to Secretary of State, 6/27/1944.

32. Smith, "Rise and Fall," 133.

33. NARA/RG59/1940-4.1, U.S. Consul Durango to Secretary of State, 6/27/1944; AGN/MAC/422/7, Arnulfo Carransco, Tamazula, to president, 12/1/1944.

34. AGN/MAV/422/5, Rosendo Ortíz to president, 6/4/1947; NARA/RG170,

box 23, Secret Agent DJCTE2646987, "Memorandum," 1/26/1948; "Complicado en el negocio de opio en Durango," *Siglo de Torreón*, November 19, 1947.

35. Smith, "Rise and Fall," 135; "Corresponsalías," *Siglo de Torreón*, June 22, 1950; "A la opinion pública del estado," *Siglo de Torreón*, August 7, 1953.

36. "Comandante Rural Asesinado," *Siglo de Torreón*, August 21, 1954.

37. Smith, "Rise and Fall," 136.

38. Nicole Mottier, "Drug Gangs and Politics in Ciudad Juárez: 1928–1936," *Mexican Studies/Estudios Mexicanos* 25, no. 1 (2009): 19–46.

39. Casa de la Cultura Jurídica Ciudad Juárez (CCJCJ), 1938/2364/E.1, Gregorio Pérez Govea; 1944/3358/E.13, Juana Alvarado; 1946/7089/E.41, Jesus Vizcarra Astorga.

40. Deborah Cohen, *Braceros: Migrant Citizens and Transnational Subjects in the Postwar United States* (Chapel Hill: University of North Carolina Press, 2013), 71, 260 note 132; Rita Arias Jirasek and Carlos Tortolero, *Mexican Chicago* (Chicago: Arcadia Publishing, 2001), 9; cf. Michael Innis-Jiménez, *Steel Barrio: The Great Mexican Migration to South Chicago, 1915–1940* (New York: New York University Press, 2013), 24.

41. Innis-Jiménez, *Steel Barrio*, 130–31.

42. Ronald L. Mize and Alicia C. Swords, *Consuming Mexican Labor: From the Bracero Program to NAFTA* (Toronto: University of Toronto Press, 2010), 148.

43. DEA, "A Tradition of Excellence, 1975–80," https://www.dea.gov/about/history/1975–1980.pdf, accessed January 23, 2017.

44. AGA/Los Herreras, Ing. Carlos Briones to Delegado del Departamento Agrario, 10/27/1938.

45. Allan Parachini and Andy Shaw, "Drugs Kings Don't Flaunt It," *Chicago Sun-Times*, September 12, 1975.

46. Gobierno Federal de México, National Census, 1930.

47. Allan Parachini and Andy Shaw, "Durango: Films, Dust – and Dope," *Chicago Sun-Times*, September 9, 1975.

48. Smith, "Rise and Fall," 136.

49. AGA/Los Herreras, "Vecinos de la comunidad de Herreras y Pascuales" to Delegado del Departamento Autónomo Agrario del Estado, 9/28/1937.

50. Lupsha and Schlegel, "Political Economy," 6.

51. "Autoridades de Tepehaunes Depuestas por un Desfalco," *Siglo de Torreón*, January 6, 1961.

52. http://www.inafed.gob.mx/work/enciclopedia/EMM10durango/municipios/10032a.html.

53. AGN/DFS (versión pública), Carlos Herrera Araluce; cf. "En el centro de la sospecha, el empresario-político Carlos Herrera," *Proceso*, November 24, 2002; "Y el presunto narco se enojó," *Proceso*, December 7, 2002; "Fallece Empresario Carlos Herrera Araluce," *Milenio*, March 2, 2016; anonymous journalist from Gómez Palacio, interview, July 26, 2017.

54. García Cabrera, *¡El Pastel!* 44.

55. Bowden, *Down by the River*, 169.

56. Lupsha and Schlegel, "Political Economy," 5; *Chicago Tribune*, April 1, 1984.

57. Smith, "Rise and Fall," 137–38.

58. U.S. Comptroller General's Office, "Report to Congress: Efforts to Stop Dangerous Drugs," December 31, 1974, 18–19.

59. Ibid.

60. "2 Traficantes de Opio Detenidos," *Siglo de Torreón*, June 10, 1963.

61. "Destrucción de Amapola," *Siglo de Torreón*, September 26, 1966; cf. "Indirecto Buen Resultado de la Criticada Operación Intercepción," *Siglo de Torreón*, October 17, 1969.

62. U.S. Comptroller General's Office, "Report to Congress," 18–19.

63. AGA/Los Herreras, "Lista de los legítimos derechantes de la comunidad," 1/20/1967.

64. Miguel Angel Vargas Quiñones, *El contexto de Durango*, November 13, 2003, https://www.cronica.com.mx/notas/2003/97441.html, accessed January 13, 2021.

65. AGN/DFS (versión pública), Policia federal Durango, 9/27/69.

66. González Anguiano's sympathies are perhaps further reflected in the fact that his son, Arturo "El Chaky" González, later became head of security for Vicente Carrillo Fuentes of the Juárez cartel (Leopoldo Mendívil, *Cronica.com.mx*, December 3, 2003, https://www.cronica.com.mx/notas/2003/97441.html, accessed January 13, 2021).

67. "Detienen a Chofer," *Siglo de Torreón*, July 27, 1968.

68. Lupsha, "Drug Lords," 45; Elaine Shannon, *Desperados: Latin Drug Lords, U.S. Lawmen, and the War America Can't Win* (London: Penguin, 1989), 59.

69. Smith, "Rise and Fall," 127.

70. Bowden, *Down by the River*, 169; cf. García Cabrera, *¡El Pastel!*.

71. Allan Parachini and Andy Shaw, "Heroin Comes Up the Pike From Mexico," *Chicago Sun-Times*, September 7, 1975.

72. "Testimony of Mary Hohler," 274.

73. Ibid.

74. AGA/Los Herreras, Ing. Carlos Briones to Delegado del Dept. Agrario, 10/27/1938.

75. "Testimony of Mary Hohler," 274.

76. Parachini and Shaw, "Heroin Comes Up the Pike From Mexico"; cf. Editorial, "12 clanes mexicanos en el tráfico de heroína," *Proceso*, June 27, 1977; Smith, "Rise and Fall," 136.

77. Lupsha and Schlegel, "Political Economy," 1.

78. Smith, "Rise and Fall," 146.

79. "Testimony of Mary Hohler," 275; cf. Lupsha and Schlegel, "Political Economy," 6.

80. "Testimony of Mary Hohler," 275.

81. Sam Quiñones, *Dreamland. The True Tale of America's Opiate Epidemic* (New York: Bloomsbury Press, 2015), 57.
82. AGN/DFS (versión pública), 8/2/1978, Oscar Flores Sánchez, 155.
83. Lupsha and Schlegel, "Political Economy," 6.
84. Parachini and Shaw, "Durango: Films, Dust – and Dope."
85. AGN/DFS (versión pública), 2/8/1978, Oscar Flores Sánchez, 155.
86. Lupsha, "Drug Lords," 49.
87. AGN/DFS (versión pública), 6/17/1978, Raúl Mendiolea.
88. Lupsha, "Drug Lords," 8; cf. Allan Parachini and Andy Shaw, "Border Traffic's Sheer Volume Favors Safe Passage for Dope," *Chicago Sun-Times*, September 11, 1975.
89. Parachini and Shaw, "Border Traffic's Sheer Volume Favors Safe Passage for Dope."
90. Parachini and Shaw, "Heroin Comes Up the Pike From Mexico."
91. Parachini and Shaw, "Border Traffic's Sheer Volume Favors Safe Passage for Dope."
92. "Family Deals Mexican Mud," *The (Port Arthur, Texas) News*, March 12, 1978.
93. "Testimony of Mary Hohler"; cf. M. Castro, "A Mexico-Canoga Park Heroin Connection?," *Los Angeles Times*, April 8, 1976.
94. Lupsha and Schlegel, "Political Economy," 9.
95. Ibid., 12; Parachini and Shaw, "Durango: Films, Dust – and Dope."
96. For more details of how such patronage networks functioned, see Alan Knight and Wil G. Pansters, eds., *Caciquismo in Twentieth Century Mexico* (London: Institute for the Study of the Americas, 2006); Paul Gillingham and Benjamin T. Smith, eds., *Dictablanda: Politics, Work, and Culture in Mexico, 1938–1968* (Durham, NC: Duke University Press, 2014).
97. Hernández, "Desplazados del narco en Durango buscan paz," *El Universal*, August 31, 2010.
98. Nathaniel Morris, "Serrano Communities and Subaltern Negotiation Strategies: The Local Politics of Opium Production in Mexico, 1940–2020," *Social History of Alcohol and Drugs* 34, no. 1: 48–81.
99. Parachini and Shaw, "Durango: Films, Dust – and Dope."
100. Parachini and Shaw, "Drugs Kings Don't Flaunt It."
101. Quinones, *Dreamland*, 57.
102. Naylor, *Wages of Crime*, 30.
103. Lupsha and Schlegel, "Political Economy," 7.
104. García Cabrera, *¡El Pastel!* 43.
105. Bowden, *Down by the River*, 169.
106. Lupsha and Schlegel, "Political Economy," 6.
107. Former DEA agent who worked in Chicago during early 1970s, interview with the author, Las Vegas, NV, May 17, 2017.
108. Ibid.

109. Allan Parachini and Andy Shaw, "Never in Custody: 3 Top Herreras Hang Tough," *Chicago Sun-Times*, September 9, 1975.

110. U.S. Comptroller General's Office, "Report to Congress," 20–22.

111. "Traficantes de drogas no acabarse; ser calamidad!" *Alarma*, February 28, 1973; "Los Judiciales Colaboran con traficantes!" *Alarma*, November 4, 1973.

112. Allan Parachini and Andy Shaw, "All Out Mexico Push to Crush Drug Traffic," *Chicago Sun-Times*, August 9, 1975.

113. Smith, "Rise and Fall," 148–49.

114. Parachini and Shaw, "Drugs Kings Don't Flaunt It."

115. Parachini and Shaw, "Durango: Films, Dust – and Dope."

116. Parachini and Shaw, "Border Traffic's Sheer Volume Favors Safe Passage for Dope."

117. Parachini and Shaw, "Never in Custody: 3 Top Herreras Hang Tough."

118. Parachini and Shaw, "Durango: Films, Dust – and Dope."

119. Parachini and Shaw, "Drugs Kings Don't Flaunt It."

120. "Drugs: Capturing a Kingpin," *Time*, September 21, 1987.

121. Lupsha and Schlegel, "Political Economy," 9.

122. Lupsha and Schlegel, "Political Economy," 8.

123. *The (Port Arthur, Texas) News*, March 12, 1978, 7.

124. John O'Brien and Ronald Koziol, "Heroin City USA – Chicago New Title," *Chicago Tribune*, January 8, 1978.

125. Cf. Gad J. Bensinger, Thomas J. Lemmer, and Arthur J. Lurigio, "The War on Drugs in Chicago," paper presented at the International Police Executive Symposium in Ayvalik, Turkey, May 26–30, 2006, 2.

126. Lupsha and Schlegel, "Political Economy," 11–12.

127. Bowden, *Down by the River*, 169.

128. Lupsha and Schlegel, "Political Economy," 6, citing "House Select Committee on Narcotics Abuse and Control, Investigation of Narcotics Trafficking Proceeds," 260.

129. Allan Parachini and Andy Shaw, "US Role in Mexico's Drug Fight," *Chicago Sun-Times*, September 10, 1975.

130. Smith, "Rise and Fall," 148–49.

131. U.S. State Department Cable, August 24, 1978, www.wikileaks.org.

132. Ibid.

133. U.S. State Department Cable, August 30, 1978, www.wikileaks.org.

134. U.S. State Department Cable, October 24, 1978, www.wikileaks.org.

135. Ibid.

136. "Detiene la justicia federal al principal distribuidor de heroina," *El Porvenir*, October 12, 1978; "Fue trasladado a Durango El Narcotraficante Herrera N.," *Siglo de Torreón*, October 14, 1978.

137. U.S. State Department Cable, October 24, 1978, www.wikileaks.org.

138. Shannon, *Desperados*, 70.

139. José Alfredo Andrade Bojorges, *La Historia Secreta del Narco: Desde Navolato Vengo* (Mexico City: Grijalbo, 1999), 72; Lupsha, "Drug Lords," 56; Jiménez de León, "Papasquiaro—Lumen gentum," *Yumka*, October 23, 2010, http://oikos-unam.blogspot.com/2010/10/papasquiaro.html.

140. U.S. State Department Cable, August 30, 1978, www.wikileaks.org.

141. U.S. State Department Cable, August 25, 1978, www.wikileaks.org.

142. Lupsha, "Drug Lords," 49.

143. Lori Santos, "Drug Agents Resign over Incident 12 Years Ago," *UPI*, November 10, 1985; cf. Bill Curry, "Dark Ending Caps Star-Bright Career Of U.S. Drug Agent," *Washington Post*, December 26, 1978; "The Case of Agent Bario," *Time*, January 29, 1979.

144. Howard Abadinsky, *Organized Crime* (Boston: Wadsworth Publishing, 2012), 154; B. B. Weidrich, "Agents Tie Chicago Heroin to Mexican 'Godfather,'" *Chicago Tribune*, April 1, 1984.

145. Lupsha and Schlegel, "Political Economy," 13.

146. Carl Manning, "Mexican Officials Break Up Drug Ring," *Associated Press*, January 7, 1985; cf. Abadinsky, *Organized Crime*, 159.

147. Manning, "Mexican Officials."

148. "Jailed Drug Trafficker May Have Ordered Murders," *UPI*, January 8, 1987.

149. "Información fue dada en México," *Siglo de Torreón*, August 23, 1987.

150. Editorial, "Guerra sin cuartel contra las drogas!" *Alarma*, October 30, 1987.

151. Ibid.

152. "Como narco 'El Jaimillo' resultó ser aprehendido," *Siglo de Torreón*, August 29, 1987.

153. "Buscan a varios complices en Durango," *Siglo de Torreón*, August 28, 1987.

154. "PJF prosigue investigaciónes en esta ciudad sobre caso de narcotraficantes," *Siglo de Torreón*, August 27, 1987.

155. "Jaime Herrera y otros prominentes empresarios de Durango, involucrados," *Siglo de Torreón*, June 30, 1985.

156. "Captura DEA 18 del Cártel de Durango," *El Porvenir*, October 27, 1993.

157. "Tribunal Segundo Unitario modificó la sentencia impuesta al 'Jimmy' Herrera," *Siglo de Torreón*, February 19, 1993.

158. Abadinsky, *Organized Crime*, 154–55.

159. "Hacen Narcos 'Limpia,'" *El Porvenir*, August 7, 1997; "Detectan un laboratorio clandestine de heroína," *Siglo de Torreón*, October 30, 1998.

PART IV

Conclusions

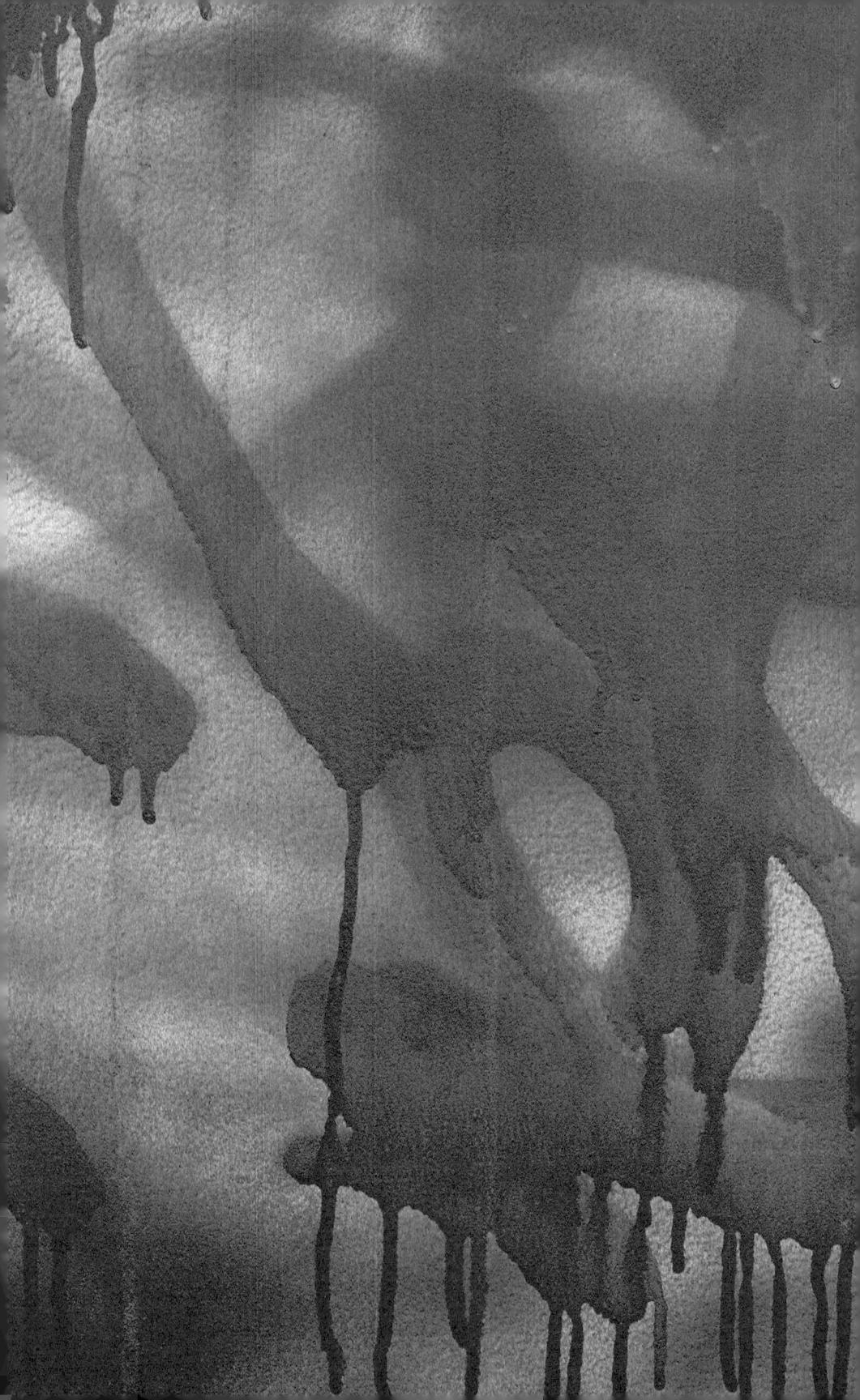

14

Drugs, Crime, and Violence in Modern Mexico

ALAN KNIGHT

Although I have dabbled in writing about violence over the years,[1] I have made only one excursion into criminal activity, that at the invitation of Wil Pansters some years ago.[2] In responding to a second, similar invitation, I should first stress that I am not a paid-up expert on drugs and crime in modern Mexico, especially regarding the past thirty years, when the concatenation of drugs, crime, violence, policing, and politics has, for obvious reasons, provoked public concern, growing debate, and—perhaps belatedly—a burst of serious academic research, of which this volume forms part.[3] The apparent neglect of the narco factor in older studies of Mexico—those, for example, that focused on the Mexican Revolution and its outcome (1910–1940)—is not surprising, nor is it prima facie evidence of academic obtuseness. Academic fashion may have favored certain approaches over others: a top-down national perspective held sway in Mexican historiography until it was subverted by "bottom-up" local and provincial history, roughly from the 1960s; and, in a parallel process, narrow political history yielded to social history, only for the latter to be in turn usurped by "cultural" history, roughly from the 1980s.[4]

But drugs and narco power had a marginal place in the older—national, political—history, for the good reason that neither played a major role in the unfolding of national political history during the Porfiriato and Revolution (1910–1940). Nor did the combined "provincial" and "social" turns make a great difference, since the principal focus of "bottom-up" and "peripheral/provincial" historians remained pre-1940, when drugs and narco power were, I repeat, marginal to the stories—for example, stories concerning popular protest, social reform, and state building—that commanded scholarly attention. Of course, there were incipient pockets of narco power: *cacicazgos* where local bosses permitted and protected drug dealing, for example, among the Chinese immigrant communities of northern Mexico, who were pioneers of the opiate trade. Esteban Cantú of Baja California, who flourished in semi-autonomy during the national upheaval of the 1910s, is a well-known case; while Chihuahua in the 1920s pioneered a turbulent blend of caciquismo, narco-trafficking and related politico-entrepreneurial criminality.[5] Both, of course, were on the frontier, and both, as it happens, have been the subjects of serious research, some of it quite old. So historians were not entirely blind to narco politics, when it reared its ugly head.

Of course, domestic drug use—of marijuana, peyote, hallucinogenic mushrooms, and other *estupefacientes*—was an old story in Mexico, as were official denunciations, prohibitions, and, at least by the nineteenth century, "moral panics" concerning the degenerative effect of these drugs (especially marijuana) and, by far the most popular and profitable "drug" of choice, alcohol.[6] The turmoil of the armed Revolution (1910–1920)—when armies roamed the country, seeking solace in "weed" and, as Pansters and Smith suggest (introduction to this volume), spreading its use—prompted more "moral panics" of this kind; certainly there were plenty of literary references to drug—chiefly marijuana—use during the Revolution (see Pérez Montfort, chapter 3 in this volume). Leaving aside, however, the lurid imaginings of Barbara Tuchman and her ilk (during the Revolution, she tells us, Pancho Villa "commanded . . . a rabble that got drunk twice a day on tequila and smoked marijuana in between"),[7] there is no evidence that drug use influenced the course of the Revolution or contributed to the careers of prominent revolutionary leaders. Cantú was, in this sense, an exception, just as the revolutionary experience of Baja California was exceptional. The 1920s and 1930s witnessed further moments of moral panic, for example, as the Bohemian avant-garde of Mexico City puffed weed or experimented with cocaine.[8] And, as Pansters and Smith also point out (introduction), Gonzalo N. Santos found that rounding up weed smokers was an easy way to burnish his dull credentials among the elite of San Luis Potosí. (Bearing in mind Santos's usual brutal modus operandi, the smokers were lucky to get away so lightly.)[9]

The burst of interest in drugs and narco-power in recent decades, then, has derived chiefly from an objective shift in Mexican reality, if such a grossly positivistic explanation can be admitted. "Constructivist" interest in sociocultural norms no doubt played a part, but only a secondary part; what Pansters and Smith call "the historically shifting cultural understandings of drugs" became important because, again in their words, powerful "empirically grounded" processes were at work, which, in terms of their scale and impact, were historically new and sociopolitically significant.[10] Constructivist "cultural understandings of drugs" comprised, we might say, the soft pulp that surrounded the hard pit of political economy.[11] (That does not mean, of course, that the pulp is irrelevant; it certainly provides plenty of juicy morsels for academic consumption.)

I begin this basic overview by reprising the big political economy story, before briefly addressing U.S.-Mexican relations—which bulk large in this volume—and, finally, some specific aspects of Mexican domestic politics.

THE POLITICAL ECONOMY OF DRUGS

The political-economic story seems fairly clear and is perhaps well-known (so apologies if I am stating the obvious). In the 1960s, Mexican drug production—marijuana and opiates—began to expand, along with the illicit trade in drugs across the border into the United States; in the 1970s the opiate (heroin) trade received a boost as the famous French Connection was severed and, a decade later, Colombian coca(ine)-trafficking routes through the Caribbean were interdicted.[12] Mexicans now supplanted the Colombian traffickers, just as they had previously supplanted the Chinese. The ensuing boom depended, as Latin American commodity booms typically did, on foreign demand, above all U.S. demand.[13]

The injection of up to $30 billion of annual demand into the Mexican economy had obvious and important consequences.[14] It handsomely rewarded drug producers and—much more—drug traffickers.[15] It fostered vast personal and family fortunes, while generating real estate booms that transformed the urban skyline in cities like Mexico City and Guadalajara. At the same time, it funneled money into what had been more bucolic—perhaps "traditional"— provincial communities, funding fancy new houses, warehouses, shiny SUVs and unprecedentedly big bets at cockfights.[16] In macro-economic terms, it bolstered what would otherwise have been a weaker peso, provided jobs (not least in rural economies hard hit by the effects of NAFTA) and thus served to dampen some of the pent-up social pressure generated by the double whammy of depression in the 1980s and post-NAFTA adjustment in the 1990s.[17] Finally, it created new domains of power that the incumbent Mexican political elite had to reckon with.[18] The older—again, perhaps, "traditional"—narco interests now gave way to bigger, richer, more ambitious organizations, with dense transnational links and access to modern technology (including transport, weaponry, and computing).

Although, even as its branches stretched across subnational and international boundaries, the pioneer Sinaloa "Cartel" retained local roots, most narco organizations tended to become increasingly deraciné, detached from the producer zones or border ports where their predecessors had plied their more modest trade. The new generation of narco "juniors" also flaunted their wealth and abandoned the more discreet anonymity of their elders.[19] Rather like the PRI itself, organized crime underwent a generational shift, with fast-living ephebocrats supplanting the grizzled veterans who had built the organization in earlier times.[20]

Or, to suggest a parallel interpretation, "social bandits"—outlaws who enjoyed genuine local or regional support—gave way to ruthlessly "unsocial" or mercenary entrepreneurs, increasingly detached from their sociospatial moorings.[21] In similar fashion, Smith argues, "narco-populism"—a syndrome involving a folksy rapport between narco bosses and local people—went into decline: as early as the 1970s Culiacán (Sinaloa) witnessed a "wave of kidnappings, robberies and murders," as narco interests "diversified" and contested for predominance.[22] Yet in Sinaloa and—perhaps to a lesser extent—elsewhere, elements of "social banditry" and "narco-populism" still lingered. Some narco bosses continued the old practice of funding churches, schools, and charities, while maintaining a large payroll (including, for example, public sector workers).[23] And "narco-bling"—the flashy dress, music, cars, women, and weaponry associated with modern Mexican criminality—continued to exert popular appeal, especially among young men pitched into a hostile labor market. But as the big cartels got bigger and richer, as violence increased, and as latter-day cartels diversified into kidnapping and extortion (often in territory where they lacked roots), so the traditional popular underpinnings of narco power eroded; the "social" dimension was stripped away, leaving a nakedly mercenary—or "antisocial"—variant. The recent and widespread mobilization of local defensas who seek to throw a cordon sanitaire around communities, denying narco access, testifies to the "deracination" of organized crime, to the demise of Mexico's long tradition of "social banditry" and, perhaps most clearly, to the downright inadequacy—or blatant corruption—of the Mexican state.[24]

Since this dynamic and destabilizing shift coincided with the rapid erosion of the legitimacy of the ruling PRI—the product, above all, of the debt crisis of the 1980s—Mexico's políticos now had to deal with the twin challenges of political realignment (sometimes simplified as "democratization") and narco political power, power which, though it certainly "grew out of the barrel of a gun," as Mao famously put it, also depended, even more, on prodigiously deep pockets. After all, money could buy the guns, hire the pistoleros who used them (who came cheap and were easily replaceable), and pay off the compliant políticos who allowed the business to flourish.

The last quarter of the twentieth century thus witnessed a boom in drug production and trafficking that, though it was not entirely "unprecedented" (few events in history really are), was on a far grander scale than in the past. The 1940s had seen a miniboom, chiefly affecting the border and the emergent "Golden Triangle," as American demand for marijuana and opiates burgeoned (some of it, of course, legitimate demand that derived from the needs of wartime medicine).[25] The 1940s miniboom also involved, necessarily, the connivance of Mexican police and políticos, both along the border and in zones of production. But the late-twentieth-century boom eclipsed anything that had gone before. Its political impact, in particular, was much greater, since it brought into unholy union a growing narco power, flush with resources, and a faltering political class that now had to cope with recurrent crises (1968, 1976, 1982, and 1994–1995), with fading legitimacy, and with a newly robust opposition, which took the form of civic movements, insurgent political parties, and sporadic armed insurrection.[26] Again, none of the latter phenomena were entirely new—there had been examples even during the *época dorada* of the PRI in the 1950s and 1960s—but the scale of the anti-PRI opposition was unprecedented and signaled a sea change in Mexican politics.

Indeed, most of the ingredients of this toxic mix were not new, as several of the studies in this volume make clear. Police, politicians, and army officers had collaborated with criminal (including narco) interests for decades. Contraband had flourished along the border for even longer. But the scale of the business was now far greater, and the quantitative shift brought a qualitative shift, since the balance between "legitimate" authorities and their illegitimate partners was decisively upset as the latter gained strength at the expense of the former. The old "plaza" system, whereby narco-trafficking franchises along the border were, crudely speaking, allocated and paid for, now began to collapse.[27] Of course, that system, by virtue of being informal, illegal, and clandestine, could not function like a well-lubricated gearbox. The history of border contraband—whether involving drugs or other tradables (alcohol, guns, cars)—was punctuated by minor turf wars, sporadic violence, recurrent revelations of official collusion, and shifting criminal leadership (which included several women).[28] Contraband certainly resembled legal commerce, since the profit motive prevailed: traffickers, then and now, were not pursuing politico-ideological goals; they did not seek revolution or orderly regime change.[29] They mixed in politics because their business required allies and protectors.

The narcos produced and exported, helped, of course, by the sustained growth in U.S.-Mexican trade that NAFTA (1994), though it did not initiate the process, further stimulated.[30] Border crossings like Nuevo Laredo hummed with activity, making it easier to make illicit shipments (drugs heading north and, increasingly, weapons heading south).[31] The políticos and police ran the racket, extracting payoffs in return for providing protection, so they were the real mafiosi.[32] Protection enabled criminal entrepreneurs to ply their trade and turn a handsome profit. Some recent analysts push the comparisons with legal big business yet further, noting that big narco organizations (often called "cartels") operate, organizationally, much like large business corporations.[33] And their operations are certainly amenable to analysis in terms of global commodity chains. But the comparison can be overdone, even when dealing with the big, rich, transnational "cartels" of today. Legality means that decision making can be relatively orderly, peaceful, and managed. Disputes can be settled and contracts enforced through the courts. Personnel can be openly recruited; corporate "head-hunting" does not involve actual decapitation. But given their illegality, narco organizations, whether the mega-cartels of today or the more modest operations of the mid-twentieth century, are, like other criminal organizations, inherently disposed to feuds, factionalism, and violent defenestrations. Informal deals, based on personal trust and family— or "clan"—networks, may work well at the local level; they have, after all, a long history in Mexican "infra-politics." But lacking legal and institutional support, they cannot easily be scaled up to national, still less international, levels.[34] Indeed, the pertinent historical parallels may be not IBM or General Motors, but the Sforzas and Borgias of Renaissance Italy.

Furthermore, the resort to exemplary violence and the proliferation of feuds may acquire, so to speak, a "relative autonomy" of the underlying commercial rationale, such that settling scores and practicing extreme brutality may start to serve "affective" rather than "instrumental" goals.[35] That is, the agents involved lose sight of the bottom line and act according to affective notions of honor, revenge, and machismo. Or, even more basically, they show themselves to be—or to have become—psychopaths. Of course, as Aviña (chapter 12 in this volume) shows, this descent into psychopathology is not confined to criminal organizations but is also evident in the ranks of the police and military. Along with collusion between state and narcos, therefore, we also see convergence in respect of brutal behavior, of which Ayotzinapa was a recent example.

One clear-cut indicator of the sea change in recent narco crime is the dramatic increase in homicides that took place in the past fifteen years. Clearly, the primary cause was incoming President Calderón's decision, in 2006–2007, to launch the army in a full-scale offensive against the narco interests, who, in turn, fought back ruthlessly, sometimes deploying superior weaponry. True, there is evidence that the old Pax Mafiosa, whereby regional narco interests maintained a measure of guarded mutual respect, thus inhibiting turf wars, had broken down long before Calderón came to power, which meant that mounting intercartel conflict preceded the state's declaration of war. At any rate, the fairly stable system of pre-1980 gave way to a kind of Hobbesian "war of all against all," involving the state (whose agents often played the field), ruthlessly hostile cartels (for example, Sinaloa versus the Tijuana, Juárez, and Gulf Cartels), and cartel breakaways (like the notorious Zetas, who split from the Gulf Cartel in 2010).[36] The homicide rate now soared, reversing the long downward trend of previous decades.[37] In other words, following the massive mortality of the Mexican Revolution (1910–1920) and the subsequent violence of the Cristero rebellion (1926–1929), large-scale warfare disappeared. Furthermore, low-intensity political conflict—for example, landlords versus *agraristas*, syndical insurgencies, intervillage feuds, student gang violence, and state repression of dissidents—all tended to decline over time.

The decline was not, of course, simple and linear. Regional conflicts—notably in states like Guerrero and Chiapas (examples, perhaps, of "México bronco")—bucked the trend.[38] But in aggregate terms, the trend line of political violence was downwards. Criminal homicides also tended to fall. For the latter half of the twentieth century, it seemed, Mexico was roughly following the "civilising process" described by Norbert Elias, or providing corroboration of Steven Pinker's more recent reformulation of that thesis.[39] Mexico's fall from grace can hardly be cited as a decisive refutation of Elias and Pinker, since they are concerned with grand global trends over the *longue durée*. But it is a crucial and—for the time being, it seems—an entrenched feature of modern Mexico, which has to be explained in terms of the rationale of state and criminal collective actors.[40]

Thus far, I have stressed discontinuity, the decisive shift brought about in the late twentieth century as narco power grew, that of the PRI waned, and the old politico-criminal collusive nexus snapped.[41] Aggravated by inept policy making (on the part of all the major parties: PRI, PAN, and now MORENA), this shift created today's homicidal Hobbesian scenario. Of course, there are also notable continuities, which several of these chapters stress: the endemic collusion of the authorities with criminal actors; the contagion of criminal contact (whereby those deployed to combat crime are drawn into collusion); the recurrent *cucaracha* (cockroach) effect, whereby criminal activity is quashed in one zone, only for it to resurge elsewhere; and, changing the metaphor, the hydra syndrome, which means that as soon as narco heads are lopped off, new heads spring up in their place.[42]

In such cases, what looks like change—occasionally even "progress"—often turns out to be deceptive. The names—of places or leaders—change, but the syndrome persists. Julián Leyzaola, police chief of Tijuana (2008–2010) and Ciudad Juárez (2011–2013), used contentiously tough measures to suppress the homicide rates in both border cities, but more recently the rates have again risen, making Tijuana and Juárez, in 2018, the two most deadly cities in Mexico.[43] Similarly, institutional churn—the creation of new agencies, programs, and "operations"—conceals underlying continuity. Portentously named "operations" come and go: Operation Intercept (1969), a unilateral U.S. initiative, morphs into the bilateral Operation Cooperation (1969), which in turn becomes Operation Canador (1970–1975), followed by the—more sustained and extensive—Operation Condor (1977–1987).[44] As already mentioned, however, attempts to seal the border, interdict the flow of drugs, or eliminate their production in Mexico, though they may produce opportunistic shifts in the commodity chain, fail to decisively stem the flow or to depress consumption.[45] Meanwhile, state actors, like Salvador Rangel, commanding the Mexican army in Michoacán in 1964, proclaim victory in their regional battles against drug producers and traffickers, only to be promptly proved wrong.[46] This leads us to an area of notable continuity that deserves brief treatment: U.S.-Mexican relations and the role of foreign actors and influences in the Mexican "drug wars."

U.S.-MEXICAN RELATIONS

In this respect, several chapters in this book seem to tell a roughly similar story. First, though the United States habitually leaned on Mexico, the United States did not determine Mexican policy; indeed, the Mexican government enjoyed a good deal of autonomy. In addition, the Mexicans—I mean Mexican officials, políticos, and policy makers—have been adept at exploiting U.S. initiatives, whether to extract resources, to mollify the U.S. government, or to justify measures in the eyes of their own sometimes skeptical population. On occasions, indeed, the Mexicans have resorted to what we could call Potemkin village policies: making a bold show of close collaboration with the gringos, when the reality is rather different (for example, in implementing Operation Condor). Hence the occasional nasty surprises—especially for the gringos—when, for example, a Mexican "drug czar" turns out to be hand-in-glove with the cartels he is meant to be relentlessly suppressing.[47]

It could be argued that this mix of compliance, pseudo-compliance, and bilateral manipulation is an old story, not at all confined to the question of drugs and narco-crime. For obvious reasons, Mexico has always had a strong incentive to try to understand, cultivate, and deceive its over-mighty northern neighbor. Leaders who got it wrong—like Santa Anna with his bullish approach to the question of Texas—paid a heavy price. Díaz, a more subtle statesman, played the U.S. more successfully, as did his revolutionary successors who, from a position of stark weakness c. 1920, managed to construct working relations with U.S. interests (both public and private) without—usually—offending nationalist opinion and incurring a political backlash at home. The Americans, for their part, recognized that Mexico was a "significant other" and—especially at times of war (1917–1918 and 1941–1945)—regarded the security of the southern border as a paramount interest.

But the United States increasingly had to juggle a global agenda, becoming, at least by 1945, the self-appointed "leader of the free world" and champion of liberal capitalism in the bipolar confrontation of the Cold War. The Americans therefore had their fingers in pies all around the world. By then, Mexico's "revolutionary" regime, its early radicalism much diluted, had mutated into a stable, effective, civilian political machine, while Mexico now enjoyed a "ripe, mature, social entente" with its once threatening northern neighbor.[48] To a large extent, the United States could regard Mexico as safe: pending questions—the bracero (migrant worker) program, the Chamizal dispute, and the Cuban Revolution—could be managed, contained, or, in the case of the Chamizal, definitively settled.[49] The Mexicans could get on with their "preferred revolution," which, as it happens, was doing rather well during the years of the Pax PRIísta and *"desarrollo estabilizador"* ("stabilizing development," c. 1954–1976). Lesser Latin American powers, like Guatemala in the 1950s, Cuba in the 1960s, and Nicaragua in the 1980s, absorbed disproportionate American attention and elicited aggressive American responses. It is perhaps significant that most U.S. ambassadors to Mexico were inexperienced placemen, not qualified career diplomats; most lacked genuine expertise in the field and few spoke fluent Spanish.[50] The Mexicans, however, had to keep close tabs on their northern neighbors, which meant maintaining an effective diplomatic presence in Washington, a tradition of U.S. expertise in the Mexican foreign policy service, and an ability, when necessary, to lobby both in Washington and in the U.S. border states. Mexico also proved adept at deploying "soft power" to cajole the Americans, feting prominent American intellectuals and capitalizing on Mexico's cultural heritage.

In short, Mexico was practiced in the difficult art of dealing with the superpower on its doorstep, while the United States regarded Mexico as a relatively safe neighbor who could, to some extent, be taken for granted. Meanwhile, although drug trafficking across the border had a long history, it was for decades a minor and manageable issue. During the 1910s and 1920s the fallout from the Revolution dominated U.S.-Mexican relations, which revolved around questions of diplomatic recognition, the payment of revolutionary reparations, the renewal of debt service, the status of U.S. direct investment in Mexico, and the plight of the Catholic Church. The illicit business activities of the likes of Esteban Cantú were of little concern. After 1919, Prohibition boosted both American "tourism" to Mexican border towns and Mexican smuggling of drink and drugs into the United States; but, again, these did not impinge much on the bilateral relationship. And in the 1930s—with Prohibition ended (1933)—cross-border trade declined and U.S.-Mexican relations continued to focus on the status of American investment (in particular, oil). Even in the 1940s, when cross-border business, "tourism," and trade revived, drug trafficking was not a major issue, however much Harry Anslinger might have wanted it to be (see Carey, chapter 5 this volume). As already noted, American demand for narcotics, boosted by U.S. border garrisons, generated the first "miniboom." But the boom petered out after the war and, during the war itself, questions of U.S.-Mexican economic and military cooperation dwarfed concerns about drug trafficking.

Thus drugs did not start to shoot up the bilateral agenda until the 1960s, when the old questions arising from the Revolution had been laid to rest, the PRIísta machine was in charge, and the contemporary youth counterculture boosted American demand, initially for marijuana. Then, as already mentioned, shifts in the global networks of heroin and cocaine trafficking, coupled with rising American demand for hard drugs, turned Mexico into a major source of supply. Drugs now became, for the first time, a significant issue in the bilateral relationship, as signaled by President Nixon's Operation Intercept, one of several acts of brash U.S. unilateralism undertaken by that—we might say—proto-Trumpian administration.[51] Apart from successive "Operations," the U.S. Congress now took a closer, critical interest in Mexican affairs, enabling the likes of Sen. Jesse Helms to strut his stuff, and U.S. agencies, such as the DEA, began to play a greater—albeit largely covert and deniable—role south of the border (see Pérez Ricart, chapter 7 in this volume). Greater political focus, coupled with growing institutional presence, was a risky combination, as the Camarena case starkly illustrated.[52] Furthermore, as the American institutional apparatus expanded, so turf wars became more common, and, Cedillo (chapter 11 in this volume) suggests, more sources of intelligence did not necessarily mean better intelligence.

The greater American presence in Mexico also presented a problem for Mexican administrations, historically leery of seeming to grovel to the gringos. And this brings me to my final set of considerations: how the growth of narco operations and related violence fed into Mexican politics.

DRUGS AND DOMESTIC POLITICS

I have already stressed the general point that, as narco power grew, the dominance of the PRI declined, for reasons largely unrelated to that growth. The old modus vivendi—the "historic compromise," perhaps?—that linked the narco interest to their PRIísta political masters thus broke down, presaging the mounting instability and violence of the twenty-first century. Political turnover—*alternancia*—tended to compound the violence, since, it has been shown, changes in local or state administration clearly correlate with violence.[53] When incumbents lose office, old pacts and *arreglos* collapse and criminal organizations jostle to replace them, which can mean both eliminating criminal rivals and scaring—or suborning—new political incumbents. In addition, democratization has stimulated electoral competition and significantly raised the costs of political campaigning, thus offering narco interests the option of funding, as well as intimidating, political candidates.

The changing bilateral relationship with the United States also had a direct impact on domestic Mexican politics. Cedillo (chapter 11 in this volume) suggests that Presidents Echeverría and López Portillo sought to "embrace" the U.S. drug agenda, thus reinforcing their—arguably declining—political legitimacy at home. But both presidents, buoyed by the windfall income of the oil boom, were quite prepared to offend the United States: Echeverría with his "Third World" rhetoric and condemnation of Zionism, and López Portillo with his outspoken critique of U.S. energy policy.[54] Indeed, it seems more likely that over the decades, Mexican políticos have typically sought domestic legitimacy on the basis of nationalist appeals that, while they may not have been outspokenly anti-American, have involved careful distancing from the *coloso del norte*. Being seen to grovel to the gringos—I repeat—was not smart politics, as President Peña Nieto found, to his cost, when seeming to defer overmuch to President Trump and his wall-building, Mexico-bashing agenda.[55]

Furthermore, Mexican official nationalism was, especially during the decades of revolutionary and old-style PRIísta rule, deeply rooted and, to some—admittedly unmeasurable—degree, authentic. It was not simply an instrumental contrivance. President Cárdenas and his expropriation of the Anglo-American oil companies in 1938 is the best example, but even presidents who, like Miguel Alemán, cooperated closely with the United States (including with the nascent CIA) were careful not to flaunt their American connections and, indeed, were at times seen in the United States as troublesomely nationalistic.[56] In respect of drugs, the first "revolutionary" president, Francisco Madero, adopted an independent policy and was no puppet of the Americans, though he may well have been influenced by broader prohibitionist trends around the world.[57] Yet more clearly, Venustiano Carranza (president from 1917 to 1920) was a stiff-necked nationalist who, in respect of drug policy, was both innovative and autonomous.[58] That is, he and his administration (which included eager technocratic reformers like Alberto J. Pani) adopted a proactively prohibitionist stance, banning drug trade and production, but they did so, it seems clear, not because the United States required them to do so—Carranza had a long history of successfully defying the United States—but because they believed it right for Mexico and because prohibition seemed the way forward; it was the international norm by which progressive countries and administrations were judged.[59] President Calles, in the mid-1920s, introduced a series of tough measures against drug trafficking, but he did so at a time when he was at loggerheads with the United States over oil, the Catholic Church, and Central America;[60] he was no pro-American patsy and there is no evidence that he cracked down on drugs in order to ingratiate himself with the gringos.

Drug prohibition thus formed part of a much broader revolutionary "ethos" that was, roughly speaking, enlightened, reformist, puritanical, and perhaps "jacobin."[61] The revolutionaries sought to "rationalize and nationalize" the backward Mexican people—particularly the backward brown people of the indigenous southeast—ridding them of the *"rancias costumbres"* ("rancid customs") that had held them back and had condemned them to oppression, while preventing them from becoming productive, patriotic Mexican citizens.[62] Similar rhetoric was deployed to justify the persecution and, finally, the mass expulsion of the Chinese, the alleged agents of opium addiction (and other supposedly related vices).[63] This discourse of "degeneration," highlighted by both Campos and Pérez Montfort (chapters 2 and 3 in this volume), was thus a genuine, autonomous force, given real impetus by the triumph of the Revolution. In earlier decades, políticos and *pensadores* had inveighed against the ingrained vices of the "degenerate" Mexican people; what was new, after 1910, was the coming to power of a new political generation, committed to a state-building, social-reformist, "jacobin" project, in a situation of unusual flux and instability. Foreign models—not necessarily American ones—were sometimes influential (President Calles, for example, was a keen student of global, especially European, politics), but the revolutionary project, of which drug prohibition was a (minor) part, derived from domestic inspiration and commitment and was in no sense a foreign import, still less a foreign imposition.

While it seems entirely correct to stress—"constructivistically"—the autonomous power of reformism and nationalism, thus the influence of "ideological" or "ideational" factors in the formulation of Mexican drug policy, it would be naive to stop there, particularly, as the analysis advances into the postwar era of the PRI and beyond. Now, reformism waned, nationalism became more formulaic, and, above all, drugs became a bigger sociopolitical issue. Now, therefore, it is essential to look beyond the "ideas" and below the formal rhetoric of the regime, rhetoric that increasingly diverged from reality, in respect of drugs and much else. As already mentioned, drug trafficking expanded—first in the 1940s, then more enduringly in the 1960s and after—permeating politics and providing new sources of power, both coercive and financial. Regarding the politics of drugs, ulterior motives now counted much more than overt discourse. The políticos of the revolutionary generation—from Madero through Carranza to Calles and Cárdenas—were, for all their sometimes ruthless pragmatism, genuinely committed to reformist national projects. So grand ideas—democracy, nationalism, anticlericalism, agrarianism—counted. From the 1940s, however, ruthless pragmatism prevailed over any lingering ideational commitment; as Womack famously observed in 1970, "the business of the Mexican Revolution is now business," a business in which drugs came to play a greater, if surreptitious, role.[64]

Again, there were precedents: the expulsion of the Chinese in the 1920s was justified in terms of social degeneration and patriotic progress, but it also served personal interests: it furthered the careers of Sinophobic politicians (especially in Sonora) and enabled Mexican interests to usurp the Chinese role in drug dealing and related vice. More generally, successive campaigns against drugs tended to enhance the role of the central (federal) government and, in particular, the executive, at the expense of local and provincial interests. In the 1920s and 1930s the aggrandizement of the "center" was served by land distribution, labor reform, and education policy; drug policy, though much less important, followed a similar path. By the 1970s, those traditional policies had lost much of their impetus, but the drug question had become more salient. Presidents Echeverría and López Portillo hiked state spending and boosted federal power. Drug policy became increasingly activist, intrusive, and "federalized" (Cedillo, chapter 11 in this volume). Specific institutions thereby stood to benefit. Gobernación, the key government ministry from the 1940s through the 1970s, extended its power by promoting and participating in antidrug campaigns (even if its officials were themselves implicated in the trade). The military, too, acquired an enhanced role, forcibly eliminating drug production and—by way of winning hearts and minds—engaging in local development projects (Maldonado, chapter 10 in this volume). After 2006, President Calderón's crackdown on the cartels involved a substantial increase in the role of the army (and navy): military personnel acquired a greater public presence, policing prisons and border ports, while military officers were drafted into local governmental positions. The military budget soared although the military payroll grew only modestly.[65]

Apart from institutional expansion, drug policy played into grander political strategies. The ruling PRI had always faced opposition and dissent. During the 1970s, that opposition became more violent and radical. Radicalization stemmed from state repression of the 1968 student movement and of regional protest movements (like that of Lucio Cabañas in Guerrero), which were driven from peaceful mobilization into armed insurrection. In addition, the example of the Cuban Revolution inspired quixotic insurrectionary movements, usually on a small scale. The PRIísta state responded by redoubling repression, thus inaugurating Mexico's Dirty War, the subject of a good deal of recent innovative research.[66] The Dirty War coincided with a more aggressive antidrug policy (e.g., Operation Condor) and the two "projects"—if we can call them that—evolved in sleazy symbiosis. The same institutions—the police, the army, Gobernación—were involved. Personnel—including pistoleros—served both causes. Under Echeverría, the DFS (Dirección Federal de Seguridad) recruited narco heavies to intimidate and even eliminate political dissidents, while the state discursively blurred the line between crime and dissent: it linked drug production and dealing to political opponents, thus promoting "the elision of drugs and dissent."[67] As Aviña (chapter 12 in this volume) shows, this strategy was particularly evident in Guerrero's long—arguably ongoing—Dirty War. Again, this was an old story: Zapata—and many other bona fide revolutionaries—had been dismissed, or demonized as mere bandits. Criminal pistoleros had been deployed against the radical cardenistas of the 1930s.[68] Now a new generation of rebels and radicals were similarly stigmatized.[69]

The explanation is not simply that there is "nothing new under the sun" (a trope that some historians like to trot out: it's good for the historical trade, of course). On the contrary, I have stressed that the scale and impact of narco crime and violence in the twenty-first century are unprecedented, and, we could say, this quantitative change has generated a qualitative sociopolitical change, evident in endemic violence, mounting public alarm, the diversification of crime, and the erosion of the state. Mexico is not—yet—an example of a classic "failed state," but it is substantially different from the "Leviathan on the zócalo" that ruled during the heyday of the PRI (c. 1946–1982),[70] and, as this book makes clear, that transformation has, in part, been brought about by drug-fueled crime and violence.

NOTES

1. Alan Knight, "War, Violence and Homicide in Modern Mexico," in *Murder and Violence in Modern Latin America*, ed. Eric A. Johnson, Ricardo D. Salvatore, and Pieter Spierenburg (Chichester: John Wiley, 2013), 12–48.

2. Alan Knight, "Narco-Violence and the State in Modern Mexico," in *Violence, Coercion, and State-Making in Twentieth-Century Mexico: The Other Half of the Centaur*, ed. Wil G. Pansters (Stanford, CA: Stanford University Press, 2012), 115–34.

3. Paul Gootenberg and Isaac Campos, "Toward a New Drug History of Latin America: A Research Frontier at the Center of Debates," *Hispanic American Historical Review* 95, no. 1 (2015), 1–35, offers a comprehensive overview of recent research.

4. I offer a similar, somewhat more detailed, sketch of the historiography of the Revolution in Alan Knight, *La revolución cósmica. Utopías, regiones y resultados, México 1910–40* (Mexico City: Fondo de Cultura Económica, 2015), chap. 1.

5. Joseph Richard Werne, "Esteban Cantú y la soberanía mexicana en Baja California," *Historia mexicana* 30, no. 1 (1980): 1–32. On Chihuahua, Mark Wasserman, *Persistent Oligarchs. Elites ad Politics in Chihuahua, Mexico, 1910–40* (Durham, NC: Duke University Press, 1993), chaps. 3, 4, describes postrevolutionary politics in the state, noting (58) the important role of "narcotic and whiskey smuggling as well as gambling." For a good recent analysis of that story, see Nicole Mottier, "Drugs Gangs and Politics in Ciudad Juárez, 1928–36," *Mexican Studies/Estudios Mexicanos* 25, no. 1 (2009): 19–46. Gabriela Recio, "Drugs and Alcohol: U.S. Prohibition and the Origins of the Drug Trade in Mexico, 1910–1930," *Journal of Latin American Studies* 34, no. 1 (2002): 21–42, describes the evolving symbiosis between U.S. prohibitionism and Mexican trafficking (of both drink and drugs).

6. On the evolving "moral panic" of the Porfiriato and after, see Isaac Campos, "Degeneration and the Origins of Mexico's War on Drugs," *Mexican Studies/Estudios Mexicanos* 26, no. 2 (2010): 379–408. The Porfirian elite's preoccupation with the incidence and ravages of alcoholism, though based on reality, also spilled over into "panic." Moisés González Navarro, *Historia moderna de México. El Porfiriato, La vida social* (Mexico City: Hermes, 1970), 72–82. Mexican concern with "degeneration" formed part of a much broader fin-de-siècle global trend. Richard Davenport-Hines, *The Pursuit of Oblivion. A Social History of Drugs* (London: Phoenix Press, 2002), chap. 6.

7. Barbara Tuchman, *The Zimmermann Telegram* (London: MacMillan, 1981), 88. The celebrated Villista corrido (ballad) *La Cucaracha* (the cockroach) contains a well-known reference to marijuana (roughly: "the cockroach now can't walk... because he has no marijuana to smoke"); the "cockroach" in question, however, is Villa's sworn enemy, the counterrevolutionary dictator Victoriano Huerta. So, far from celebrating the drug, it is invoked to lampoon an enemy; Isaac Campos, *Home Grown. Marijuana and the Origins of Mexico's War on Drugs* (Chapel Hill: University of North Carolina Press, 2012), 162–63. Curtis Marez, *Drug Wars. The Political Economy of Narcotics*

(Minneapolis: University of Minnesota Press, 2004), 142–44, 186, 209–15, harks back to Tuchman, seeing the "lowly cockroach" as a "revolutionary subaltern," a "figure for Villa's soldiers who . . . cannot keep marching because they have no more marijuana to smoke." This seems an odd and unconvincing interpretation, but then the book itself—supposedly dealing with the "political economy of narcotics"—is nothing of the sort, being an imaginative, interesting, but sprawling cultural history.

8. On the emergence of Mexico City's "dark Bohemia," where "intellectual creativity" conspired with "drugs, alcohol (and) sex," see Mauricio Tenorio, "Around 1919 and in Mexico City," CIDE Documentos de Trabajo n. 56 (Mexico City: CIDE, 2009), quote from page 55.

9. Gonzalo N. Santos, *Memorias* (Mexico City: Grijalbo, 1984), gives plenty of examples.

10. Pansters and Smith, introduction to this volume. The "constructivist" (or "constructionist") approach seems to derive, in the Latin American context, from Gootenberg and Campos, "Toward a New Drug History," 20–22. Its provenance appears to be U.S. drug research, and, I suspect, it is rather more useful and pertinent when considering drug consumption and related drug policy (e.g., in the United States), since it may help us understand the conceptual universe—including the "moral panics"—that are involved. And they, of course, are empirical facts like any others in history. I am less persuaded that "constructivism" offers a crucial explanatory key to drug production, crime, and violence in Mexico. It is worth noting that "constructivism" has become a fashionable, but also contentious, approach in international relations theory. Christopher Hill, *The National Interest in Question. Foreign Policy in Multicultural Societies* (Oxford: Oxford University Press, 2013), 2, 5–6.

11. I am appropriating a fairly old metaphor, coined by Sir George Clark (1952) and recycled by E. H. Carr, *What Is History?* (Harmondsworth: Penguin, 1964), 9–10.

12. Alexandre Marchant, "The French Connection: Between Myth and Reality," *Vingtième Siècle. Revue Historique* 115, no. 3 (2012): 89–102, offers a sober revision. See also Luis Astorga, "Cocaine in Mexico," in *Cocaine: Global Histories*, ed. Paul Gootenberg (London: Routledge, 1999), chap. 9.

13. From a global perspective, European demand has also become more salient, but since the focus here is Mexico, it is U.S. demand that is key. Like previous waves of drug use and dependency (e.g., laudanum in the nineteenth century), those of the twentieth and twenty-first centuries have their own dynamics, deriving from changing American culture and consumption. However, I take those dynamics—and the resulting demand—as givens, which, for want of space and expertise, I don't explore.

14. Ioan Grillo, *El Narco: Inside Mexico's Armed Insurgency* (New York: Bloomsbury, 2011), 8, 147, suggests (without citing sources) that Mexican drug exports are worth up to $30 billion a year. I assume this is based on U.S. street value, which embodies a huge (80–90 percent) markup on the wholesale import price, which in turn is substantially greater than the price paid to local Mexican producers. See the persuasive analysis of

Peter Reuter and Victoria A. Greenfield, "Measuring Global Drug Markets: How Good Are the Numbers and Why Should We Care About Them?," *World Economics* 2, no. 4 (2001): 159–73, which suggests that the export price of Mexican drugs may be no more than $3 billion (c. 2000). But that is still a lot of money.

15. As already suggested (note 14), global commodity chains involve hefty markups along the way: e.g., a $3 cup of Starbucks coffee generates only eight cents for the Brazilian coffee beans, of which one cent goes to the farmer. But in drug production, export and retailing the markups are exceptional (for example, 30,000 percent in the case of Colombian cocaine sold in Los Angeles), which is not surprising, given the risks and bottlenecks involved along the way. Two conclusions follow: first, drug busts that are assessed in terms of "street-value" (e.g., in the United States) vastly inflate the value of the product "upstream" (but they make the drug busters look good). And elimination programs in producing countries often have little or no effect on the final "street price," since that price factors in a whole range of risks and losses along the way. See Tom Wainwright, *Narconomics. How to Run a Drug Cartel* (London: Ebury Press, 2016), chap. 1.

16. See James A. MacDonald, "The Narco Economy and Small Town Rural Mexico," *Human Organisation* 64, no. 2 (2005): 115–25, which describes the impact of narco money on a minor provincial town ("Buenavista": a pseudonym) in west-central Mexico c. 2000. Given that "Buenavista" was historically a conservative, Catholic, and Cristero town, it seems fair to use the loose term "traditional" (a term I usually prefer to avoid).

17. The economic impact of the narco business raises a host of complicated questions. In "Buenavista" (and elsewhere), narco money was recycled through the local economy, generating—via the multiplier—jobs, income, and investment. It thus performed a roughly similar role to migrants' remittances, which have been crucial to many Mexican communities and families. Both, of course, involve hard currency channeled from the north. And this income became particularly vital during the depression years of the 1980s. Salvador Maldonado Aranda, "Stories of Drug Trafficking in Rural Mexico. Territories, Drugs and Cartels in Michoacán," *European Review of Latin American and Caribbean Studies* 94 (2013): 63. On the other hand, narco income may have introduced elements of "Dutch disease" (export-led currency overvaluation) into the Mexican economy, and though it provided income, it did nothing for overall socioeconomic equality (indeed, MacDonald, "The Narco Economy," 117, argues that it promoted "dramatic inequality"). It is also generally supposed that the mounting violence of post-2007 deterred investment and thus inhibited the legal economy. The evidence, however, is variable. Nathan Ashby and Miguel Ramos, "FDI and Industry Response to Organized Crime," *European Journal of Political Economy* 30 (2013): 80–91, argue that violence—represented by the homicide rate—correlates *negatively* with foreign direct investment (FDI) in agriculture, services, transport, and communications; that there is no significant correlation between violence and

FDI in manufacturing; and that violence correlates *positively* with FDI in extractive industries (oil and mining). This positive correlation might arise, as Dawn Paley polemically suggests, because extractive interests thrive on local violence (see *Drug War Capitalism* [Oakland: AK Press, 2014]), or, more likely, because mining involves fixed assets that cannot move out of harm's way, and which can therefore be more easily extorted, parasitically, by criminal interests.

18. Having exculpated historians of the revolutionary period (1910–1940) from the charge of obtusely neglecting the narco issue, I would suggest that political scientists of the PRIísta heyday (c. 1946–1982) did, in the main, neglect it, even as it became more significant. One creditable exception was Kenneth F. Johnson, *Mexican Democracy: A Critical View* (New York: Praeger, 1978), chap. 7, which, by stooping to analyze the seamy side of local Mexican politics (in Nogales, Sonora), paid due attention to official drug-related corruption.

19. For a journalistic take on "narco-juniors," see Julian Borger and Jo Tuckman, "Blood Brothers," *The Guardian*, March 15, 2002, describing Benjamín and Ramón Arellano Félix. Ramón "would drive around in red Porsche, garishly dressed in a mink jacket and heavy gold jewellery, cruising the streets of Tijuana, where his cocky style became a magnet for the bored sons of the city rich. Some of them became Ramón's 'narco-juniors,' trust-fund hitmen who, when they were not killing for business, killed out of simple ennui." Compare the modest and discreet lifestyle of La Nacha, a border drug-dealer of a previous generation (and gender), described by Carey, chapter 5 in this volume.

20. The Mexican state's "ephebocratic" turn (i.e., its tendency to promote young political high-flyers) arguably began with President Echeverría (1970–1976). See Miguel Angel Centeno, *Democracy Within Reason. Technocratic Revolution in Mexico* (University Park: Penn State Press, 1994), 150–53. But it then resurfaced, in a different guise, as Presidents Salinas (1988–1994) and Zedillo (1994–2000) engineered Mexico's neoliberal turn, which involved an enhanced reliance on young, highly trained technocrats and a corresponding demotion of the old PRIísta bosses (the so-called "dinosaurs").

21. Narco "social banditry" gets short shrift in this volume, so I insert this bulky footnote by way of balance. While, as a category of historical analysis, "social banditry" is not as innovatively sexy as once it was, I don't think it's an analytical lost cause, as I have suggested elsewhere: Knight, "Narco-Violence and the State," 131–33; and Alan Knight, "Eric Hobsbawm, la historia mexicana y el bandolerismo social," in *Los historiadores y la historia por el siglo XXI: Homenaje a Eric J. Hobsbawm*, ed. Gumersindo Vera Hernández et al. (Mexico City: CONACULTA/INAH, 2007), 455–58. And for a fuller discussion regarding Mexico, see the interesting work of Mark Cameron Edberg, "Drug Traffickers as Social Bandits: Culture and Drug Trafficking in Northern Mexico and the Border Region," *Journal of Contemporary Criminal Justice* 17, no. 3 (2001): 259–77; and *El Narcotraficante. Narcocorridos and*

the Construction of a Cultural Persona on the U.S.-Mexican Border (Austin: University of Texas Press, 2004). Of course, not *all* narco bosses can be considered "social bandits," and those who might qualify are certainly fewer now than they were in the past, at least in Mexico. But no one—I hope—ever suggested that *all* such bosses were social bandits, just as Hobsbawm, who coined the term, never argued that *all* bandits, in all times and places, were "social." True, he cast the net too widely and relied overly on literary—constructivist?—sources; hence Anton Blok's cogent and influential critique of Hobsbawm's rosy portrait of Sicilian bandits ("The Peasant and the Brigand: Social Banditry Reconsidered," *Comparative Studies in Society and History* 14, no. 4 [1972]: 494–503). But to deny or downplay Sicilian social banditry is not to ditch the concept altogether. Two further caveats are in order. First, like many such social-scientific debates, it is better to deal in *degrees* of "social banditry" (or "populism," "fascism," "liberalism," etc.) rather than to create a binary universe of "social" sheep and "antisocial" goats. Individuals and organizations can shift along a social/antisocial continuum, depending on circumstances. Second, "social" does *not* mean "socialist" or even "social reformist": "social bandits" don't have to demonstrate formal politico-ideological credentials; they reveal their "social" dimension by their actions and by the active popular sympathy and support they elicit. Robin Hood never published a political manifesto denouncing feudalism.

22. Benjamin T. Smith, "The Rise and Fall of Narco-populism: Drugs, Politics and Society in Sinaloa, 1930–80," *Journal for the Study of Radicalism* 7, no. 2 (2013): 138.

23. On traditional perks and patronage, see Morris, chapter 13 in this volume, and Mottier, "Drug Gangs," 29–30, 38, which notes how, in Juárez in the 1930s, Enrique Fernández "scattered money, by the handful" while maintaining truck drivers, carpenters, electricians, and street cleaners on his payroll.

24. Salvador Maldonado Aranda, "'We Are Men of War': Self-Defense Forces, Para-militarism and Organised Crime on the Mexican Periphery," *Global South* 12, no. 2 (2018): 148–65; Nathaniel Morris, "Serrano Communities and Subaltern Negotiation Strategies: The Local Politics of Opium Production in Mexico, 1940–2020," *Social History of Alcohol and Drugs* 34, no. 1 (2020): 76–79. As Morris points out, the practice of community armed self-defense is an old tradition in Mexico, particularly among serrano ("highland")—remote and semiautonomous—communities, who played a major role in the Mexican Revolution (1910–1920), a period when local defense forces were also a common community response to the prevalent upheaval (see, for example, Alan Knight, *The Mexican Revolution* [Cambridge: Cambridge University Press, 1986], 2:437–39).

25. On U.S. demand and Mexican response in the 1940s, see Smith and Pansters, chapter 6 in this volume; Smith, "The Rise and Fall"; and Luis Astorga, *El siglo de las drogas. Del Porfiriato al nuevo milenio* (Mexico City: Delbolsillo, 2016), chap. 3.

26. There is a large literature on the decline of the PRI and the rise of a variegated opposition. The electoral story (which is only one theme among many) is well told by

Miguel Basáñez, *El pulso de los sexenios. Veinte años de crisis en México* (Mexico City: Siglo XXI, 1990) and Jorge I. Domínguez and James A. MacCann, *Democratizing Mexico: Public Opinion and Electoral Choices* (Baltimore: Johns Hopkins University Press, 1996).

27. Terrence E. Poppa, *Drug Lord: The Life and Death of a Mexican Kingpin* (Seattle: Demand Publications, 1998), offers a good case study of the how the plaza system operated in its heyday; see also Flores Pérez, chapter 9 in this volume, on Juan N. Guerra's operations in Tamaulipas.

28. On the important role of women in the drug trade, see Smith, "The Rise and Fall," 134; Mottier, "Drug Gangs," 26, 29; Poppa, *Drug Lord*, chap. 13; and Carey, chapter 5 this volume.

29. John Ross, "Mexico's Modern Revolutionaries," *The Guardian*, September 12, 2010, argues that "if revolution can be defined as an armed uprising to overthrow an unpopular government, then the new Mexican revolution has already begun"; and, while the narco bosses are not exactly Bolsheviks, "a narco-insurgency may be the best revolution this lacerated nation is going to get." There are, as they say, more holes in this argument than in a string vest.

30. In the ten years following the inauguration of NAFTA in 1994, Mexican trade with the United States grew by 168 percent (in nominal terms), from $100 billion to $268 billion (so by about 140 percent in real terms). Ismael Barajas et al., "Trade Flows Between the U.S. and Mexico: NAFTA and the Border Region," *Artículo. Journal of Urban Research* 10 (2014), table 2. Increased Mexican migration to the United States—which the 1980s recession encouraged—also facilitated trafficking. Maldonado, "Stories of Drug Trafficking," 52.

31. Guadalupe Correa-Cabrera, *Los Zetas Inc. Criminal Corporations, Energy, and Civil War in Mexico* (Austin: University of Texas Press, 2017), 23. Smith, "The Rise and Fall," 142, shows that the phenomenon of drug exports piggybacking on legitimate border trade goes back at least to the 1970s. At the same time, the cartels also deployed their ample resources, manpower, and ingenuity to transport drugs from South America to Mexico and from Mexico to the United States by means of airplanes, submarines, catapults, tunnels, and improvised bridges.

32. I base this on the notion that the original (Italian) mafia was essentially a "system of organized protection." Raimondo Catanzaro, *Men of Respect. A Social History of the Sicilian Mafia* (New York: The Free Press, 1988), 17. More recently, of course, the mafia has also entered the business of drug trafficking.

33. The term "cartel" is often bandied about casually; for that reason, some analysts—e.g., Correa-Cabrera, *Los Zetas*, 8—choose to avoid it when referring to "drug-trafficking organizations in contemporary Mexico." This seems to me overly scrupulous. Clearly, such organizations are very different from the original "cartels" (market-rigging associations among big corporations, for example, in Gilded Age America or Bismarck's Germany); but that, I would have thought, is quite obvious. It's

obvious, too, that the drug "cartels" operating in contemporary Mexico are sprawling, shifting criminal entities, not tightly organized legal corporations. Some umbrella term, however, is needed to describe those entities—however loose and variable they may be—and "cartel" has the merit of being succinct, commonly understood, and, on balance, an aid to communication. In this context, newly coined acronyms may sometimes have their use, but they are not necessarily "aids to communication": for example, "TOC" ("Transnational Organized Crime") has 107 other acronymic meanings.

34. Paul Gootenberg, "More and More Scholars on Drugs," *Qualitative Sociology* 31, no. 4 (2008): 426, applauds scholars who "transcend the artificial or politically-imposed distinctions between legitimate legal goods and flows and now illicit ones." We can all agree that the legal/illegal distinction is a political one and, to that extent, "artificial" (or, we might say, "arbitrary"), and that scholars of the subject should certainly survey both sides of that official frontier. But the existence—and precise location—of that frontier is crucial, since legal and illegal commerce necessarily follow quite different patterns, which is why debates—past and present—about drug legalization and decriminalization are of real consequence.

35. The instrumental/affective—or /expressive—dichotomy crops up in psychology, criminology, and political science. For example, Geoffrey Brennan and Loren Lomasky, *Democracy and Decision: The Pure Theory of Electoral Preference* (Cambridge: Cambridge University Press, 1993), 25, contrast "instrumental" or "outcome-causal" action with "expressive or symbolic action," which is "undertaken for its own sake rather than to bring about particular consequences." The distinction could be traced back—or, at least, related—to Weber's discussion of *Zweckrationalität* (goal-rationality) versus *Wertrationalität* (value-rationality). Those of Freudian persuasion might also see instrumental conduct as obeying the strictures of the superego, while affective/expressive actions bubble up from the depths of the id . . .

36. Correa-Cabrera, *Los Zetas*, chap. 1. See also the excellent analysis of cartel conflict (including the Zetas), in Michoacán in Maldonado, "Stories of Drug Trafficking."

37. Paul Gillingham, "Who Killed Crispín Aguilar? Violence and Order in the Postrevolutionary Countryside," in *Violence, Coercion, and State-Making in Twentieth-Century Mexico: The Other Half of the Centaur*, ed. Wil G. Pansters (Stanford, CA: Stanford University Press, 2012), 108, charts the steady long-term decline in homicides (from thirty-eight per 100,000 population in 1940 to six in 2000). Recent trends are captured by David A. Shirk and Joel Wallman, "Understanding Mexico's Drug Violence," *Journal of Conflict Resolution* 59, no. 8 (2012): 1348–76, who note that the Mexican homicide rate had fallen to as low as eight per 100,000 in 2007 (and was thus converging on the then U.S. figure of five); but thereafter it shot up, reaching twenty-three by 2011. In other words, the homicide rate nearly tripled in four years.

38. Gillingham, "Who Killed Crispín Aguilar?," 108, shows significant long-term fluctuations in homicide rates in particular states (Guerrero, Veracruz, and San Luis Potosí); Correa-Cabrera, *Los Zetas*, 188, shows short-term (2000–2015) fluctuations in

Tamaulipas. On "México bronco"—"untamed Mexico"—see Wil G. Pansters, "Zones of State-Making," in *Violence, Coercion, and State-Making in Twentieth-Century Mexico: The Other Half of the Centaur*, ed. Wil G. Pansters (Stanford, CA: Stanford University Press, 2012), 5–6, and Alan Knight, "México bronco, México manso: Una reflexión sobre la cultura cívica mexicana," *Política y Gobierno* 3, no. 1 (1996): 5–30.

39. Norbert Elias, *The Civilizing Process: The History of Manners and State Formation and Civilization* (Oxford: Blackwell, 1997 [1939]); Steven Pinker, *The Better Angels of Our Nature: A History of Violence and Humanity* (London: Penguin, 2011).

40. And not grand politico-cultural attributes (for example, Mexico's supposed "Aztec" or "Conquistador" legacies), since they are largely incapable of explaining the dramatic variations in violence over time (and place). Knight, "War, Violence and Homicide," 16–19. Current trends are beyond the scope of this chapter, but it is worth noting that incumbent president Andrés Manuel López Obrador, having initially promised a new approach to endemic violence (summed up in the catchy phrase "abrazos no balazos": "bearhugs instead of bullets"), has failed to dent the trend and, in fact, has presided over rising rates of homicide. His government has also widely deployed the army.

41. I mean the old pyramidal system, in which the políticos, lodged within the stable PRIísta hierarchy, called the shots, discreetly colluding with subordinate narco interests. Collusion is still endemic, of course, but it is now a more messy, decentralized and unstable "system" (if it can be called a "system" at all; perhaps "syndrome" would be a better description).

42. A phenomenon that was noted some time ago. Peter A. Lupsha, "Drug Lords and Narco-Corruption: The Players Change but the Game Continues," *Crime, Law, and Social Change* 16, no. 1 (1990): 41–58; and Poppa, *Drug Lord*, chap. 8. See also Morris, chapter 13 in this volume, which recounts how, despite the elimination of the "two Jaimes" in Durango in the 1980s, the multicellular Herrera organization regrouped and carried on. George W. Grayson, *The Impact of President Calderón's War on Drugs* (Carlisle, PA: Strategic Studies Institute, 2013), 4–11, provides a long list of narco bosses arrested or killed between 2007 and 2012, years in which violence soared.

43. Critics of Leyzaola point not only to his many infringements of human rights and the rule of law; they also suggest that some of his success derived not from the prowess of the police, but from the coincidental occurrence of intercartel truces. On Leyzaola's regime in Tijuana, see William Finnegan, "In the Name of the Law," *The New Yorker*, October 18, 2010 (and other reports from the same source). In 2008 there were 844 reported homicides in Tijuana; by 2012 this number had fallen to 312. By 2018 it had again shot up to 2,506, which, some said, made it the most homicidal city in the world. Wendy Fry, "Drug Violence Continues to Grip Tijuana," *San Diego Union-Tribune*, January 6, 2020. For what it's worth, I spent a week in the "world's most homicidal city" in May 2019 to take part in an academic event. This confirmed my recent personal experience of several troubled Mexican cities (Culiacán,

Monterrey, Torreón), which is that transient visitors, shepherded to and fro by sensible local hosts, are at little risk and, indeed, could be deceived into thinking that things are not nearly as bad as depicted in the media. To put it another way: violence tends to be concentrated in particular city districts, and while there is certainly plenty of collateral damage (including for example, journalists, political activists, and hapless migrants), the victims of violence are often those directly involved in the armed conflict (police and criminals).

44. Cedillo, chapter 11 in this volume.

45. More systemic change seems to derive from shifts in consumption. Thus in recent years, U.S. demand for methamphetamines and synthetic opioids like fentanyl has sharply risen (and, with it, drug-related deaths); both are produced or trafficked through Mexico, where domestic consumption of methamphetamines has also increased. Meanwhile, the fentanyl boom has depressed demand for Mexican heroin, affecting local producers. See R. Le Cour Grandmaison, N. Morris, and B. Smith, "The Last Harvest? From the U.S. Fentanyl Boom to the Mexican Opium Crisis," *Journal of Illicit Economies and Development* 1, no. 3 (2019): 312–29.

46. Maldonado Aranda, chapter 10 in this volume, which quotes Rangel hubristically declaring, in November 1964, that "drug-trafficking has ended in the tierra caliente (hot country of Michoacán)" and that "planting drugs is a thing of the past." For similarly exaggerated claims of eradication, see Peter Reuter and David Ronfeldt, "Quest for Integrity: The Mexico-U.S. Drug Issue in the 1980s," RAND Note (Santa Monica, 1992), 21–22.

47. As was the case with General José de Jesús Gutiérrez Rebolledo, a man of "impeccable integrity," in the words of Barry McCaffrey (director of the Office of National Drug Control Policy in the United States). Newly promoted to head Mexico's INCD (Instituto Nacional para el Combate de las Drogas) in 1997, Gutiérrez was promptly arrested and jailed for forty years. The events—and the irate American reaction—are recounted by Carlos Fazio, "Mexico: The Narco General Case," in *Crime in Uniform: Corruption and Impunity in Latin America*, ed. Theo Roncken (Amsterdam: Transnational Institute, 1997). For a detailed discussion of the Mexican military and drug policy, see Luis Astorga, *Seguridad, traficantes y militares. El poder y la sombra* (Mexico City: Tusquets, 2007).

48. Howard F. Cline, *The United States and Mexico* (Cambridge, MA: Harvard University Press, 1953), 388.

49. The Chamizal concerned a strip of border land in El Paso that Mexico claimed and, in 1963, recovered. For a good eyewitness account of these years—and disputes—see Paul Kennedy, *The Middle Beat* (New York: Teachers College Press, 1971), 96–114.

50. Dolia Estévez, *U.S. Ambassadors to Mexico: The Relationship Through Their Eyes* (Washington, DC: Woodrow Wilson Center, 2013), covers nine ambassadors between 1977 and 2011, a period when Mexico was a growing American priority. Yet the majority were chosen, it seems, for short-term political reasons and lacked back-

ground experience. With few exceptions (such as George S. Messersmith, ambassador 1942–1946), the previous generation was no better. To be fair, William O'Dwyer, U.S. ambassador from 1950 to 1952, and a former mayor of New York City, spoke Spanish (he'd studied for two years at the Jesuit University of Salamanca) and appears to have liked Mexico; indeed, he lived and practiced law there after his brief diplomatic career ended in 1952. But his Mexican sojourn, some said, was prompted by the fear of facing charges for colluding with racketeers during his mayoralty. "Former Mayor O'Dwyer Dies," *New York Times*, November 25, 1964, 1, 33.

51. Perhaps this is unfair to Richard Nixon (a sentence I never thought I would write). Like Trump, however, Nixon appealed to the "silent majority," liked red baiting, and favored unilateral economic démarches: for example, closing the gold window, devaluing the dollar, and arbitrarily imposing import surcharges. But, more paranoid than narcissistic, he at least pioneered a sensible policy toward China.

52. Enrique Camarena, an undercover agent of the DEA, was abducted and murdered by members of the Guadalajara Cartel in 1985. The incident prompted a robust response from the Reagan administration: a partial closure of the border, a heightened American police-security presence in Mexico, and the formulation of NSDD (National Security Decision Directive) 221, which established counternarcotic policy as a key item in U.S. foreign policy. See Aileen Teague, "The U.S., Mexico and Mutual Securitization of Drug Enforcement," *Diplomatic History* 43, no. 5 (2019): 785–812.

53. In short, rival cartels "went to war when they lost access to informal networks of subnational government protection," as a result of *alternancia*. Guillermo Trejo and Sandra Ley, "Why Did Drug Cartels Go to War in Mexico? Subnational Party Alternation, the Breakdown of Criminal Protection, and the Onset of Large-Scale Violence," *Comparative Political Studies* 51, no. 7 (2018): 900–37.

54. On Echeverría's *"tercermundismo"* ("Third-Worldism"), see Samuel Schmidt, *The Deterioration of the Mexican Presidency: The Years of Luis Echeverría* (Tucson: University of Arizona Press, 1991), chap. 5. When President Carter visited Mexico in February 1979 he encountered a "Mexico gripped by a wave of nationalism and determined to resist [U.S.] pressure" regarding oil and gas; during the visit, President López Portillo "repeatedly criticized the U.S." Alan Riding, "Mexico Angry at U.S.," and Martin Tolchin, "Carter Ends Mexican Visit," *New York Times*, February 11, 1979, 1, and February 17, 1979, 1.

55. Jesus Velasco, "The Future of U.S.-Mexico Relations: A Tale of Two Crises," Baker Institute for Public Policy, Rice University, August 2018, 13–14, gives polling data and examples of critical comment from across Mexico's political spectrum.

56. For a good recent resumé of Alemán's project, stressing its careful balancing of economic nationalism and collaboration with the United States, see Vanni Pettinà, "Adapting to a New World: Mexico's International Strategy of Economic Development at the Outset of the Cold War, 1946–52," *Culture and History Digital Journal* 4, no. 1 (2015).

57. Campos, chapter 2 in this volume. Of course, during his short and shaky presidency (1911–1913), Madero had a great many major worries and drug trafficking was not one of them, so drug policy was hardly a key plank in the Maderista platform.

58. Pérez Montfort, chapter 3 in this volume.

59. On global prohibitionism in the early twentieth century, see Davenport-Hines, *The Pursuit of Oblivion*, chap. 7.

60. Regarding Calles's crackdown on drug imports and trafficking—which formed part of a broader project of public health reform—see Ricardo Pérez Montfort, *Tolerancia y prohibiciones. Aproximaciones a la historia social de las drogas en México* (Mexico City: Penguin Random House, 2016), chap. 6. Olvera Hernández, chapter 4 in this volume, shows how, yet again, actual practice—e.g., on the part of the police—diverged from proclaimed public norms.

61. Alan Knight, *Mexican Revolution*, 2:500–12, on the origins and character of this revolutionary "ethos."

62. I have touched on this theme of high-minded, top-down, jacobin reformism elsewhere: "Revolutionary Project, Recalcitrant People: Mexico, 1910–40," in *The Revolutionary Process in Mexico: Essays on Political and Social Change*, ed. Jaime E. Rodríguez O. (Los Angeles: UCLA Publications, 1990), 227–64.

63. José Jorge Izquierdo, *El movimiento anti-chino en México (1871–1934)* (Mexico City: INAH, 1991).

64. John Womack Jr., "The Spoils of the Mexican Revolution," *Foreign Affairs* 48 (July 1970): 677–88.

65. Grayson, *The Impact*, offers a useful resumé of the diverse and growing roles of the military; see also Sabina Morales Rosas and Carlos A. Pérez Ricart, "Más allá del gasto militar: en búsqueda de un concepto para entender la militarización en México," MéxicoVíaBerlin, documento no. 1, April 2014. Mexican military expenditure—historically low by Latin American standards—fell in real terms under President Fox (2000–2006), but the trend was sharply reversed by his successor, with expenditure increasing from US$2.8 billion in 2006 to US$5.0 billion (in 2018 U.S. dollars). As Morales Rosas and Pérez Ricart show, there was also a fourfold increase in spending by the Public Security Ministry (Secretaría de Seguridad Pública) between 2007 and 2011. Under President Peña Nieto (2012–2018) military spending initially flatlined, then rose again, reaching $5.8 billion in 2018. Stockholm International Peace Research Institute database, https://www.sipri.org/databases/milex, accessed June 2020. Mexico's military buildup was bolstered by the Mérida initiative (2008), whereby the United States pledged $1.6 billion of nonlethal aid to Mexico and Central America, with Mexico receiving the lion's share. It is hard to establish reliable figures for the army payroll: Grayson, *The Impact*, suggests an increase of only 7 percent between 2006 and 2012.

66. Laura Castellanos, *México armado, 1943–1981* (Mexico City: Ediciones Era, 2007), offers a good survey; Kate Doyle, "'Forgetting Is Not Justice': Mexico Bares Its

Past," *World Policy Journal* 20, no. 2 (2003): 61–72, addresses the research agenda and the obstacles it faces. See also Alexander Aviña, *Specters of Revolution: Peasant Guerrillas in the Cold War Mexican Countryside* (New York: Oxford University Press, 2014).

67. Smith, "The Rise and Fall," 149–50.

68. Smith, "The Rise and Fall," 134.

69. There are, of course, paramilitary organizations—like Colombia's FARC and Ireland's IRA—that have combined criminality (including drug trafficking) with politico-ideological programs. As a young Bolshevik, Stalin was a successful bank robber.

70. As several chapters in this book indicate, the old image of a highly efficient, centralized PRIísta leviathan is misleading since, even in its heyday, the PRIísta state was factionalized and the "center" did not exercise seamless control over a docile periphery. I think we have known this for some time; it is, perhaps, the—correct—new orthodoxy. That system, however, was more stable, predictable, and, over time, more peaceful than the current status quo.

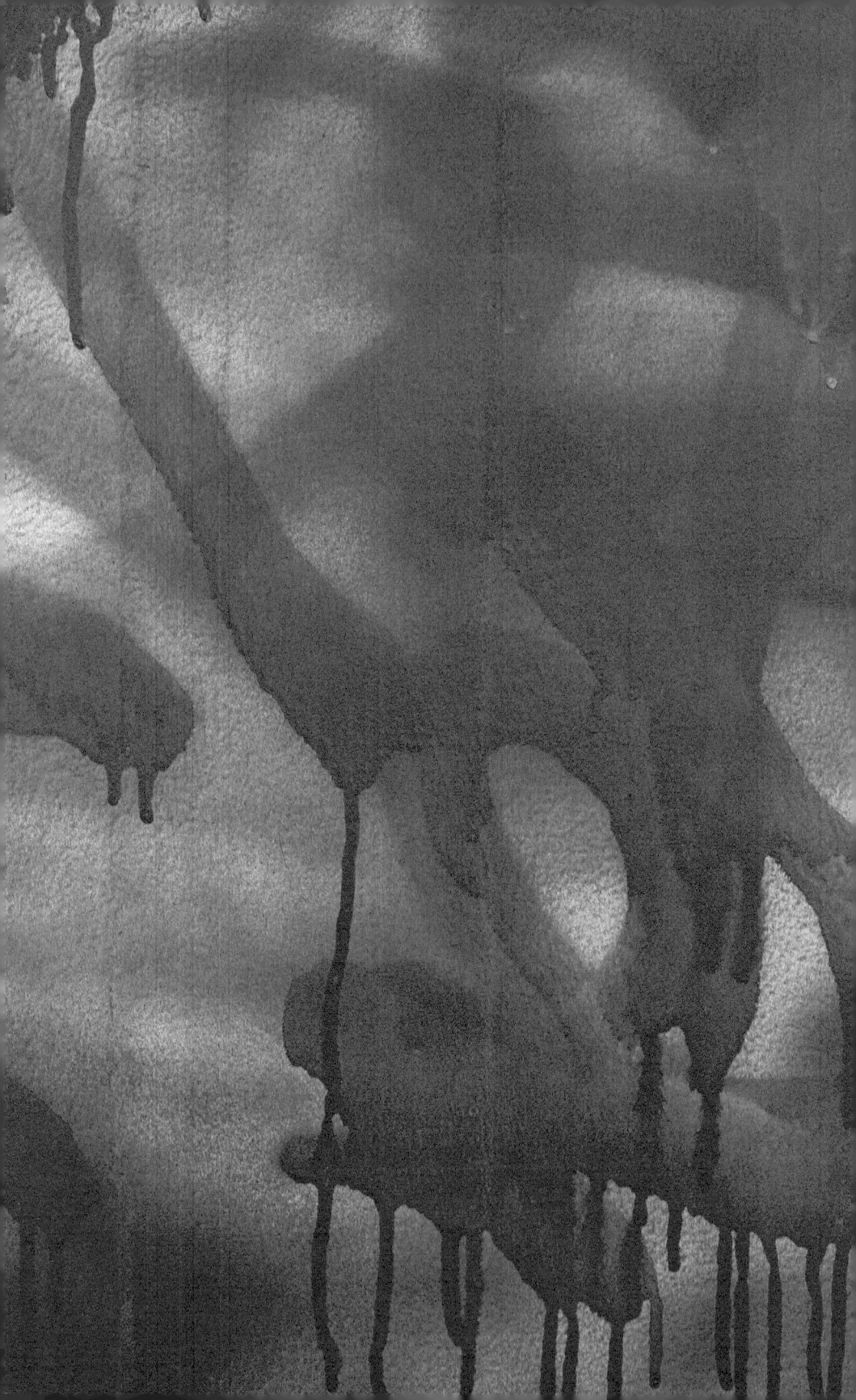

Contributors

ALEXANDER AVIÑA is an associate professor of history in the School of Historical, Philosophical and Religious Studies at Arizona State University. He received his PhD in history from the University of Southern California in 2009. His book, *Specters of Revolution: Peasant Guerrillas in the Cold War Mexican Countryside* (2014) was awarded the María Elena Martínez Book Prize for Mexican History by the Conference on Latin American History in 2015.

ISAAC CAMPOS teaches history at the University of Cincinnati. He is author of *Home Grown: Marijuana and the Origins of Mexico's War on Drugs* (University of North Carolina Press, 2012) along with articles published in the *Hispanic American Historical Review*, *Mexican Studies*, *Third World Quarterly*, and *The Social History of Alcohol and Drugs* among other outlets. He holds degrees from Harvard and the University of Michigan.

ELAINE CAREY is professor of history and Dean of the College of Humanities, Education, and Social Science at Purdue University Northwest. She is the author of *Plaza of Sacrifices: Gender, Power, and Terror in 1968 Mexico* (2005) and the award-winning *Women Drug Traffickers: Mules, Bosses, and Organized Crime* (2014). She is also coeditor with Andrae Marak of *Smugglers, Brothels, and Twine: Transnational Flows of Contraband and Vice in North America* (2011) and the editor/author of the textbook *Protests in the Streets: 1968 Across the Globe* (2016).

ADELA CEDILLO works as an adjunct professor at Syracuse University. She earned her PhD in Latin American history at the University of Wisconsin-Madison. She is the author of *El Fuego y El Silencio, Historia de las Fuerzas de*

Liberación Nacional (Comité '68 Pro Libertades Democráticas, 2008) and the coeditor of *Challenging Authoritarianism in Mexico. Revolutionary Struggles and the Dirty War, 1964–1982* (Routledge, 2012). Her research interests center around revolutionary movements, counterinsurgency warfare, drug wars, human rights, and women's activism in Latin America.

JUAN ANTONIO FERNÁNDEZ VELÁZQUEZ is a doctor in history and regional studies from the Instituto de Investigaciones Histórico-Sociales of the Universidad Veracruzana. He is currently professor-researcher at the Universidad Autónoma Indígena de México, in Sinaloa. His research interests include the social history of violence and criminality in twentieth-century Mexico. He is a current candidate for the Sistema Nacional de Investigadores del Consejo Nacional de Ciencia y Tecnología (México).

CARLOS ANTONIO FLORES PÉREZ is research professor in the Center for Research and Postgraduate Studies in Social Anthropology (CIESAS) in Mexico City. He has a PhD in political science from the National University of Mexico (UNAM) and conducts sociohistoric research on drug trafficking in Mexico. He authored *Historias de polvo y sangre. Génesis y evolución del tráfico de drogas en el estado de Tamaulipas* (CIESAS, 2013) and *El Estado en crisis: crimen organizado y política. Desafíos para la consolidación democrática* (CIESAS, 2009). His new book *Negocios de sombras. Red de poder hegemónica, contrabando, tráfico de drogas y lavado de dinero en Nuevo León*, also with CIESAS, was published in 2020.

ALAN KNIGHT is emeritus professor of the History of Latin America at Oxford University. Apart from Oxford, he has held positions at Essex University and the University of Texas at Austin. He is the author of *The Mexican Revolution* and several volumes dealing with modern Mexican—and Latin American—history, including *Repensar la Revolución mexicana* and *Revolución, democracia y populismo en América Latina*.

SALVADOR MALDONADO ARANDA is professor and researcher at El Colegio de Michoacán. He holds a PhD in anthropology from the Universidad Autónoma Metropolitana in Mexico City, and specializes in violence, security, and governance. He has published three books and more than fifty book chapters and articles in (inter)national journals. His work was awarded the prize for best book in anthropology by the Instituto Nacional de Antropología e Historia (2011) and the Premio Iberoamericano granted by the Universidad Nacional Autónoma de Mexico (2012). He is currently codirecting an international project about the improvement of collaboration in security matters.

NATHANIEL MORRIS is a historian of modern Mexico. He researches the drugs trade, revolutionary state formation, indigenous politics, and rural violence. He is currently a Leverhulme Early Career Research Fellow at University College London, where he is investigating the role of militia forces in both the Mexican Revolution and Mexico's ongoing "Drug War." His first book, *Soldiers, Saints, and Shamans: Indigenous Communities and the Revolutionary State in Mexico's Gran Nayar*, was published by the University of Arizona Press (2020).

NIDIA A. OLVERA HERNÁNDEZ earned a bachelor's degree in ethnohistory from the National School of Anthropology and History (ENAH) and a master's in social anthropology from the Center for Research and Postgraduate Studies in Social Anthropology (CIESAS) in Mexico City. Her main area of interest is the modern history of psychoactive substances and drug policies. She is a professor at ENAH, at the Autonomous University of Mexico City (UACM), and the author of several peer-reviewed articles. As a PhD candidate in history at the Instituto Mora in Mexico City she is currently researching drug control in the middle of the twentieth century in Mexico.

WIL G. PANSTERS is professor at the Department of Cultural Anthropology at Utrecht University. He has published widely on political culture, regional history, democratization, violence, and drug trafficking. He is the editor of *Violence, Coercion and State-Making in Twentieth-Century Mexico. The Other Half of the Centaur* and *La Santa Muerte in Mexico. History, Devotion and Society*. His articles have appeared in *Global Crime, Bulletin of Latin American Research, Conflict & Society, Foro Internacional, Journal of Contemporary History*, and *European Review of Latin American and Caribbean Studies*.

RICARDO PÉREZ MONTFORT is research fellow at the Center for Research and Postgraduate Studies in Social Anthropology (CIESAS) and professor at the Faculty of Literature and Philosophy at UNAM, both in Mexico City. He is a member of the National Research System (SNI), Level III. His academic interests include nationalism, cultural history of Mexico and Latin America during the nineteenth and twentieth centuries, Mexican historiography, history of photography in Mexico and Latin America, and the history of drugs in Mexico. He has written twenty-seven books and more than 130 scientific articles. With a special interest in cinematography he has made various documentaries on Mexican history and culture. His most recent publications are *Tolerancia y prohibición. Aproximaciones a la historia social y cultural de las drogas en México 1840–1940* (2015) and *Lázaro Cárdenas, un mexicano de siglo XX*, two volumes (2018, 2019).

CARLOS A. PÉREZ RICART is assistant professor in International Relations at the Center for Research and Teaching in Economics (CIDE) in Mexico City. Prior to joining CIDE, he was a postdoctoral fellow at the University of Oxford, where he worked between 2017 and 2020 at both the History Faculty and the Latin American Centre, St. Antony's College. Pérez Ricart holds a PhD in political science from the Freie Universität Berlin and has a degree in international relations from El Colegio de México.

BENJAMIN T. SMITH (PhD Cambridge, 2006) specializes in the history of modern Mexico. He has published three monographs, three edited volumes, and dozens of academic articles. His most recent book—*The Dope: The Real History of the Mexican Drug Trade*—was released by Ebury/W. W. Norton in 2021.

Index

107th Street Mob 155

Abarca Alarcón, Raymundo, 270
Abraham Pérez, Salvador, 159
Acapulco, 12, 263, 264, 267–81
Acosta Chaparro, Mario, 276–79
Acuña Carmona, Juan, 133
Adelson, Morris, 149
Afghanistan, 12, 28
Aguilar Garza, Carlos, 246, 247, 250, 255
Aguilar Mora, 134
Aguililla, 222–24, 231
Ahome, 177
Alcalá, Jaime, 249, 250, 255
alcohol, 13, 17, 50, 58, 63, 73, 74, 77, 78, 81–83, 91, 96, 114, 129, 148, 150, 151, 194, 201, 222, 230, 318, 322
Alemán Valdés, Miguel, 18, 21, 97, 98, 136, 195, 197–99, 204, 328
Almázan, Leónides, 89
Alvarado Barrón, Gustavo, 185
Alvarado, Gustavo, 185
Ameca, 13
Amsterdam, 29
Anslinger, Harry, 16, 21, 96, 109, 112–16, 119, 122, 137, 149, 153, 154, 156, 157, 160, 161, 166, 326
Anti-Saloon League, 81

Apatzingán, 220, 221, 224, 228, 230–33
Aquila, 222, 231, 233
Aragón, Edmundo, 80
Arellano, Hector Román, 272
Arias, Justo, 133
army, 9, 13, 16, 18, 19, 22, 25, 57, 71–76, 86, 96, 97, 119, 143, 151, 176, 180, 183, 184, 186, 195, 196, 200, 217, 218, 220–38, 272, 277, 286, 321, 323, 324, 330, 331, 339, 342
Arpaio, Joseph, 158
Arteaga, 225
Asaf y Bala, Jorge, 160, 161, 167
Astorga, Luis, 3, 289
Atlixco, 13
Atoyac, 272, 273
Attie, James, 160, 161
Attorney General's Office (PGR), 19, 93, 94, 96–99, 118, 150, 161–64, 176, 188, 199, 201, 229, 230, 232, 244, 245, 256, 272, 298, 301, 303–5
Australia, 45
Avila Camacho, Manuel, 97, 98, 145, 192
Avilés Pérez, Pedro, 176, 250
Azuela, Mariano, 71, 75

Bacacoraguá, 181, 182
Badiraguato, 17, 26, 133, 177–85, 188, 189, 247, 251–53, 259, 290

Baja California, 14, 16, 17, 20, 23, 24, 57, 69, 78, 127–42, 155, 156, 161–63, 185, 205, 250, 291, 318
Barajas Lozano, Ignacio, 270
Barberena, Octavio, 159
Barquín Alonso, Francisco, 277–79
Barragán, Miguel "Big Mike," 10, 14, 138–42
Barrera González, Germán, 195, 198
Batíz, Bernardo, 132
Batopilas, 247, 251
Bautista, Jorge, 272, 273
Beltrán Bustamante, Francisco, 187
Beltrán, Reinaldo, 99
Bermúdez, Antonio J., 111–13
Board of Health, 68, 79
Bolivia, 28, 29, 44
Brazil, 29, 275
Brent, Charles Henry, 68, 83
Buenavista, 231
Bureau of Narcotics and Dangerous Drugs (BNDD), 122, 167

Caballero Aburto, Raúl, 270
Cabañas, Lucio, 234, 237, 263, 273, 274, 276, 331
cacicazgo, 25, 26, 218, 269, 272, 305, 219
cacique, 9, 25–27, 183, 217–23, 226, 234, 235, 245, 264, 268–76, 294, 296, 297, 299
caciquismo, 25, 217, 219, 228, 233, 299, 318. See also *cacicazgo*; *cacique*
Cajeme, 134
Calderón, Alfonso G., 247, 249, 250
Calderon, Felipe, 1, 5, 16, 323, 330
Caldwell, Philip M., 152
California, 10, 16, 22, 46, 59, 117, 118, 138–42, 148, 155, 157–60, 218, 267, 287, 288, 291
Camarena, Enrique, 18, 287, 305, 307, 327

Camargo, Raúl, 92
Campos González, Agustín, 95
Canada, 29, 45, 110, 118
Canavati family, 206–8
Candelaria de los Patos, 94
cannabis, 16, 62, 71, 175, 176, 267
Cansino, Margarita (aka Rita Hayworth), 129
Cantú, Esteban, 14, 16, 17, 24, 34, 57, 69, 70, 127, 132, 318, 326
Capirato, 186
Cárdenas, Dámaso, 218–21
Cárdenas, Lázaro, 16, 96, 151, 196, 218, 228, 234, 235, 328, 330
Carli, Victor D., 149
Caro, Gil, 184
Caro, Manuela, 184
Caro, Porfiria, 187
Caro Quintero, Rafael, 174, 184, 255, 305, 306
Carrancistas, 50, 78
Carranza, Venustiano, 16, 58, 67, 78–81, 85, 127, 328, 329. *See also* Carrancistas
Carrillo Fuentes, Amado, 278, 279
Carrola Antuna, Enrique, 203
Casey, Daniel, 158
Castellanos Tuexi, Francisco, 198, 203
Castillo Nájera, Francisco, 75, 76
Castro Flores, Alejo, 159
Cavazos Lerma, Manuel, 199
Cazares, Alejo, 188
Cazares, Enrique, 188
Central Campesina Independiente (CCI), 228
Central Intelligence Agency (CIA), 8, 29, 248, 257, 266, 328
Cervantes, Ricardo, 247, 249
Cervantes Aguirre, Enrique, 276, 278
Chamizal, 325, 326
Chappell, Howard, 157, 162, 164, 165
Chávez León brothers, 292

Chávez Ortiz, María, 185
Cherrington, Ernest, 81
Chiapas, 14, 175, 323
Chicago, 10, 26, 112, 118, 160, 288–308
Chihuahua, 14, 16–20, 26, 27, 78, 81, 116, 123, 129, 133, 135, 156, 157, 178, 185, 241–47, 266, 288, 290, 293, 296, 298, 303, 318, 268
Chihuahua Judicial Police (PJC), 242
Chile, 29
Chilpancingo, 267, 271, 274
Chin, José Luis, 165
China, 44–46, 49, 52, 68, 118, 119, 132, 134
Choix, 140, 177, 247
Chopson, Luis, 58
Ciudad Juárez, 10, 14, 19, 20, 23, 29, 81, 109–23, 155–57, 160, 185, 279, 293, 296, 298
Coahuayana, 224, 230
Coahuila, 17, 20, 57, 67, 80, 115, 159, 165, 194, 290
Coalcomán, 222, 230, 233
cocaine, 8, 9, 13–15, 19, 20, 30, 44, 54, 55, 58–61, 69, 71, 78–80, 83, 84, 88, 90, 128, 133, 157, 158, 160, 208, 210, 253, 254, 260, 278, 287, 300, 305–7, 318, 327, 334
Cochran, John J., 111, 113
Coire, 233
Cold War, 5, 12, 27, 28, 29, 241, 273, 289. *See also* counterinsurgency
Colima, 244
Colombia, 5, 8, 10, 11, 13, 15, 28, 29, 269, 278, 305, 306, 319, 334, 343
Conant, Kenneth W., 162, 165
Confederación de Trabajadores Mexicanos (CTM), 231
Consejo Superior de Salubridad, 49. *See also* Board of Health
corridos, 71, 72, 75, 82

Cosalá, 177
Cossman, Max, 136, 155, 156
counterinsurgency, 12, 27, 29, 240–56, 264–68, 273–79. *See also* Cold War
Creighton, Harry S., 150–52
Crook, W. H., 110, 111, 156
Cuban Revolution 27, 219, 220, 326, 331
Cuén, Antonio, 184
Cuén Cásarez, Melesio, 26
Cuenca Díaz, Hermenegildo, 265, 276
Culiacán, 16, 20, 35, 133, 138. 174, 177–82, 184–89, 246–49, 252, 259, 261, 271, 291, 297, 205, 307, 320
Customs Bureau (U.S.), 14, 110, 111, 115, 120, 128, 132, 133, 136, 136–38, 147–57, 162–67, 176, 292, 298
Customs Office (Mexico), 196–203, 207, 208

Dallas, 299
Davalos, Marcelino, 71, 72, 74
Dawson, Alexander, 5
degeneration, 16, 50, 78, 80, 329, 330, 332
degeneration theory, 16, 50, 78, 90, 329, 330
De la Madrid, Miguel, 19, 242, 305, 206
De la Rocha clan, 292
Delgado, Pablo I., 116
Demara, Jesús, 137
Demaris, Ovid, 127, 140
Denny, J. W., 131
Departamento de Correos, 52, 53, 56. *See also* Postal Service
Detroit, 110, 112, 118, 299
Diarte, Enrique, 135, 136, 140
Diarte brothers, 179
Díaz García, Enrique, 297
Díaz, Gustavo, 300
Díaz, Porfirio, 268, 325
Díaz Ordaz, Gustavo, 240, 243, 270

Index 351

Dirección Federal de Seguridad (DFS), 8, 18, 19, 24, 25, 195, 201, 203, 204, 208, 211, 242, 245, 248–50, 255, 256, 264, 265, 269, 270, 276–78, 298, 304–8
Dirty War, 27, 24, 254, 256, 263–65, 273, 274, 276–79, 331
Drug Enforcement Administration (DEA), 8, 13, 15, 18, 152, 167, 241, 244, 248, 253–55, 287, 293, 294, 298, 299, 300–307, 327
Duarte Araujo, Manuel, 200
Durango, 7, 10, 14, 23, 26, 75, 123, 133, 134, 178, 241, 244, 245, 247, 266, 268, 287–307
Durango Judicial Police, 296
Durazo Moreno, Arturo "el Negro," 15, 19, 23
Durkin, William, 166

Echeverría, Luis, 234, 241, 243, 244, 265, 301, 328, 330, 331, 335
El Altar, 14
El Fuerte, 177
Elias, Norbert, 323
Eliopoulos, Elias, 156
Elizalde, Pedro, 95
Elizondo, Ernesto, 204, 209
Elota, 177
El Paso, 109–12, 115–22, 288
El Tahuachal, 198
Ensenada, 70, 128, 131, 132, 134, 148
Escabi, Salvador, 160, 161
Escalate, Fernando, 5, 6
Espinosa de Olea, Celia, 272
Esquivel Méndez, Eligio, 161
Estévez Zulueta, Dolores (aka "Lola la Chata"), 88, 95, 116
Ezeroi, Manuel, 131

Farías, José Antonio, 159
fayuqueros, 17, 29

Federal Bureau of Narcotics (FBN), 8, 9, 113, 117, 123, 141, 147–67, 183
Felix Gallardo, Miguel Angel, 174, 255
fentanyl, 9
Fernández, Eduardo "Lalo," 184, 188
Fernández, Fermín, 183
Fernández gang, 188
Figueroa, Rubén, 276, 277
Finger, Henry, 46, 59
Flores, Manuel, 199
Flores Sánchez, Oscar, 19, 245, 246, 298, 303, 304
Fonseca Carrillo, Ernesto, 174, 255, 305–7
Ford, Gerald, 243, 244
Foster, Ben, 112
France, 14, 29
Franco Rodríguez, David, 219
French Connection, 14, 139, 205, 240, 297, 319
Frost, John A., 159
Fu, Chan, 70

Galindo, Al, 139
Galindo, Imelda, 139
Gamboa, Federico, 47, 71, 74, 75
Gárate Legleu, Raúl, 196, 199, 204, 205
García, Teodoro, 110
García Abrego, Juan, 206, 209, 210
García Barragán, Marcelino, 234, 258, 274
García Cantín, José, 98
García González, Guillermo, 200
García Paniagua, Javier, 245, 255
García Segovia, Felipe, 200
Garduño, Eduardo, 202
Garza Zamora, Tiburcio, 18, 195–207, 210
Gastélum, Leonardo, 188
Germany, 68, 69, 79, 131
Gertz Manero, Alejandro, 244, 247, 257
Giordano, Henry L., 157, 164

Gómez Palacio, 290, 294–96, 298
Gómez Vidal, Victor, 250
Gónzalez Anguiano, Arturo, 295
González, E. A., 56
González, Hugo Pedro, 17, 18, 196, 204
González, Pablo, 78
González, Pablo El "Pablote," 114
González Chavando, Bulmaro, 274
González Garza, Juan Manuel "El Chapeado," 208, 209
González Sánchez, Oscar, 203
Gootenberg, Paul, 5, 8
Great Britain, 44, 45, 47–56, 236
Grupo Sangre, 27, 263–66, 274–79
Guadalajara, 7, 19, 20, 79, 98, 111, 117, 136, 156, 174, 184, 256, 271, 287, 304, 305, 307, 319
Guadalajara Cartel, 19, 174, 255, 256, 287, 304, 307
Guadalupe y Calvo, 247, 251, 252
Guatemala, 29, 326
Guaymas, 134, 135
Guerra, Juan Nepomuceno, 17, 193–210
Guerra, Plácido, 198, 199
Guerra, Venustiano, 199
Guerra Cárdenas, Roberto, 201, 204, 206, 210
Guerrero, 16, 26, 27, 167, 205, 233, 234, 244, 247, 263–79, 323, 331
Guerrero Guajardo, Anacleto, 199, 205
Gulf Cartel, 193, 209, 210, 279, 323
Gutíerrez, Hector, 185
Guzmán, Guadalupe, 110
Guzmán, Joaquín "El Chapo," 6, 174
Guzmán, Regina, 111
Guzmán Loera, Joaquín "el Chapo," 6, 30, 174

Hague International Opium Convention, 43–48, 54–59, 68, 69, 80, 83
Harmon, W. J., 152

Harrison Narcotics Act, 109
Havana, 29, 150
Health Department, 80, 88, 91–97, 113, 149. *See also* Secretaria de Salubridad Pública
Heath, Edward, 243, 253, 254, 257, 304
Heine Rangel, Roberto, 276
Helms, Jesse, 327
Hernández, José, 166
Hernández González, Arturo, 279
Hernández Rodríguez, Salvador, 159
Hernández Toledo, José Francisco, 247
Herrera, Edmundo, 23
Herrera Araluce, Carlos, 296
Herrera-Chávez, Asunción, 300
Herrera Díaz, Jesús, 288
Herrera drug ring, 7, 8, 287–307
Herrera Herrera, Jaime, 288, 305–7
Herrera Herrera, Manuel, 297
Herrera Nevárez, Alfredo, 288
Herrera Nevárez, Jaime, 23, 288, 294–97, 298–307
Herrera Nevárez, Reyes, 300, 301
Herrera Nevárez, Rodolfo, 303, 304
Hidalgo del Parral, 245
Hill, Benjamín R., 198
Hill, Robert C., 160
Hong Kong, 45, 51, 268
Hospital de Toxicómanos, 94–96
Houston, 150, 159
Huerta, Victoriano, 56, 68, 69, 71–75
Huesca de la Fuente, Luis, 88, 89, 95, 96
Hussong family, 131

Idaho, 135
Iguala, 233, 268, 270, 271
Illinois, 287, 300
Imperial Valley, 129
Indiana, 287
Ireta, Feléix, 221, 233
Islas Marias, 98, 115, 116

Index   353

Jalisco, 13, 26, 11, 134, 141, 167, 218, 244, 255, 270
Jamaica, 13
Jasso, Ignacia "La Nacha," 14, 20, 109–23, 156, 335
Jiménez, Adolfo, 159

Kamstra, Jerry, 176, 186, 270
Kee, Yon, 131
Kelly, J., 159
Kennedy, John K., 218

La Merced, 94, 95
Landell, Ignacio "Nacho," 178, 183, 187, 189
Landell, Onofre, 184
Landeros, Gloria, 199
La Piedad, 133, 135
Lara, Rosa Lilia, 184
Lascurain, Pedro, 51
Lavat, Luis, 157
Lazcano y Ochoa, Manuel, 176
Leyva Mancilla, Baltasar, 269
Leyva Valenzuela, Teresa, 187
Leyzaola, Julián, 324
Leyzaola Salazar, Alfonso, 17, 184
Licuanan, Jayme R., 164
Lilliestrom, T. L., 115
Livas Villareal, Eduardo, 210
Loaiza, Rodolfo T., 136, 137
López, Esperanza, 88
López, Leonicio, 133
López Arias, Fernando, 164
López Mateos, Adolfo, 200, 202, 207, 208, 217–20, 234
López Portillo, José, 241, 245, 247, 250, 254, 303, 328, 330
Los Angeles, 117, 118, 132, 136–41, 155, 157, 162, 299
Los Herrera, 288, 293, 294, 295, 297
Los Limones, 186

Los Mochis, 140, 141, 156, 175, 183, 185
Lozano, Angel, 199
Lozano, José Luis, 199
Luciano, Lucky, 111
Lugo, Conrado, 95

Macao, 45, 50–52
Macías, Cruz, 140, 141
Macias, Ramón, 55
Macías Valenzuela, Pablo, 136
Madero, Francisco, 47, 48, 72, 73, 328, 330
madrinas, 153, 250
Maduro, Reynaldo, 160, 161, 167
Malda, Gabriel, 92
Maldonado, Braulio, 141
Maldonado, Caritano, 272
Maldonado Rosas, Emilio, 165
Mancilla, Ignacio, 155
marijuana, 8–16, 19–21, 26, 27, 29, 58, 61, 71–83, 90, 93–95, 98, 99, 110, 116–18, 134, 135, 139, 141, 142, 154, 157, 160, 175–80, 185, 186, 188–90, 205, 219, 223, 225, 232, 234, 240, 241, 247, 252, 264–79, 287, 301, 308, 318–21, 332
Marlowe, Philip, 127
Marseilles, 138
Martínez, Domingo, 200
Martínez, Jesus M., 166
Martínez Montenegro, Roberto, 249, 250
Martínez Salgado, Filberto, 272
May, Francis Henry, 51
McGovern, Roger, 269
Medellín, 29
Medina Lugo, Jesús, 186
Medina Villa, Dolores, 185
Medrano Suárez, Ramón, 185
Méndez, José, 135, 138
Mendez, Roberto, 183
Mendiolea Cerecero, Raúl, 19, 246, 258, 298, 303, 304

Mendoza, Arnalfo, 155
Mendoza, Everardo, 231
Mendoza, Vicente T., 77
Meneses, Juan, 137
Merza Terán, Jesús, 92
Messersmith, George, 113, 122
Mexicali, 15, 20, 22, 69, 70, 78, 127–37, 149, 155, 161–65, 185
Mexico City, 17, 19, 23, 48, 71, 79, 84, 88–100, 122, 124, 139, 149, 150, 152, 160, 162, 163, 166, 205, 207–9, 250, 273, 274, 306, 318, 319
Miami, 15
Michoacán, 10, 22, 26, 27, 133–38, 217–33, 244, 269–70, 346
Miguel Alemán, 195, 201, 205–8
Minas, Steve, 166
Ministry of National Defense (SEDENA), 97, 220, 221, 224, 227, 243, 251, 254, 259, 275
Ministry of the Interior, 92, 96, 163, 227, 296. *See also* Secretaria de Gobernación
Minjares Perea, Daniel, 114
Mixhuca, Magdalena, 94
Mocorito, 133, 157, 140, 157, 177, 182, 183, 185, 189
Monroy, José, 94
Monterrey, 7, 166, 167, 194, 195, 199, 203, 205–8, 340
Montreal, 270
Monzón-Terrazas gang, 188
Morales, Mariano, 111
Morales Cadena, Raúl, 199
Morales Farías, Raúl, 199, 200, 204
Morelia, 220, 221, 223, 225, 229
Morena, 324
Moreno, María Luisa, 98
Movimiento de Liberaciión Nacional (MLN), 228
Nacaveva, A., 180, 181

NAFTA, 21, 22, 319, 322
narcocorrido, 22, 174
Narcotics Police, 89–100
National Revolutionary Civic Association (ACNR), 264, 266
Nayarit, 10, 26, 134, 151, 175, 244, 270
Nazar Haro, Miguel, 249, 250, 277
Nevada, 157
New York, 11, 81, 110, 112, 118, 124, 130, 138, 155, 155, 160, 210, 270, 288, 299, 300
Nicaragua, 326
Nixon, Richard, 13, 15, 240, 327
Nogales, 150, 155, 185, 189
Nuevo Laredo, 17, 157, 159, 207, 322
Nuevo León, 73, 157, 194–207

Oaxaca 5, 26, 79, 244, 267, 281
Ojeda Paullada, Pedro, 301
Oklahoma City, 299
Olachea, Agustín, 132, 220, 221
Operation Canador, 240, 243, 324
Operation Condor, 13, 20, 21, 27, 240–56, 266, 278, 324
Operation Cooperation, 240, 243, 324
Operation Friendship, 275
Operation Intercept, 15, 240, 243, 275, 324
Operation Spider Web, 275
Operation Trizo, 241, 244, 258, 278
opium, 9–17, 20, 26, 29, 43–59, 67–71, 74, 78–84, 90, 93, 94–98, 100, 109–12, 124, 127–41, 148–51, 155–58, 160, 175–90, 205, 222, 243, 245, 253, 264–73, 276, 279, 289–301, 305, 329
Opium Exclusion Act, 45, 54
Orbe, Francisco, 136
Ortega, Melchor, 272
Ortiz Mena, Antonio, 202, 210
Ortiz Pinchetti, Francisco, 251
Oviedo, Francisco, 72

Index 355

Padilla, Ezequiel, 112, 113, 122
Paez, Natividad, 178
Palacios Vargas, Ramón, 203
Palm, Oscar, 139
Palomar, Rafael, 155
paraquat, 13, 244, 252
Parra Cosío, Ester, 185
Parral, 296, 298
Parra López, Telesforo, 140, 141, 161, 171
Partido Acción Nacional (PAN), 6, 160, 324
Partido Revolucionario Institucional (PRI), 15, 16, 27, 199, 204, 240–45, 249, 254, 264, 265, 268, 269, 272, 273, 294, 320, 321, 324, 327, 329, 331
Party of the Poor (PDLP), 263, 264, 266, 273–77
Pasquel, Jorge, 206
Pedroza, José, 94
Pemex, 195
Peña, Salvador, 152
Peñuelas, Miguel Angel, 182, 186, 188, 189
Pershing, General John, 77
Peru, 8, 15, 28, 29, 44, 61, 254
Peterson, Carl, 152
Philippines, 68
Phoenix, Bebe, 139
Piedras Negras, 159, 199–202, 208
police, 9, 15–19, 22–26, 70, 79, 88–100, 110–15, 119, 123, 131, 132, 134–41, 147, 150, 152, 153, 156, 158–67, 179–86, 189, 196, 198, 202, 205, 206, 209, 220, 227, 229, 230, 238, 242, 245, 246, 248–50, 258, 259, 264, 265, 270–74, 276–80, 293, 295, 298–308, 321, 322, 324, 331
Polina Limón, Luis, 95
Pómaro, 233
Porfiriato, 69, 72, 75, 83, 317
Portes Gil, Emilio, 17, 196
Postal Service, 55. *See also* Departamento de Correos

Price Daniels hearings, 117, 118
Procuraduria General de la República (PGR), 99, 162, 201, 246–50, 253, 254. *See also* Attorney General's Office
Pruneda, Alfonso, 92
Puebla, 13, 268
Puente, Ramón, 72–74
Puerto Peñasco, 135
Puerto Vallarta, 267
Pyes, Craig, 253, 254

Querétaro, 79, 80
Quevedo, Rodrigo, 17, 115
Quezada, Luciano, 155
Quezada Fornelli, Antonio, 245, 246
Quiñonez Valenzuela, José Luis, 185
Quintanar, Alberto, 249
Quintana Roo, 73
Quintanilla González, Hector, 305
Quintero Aguilar, Mariano, 135, 138
Quirós Hermosillo, Francisco, 276–79

Rabasa, Oscar, 118, 160, 166
Rafael Buelna, 187, 188
Ramírez y Ramírez, Enrique, 273
Rangel Escamilla, Manuel, 203
Rangel Medina, Salvador, 220–29, 232–35
Reyes Curiel, Alfredo, 248
Reyna Celaya, Jesús, 137
Reynosa, 195, 196, 198, 200, 201, 205, 206
Rivera Urias, Celia, 185
Rock, Richard D., 162, 166
Rodríguez, Abelardo, 17, 127
Rodríguez, Daniel, 114
Rodríguez, José María, 58, 80
Roosevelt, Theodore, 45, 68
Rosas, Emilio, 159
Ruacha, Sabas, 155

Rueda Magro, Manuel, 94
Ruiz Cortines, Adolfo, 121, 219

Sáenz Garza, Aarón, 1978
Sahagún Baca, Francisco, 19
Salazar, Ruben, 117, 119–22
Salazar Viniegra, Leopoldo, 88, 89, 96, 100, 151
Salcido Uzeta, Manuel "el Cochiloco," 248, 249, 255
Salinas de Gotari, Carlos, 209
Salinas Domínguez, Francisco, 159
Salinas Leal, Bonifacio, 18, 196, 198, 204, 209
Salinas Lozano, Carlos, 209
Salinas Lozano, Raúl, 209, 210
Saltillo, 71, 159
Sámano Gustavo, 248, 249
Sanalona, 186
Sánchez, Herlinda, 94, 95
Sánchez, Saturnino, 272
Sánchez Celis, Leopoldo, 17, 24, 245, 250
Sánchez Taboada, Rodolfo, 129
Sandez Jr., Salomón, 141, 165
San Diego, 56, 131, 133, 135, 149, 185
San Felipe, 134
San Francisco, 46, 155, 157
San Ignacio, 177
Sanitary Code, 48, 49, 55, 93
Sanitary Police, 23, 89–99
San Luis Potosí, 23, 194
San Luis Río Colorado, 176, 185
Santa Anna, 325
Santa Rosalia, 141
Santiago de los Caballeros, 179, 184
Santiago Papasquiaro, 10, 26, 293, 294, 299
Santos, Gonzalo, 23, 318
Scharff, Alvin E., 147, 149–51
Schultz, "Dutch," 111

Schuyler Jr., Montgomery, 47
Seattle, 110
Secretaria de Gobernación, 49, 52, 54, 56, 330, 331. *See also* Ministry of the Interior
Secretaria de Hacienda, 49, 52, 53, 55, 56
Secretaria de Salubridad Pública, 49, 51–58, 91. *See also* Health Department
Serbia, 69
Siegel, Bugsy, 136
Simbras, Alejandro, 273
Simpson, T. S., 152, 155
Sinaloa, 7, 9, 11, 13, 16–20, 24, 26–29, 78, 98, 133–41, 144, 151, 157, 174–90, 241–55, 266–70, 279, 287, 290–94, 299, 303, 305–9, 320, 323
Sinaloa de Leyva, 177, 247
Sinaloa Judicial Police (PJS), 242, 243, 248, 249, 250
Sinaloa's Bar Association "Eustaquio Buelna," 250
smoking opium, 14, 49, 54, 69, 78, 110, 111, 127, 128, 137, 176, 206
social bandit, 289, 294, 320, 331
Solís Alemán, Miguel, 198
Solís Bolaños, Alfonso, 203
Sonora, 14, 129, 130, 131, 133–38, 141, 144, 150, 185, 205, 244, 250, 330
Soto, Baldemar, 161–64
Soza, Jesús, 23
Stronge, Francis, 51, 52
Suárez Buelna, Francisco, 133
Suárez Domínguez, Manuel, 160

Taft, William Howard, 69
Talent, Terry, 115
Tamaulipas, 17, 18, 20, 24, 28, 193–205, 208, 246
Tamazula, 247, 251, 252, 290, 292, 296, 297

Tampico, 196
Tecate, 139
Tehuixtitlán, 99
Tellez, Frank H., 141
Teloloapan, 274
Tepalcatepec, 225, 228
Tepehuanes, 292–97
Tepito, 94
Texas, 16, 20, 77, 81, 109, 117–21, 148–50, 159, 160, 193, 194, 205, 207, 208, 255, 278, 282, 287, 325
Thailand, 13
Tierra Blanca, 184, 186, 188
Tierra Caliente, 16, 29, 223, 225, 228, 232, 236, 269, 271, 272, 274, 279
Tijuana, 10, 14, 15, 20, 22, 28, 29, 69, 70, 127–42, 149, 155, 161–65, 182, 185, 186, 198, 250, 307, 323, 324
Tlalpan, 94
Tlaxcala, 268
Toca Cangas, Amador, 162, 164, 165
Topia, 251, 290, 297
Torreón, 13, 67, 115, 290, 291, 293, 306
Torres Ibarra, Alberto, 111
Treglia, Joseph L. V., 149
Treviño, Alfonso, 17
Treviño Rios, Oscar, 161, 162, 164
Tuchman, Barbara, 318
Tumbiscatío, 233
Turkey, 156–58, 240

United States, 5, 10, 14–22, 30, 44–47, 50, 52, 55–59, 65, 78, 81, 82, 96, 98, 109–18, 121–23, 129, 131–40, 148–67, 176, 186, 189, 193, 194, 209, 217, 218, 223, 235, 238, 240–45
Universidad Autónoma de Sinaloa, 181
Uriarte Obeso, Micaela, 182
Urias Uriarte, Miguel, 181, 182

Urique, 251
Urquizo, Francisco L., 73, 74
Uruapan, 220, 224
U.S. Treasury Department, 97, 151
Utah, 135

Vaca Corella, Gastón, 98
Vázquez, Genaro, 234, 272, 273
Vázquez, Luis Manuel, 111
Vega Cantú, Zeferino, 200, 202
Veracruz, 69, 150, 194
Vietnam, 244
Villa Coss, Octavio, 200–206
Volstead Act, 81, 194

Wadsworth, R. M., 155
Washington, D.C., 47, 112, 118, 149, 163, 169, 171, 283, 286, 305, 326
Webb, Lake T., 152
Westover, H. B., 110, 111, 156
Wheeler, Wayne, 81
White, George H., 156, 166
White Brigade, 248, 265, 277, 279
Williams, Holvey, 117
Wilson, Henry Lane, 47
Wilson, Huntington, 47, 62
Wright, Hamilton, 46, 83
Wyoming, 135

Xalisco, 10
Xochimilco, 94, 97

Yárrington Ruvalcaba, Tomás, 24
Yarritou, Francisco, 200

Zacatecas, 244, 290
Zambada, Ismael "el Mayo," 174
Zamora, 231
Zavala, Alfredo, 305

www.ingramcontent.com/pod-product-compliance
Lightning Source LLC
Chambersburg PA
CBHW021334230426
43666CB00006B/292